India Since 1947

India Since 1947

Looking Back at a Modern Nation

Edited by:

Atul Kumar Thakur

Foreword:

B.G. Verghese

NIYOGI BOOKS

Published by

NIYOGI BOOKS

D-78, Okhla Industrial Area, Phase-I
New Delhi-110 020, INDIA
Tel: 91-11-26816301, 49327000
Fax: 91-11-26810483, 26813830
email: niyogibooks@gmail.com
website: www.niyogibooksindia.com

Editor: Gita Rajan
Design: Shashi Bhushan Prasad/Niyogi Books

ISBN: 978-93-81523-92-6
Publication: 2015

Printed at: Niyogi Offset Pvt. Ltd., New Delhi, India

For Maa, Papa and brother Ashutosh…

Contents

Foreword

On the midnight of 14-15 August, Jawaharlal Nehru spoke of India's tryst with destiny. How far have we travelled down that road in fulfilling the promise of the Constitution? *India Since 1947* admirably addresses this question through a series of thirty essays on governance, development, external relations and security, and culture by men and women who have not merely watched the pilgrim's progress but played some part in advancing that journey.

Prem Shankar Jha dwells on 'Where Indian Democracy has Gone Wrong'. After Nehru's 'years of empowerment', the prevailing regime of single party dominance was challenged in 1967 when a series of coalitional Samyukta Vidhayak Dal (SVD) formations took office. The Parliamentary process got stultified with the rise of personalised, 'clientelist' politics under Indira Gandhi who beat the regionalised money-powered control of the Congress machine by what later came to be known as the 'Syndicate'. Her resort to leveraging the Permit-Licence Raj System to raise funds aggravated trends towards the criminalisation of politics. This gradually stultified the parliamentary process—which was itself corrupted by the demands of electoral funding—giving rise to civil society and people's movements from JP to Anna Hazare. Lohia had even earlier preached 'socialism of the streets' whereby public policy would evolve through street action, leaving it for legislatures merely to endorse what the 'people' desired. This path threatens anarchy. The fertiliser (Thal Vaishet) and Bofors scams, among others, were precursors of what has more recently followed.

Jha's remedy is restoration of tax-deducible company donations to political parties and state funding. The Election Commission and students of electoral politics have suggested several other structural changes in the electoral system to make them more representative and transparent.

The same criminalisation of politics, coalition blackmail by small parties in and outside the government and the rapid turnover of governments is cited by Bimal Jalan. He too speaks of criminalisation of politics and of the permanent bureaucracy that has affected decision-making and spawned protection systems. The balkanisation of ministries has snarled clearance procedures and affected coherence and coordination. Collective responsibility has been a casualty. However coalition politics is here to stay for some time as the process of continuous empowerment from below is yet to exhaust itself. The answer is not to cavil at objective realities but to ensure firm governance. Swift and condign action against those violating established codes of behaviour will send a strong message and help stem the rot as tolerance of political and criminal misconduct has encouraged malfeasance. Smaller and more coherent ministries are in order and the current spoils system in the distribution of portfolios must end. Economic reform is necessary but perhaps administrative and system reform is even more urgent.

Shashi Tharoor laments the flight of the middle class from the civil services to the corporate and professional world. He however expects that the balance will right itself over the next decade as the Indian middle class rapidly increases in size. It is true that the middle class provides leadership of every kind, but if criminalisation of politics and politicisation of the civil service is not arrested, then Gresham's Law will prevail and the bad will drive out the good. On the other hand, Rakshanda Jalil is concerned about the continuing great divide between rural and urban, rich and poor, regions and gender and would have the country relearn the wisdom of Gandhi. Udaya Narayana Singh echoes this in terms of Centre and Periphery, we and they, English and the vernacular, and arrogant concepts of the mainstream. He would celebrate pluralism.

India however has come together despite its enormous diversity. Ramchandra Guha offers the example of language but laments that the bilingual intellectual has been in decline. Hindi or Hindustani is now quite widely spoken, less because of a stilted official language policy but more on account of Bollywood and the allure of commerce and employability over culture. Macaulay was not right in his scornful dismissal of the vernacular but he was not entirely wrong about the virtues of learning English, now the world's language. The vernacular in all its variety may have declined in commerce but must surely be encouraged to flourish as culture and the plea on 'lost tongues' should not go unheeded.

Communication, the media—print, radio, television and film—have bonded India but the telecom revolution, taken at the flood, has truly connected ordinary people and empowered them. With the right to information, those in authority are increasingly accountable and there is pressure for greater transparency. Broadcasting must serve the marginalised citizen as much as the high-spending consumer. Hence the importance of public service broadcasting which has been shabbily treated, by successive governments and the public, and disabled from setting standards in an overly market-oriented media environment.

Inclusive development was obviously one of the principal goals of freedom whose purpose, Gandhi said, must be to wipe the tear from every eye. We have made some headway but are nowhere near there. Indeed, our record is unflattering, with India's HDI and poverty indices ranking among the lowest even in sub-Saharan Africa and, latterly, within South Asia. Amartya Sen and Jean Drèze dwell on India's high growth, low HDI syndrome, dwell on China's superior record and call for inclusive growth. Brazil is held out as an example in its more recent reforming years. High growth is important as it provides the wherewithal to thrust forward, but that growth must be shared. India's democratic tradition cannot be pleaded as an excuse as its high growth over a considerable span of years disproves that 'discipline' yields greater dividends. Bibek Debroy looking at the time ahead cites the danger of India missing its demographic dividend unless it reforms its labour laws and legal structures to make production and regulatory procedures more efficient and investor friendly. He remarks on the country's rural to urban transition being impeded by hurdles to the creation of a rural land market. Sunita Narain argues in favour of the 'environmentalism of the poor' that would seek to prevent pollution, waste disposal and unsustainable development prior to allowing all this to happen and then striving to clean up the mess. Anupam Mishra concurs. He pleads the Gandhian axiom that if people own something, such as their own environment, they will protect it.

The Nehruvian foreign policy consensus on non-alignment, universal nuclear disarmament, decolonisation and UN reform is applauded by K. Natwar Singh. He however deplores that this framework has been jolted by Dr Manmohan Singh's moves to embrace the United States. Ninad D. Sheth however is aghast at India's lack of any grand strategy and flawed diplomacy over Kashmir, Tibet and the Simla Agreement. He traces non-alignment's roots to non-violence and pleads that India give up its continental posture and align with maritime democracies, including the US, in warding off China. He would develop India's indigenous military hardware capability, two-thirds of which is currently imported, and involve the armed forces in apex strategic decision making. Even so, the role and uses of soft power are not to be despised, as Mayuri Mukherjee reminds us.

There are other essays on the Naxal menace, Jammu & Kashmir and the Northeast. The Naxal problem will not be resolved unless the country understands the centrality of and implements the Fifth Schedule. Jagmohan is critical of Article 370 which, he feels, fosters separatism in Jammu & Kashmir, and would rather work towards some kind of India, Pakistan, Bangladesh confederation or economic union. The former proposition is problematic but many would say amen to the latter.

There is an engaging piece by Sumana Roy on the Chicken's Neck, a geo-strategic choke point. However, other essays on the Indian novel, comics, cinema, music and art, sport, gender budgeting and the changing city of Delhi, though interesting in themselves, belong slightly differently to this volume. Overall, the book speaks on how India has changed since 1947.

There certainly are many promises to keep and much might seem to be going wrong. There is however no reason to despair. India's democracy that binds its amazing plurality and civilisational roots gives us a resilience and strength to weather the critical transition we are making from an agrarian to an urbanising society with demography overwhelming geography. With the upthrust from below of vast cohorts getting empowered year by year, as millions graduate from 'Bharat' to 'India', the pressures are obviously great, progress tardy and disparities many. There is understandable impatience and anger at corruption and the need of the hour is for more and wider reform. At the same time much that is positive is happening too though not reported as such by a cynical media as 'breaking news'. Transitions are always difficult. But we shall overcome.

—B.G. Verghese
30 October 2012

Introduction

This book establishes the interface in diverse domains and presents an overview of modern India from the social history angle. The use of the social history perspective supports the narrative side and makes it more than a monotonous repetition of events from the recent past.

Writing contemporary history can be an adventure, especially on a country as diverse as India, where much happens but little is documented due to the lack of a culture of documentation of its past—both splendid and horrific. This anthology attempts to fill in this gap through a collection of thirty incisive essays—some by India's top scholars and others by young but insightful minds.

It was felt that alien perception, not being rooted in the complexities of this multi-cultural and multi-lingual country, could not present a true picture of things and events to readers—both from the east and the west.

The contributors' attempt is to counteract the trend of looking at India's history through an outsider's perspective. Such a sound research on modern Indian history, written by the Indians for India enthusiasts and Indophiles, was felt essential to portray *an Indian perspective* on India's history as a balance and a counterpoint to the outsiders' *perspective or viewpoint.*

This work attempts to describe how India progressed further with radical changes in its socio-economic order, overcoming the trauma of Partition. India's Constitution, based on progressive macro ideas, notionally secures the nation's egalitarian mandate. Under it, the Indian nation and system continued to grow over the years despite innumerable flaws.

Modern day India is very different from what it was in 1947, when the nation faced the challenges of existence. Now it struggles to develop, improve and clean up its systems in order to maximise its potential.

While some of the contributors to this anthology include the foremost architects of the new social history and need no formal introduction, others are known, through their work in journalism and academics, for their clear understanding of modern India. Every writer develops a specific theme from 1947 onwards and provides an analysis.

The essays have been written with a view to provide, in totality, an alternative narration on modern India, without distorting events or facts. Nonetheless, this anthology is far too serious to be attacked by the vociferous academic critics and carries the required facts, so that even the historians of different genre and intellectual taste would abstain from seeing this project of modern history, as a bit 'ahistorical'.

Ramchandra Guha's *The Rise and Fall of the Bilingual Intellectuals* goes into the details of what implication the process of displacing the vernaculars by the British connection has left on India as a modern nation.

In *India: Where Democracy Has Gone Wrong,* Prem Shankar Jha points out the origins of the corruption, extortion and lack of accountability to the people that bedevils governance in the country today. Bimal Jalan takes the matter forward with *India's Polity: Crisis of Governance.*

B.G. Verghese strikes the chord with investigating the actual function of public broadcasting in *Revisiting Public Service Broadcasting*. Shashi Tharoor's *Politics and the Indian Middle Class* reflects how the participation of middle class youth would be fateful for the Indian democracy in the days to come.

K. Natwar Singh recounts the main trends of India's external policy with *The First Sixty-Five Years of India's Foreign Policy*. Mayuri Mukherjee supplements the strategic dimension and furthers the debate through *Chess 3.0 in the Jungle: Mapping India's Engagement with the World in the 21st Century*. Ninad D Sheth's *India Adrift: Great Power Aspiration Without Grand Strategy* reminds India's insufficient strategic preparation under the changed global scenario.

While writing on Kashmir, *Kashmir: Past, Presents and Future*, Jagmohan touches the core issues, which media often categorised in the blocks of secularism and its alter shades. My own piece, *India: Underlined in Red!* focuses on the state of radical dissents in India, introspecting the last six decades, for finding the genesis and the causes of its persistence.

Sumana Roy's *In the Chicken's Neck* brings the lively truth from unexplored Siliguri Corridor, better known as the chicken's neck—a stretch of land that connects India's north-eastern states to what is called its "mainland" and to the crucial international borders. The North East has been given a fair portrayal by Ratnadip Choudhury in *The Seven-Sisters Plight.*

Over the decades, the politics of environmentalism has been evolving through two known factors–degradation of natural resources and activism for or against it. Sunita Narain's *The Decade of Environmentalism of the Poor* and Anupam Mishra's *Sadhya, Sadhan aur Sadhna* unleashes many shades on this front.

Jean Drèze and Amartya Sen put forth their concern on the inequitable economic growth of India in *Putting Growth in Its Place.* Bibek Debroy's *The Time Ahead for India* presents a sound projection on the Indian economy, taking into account the precedents that impacted its growth. Yamini Mishra and Navanita Sinha broadly forward the gender discourse in India with *Gender Responsive Budgeting in India: What has gone wrong.*

Rakhshanda Jalil's *Looking back: 64 Years of Independence* aims to see India, as it was in the making and now, through her own personal experiences and active drawing from collective memory. Rafia Zakaria's *A Woman Named Honour: The Good, the Bad and the Remembered* explores new understandings of how tthe good, the bad and the honourable have changed or remained the same in contemporary culture. Bishal Thapa's *In Search of India's Destiny* figures out the actual progress India has made over the decades.

Udaya Narayana Singh's *Another India: Voices from the Periphery* searches for the plural space for languages, along with looking on the conditions that are less supportive. Saugata Ghosh's *Litany of Lost Tongues* furthers the broad debate on languages. The literary part of the book revolves around the swiftly growing Indian English writing. Banibrata Mahanta's *The Indian Novel in English and National Identity* systematically recounts the influx and growth of English writing in India.

Pran Nevile has recalled modern India's most prominent musical genius in *K.L Saigal's Legacy*. Benoy K Behl's *The Art in Modern India* focuses on the various paradigms of art in modern India.

Santanu Banerjee and Subhadeep Ray's *Hunger on Celluloid: Through Satyajit Ray's Ashani Sanket and Beyond* is a serious quest to get back to those rich cinematic works, which overtured on meaningful issues like, famine, poverty, rural isolation, etc. Subhadeep Paul informs holistically on India's sports culture in his essay, *India's Tryst with Destiny in Sports.*

Alokita Datta's *Love, Loss and Longing: A Capital Affair* tells the modern history of New Delhi, as a capital of the world's largest democracy. Mahima Kaul's *Connecting India* concentrates on the digital inclusion efforts in India and tries to catch both its momentous and long term effects. And lastly, a growing child's point of view on India comes to the fore with Aditya Mani Jha's *Immortal Picture Stories: Growing Up with Indian Comics.*

To sum up, this anthology is an outcome of a painstaking preparation with which I remained associated for years. I am glad the way it has shaped up, and am hoping for an engaged debate following the readers' valuable comments and reviews and the message it sends across.

India, the world's largest democracy is a complex yet charming set of systems, which need a thorough looking back. The present anthology is an attempt to fulfil some of those needs on the idea-front. 'Action' too may be the order of the day. And that will remain a strong hope!

—Atul Kumar Thakur
06 March, 2013

The Rise and Fall of the Bilingual Intellectuals*

—*Ramachandra Guha*

This essay is inspired by an argument between the scholar-librarian B.S. Kesavan and his son Mukul that I was once privy to. I forget what they were fighting about. But I recall that the father, then past ninety years of age, was giving as well as he got. At periodic intervals he would turn to me, otherwise a silent spectator, and pointing to his son, say: '*Makku!*' '*Paithyam*!' Those were words that Mukul, born in Delhi of a Hindi-speaking mother, did not himself understand. But I did. They meant, roughly and respectively, 'imbecile' and 'lunatic'.

B.S. Kesavan knew that I lived in Bangalore, that both my parents were Tamil, and that one of my great-uncles had been a Tamil scholar. Thus, when his son's stupidity (real or alleged) could not be adequately conveyed in their shared language, namely, English, he took recourse to his mother-tongue, which was also theoretically mine. The emphasis must be on 'theoretically'. My great-uncle the Tamil scholar used to write postcards asking me to 'learn Tamil and lead a simple life'. I failed him wholly in the second respect, but have down the years managed to pick up a few dozen words of Tamil, among them *makku* and *paithyam*.

B.S. Kesavan was formidably multilingual. He was fluent in Tamil, Kannada and English, spoke Bengali adequately and Hindi passably, and had a good grasp of Sanskrit. No doubt his multilingualism came in handy in his work as the first Indian Director of the National Library, his nurturing of a National Information System, and his pioneering histories of publishing and printing. However, his taste for languages

* This is the revised version of the piece published under the same title in *Economic and Political Weekly* (EPW) dated 23 January 2010...the changes made are by the author himself.

was shared by many other Indians of his generation who did not necessarily require those skills in their jobs or careers. My own father, for instance, was a paper technologist by profession, speaks English and Tamil well, and Kannada and Hindi passably. He also has a reading knowledge of French and German. On the other hand, Mukul Kesavan and I are essentially comfortable in English alone. We can speak Hindi conversationally, and use documents written in Hindi for research purposes. But we cannot write scholarly books or essays in Hindi. And neither of us can pretend to a third language at all.

Let me move now from the personal to the historical, to an argument on the question of language between two great modern Indians. In the month of April 1921, Mahatma Gandhi launched a broadside against English education. First, in a speech in Odisha (now Odisha), he described it as an 'unmitigated evil'. Bal Gangadhar Tilak and Rammohan Roy would, said Gandhi, have 'been far greater men had they not the contagion of English learning'. In Gandhi's opinion, these two influential and admired Indians 'were pigmies who had no hold upon the people compared with Chaitanya, Sanker, Kabir, and Nanak'. Warming to the theme, Gandhi insisted that 'what Sanker alone was able to do, the whole army of English-knowing men can't do.' I can multiply instances? Was Guru Gobind a product of English education? Is there a single English-knowing Indian who is a match for Nanak, the founder of a sect second to none in point of valour and sacrifice? If the race has even to be revived it is to be revived not by English education.

A friend, reading the press reports of this talk in Odisha, asked Gandhi to explain his views further. Writing in his own newspaper, the Mahatma clarified that 'it is my considered opinion that English education in the manner it has been given has emasculated the English-educated Indian, it has put a severe strain on the Indian students' nervous energy, and has made of us imitators. The process of displacing the vernaculars has been one of the saddest chapters in the British connection. 'Rammohan Rai would have been a greater reformer', claimed the Mahatma, 'and Lokmanya Tilak would have been a greater scholar, if they had not to start with the handicap of having to think in English and transmit their thoughts chiefly in English'. Gandhi argued that 'of all the superstitions that affect India, none is so great as that a knowledge of the English language is necessary for imbibing ideas of liberty, and developing accuracy of thought'. As a result of the system of education introduced by the English, 'the tendency has been to dwarf the Indian body, mind and soul'.

One does not know whether the Mahatma's anonymous friend was content with this clarification. But someone who was less than satisfied with Gandhi's views was the poet Rabindranath Tagore. He was then travelling in Europe, where he received, by post, copies of Gandhi's articles. Tagore was dismayed by their general tenor and by the chastisement of Rammohan Roy in particular. On 10 May, 1921, he wrote to their common friend C.F. Andrews saying, 'I strongly protest against Mahatma Gandhi's depreciation of such great personalities of Modern India as Rammohan Roy in his zeal for declaiming against our modern education'. Gandhi had celebrated the example of Nanak and Kabir, but, as Tagore suggested, those saints 'were great because in their life and teaching they made organic union of the Hindu and Muhammadan cultures—and such realisation of the spiritual unity through all differences of appearance is truly Indian'.

In learning and appreciating English, argued Tagore, Rammohan Roy had merely carried on the good work of Nanak and Kabir. Thus in the modern age, Rammohan Roy had that comprehensiveness of mind to be able to realise the fundamental unity of spirit in the Hindu, Islamic and Christian cultures. Therefore he represented India in the fullness of truth, and this truth is based, not upon rejection, but on perfect comprehension'. Tagore pointed out that 'Rammohan Roy could be perfectly natural in his acceptance of the West, not only because his education had been perfectly Eastern—he had the full inheritance of the Indian wisdom. He was never a school boy of the West, and therefore he had the dignity to be the friend of the West. If he is not understood by modern India, this only shows the pure light of her own truth has been obscured for the moment by the storm-clouds of passion'.

Tagore's letter to Andrews was released to the press, and read by Gandhi. His answer was to say that he did 'not object to English learning as such', but merely to its being made a fetish, and to its being preferred as a medium of education to the mother-tongue. 'Mine is not a religion of the prison-house', he insisted: 'it has room even for the least among God's creation'. Refuting the charge that he or his non-co-operation movement was a manifestation of xenophobia, he said: 'I hope I am as great a believer in free air as the great Poet. I do not want my house to be walled in on all sides and my windows to be stuffed. I want the cultures of all the lands to be blown about my house as freely as possible. But I refuse to be blown off by any'.

These words are emblazoned in halls and auditoria across India, but always without the crucial first line: 'I hope I am as great a believer in free air as the great Poet'. Tagore had convinced Gandhi, but to make sure the conversion was permanent, he brought back into circulation some early essays warning against a xenophobic nationalism, published in Bengali in 1908-09. Tagore was worried that the non-co-operation movement would produce, among the young especially, an atavistic hatred of the West and of modern ideas. He was then travelling in Europe, raising funds for his university in Santiniketan. To instruct the over-zealous Gandhians, he instructed Satyendranath Tagore to translate his *Prabasi* essays for publication in English by the Madras firm of S. Ganesan (Had he the time he might very well have done the job himself).

In truth, despite this argument in theory, in practice Gandhi and Tagore were more-or-less on the same side. Gandhi wrote his books in Gujarati, but made certain that they were translated into English so as to reach a wider audience. And when required he could use the conqueror's language rather well himself. His first published articles, that appeared in the journal of the Vegetarian Society of London in 1891, were written in the direct and unadorned prose that was the hallmark of all his work in English, whether petitions to the colonial government, editorials in his journals *Indian Opinion, Young India,* and *Harijan,* or numerous letters to friends. In writing in more than one language, Gandhi was in fact merely following in the footsteps of those he had criticised. For Bal Gangadhar Tilak's mother-tongue was Marathi, a language in which he did certainly publish essays. On his part, Rammohan Roy had published books in Persian and essays in Bengali before he came to write in English (he was also fluent in

Sanskrit and Arabic). As for Tagore, this man who shaped and reshaped the Bengali language through his novels and poems, made sure that his most important works of non-fiction were available in English. His major political testament, *Nationalism,* was based on lectures he wrote and delivered in English. His important and still relevant essays on relations between East and West were either written in English or translated by a colleague under his supervision. Tagore understood that while love and humiliation at the personal or familial level were best expressed in the mother tongue, impersonal questions of reason and justice had to be communicated in a language read by more people and over a greater geographical space than Bengali.

By writing in English as well as their mother-tongue, Gandhi and Tagore were serving society as well as themselves. They reached out to varied audiences—and, by listening to their views, broadened the bases of their own thought. This open-mindedness was also reflected in their reading. Thus Gandhi read (and was influenced by) thinkers who were not necessarily Gujarati. The debt he owed to Ruskin and Tolstoy was scarcely less than that owed to Raychandbhai or Narsingh Mehta. Gandhi was also enriched by the time he spent outside Gujarat—the several years in England, the several decades in South Africa, the millions of miles travelling through the Indian countryside.

On his part, Tagore was widely read in European literature. When he visited Germany in the 1920s at the invitation of his publisher, Kurt Wolff, his host remembered the 'universal breadth of Tagore's learning', their conversations revealing 'without doubt that he knew far more of the West than most of the Europeans he encountered knew of the East'. Tagore had spoken, among other things, of the work of T. S. Eliot. 'It is quite remarkable', said Wolff, 'that someone born in India in 1861 should display such an interest in and grasp of an Anglo-American poet thirty years his junior'.

Like Gandhi, Tagore learnt as much from his travels as from his books. He spent long periods in Europe, visited Japan and the United States several times, and also went to China, South-east Asia, Iran, and Latin America.

For Gandhi, and for Tagore, the foreign language was a window into another culture, another civilisation, another way (or ways) of living in the world. For them, the command of a language other than their own was a way of simultaneously making themselves less parochial and their work more universal. Their readings and travels fed back into their own writing, thus bringing the world to Bengal and Gujarat, and (when they chose to write in the foreign language) Bengal and Gujarat to the world. Bilingualism was here a vehicle or something larger and more enduring—namely, multiculturalism.

In these respects Gandhi and Tagore were wholly representative. Before them there was Sir Syed Ahmad Khan, who moved between Urdu and English as he strove simultaneously to make the British more sensitive to Muslim interests and Muslims more willing to engage with modernity. After them there was B.R. Ambedkar, who wrote in Marathi for a local constituency; and in English for the rest of India and for the world. Ambedkar knew his Tukaram, but also his John Stuart Mill. To take another example, C. Rajagopalachari is still admired for his English style; but few now know that he was a pioneering essayist and short-story writer in Tamil. He knew his Kural, but—as he once reminded an interviewer—he had also read Thoreau well before he met Mahatma Gandhi. Rajaji's contemporary V.D. Savarkar also wrote books in English, as well as plays and polemical tracts in Marathi. From the other end of the political spectrum, consider the communist E.M.S. Namboodiripad, who was a prolific writer and polemicist in both Malayalam and English.

Possible exceptions to this trend are M.A. Jinnah, Jawaharlal Nehru, and Subhas Bose, who were also all thinker-politicians, albeit of a monolingual variety. Jinnah, as is well known, was not exactly fluent in Urdu. Nehru could give a public lecture in Hindustani and Bose in Bengali; however, their major writings, like Jinnah's, are all in English.

A thinker-politician who, at first glance, may seem to have been an aberration is Rammanohar Lohia. To be sure, Lohia called for the abolition of English from educational institutions and in public life, and, at the same time, for the countrywide promotion of Hindi. However, Lohia advocated not monolingualism but multilingualism. He asked for school instruction to be provided in the mother tongue, but insisted that children must, in addition, learn two other languages—Hindi, and either a foreign language or another Indian language. He saw the need for an international language, to be used in communications between nations, but was not convinced that this had necessarily and for all time to be English. The role had been played by French in the past; and would, he thought, perhaps be played by Russian or Chinese in the future. Lohia himself knew German (he had taken his PhD at the University of Berlin), while some of his finest polemical essays against the use of English were written in that language itself.

So in fact Lohia was not an exception after all. Bilingualism and multiculturalism came naturally to him, as it did to the other leaders of his generation. It also came naturally to the social scientists who were their contemporaries. Of those active in the 1940s and 1950s, the anthropologists Nirmal Kumar Bose and Irawati Karve, the economist D.R. Gadgil, and the sociologist D.P. Mukerji—all made a name for themselves for their work in English as well as for their writings in their mother tongue. They tended to publish academic papers in English, and more popular or literary essays in Bengali or Marathi. Sometimes the work in the local language was translated into English, and made a considerable impact (as for example with Karve's re-rendition of the Mahabharata, *Yuganta*.) As with Gandhi and Tagore, the process of enrichment was two-sided—they themselves became less parochial, while through their writings they allowed their parish to feel palpably part of a wider world.

The bilingualism of the politicians and scholars was matched by the writers and critics. It was, I think, Harish Trivedi who first noted that many of the finest creative writers of the middle decades of the twentieth century were Professors of English, yet wrote their poems and stories in other languages. His essay is not at hand as I write, but among the names Professor Trivedi may have mentioned were the poet Gopalkrishna Adiga and the novelist U.R. Anantha Murty in Kannada; the poet Harivanshrai Bachchan and the short story writer Nirmal Verma in Hindi; and the poet Firaq Gorakhpuri in Urdu. All taught English literature; some even had PhDs in the subject from the best British Universities. Literary historians could doubtlessly add many other names to the list—of established writers in Assamese, Oriya,

Bengali, Tamil, Telugu, etc, who made their living teaching English yet wrote in the mother tongue in order to live.

Here, too, facility with more than one tongue was a matter not just of skill but also of sensibility. The writer, his work, and his audience, all benefited from the fact that the person in question was in command of more than one linguistic or cultural universe. Surely Bachchan's Hindi verse must have at some level been influenced by, or been a response to, his doctoral work at Cambridge on W.B. Yeats. By the same token, his classroom teaching and the occasional essays he wrote in English must certainly have been enriched by his immersion in the world of Hindi letters.

Perhaps the most striking instance of this bilingualism concerns the crafting of Premchand's *Godan*. This work, published in 1936, is considered the very archetype of the modern Hindi novel, yet the author first outlined the plot in English!

In the inter-war period, no Indian town better expressed this multilinguality than the town where B.S. Kesavan spent some of his best years, Mysore. Among the town's residents then were the Kannada poet K.V. Puttappa (Kuvempu), who wrote political essays in English; the English novelist R.K. Narayan, who was equally fluent in Tamil and Kannada; and the journalist H.Y. Sharada Prasad, who thought and wrote in Kannada, but whose command of English was later put to good effect in the many speeches he ghosted for successive Prime Ministers of India. A somewhat younger resident was A.K. Ramanujan, who later recalled that, growing up in Mysore, he had necessarily to become equally familiar with the language of the street (Kannada), the language of the kitchen (Tamil, spoken by his mother), and the language of the study upstairs (occupied by his father, who liked to converse in English). Ramanujan was an accomplished poet in both Kannada and English, and achieved undying fame for his translations into English of Kannada and Tamil folklore and folk poetry—work that was enabled, in the first instance, by his growing up in the multilingual intellectual universe of Mysore.

Mysore was here representative of other towns in colonial India. The intellectual culture of Dharwad, Cochin, Allahabad, etc, was likewise bilingual, with writers and professors operating both in English and in the language of the locality or province. There was a cultural continuum that ran between *qasba* and *mahanagar,* between the smaller urban centres and the great cities of the Presidencies.

The bilingualism I have described was a product of a particular historical conjuncture—namely, the advent first of colonialism, and later, of nationalism. The British required some Indians to learn English, to interpret between them and their subjects, and to assist in governance and administration (as well as in commerce and trade). However, over time the language of the rulers also became a vehicle to demand equal rights from them. Thus, from being an accessory in the process of conquest and control, English became an ally in the process of protest and profanation. It was the language in which Indian nationalists' chastised the British for not living up to their own best traditions. Simultaneously, it also became the language in which intellectually or politically minded Indians could communicate across the different linguistic zones of the Empire. Notably, even as they acquired a working knowledge of English (or better), these reform-minded Indians continued to operate in their mother tongue. The latter served best for creative literary expression, and when focusing on the abolition of reactionary social practices; the former was necessary for nurturing or deepening cross-provincial networks of political action.

Between (roughly) the 1920s and 1970s, the intellectual universe in India was—to coin a word—'linguidextrous'. With few exceptions, the major political thinkers, scholars and creative writers—and many of the minor ones too—thought and acted and wrote with equal facility in English and at least one other language. It appears that this is no longer the case. The intellectual and creative world in India is increasingly becoming polarised—between those who think and act and write in English alone, and those who think and write and act in their mother tongue alone.

The state of West Bengal appears to have held out best (and longest) against this separation of literary and intellectual discourses. At least in Kolkata, there are still very many intellectuals who are properly linguidextrous. In 2009, Ranajit Guha was awarded the prestigious Ananda Puraskar for a book on Tagore in Bengali. Coincidentally, his collected essays in English were published in the same week. Ranajit Guha is of course a *prabasi*, but of those still resident in Kolkata, Supriya Chaudhuri, Sukanta Chaudhuri, Partha Chatterjee, and Swapan Chakravarty are all world-renowned scholars for their writings in English—and they have written first-rate essays and books in Bengali as well. These scholars are all the wrong side of fifty, but there are, I am reliably told, some Bengali men and women now in their thirties and forties who likewise move effortlessly between the language of the world and the language of the locality.

In a life lived in-between the interstices of the academy and the press, I have had the privilege of knowing and befriending many linguidextrous intellectuals. Some are *prabasi* Bengalis, such as those remarkable couples Tanika and Sumit Sarkar, Kalpana and Pranab Bardhan, and Meenakshi and Sujit Mukherjee. Others have come from more subaltern linguistic zones, for example Kumar Ketkar, Madhav Gadgil, Dilip Chitre, and Rajendra Vora (Marathi), Shahid Amin (Hindi), Girish Karnad and D.R. Nagaraj (Kannada), C.V. Subba Rao (Telugu), Jatin Kumar Nayak (Oriya), and N.S. Jagannathan (Tamil). Like me, all these writers have written a great deal in English; unlike me, they have published important work in their other language too. In countless conversations down the decades, I have been to them what the readers of Gandhi and Tagore were to those great Indians—namely, a grateful recipient of knowledge and understanding derived from languages that I do not myself speak or read.

Notably, the individuals mentioned in the preceding paragraph were all born more than fifty years ago. Speaking of the younger generation, linguidextrous intellectuals run more thinly on the ground—at least outside of Bengal. Of scholars in their forties, I can think easily of only three who would qualify—A.R. Venkatachalapathy, Tridip Suhrud, and Yogendra Yadav. All have considerable and independently won reputations for their writings in their language (Tamil in the one case, Gujarati in the second, Hindi in the third) as well as English. A fourth name might be that of the young historian Arupjyoti Saikia, who writes in both Assamese and English.

In general, though, the gap between the generations is telling. Consider thus the career of Sadanand More, whose major works include a reception history of the poet-saint Tukaram and a study of the transition from Tilak to Gandhi in the politics of western India. As I have discovered on several visits to Pune, he is something of a cult figure in Maharashtra, because of his books and his columns in newspapers. Had he written in English, he might have been considered the Partha Chatterjee of Maharashtra—he is comparable in the range of his interests and the originality of his mind.

A distinction must be made here between reading a language and knowing it through and through. There are those who are *functionally* bilingual; and yet others who are *intellectually* and *emotionally* bilingual. I use letters and news reports written in Hindi for my research, raiding them for facts and opinions. But I do not read Hindi for pleasure, nor could I think of writing an essay in Hindi in a quality journal. In this I believe I speak for many other social scientists of my age or younger. These too may be able to use an Indian language as source material, but—unlike their predecessors N.K. Bose and Irawati Karve—cannot see themselves as contributing to literary or academic debate in that language. They, and I, are admittedly cosmopolitan, but in a somewhat shallow sense, knowing the world well without knowing the locality much—or at all.

At the same time, at the other end of the linguistic spectrum, many—perhaps most—of the best poets and novelists in Tamil, Kannada, Hindi, Oriya, Gujarati, etc., are likewise completely comfortable in one language only. They may occasionally read a novel or tract in English, but most of their reading—and all their writing—is confined to a single language, their own. No Kannada novelist of the younger generation has anything like the acquaintance with Western literature and social theory once commanded by U.R. Anantha Murty. The Hindi writers I meet are all deeply rooted in their environment, yet few follow Nirmal Verma in his curiosity about, or knowledge of, the wider world.

My evidence is somewhat anecdotal, but I believe most observers will agree with the thrust of my conclusions—namely, that there has been a decline in the number and visibility of scholars and writers who are properly linguidextrous. The third class of bilingual thinkers, the politicians, is wholly depopulated now. In my view, the last active politician to have any serious claims to intellectual originality was Jayaprakash Narayan, who, of course, wrote and thought and argued in both Hindi and English. (Critics with more lax standards may offer the names of Mani Shankar Aiyar and Arun Shourie. In any case, whether intellectual or not, original or not, they operate in English alone.)

One sphere of life which has somewhat retained its linguidextrouness is the theatre. Playwrights and stage directors such as (among others) Arundhati Nag, K.V. Akshara, and Sudhanva Deshpande move easily between the worlds of Kannada or Marathi or Hindi theatre on the one hand and English theatre on the other. All across the subcontinent, plays written in one language are regularly performed in another. Among stage actors who are multilingual, Naseerudin Shah is perhaps the best known and most widely admired; but there are many others, among them even some in their twenties and thirties.

There is still a certain amount of functional bilinguality among India's intellectual class; but emotional or intellectual bilinguality, once ubiquitous, is now present only in pockets, these too of chiefly older women and men. What are the reasons for this? A key reason, in retrospect, was the creation and consolidation of linguistic states after 1956. I have argued elsewhere that linguistic states have helped save the unity of India. Had we not allowed states to be constituted around language, and had we instead imposed Hindi on the whole country, we might have gone the way of a now divided Pakistan and a war-torn Sri Lanka.

I believe that on balance, linguistic states were indeed a good thing. Even in the particular context of intellectual work, they have had good as well as bad effects. The expansion of the school network, and the entry into the political system of previously excluded groups, has greatly deepened the social bases of the intellectual class. Literature and scholarship across India was once dominated by Brahmins, Banias, Kayasths, and well-born Muslims. But from the 1950s, very many Dalits and OBCs began entering schools and colleges. Some went on to become professors and writers, taking to jobs and careers that would have been closed to men and women of their background half-a-century previously.

In most states, however, instruction in government schools was conducted in the official language of the state alone. There was little room for English—sometimes, no room at all. English was removed from Gujarati schools in the 1950s and from schools in West Bengal in the 1970s—each time, at the instance of men (Morarji Desai in the first case, Jyoti Basu and Ashok Mitra in the second case) who were themselves superbly fluent in English. It has been claimed—not altogether implausibly—that the parochialism and xenophobia that underlies the rise of a certain Gujarati politician is not unrelated to the banning of the one language which, to quote that other and more broad-minded Gujarati politician, would have best allowed the cultures of other lands to be blown freely around and about the west coast of India. Similarly, the decline of West Bengal as a centre of science and scholarship is not unconnected to the equally misguided decision to ban English-teaching in the state-run schools of the province.

In the 1960s and 1970s, at the same time as the subaltern classes were producing their first major crop of scholars and writers, the elites were choosing to patronise English-language schools alone. In the North Indian public school I studied in, Hindi was *verboten*—the boy most badly ragged in my time spoke ungrammatical English with a Hindi accent. The experience was representative—in other towns and cities across India, upper caste children whose fathers may have, in colonial times, studied in government schools where both Sanskrit and the local language had an important place, were sent to 'convent' or public schools where English was the preferred language of communication, with Hindi (or its equivalent) allotted a minor, residual and contemptible place in the curriculum.

English in post-colonial India was the language of status and prestige. With the opening of the economy after 1991 it also became the language of economic and material advancement. The spread of English was further helped along by the growing number of inter-caste and inter-community marriages in urban India. If, for example, a Tamil-speaking girl met a Bengali-speaking boy in an office which functioned in English, and the two fell in love and later married, the chances were, and are, that the home language would, by default, be English, this becoming, in time, the first, preferred and perhaps also sole language of the children of the union. Cases like these must, by now, number in the hundreds of thousands. And it is from professional unions such as these that some of India's most prominent scholars and writers have been and will be born.

This separation of discourses is reflected in the growing distance—cultural as much as geographical—that now exists between the *qasba* and the *mahanagar*. Smaller towns tend to produce thinkers and writers who operate in the local language alone, whereas professors and students in the elite colleges of the metropolis are often comfortable only in English. In a cultural and linguistic sense, Karnatak College, Dharwar, is worlds removed from Christ College, Bangalore; D.A.V. College, Dehradun, from St. Stephen's College, Delhi.

The Kannada writer U.R. Anantha Murthy uses the term 'vernacular anxiety' to describe the condition of many writers in Indian languages. There may perhaps be a comparable 'cosmopolitan anxiety' among those who write in English alone. Sometimes, this anxiety masquerades as arrogance (as, in the case of Salman Rushdie, who once claimed that all the best writing about India appeared in English); at other times, as defensiveness.

Notably, the decline of intellectual bilingualism has been accompanied by a rise of functional bilingualism among the population at large. Many more Indians now speak more than one language than they ever did in the past. The universe of the farm and village is classically monolingual, whereas the universe of the office and factory emphatically is not. Thus, industrialisation and urbanisation have brought together millions of people speaking different languages at home. Migrants to cities and towns find that the *lingua franca* of their workplace is, as often as not, something other than their mother tongue. Bihari labourers in the informal sector in Kolkata have perforce to speak Bengali, while Malayalam workers in public sector units in Bangalore have necessarily to learn some Kannada.

Meanwhile, Hindi and English have emerged as pan-Indian languages of communication and conversation. Where official attempts to promote Hindi in southern and eastern India conspicuously failed, the language has nonetheless spread through the more informal, and hence more acceptable, medium of television and film. In cities like Bangalore and Hyderabad, in Mumbai, and now even in Kolkata, Hindi is widely used as the default language of conversation between two Indians reared to speak other tongues. The spread of English owes itself to more instrumental factors—the fact that it is the language of the international market-place and of the larger companies and firms that operate in it. Since the best-paying and often most prestigious jobs demand knowledge of English, there is a huge incentive to acquire it.

And so, while intellectuals tend increasingly to operate in a single linguistic sphere, millions of Indians in other jobs, trades, and professions are acquiring proficiency in tongues other than their own.

In those essays of 1921, Gandhi had hedged his opposition to English with a series of caveats. 'I am opposed to make a fetish of English education, I don't hate English education', he said. 'I know what treasures I have lost not knowing Hindustani and Sanskrit', he continued. We may endorse these sentiments while recognising, sixty years after Gandhi's death that an equal danger lies in making a fetish of the opposition to English. Those who banned English in West Bengal deprived millions of schoolchildren of a wider education. Now, to those Kannada writers who ask for instruction in the mother tongue alone, the Dalits answer—first you did not allow us to learn Sanskrit, now you want to deny us access to English.

The decline of the bilingual intellectual in contemporary India is thus a product of a combination of many factors: public policy—which emphasised the mother tongue alone; elite preference—which denied or diminished the mother tongue altogether; social change—as in new patterns of marriage; and economic change—as in the material gains to be had from a command of English.

The temporal sphere of my arguments is restricted to the twentieth century; the spatial sphere, to my country alone. Those who know the history of pre-colonial India may have interesting and important things to say about the multilingual nature of intellectual discourse in past times. Meanwhile, as someone who has a casual acquaintance with contemporary Europe, let me suggest that the intellectuals in that continent have gone in exactly the reverse direction to ours. Once, they operated mainly or even exclusively in the language that defined their nation—the French in French, the Spanish in Spanish, etc. Now, with the emergence of the European Union and the growth of English as a global language, these French and Spanish and German thinkers have abandoned their opposition to the foreign tongue without disavowing their own. The best (or at rate most successful) French thinkers now are linguidextrous, writing essays and books in their own language as well as in English. Scholars in other European nations have gone even further. Thus the distinguished ecological thinker J. Martinez-Alier writes in English for a global audience, in Spanish for his compatriots, and in Catalan for the people of his own province.

I shall end this essay with two stories which illustrate the sometimes unanticipated glories of the best kind of linguidextrousness. When H.Y. Sharada Prasad died in 2009, a letter-writer in *Outlook* magazine complained that in all his years in New Delhi, serving Prime Ministers and earning their trust and respect, Sharada Prasad had never lifted a finger for a single Kannadiga. The parochialism was characteristic of our times. For what the letter-writer did not recognise is that by translating the novels of Shivarama Karanth into English, Sharada Prasad had done a far greater service to the Kannada language, and to Kannadigas, than had he got some of them ten minutes with Indira Gandhi or an out-of-turn gas connection.

Sharada Prasad spoke Kannada, Tamil, Telugu, and English very well—and knew some Sanskrit and Hindi too. The other Indian of my acquaintance who comes closest to this multi-lingual dexterousness is the writer and public servant Gopalkrishna Gandhi. Literary critics know Gopal Gandhi as the translator into Hindi of Vikram Seth's novel *A Suitable Boy*. He has also written his own books, in English. However, these are only two of the languages this good man can fluently read, write, and speak. I recently discovered that his first literary production was undertaken as a boy of seventeen, when he translated the memoirs of Manu Gandhi from Gujarati into English. He speaks Tamil, which was the language of his mother, quite beautifully. More recently, he has acquired an adequate knowledge of Bengali.

For all his achievements, among Indian intellectuals at any rate Gopal Gandhi can only be known as the younger brother of the philosopher, Ramchandra (Ramu) Gandhi. Although he wrote several important books, Ramu Gandhi was at his best at the lectern. I have never heard a more brilliant lecturer—a judgement that would I think be endorsed by most people who heard him speak in either Hindi or English, among them the very many students he trained and inspired at the universities of Rajasthan, Delhi, Hyderabad and Santiniketan. After he quit academic life, Ramu Gandhi's main theatre of operation was the India International Centre (IIC), where he would lecture occasionally in the auditorium, and more informally—if to equal effect—in the lounge or the bar.

Ramu Gandhi was the son of Mahatma Gandhi's youngest son, whereas his mother was the daughter of C. Rajagopalachari. In the mid 1950s, when Ramu was entering university, Rajaji took an extended holiday from politics to write modern renditions of the Ramayana and the Mahabharata. He wrote them first in his native Tamil, and then translated them into English.

These modern versions of the epics proved so popular that a demand arose for translations into other languages. Rajaji's daughter, Lakshmi Devadas Gandhi, volunteered to do them in Hindi, a language she knew well in part due to long residence in New Delhi. The Hindi versions sold briskly and continuously—they were still selling in the 1960s, and well into the 1970s. Sometimes towards the end of that decade Mrs Devadas Gandhi decided to make a will. However, as the daughter and daughter-in-law of ascetic and incorruptible politicians, she had no worldly possessions to speak of.

Of course except for the royalties from those translations. Who then to will them too? Mrs Gandhi had three sons. The first, Rajmohan was a journalist and author of popular works of biography and history—surely the Fourth Estate and his publishers would take care of him where he ever in distress? The youngest son, Gopal, was a member of the Indian Administrative Service—he would, in time, get a *sarkari* pension linked to the cost-of-living index. That left the middle son, the dreamy philosopher who had left six jobs and declined to accept six others.

So it was to Ramu Gandhi that the royalties were willed, and to him, after his mother's death in 1983, which they came. Every year, without fail, Ramu would get a cheque for several thousand rupees that would comfortably cover the cumulative bills, for that year from the IIC bar. And, so, in this manner, works originally composed in Sanskrit, then rendered in Tamil and still later translated into Hindi, were to fuel the belly and the mind of the most brilliant man to have walked the lawns or entered the bar or spoken in the auditorium of the India International Centre.

The story may be apocryphal, but it deserves to be true. For it illustrates like nothing else the beauty and potency of intellectual and literary bilingualism—practised in this case across three successive generations—father, daughter, and grandsons.

India: Where Democracy has Gone Wrong

—Prem Shankar Jha

On 27 August 2011, when the Indian parliament agreed to include three key clauses in the bill to set up the Lok Pal that had been demanded by Anna Hazare, the leader of the Bhrashtachar Virodhi Andolan (India Against Corruption) movement, as a precondition for ending his fast-unto-death, all of India hailed it as a victory for democracy—perhaps the greatest in India's sixty-five years of freedom. But a year later the victory of August had become a dim memory. The Lok Pal Bill lay marooned in the parliament because state governments like that of West Bengal decided that a clause requiring them to set up Lok Ayuktas (State Ombudsmen) that would work under the supervision of the Lok Pal was an infringement of their rights under the Indian Constitution. A year later, with the Indian economy in a tailspin, small factories pulling down their shutters and employment declining, the attention of the public had shifted from longer term issues of empowerment to a growing concern for their economic future.

India's power elite has heaved a sigh of relief. But the dissatisfaction with the Indian State which brought millions out on the streets in support of Anna Hazare when he went on his first and second fasts in April and August 2011 has not abated. This dissatisfaction is not new. The Nehru years were undoubtedly years of empowerment: the government was honest; it drew up grand plans for ending poverty, and the people believed in them. But the euphoria did not last. Disillusionment first revealed itself in a so-called protest vote in the 1967 General Elections. In these elections which were the last to be held simultaneously for the parliament and the state assemblies, a clear pattern emerged in which higher than normal turnouts to vote were invariably associated with setbacks for the then-dominant Congress party.

This dissatisfaction became endemic in the 1980s. Voters threw out incumbent governments so regularly that this came to be known as the 'anti-incumbency factor'. But people soon realised that changing governments made no difference to their lives. No matter who came to power, the same, extortionate and oppressive *Mai Baap sarkar* continued to rule their lives. Gradually, concerned citizens realised that to change things they would have to exert pressure from outside Parliament. That was when the civil society movement, as it has now come to be called, was born.

Where Did Indian Democracy Go Wrong?

The origins, the corruption, extortion and lack of accountability to the people that bedevils governance in the country today can be traced to two deep flaws in the Constitution India adopted in 1950. The first is the omission of a system for meeting the cost of running a democracy, i.e. the entire process of selecting and then electing the people's representatives. The second is the failure to enact provisions that would convert a bureaucracy that had been schooled over a century into believing that its function was to rule the people into its servants.

The first arose from an unthinking emulation of the British practice. What the members of the Constituent Assembly forgot was that whereas the average British constituency was 375 sq km in size, and today has an electorate of 60,000, the average parliamentary constituency in India is 6,000 sq km in size and has 1.2 million voters. In Britain, a candidate for Parliament can therefore get into his car every morning, visit two or three towns and villages, and return home every night. But in its Indian counterpart, the typical constituency has more than a thousand villages. To man its 1,000-1,200 polling booths, every serious candidate has to employ at least 8,000 persons on polling day. The cost is, quite simply, enormous. The failure of the Constituent Assembly to understand how this difference in size made it impossible to copy the British model in India was surprising, to say the least.

The oversight could have been remedied with a constitutional amendment at a later date, but instead, in 1967, Indira Gandhi took the country in the opposite direction and choked off the only legitimate source of funds that had sprung up in the intervening years. This was the donations from corporations that all parties, except the Communists, had begun to depend upon.

Gandhi took this decision, weeks after the Congress party came close to defeat in the General Election of 1967. Not only did its tally in the Lok Sabha fall from 353 to 282—only 10 more than what it needed for a majority but for the first time, it also lost the Assembly elections in six major states. It first repealed the tax concessions on donations to political parties and followed it up three years later with a complete ban on company donations to political parties. But while choking the political system's main source of funds, she deliberately did not create an alternative.

She did this because her purpose was not, as her party claimed, to reduce the influence of big business on policy-making. The second Industrial Policy Resolution of 1956 had already done this. It was to cripple a rising threat from the right by depriving it of funds. In 1967, the pro-market Swatantra Party, formed by C Rajagopalachari in 1961, and the Bharatiya Jana Sangh (BJS) had fought the elections jointly and become a serious threat to the Congress in three states. These were Madhya Pradesh, where the BJS won 78 out of the 296 seats, Gujarat, where the Swatantra Party won 66 out of 168 seats, and Rajasthan, where, by winning 72 seats, they succeeded in reducing the Congress to a minority.

More than their share of the seats, the Congress feared their much larger share of the vote, for this threatened to turn them into a magnet for the then numerous smaller parties and independents. A two-party, or at least two-coalition, political system, therefore, seemed on the point of being born, but the threat that a second national party could pose to the Congress was too much for its leaders to stomach. It therefore, knowingly, passed a law designed to starve the Opposition of funds that only it, by virtue of being in power, could flout with impunity.

Birth of the Predator State

The ban on company donations closed the only honest, open and transparent avenue for raising funds to fight elections, which had come into being since Independence. Like Solomon Bandaranaike's Sinhala-only language policy of 1956, it was entirely opportunistic. And as in Sri Lanka, the harm it has done is beyond measure. For it has deprived all political parties, including the Congress, of the option of remaining honest. It therefore, opened the gates for the entry of crime and black money into politics.

Over almost half a century, we have become familiar with the corruption and extortion that this has bred. But few understand the deadly impact that it has had on Indian politics. Its immediate effect was to all but destroy the centrist Opposition in Indian politics, and strengthen its ideological extremes. The Swatantra, being the most dependent on funds from the corporate sector, simply threw in the towel: most of its members merged with the Jana Sangh. The two socialist parties, the Praja Socialist Party (PSP) and the Samyukta Socialist Party (SSP), weakened rapidly, merged, then joined the Janata Party in 1977 and finally, disappeared altogether. Their place was taken by a host of caste and ethnicity-based political parties that we are familiar with today.

Only the Jana Sangh and the two Communist parties survived relatively unscathed. By the late 70s, therefore, the dream that India would one day develop a bipolar political system similar to that of Britain had vanished.

A second, more serious effect has been to stifle intra-party democracy. The ban on company donations made it harder even for the Congress to raise funds, for its managers had to replace a relatively small and stable cadre of large donors with a much larger number of widely dispersed donors, who were prepared to contribute small sums in cash. Over time, the sheer difficulty of doing this every few years has made them extremely reluctant to disturb a financing network once it had been established. In 80 per cent of the constituencies, these networks are inevitably local. All the favour-swapping that has to be made to establish them centres on gaining the favour of not only the party in power, but more specifically, the candidate who represents it in the legislature. This is the origin of clientelist politics.

The actual deals are struck by self-appointed lieutenants, who give candidates the elbow room necessary to modify, or get out of, conflicting commitments. Once a network is established, and especially once it has succeeded in getting its candidate elected, the lieutenants have the most powerful of interests in making sure that it is not threatened by a rival. New entrants into politics determined to change things stand little chance of breaking these clientelist networks. Thus, the more Indian democracy has matured, the more it has succeeded in shutting new people out of politics unless they too are prepared to become a part of the existing clientelist networks.

A corollary to this has been the rise of the so-called princelings, a second generation of leaders in Indian politics who have inherited and not earned their constituencies. In western democracies, when a long-term Member of Parliament, National Assembly or Congress dies, the party almost always chooses a successor on the basis of his or her standing in the constituency. In India, by contrast, the death of a senior politician triggers a rush by the operators of his clientelist network (who have all been inducted into the party by then) to Delhi or the state capital to make sure that there is no contest for the vacant seat, and that the dead leader's wife, son or daughter is nominated to take the parent's place. They do this because, sentiment apart, this is the one way of making sure that the clientelist network will not be disturbed. While some princelings regularly capture headlines, they make up only a small visible fringe of the tribe. A study by Patrick French of the composition of the 2009 Lok Sabha showed 156 MPs (28.5 percent), including 78 from the Congress (37.5 percent), were selected as candidates because of their family connections. What is still more significant is the preponderance of princelings in the younger members. What is more, French found that 'nearly half of all MPs aged 50 or under, are hereditary selected to contest a seat primarily because they are the children of politicians. Thirty-three of the youngest 38 MPs and every Congress MP under the age of 35 entered Parliament because of their birth.

These figures are disturbing not because of their character and ability, which is much higher than the average, but because, as French concluded: If you do not come from an established ruling family, you have almost no chance of progressing in national politics, unless you join an ideological party such as the Bharatiya Janata Party

(BJP) or the Communist Party of India (Marxist), where lineage is not important.'

A third, unforeseen consequence has been the weakening of national leaderships of the main, non-ideological parties. In this too, the Congress was the first sufferer. When donations were legal, the money used to come directly to the president or treasurer of the political party. This ensured that the reins of financial power remained in the hands of its leaders whom the public recognised and could hold accountable for the way it was collected and spent. But once money began to be raised clandestinely, financial power slipped into the hands of anonymous, unaccountable and, more often than not, unsavoury characters. What is more, control over these new money collectors passed more and more out of the hands of the central party leaders into those of the leaders in the states.

Over time, the price that fundraisers demanded kept growing and, with it, the power of the elected leaders to choose candidates or determine policy, declined. One of the first victims of the change was Indira Gandhi herself. Scholars have severely criticised the way in which she concentrated power within the Congress in her own hands during the Emergency, but in reality, this was a defensive action to stem a weakening of her control over the party that only she fully sensed. For by the mid-1970s; she had all but lost control of several charismatic Congress chief ministers, including H.N. Bahuguna in UP and V.P. Naik in Maharashtra. Both were able administrators, and Bahuguna in particular, had restored efficient governance in UP after a lapse of several years. The main reason why Gandhi felt obliged to withdraw her trust from them was that they were no longer obeying the Centre's directives. In all, Gandhi changed the chief ministers in the Congress-ruled states no fewer than 15 times between 1975 and 1977. That she did this during the 21 months of the Emergency, when, in theory, she was at the peak of her powers, shows how much the Centre had been weakened by the changes that had occurred within the party.

The weakening of the central leadership of the Congress has reduced the capacity of the national leaders to take hard decisions in national interest. In 1967, Gandhi was able to overcome the resistance of a powerful regional chief minister in Assam, B.P. Chaliha, and separate

Meghalaya from Assam. Sixteen years later, her inability to control the Punjab Congress precipitated the Khalistan insurgency in the state. Not only was the Punjab Congress responsible for the rise of Jarnail Singh Bhindranwale, whom it actively fostered in an attempt to break the Akali Party, but three meetings between Gandhi and Sant Longowal in 1983 failed to produce an agreement over four long-standing demands that, if conceded, would have stemmed the rise of separatism in Punjab. This was because she was unable to persuade the state Congress party's leaders in Punjab (and Haryana), to endorse anything that would give the Akalis an edge over them in the next election. The country paid the price for her failure with ten years of insurgency and 61,000 civilian lives. Two thirds of the victims were Sikhs.

The fourth consequence is the entry of criminals into politics. Members of the current Parliament (29 per cent) are facing serious criminal charges including murder, arson, rape, kidnapping, dacoity and illegal possession of arms. In the current Bihar legislature, the ratio is 44 per cent and in the recently elected West Bengal Assembly, it is 35.1 per cent. To think that West Bengal is one of the most law-abiding states in the country!

The final act in the cementing together of the clientelist State and denying access to power to outsiders' was the establishment of the MPs and MLAs Local Area Development Scheme (MPLADS and MLALADS) under which they are allotted Plan funds to spend on development projects in their constituencies at their discretion. On paper, this power is hedged with elaborate safeguards to prevent misuse, but in practice there is no effective monitoring of how much of the allocated money is spent on projects and how much finds its way back into the MP or MLA's pocket. This scheme has completed the conversion of constituencies into zamindaris. But when the allocations for it was raised from Rs two crore to Rs five crore a year for each MP and from Rs one crore to Rs two crore for each MLA in the middle of the 2G scam furore, no one, not even Team Anna, voiced a single murmur of protest.

Economic Consequences

The economic consequences of the total denial of honest funding to political parties has been, if anything, even more devastating, for it has transformed what was intended to be a developmental State into a predatory one. This has taken place in four stages.

In the immediate aftermath of the ban on company donations, the Congress party's fund managers also found themselves at a loss for where to raise the money to fight elections. In the 1971 Lok Sabha and 1972 Assembly elections, they therefore went back to the same companies and trade organisations from whom they used to accept tax-deductible cheques in the past, and demanded cash. Although most of them complied, they did so unwillingly. Raising money to meet electoral and administrative expenses therefore became more difficult than it had been before. But the gap was filled by owner-managers of small and medium-sized enterprises, traders and shopkeepers, moneylenders, and others in the informal sector with cash to exchange for entitlements and allocations from the government. This was the base of the shift of power from the central to state units of the Congress described earlier.

But small enterprises needed space to grow and rich farmers needed subsidies. The former played a significant role in providing the rationale for Gandhi's second round of socialist controls on big business enacted between 1970 and 1973. The latter converted support prices in agriculture that were designed to protect farmers from loss into procurement prices that regularly elevated the market price of cereals and ensured a steady and rising stream of profits for rich farmers. The political power of this intermediate class not only caused a further fall in the GDP growth rate from 3.7 percent between 1956 and 1967 to 3.1 percent from 1967 to 1975, but prolonged the life of the command economy by another 15 years till 1991.

The defeat of the Congress in the post-Emergency 1977 elections triggered something close to a financial collapse in the central Congress party, but left more than half of its state units relatively unaffected. This triggered the second phase of the development of the predatory state, for when the Congress returned to power in 1980, restoring the financial autonomy and pre-eminence of the central command of the party became one of Gandhi's first preoccupations. It did this by institutionalising a system of commissions and kickbacks on foreign contracts, notably in infrastructure and defence.

Over four decades, the cost borne by the people, in terms of opportunities foregone, has been astronomical. Two examples, highlighted in the media at the time when they occurred, show how it has been paid. In the late 70s, the Janata government had obtained World Bank financing for the first of a new generation of fertiliser plants based upon the natural gas from Bombay High to be set up at Thal-Vaishet, south of Mumbai. Based upon international bidding, the consultants employed by the World Bank had recommended that the contract be given to an American firm, CF Braun. But when the Congress returned to power in 1980, it began to negotiate independently with several firms, including Toyo Engineering of Japan and Haldor Topsoe of Denmark, a subsidiary of the state-owned Italian engineering giant, Snamprogetti. When the World Bank refused to reopen the bid, and pulled out of the project, the government went ahead nonetheless, beating the nationalist drum against foreign dictation, hinting at the World Bank's subservience to the US government, and hence, partiality to CF Braun, proclaiming that it would finance the plant from its own (non-existent) foreign exchange resources.

Eventually, it awarded the contract not only for the Thal-Vaishet Plant, but for four others, to Haldor Topsoe. At the time, it was common knowledge that the government had given the contract to Haldor Topsoe in exchange for a handsome kickback. Only later did the public come to know how much the country had to pay for that deal.

CF Braun had been chosen because of all the bidders, it had by far the most energy efficient technology and lowest overall manufacturing cost. Had the original project been implemented with all the safeguards of the World Bank, it would have set the benchmark for the entire future generation of gas-based plants. But it would, unfortunately, have made kickbacks on future projects much harder to obtain.

The award of a single contract for five plants without any international bidding led to an inflation of the capital costs of all the plants. To make matters worse, Haldor Topsoe's ammonia making technology used 15 per cent more energy per tonne of output. These two disadvantages ensured that these plants would never be able to produce urea at internationally competitive prices. The Thal-Vaishet project therefore created a much higher benchmark for capital costs in later plants. These and its higher energy costs had to be offset by subsidies. Since subsidies were designed to ensure a minimum return on capital invested, it ensured that the cost of all future plants would be gold-plated. Indian taxpayers have been paying the resulting, inflated, subsidies till this day.

Even while the Thal-Vaishet project was being renegotiated, the Ministry of Defence had begun a similar renegotiation of major defence contracts entered into by the Janata government. Two that were eventually reinstated at immensely higher prices (and much higher kickbacks) were the purchase of groundhugging long-range Jaguar fighter bombers for the Indian Air Force and the Harrier vertical/short take-off aircraft for the Indian Navy from British companies.

But the country had to wait another five years to gain its first unequivocal understanding of the direction in which the political system had evolved. It got this from an exposé in the Swedish newspaper *Dagens Nyheter* in 1987 of what came to be known as 'The Bofors Deal'. And in much the same way as is happening now, the details only came to light because of the then Prime Minister, Rajiv Gandhi's determination to clean up the system he had inherited. The investigations that followed the Swedish exposé revealed no fewer than three layers of kickbacks, totalling a mammoth 17 per cent of the $1.3 billion contract. So great was public indignation over the deal and its aftermath that the revelation of yet another massive kickback, of 6 per cent on the purchase of submarines from the German firm Howalds Deutsche-Werke went virtually unnoticed.

The loss of money is, however, the least part of the harm that the institutionalisation of kickbacks has done. Kickbacks take time to negotiate. This has meant escalations in cost and a loss of valuable time. The last is unforgivable in defence contracts because it has left the country vulnerable for long periods while kickbacks are being struck. For instance, both Pakistan and India decided to equip their armies with 155 mm Howitzers at more or less the same time in the late 1970s. The Pakistan Army got its guns by the early 80s. The Bofors deal was only finalised in 1985.

The need to arrange the kickbacks has led to an unhealthy centralisation of even routine procurement in the hands of the civilian staff of the Ministry of Defence. Today, senior armed forces officers openly lament that it takes an average three years for their requisitions to be met.

The institutionalisation of kickbacks has also meant that contracts have often not gone to the most qualified bidders because these have the least need to pay kickbacks in order to secure orders. This was the probable cause of the cancellation of the agreement with CF Braun.

But by far, its biggest effect has been to put the State up for sale. And in doing so, align it with the predators in society. For once it takes a bribe from a bidder, it makes itself a party to whatever the bribe-giver has to do to recover his costs. The State, thus, ceases to be the people's watchdog.

This is the source of all the abuses that have crept into the tendering system—the omission of time schedules, the obfuscation of penalty clauses and, once the deal has been struck, the repeated modification of tenders to ensure that only the pre-determined bidder secures the contract. In addition, since the presence of independent consultants makes deal-making more difficult and fraught with risks, government departments have been found to be shy of employing them to plan and execute projects and have insisted on doing so themselves. This has not only removed the last remaining safeguard against graft but contributed to it.

State governments in particular, have taken advantage of this by developing a stratagem for extracting money from projects that only Indian ingenuity could have dreamt up: they chop up large projects into numerous smaller parts in the name of preserving competition, and invite separate tenders for each part. This allows ministers and bureaucrats to award contracts to small companies without the capital base, equipment or track record required to qualify for large projects, but willing to offer almost anything in return for getting a piece of the cake. Highway projects, and more recently a rash of tiny solar power projects, are the most obvious examples of such parsing for profit. The cost in terms of delays, inflation and shoddy work can be judged from the fact that the Golden Quadrilateral highway project, to link Mumbai, Delhi, Kolkata and Chennai—started by former prime minister Atal Bihari Vajpayee in 1999 with the express purpose of providing a fiscal stimulus to the Indian economy after two years of recession—intended to be completed by 2004, is not even half complete in 2011. What is more, it is incomplete because there were unfinished portions in each and every section of the four highways! By contrast, Chinese companies have built 1,000 km of four-lane highways that measure up to European specifications in Kenya, and another 500 km of high-grade two-lane roads in just three years.

In the three decades or more, since kickbacks became the norm for financing political parties, these practices have spread to every corner of the country and every level of its government. Today, there is hardly a contract from the purchase of a new generation of Main Battle Tank to the construction of a rural road, which is not being preyed upon to extract money. Over the years, bureaucrats at every level, from the secretariats in New Delhi to Block Development Offices in each sub-division, have learnt that they can do with even greater impunity for themselves what their political bosses want them to do for their parties.

Economic liberalisation in 1991 ushered in the third phase of development of the predator-clientelist State. The ban on company donations was finally lifted in 2003, but by then the need for funds far outstripped what industrialists, in the new, fiercely competitive economy, with its vastly reduced scope for favour-swapping, were prepared to pay.

According to a recent study by Indira Rajaraman in 2009-10, corporates, large and small, donated only Rs 130 crore to political parties. But industrialists have found more direct ways of influencing government decisions: they now just buy the concerned decision-makers. This is what the spate of scams in the 1990s and 2000s has shown.

The fourth and final stage of development of the mature clientelist State occurred when coalition rule at the Centre became the rule. Look at all the five governments formed since 1996 and you will find that while the 'national' party, be it the Congress or the BJP, has retained the power portfolios, defence, home, external affairs and the prime ministerships, all but a few of the money portfolios have been taken by its regional coalition partners. That is the root of the 2G scam. But the 2G scam is only an extreme case of what is now everyday routine business.

Team Anna would be indulging in wishful thinking if it believed that even the Lokpal of its dreams will make more than a dent in this awesome edifice of corrupt power. Nothing will change till political parties are once more freed from the need to break the law to stay in business and given the option to be honest once again. The only way to do this is to start a very large State fund for financing the electoral expenses of recognised political parties. This requires a much-strengthened Election Commission with a powerful auditing wing, and the adoption of strict and transparent criteria for awarding recognition to political parties. Other reforms can be built upon this foundation. But without it, all the rest will fail.

The First Sixty-Five Years of India's Foreign Policy

—K Natwar Singh

A united independent India would have been a world power in her own right. A divided India was required to work overtime to play any effective part in world affairs. Jawaharlal Nehru's authority and eminence ensured that the Indian point of view was heard with a certain amount of, no doubt, grudging respect in world capitals. It is a great tribute to the foresight and wisdom of Jawaharlal Nehru that the foreign policy framework crafted and created by him has stood the test of time. For fifty years a broad national consensus has existed on India's foreign policy. The non-Congress governments of Morarji Desai, Charan Singh, V.P. Singh, Chandra Shekhar, Atal Bihari Vajpayee, Deve Gowda and I.K. Gujral have followed the foreign policy parameters laid down by Nehru, Indira Gandhi and Rajiv Gandhi. Why? Simply because there was and there is no better or more honourable course to follow, unless we wish to become a client state or a camp follower. This, the proud people of India will not countenance.

Nehru was ideally equipped to be Foreign Minister of India. From his early youth he was a diligent student of international affairs. After his return in 1927 from his second visit to Europe, he drafted the foreign policy resolutions of the Indian National Congress at its annual sessions. He made the Congress party take interest in foreign affairs. In his presidential address at the 1929 session at Lahore, he pronounced his vision of India's foreign policy:

'India today is a part of the world movement. Not only China, Turkey, Persia and Egypt, but also Russia and countries of the west are taking part in this movement. We have our own problems—difficult and intricate–and we cannot run away from them and take shelter in the wider problems that affect the world. But if we ignore the world, we do so at our peril…if India has a message to give to the world, as I hope she has, she has also to receive and learn…'

It is generally believed that non-alignment was a post-1947 phenomenon. Not so. The principle of non-alignment was accepted by the Congress at the Haripura session in 1938. The resolution on foreign affairs said that a free India would keep aloof from both imperialism and fascism. The resolution stated that, 'India was resolved to maintain friendly and co-operative relations with all nations and avoid entanglement in military and similar alliances which tend to divide up the world in rival groups and thus endanger world peace.'

By the time Nehru became the Vice-President of the interim government on 2 September 1946, he had, between 1927 and 1946, visited the U.S.S.R, Germany, France, Switzerland, Czechoslovakia, Hungary, Spain, Egypt, Malaya, Ceylon, Burma, China and England. No other Indian politician could match this record. He, therefore, lost no time in articulating the features of free India's foreign policy. This he did in his first broadcast to the nation on 7 September 1946:

> 'We propose, as far as possible, to keep away from the power politics or groups aligned against one another, which has led in the past to two world wars and which may again lead to disasters on an even vaster scale. We believe that peace and freedom are indivisible and the denial of freedom anywhere must endanger it elsewhere and lead to conflict and war. We are particularly interested in the emancipation of colonial and dependent countries and peoples and in the recognition in theory and practice of equal opportunities for all races. We repudiate utterly the Nazi doctrine of racialism wherever and in whatever form it may be practised. We seek no domination over other peoples and we claim no privileged position over other peoples, but we claim equal and honourable treatment for our people wherever they may go, and we cannot accept any discrimination against them.'

India's independence in August, 1947, was a world event. The era of colonialism and imperialism was nearing its final phase. India's freedom movement had inspired other people under foreign rule. They now looked to India to fight for their cause at the United Nations and the Commonwealth. If Nehru had died in 1960 instead of 1964, he would have gone out on a triumphant heroic wave. The perfect symmetry of his life was disfigured in 1962 by the Sino-Indian border clash. Nevertheless, for half a decade (1950-1955), Nehru achieved something unique. He lit the international sky and the glow raised the sights of humankind. He passionately believed in peace, peaceful co-existence, in co-operation, in creative non-alignment, in nuclear and conventional disarmament and development. He was no starry-eyed ivory tower idealist. He had his feet firmly on the ground. More importantly, India meant something very special to him. It was something more than a country or a nation. Out of his historical awareness emerged certain fundamental elements of our foreign policy which he spelt out from time to time. He was acutely aware of the nexus between foreign policy and internal cohesion: 'Foreign policies depend ultimately on internal conditions and developments. Internal progress for us, therefore, becomes essential if we are to play any effective part in world affairs.'

Few examples of his success will suffice from Korea, Indo-China, Congo, Cyprus, and Gaza. Also his call for nuclear disarmament, his assault at the United Nations and the Commonwealth on Apartheid and colonialism. The birth of NAM at Brioni and its launching at Belgrade owe much to Nehru. Without him there would have been no Bandung, no Panchsheel. How ironical it is that Nehru, who pushed for an invitation to China at Colombo to Bandung, should, towards the end of his life, have been broken on the Sino-Indian frontier.

In 1947, India's G.N.P was not worth calculating. Yet India was a factor in world affairs. Till 1962, India was undoubtedly the most important U.N. member from the countries of Asia, Africa and Latin America. At the end of World War II, an exhausted humanity looked to India to give a lead, a moral lead. The distinctive character of our freedom movement under Gandhi was much admired. The absence of Mao's China from world bodies went in favour of India. By 1964, more than 60 per cent of Africa was free of colonialism. The U.N. bench began to be crowded. We were no longer the only country opposing colonialism and Apartheid at the U.N., the NAM or the Commonwealth. If we had been a bit more worldly wise, we might have got a permanent seat in the Security Council in 1955-60, because the Americans were at that time on a crusade against Mao's China. Substituting India for Taiwan was not all that unreal. Be it said to Nehru's credit that he would have none of it.

Nehru did not subscribe to the assumptions of the Cold War. There was an Indian way of looking at issues and events and if that meant standing alone, so be it.

On the Cold War

Nehru was unambiguous about this:

> 'I can understand some of the smaller countries of Europe or some of the smaller countries of Asia being forced by circumstances to bow down before some of the great powers and becoming practically satellites of those powers, because they cannot help it. The power opposed to this is so great that they have nowhere to turn. But I do not think that consideration applies to India...India is too big a country herself to be bound down to any country, however big it may be.'

On another occasion he was equally specific:

> 'The world seems to be divided into two mighty camps, the Communist and the anti-Communist, and either party cannot understand how anyone can be foolish enough not to link up with itself. That just shows what little understanding these people have of the mind of Asia. Talking of India only, and not at all of Asia, we have fairly clear ideas about our political and economic structure. We function in this country under a constitution, which may be described as a parliamentary democracy. It has not been imposed upon us. We propose to continue with it... we have no intention to turn Communists. At the same time, we have no intention of being dragooned in any

> other direction...we have chosen our path and we propose to go along with it and to vary it as and when we choose, not at anybody's dictate or pressure, and we are not afraid of any other country imposing its will upon us by military method or any other methods...our thinking and approach do not fit in with the crusade of Communism or crusade of anti-Communism.'

From the very beginning, Nehru's approach to the USSR and USA was friendly. He paid three visits to the USA. The outcome was mixed. The US military aid to Pakistan adversely affected Indo-US relations. Kennedy admired Nehru and spoke of his 'soaring idealism'. In spite of his partial disillusionment after the 1961 visit of Nehru to the USA, Kennedy promptly responded to the call for help from Nehru in 1962.

The USSR had, during Stalin's time, not been at all friendly towards India. After his death, there was a change. Nehru's visit to the USSR in 1955 was a spectacular triumph. Bulganin and Khruschev came to India in December 1955 and met with a tumultuous welcome. It was during this visit that Khruschev announced that Kashmir was an integral part of India. Indo-Soviet relations intensified in every field. From now on, the Soviet Union could be depended upon not to permit any resolution, unfair or hostile to India, to be passed in the Security Council.

Nehru was both Prime Minister and Foreign Minister for seventeen years. Throughout he relied on Krishna Menon and a few Civil Servants. Girija Shankar Bajpai was by all accounts outstanding. N.R. Pillai had his good points. S. Dutt was sensible, sound and unflappable. But it was Krishna Menon who had the last word. No institution could cope with so erratic, abrasive, unreasonable and demanding an individual. Instead of managing our foreign affairs, our diplomats in London and New York were spending time and energy to manage Krishna Menon. B.K. Nehru in his recently published memoirs has, in great detail, described the harm Menon did to Indo-US relations. The first serious doubts on our non-alignment were expressed when Menon disregarded instructions and voted the way he did in the debate on Hungary in the Security Council. The good that Menon had done on Korea and Indo-China was soon forgotten. Next came his Kashmir performance. His nine-hour speech did one thing—it internationalised the issue. It also made people ask—if your case needs nine hours of advocacy, it must be weak. In India he became a hero, but we had lost the Kashmir round at the U.N.

It is now generally agreed that it was a mistake to refer Kashmir to the Security Council and that too under Chapter VI of the U.N. Charter. Nehru approached the U.N. in good faith. He expected justice. All he got was a very cold, Cold War shower. Over the years, the Kashmir question sapped the energies of our diplomats. Too much time had to be devoted just to Kashmir. It must be said in defence of Nehru that he got Gandhiji's and the Cabinet's approval for taking the matter to the U.N. It must also be remembered that if India had not taken Kashmir to the U.N., Pakistan would have.

Nehru with his great knowledge of history, his faith in international goodwill and co-operation, misread the minds of the Chinese communists. They were a new brand in China, arrogant, confident, and ruthless. China as a nation was familiar with statecraft. We were not. Nehru took them at face value. An in-depth examination of the 1962 events cannot be made till the Peoples Republic of China open their archives.

What we do know is that even on so vital a matter ad-hocism ruled. Ambassador K.M. Panikar, at Peking, carried on his own brand of diplomacy and misinformed the Chinese of our position. At Delhi, there was no integrated or well thought through plan or policy. K. Subramanyan has written that:

> 'there were plenty of anecdotal accounts, but not "a comprehensive hypothesis" of what went wrong and why. The April 1960 visit of Chou En Lai was grossly mishandled by us. His meeting with Morarji Desai was a disaster. Chou En Lai, the suavest of men, was so put out that he actually walked out of the meeting. It was not a happy chapter of Indian diplomacy. As a young diplomat, I was aghast at Shri Desai's performance. I was not a taker!!'

It was not an easy act to follow Nehru as Prime Minister. Lal Bahadur Shastri's tenure was far too short to make a lasting impact on international affairs. He shed the external affairs portfolio and appointed Swaran Singh to the job, who had cut his diplomatic teeth during Chou En Lai's fateful visit to Delhi in April, 1960. Shastri himself proved a man of courage, when he responded to Pakistan's aggression in 1965 with vigour and a clear head. His Tashkent foray has been excessively praised. By accepting Soviet brokerage he departed from the established pattern. However, he deserves much credit for allowing Swaran Singh and his delegation to walk out of the Security Council in October 1965, when Bhutto resorted to abuse. Thereafter, the Security Council did not again take up Kashmir.

Indira Gandhi succeeded Lal Bahadur Shastri in January 1966. She had no direct experience of government, but her name was well known. It did not take her long to get to the top on her job and make her presence felt in the world. On the homefront, she made sure that India became self-sufficient in foodgrains. India's relations with the USSR had been greatly improved during Nehru's lifetime and she carried the process further, without in any way compromising on any aspect of our foreign policy. With the USA, relations remained strained due to differences over Vietnam, Pakistan, Southern Africa and West Asia.

A couple of events in her sixteen years as Prime Minister assure her a high place in history. There would have been no Bangladesh without her. For almost nine months, she showed extreme restraint under massive provocation. She went on a seven nation tour in September-October 1971 to explain what was happening in East Pakistan and the burden it placed on India.

Her diplomacy was eminently successful. The USA was isolated as even her NATO allies supported the Indian view of the crisis in East Pakistan. In her talks with western leaders and Messers, Nixon and Kissinger, she made it clear that there was no Indo-Pak dispute involved. The quarrel was between Pakistan's two wings–between the freely elected Awami League leadership and Yahya Khan's ruthless military dictatorship.

After the surrender of the Pakistani Army in Bangladesh on 16 December, 1971, she did not extend the war to West Pakistan. 93,000 officers and men of the Pakistan Army surrendered. In the aftermath, she acted in a statesman-like manner. She did not humiliate a defeated

Pakistan. By signing the Simla Agreement in July 1972, she ensured durable peace between the two countries. Her world stature grew. She had altered the map of the sub-continent and the geo-politics of the region. Having signed a treaty of friendship with the Soviet Union in August 1971, she ensured that China would not intervene on behalf of Pakistan. The Americans were too busy courting China clandestinely to do anything till it was too late. Even the Seventh Fleet was rendered useless by the speed with which India acted in December, 1971.

The next great event was that she took a significant step in raising the level of our diplomatic representation in China, from Charge d'Affaires to Ambassador. She wanted a non-adversarial relationship with China. This step eventually led to Rajiv Gandhi's successful visit to China in 1988.

Her second tenure (1980-84) though less eventful, was marked by an improvement in Indo-US relations. She also made her displeasure, on the Soviet intervention in Afghanistan, known to Brezhnev in no uncertain terms.

When she was assassinated, India's foreign policy and diplomacy were in a healthy state. There was internal unity and political stability, social and economic progress and a defence capability not to be scoffed at. She had proved that India had an independent foreign policy. She achieved a brand balance in our relations with the major nations. She gave our policy a certain and desirable flexibility. She also put new life in the NAM during her chairmanship following the seventh summit in Delhi. She was without doubt the most respected head of government in the Commonwealth and her presidency over the Commonwealth summit in November 1983 was the culmination of her ascendency on the world stage.

From March 1977 to January 1980, the governments of Morarji Desai and Charan Singh were too busy reconciling contradictions to have much time for conducting a meaningful diplomacy and a forceful foreign policy. It is noteworthy that there was no U-turn in the foreign policy arena. The phrase 'genuine non-alignment', when used by the Desai government, invited derision and Atal Behari Vajpayee soon dropped it. He, it must be said to his credit, invoked the names of Gandhiji and Pandit Nehru in several of his foreign policy pronouncements. His serious attempt to further improve relations with China was aborted by China attacking Vietnam during his visit to China.

In a celebrated article that Indira Gandhi wrote in the October 1972 issue of Foreign *Affairs,* she outlined for her American audience the tenets of our foreign policy, and what made us tick:

> 'India's foreign policy is a projection of the values which we have cherished through the centuries as well as our current concerns. We are not tied to the traditional concepts of foreign policy designed to safeguard overseas possessions, investments, the carving out of areas of influence, the erection of Cordons Sanitaires. We are not interested in exporting ideologies.'

She further stated that:

> 'our first concern was to prevent the erosion of our independence. Therefore, we could not be camp followers of any power, however rich and strong. We had equal interest in the maintenance and safeguarding of international peace as an essential condition of India's economic, social and political development. In the bipolar world, which existed in the immediate post-war era, Jawaharlal Nehru refused to join either bloc. He decided to remain non-aligned as a means of safeguarding of our independence and contributing to the maintenance of world peace. Non-alignment implied neither non-involvement nor neutrality. It was an assertion of our freedom of judgment and action. We have not hesitated to express our views on any major controversy or support for just causes.'

Such was the high minded yet practical legacy Rajiv Gandhi inherited, when he became Prime Minister on 31 October 1984.

Rajiv Gandhi took to foreign affairs as a duck takes to water. He had brio, flair and relished the sophistication that made diplomacy both an art and a craft. His first real exposure on the world scene was at the Nassau Commonwealth Summit in the Bahamas in October 1985. At the Harare NAM Summit in September 1986, Rajiv Gandhi played a crucial role in reconciling opposing positions, establishing the Africa Fund and preventing a 'local war' between Iran and Iraq at the summit. He and Fidel Castro were the two heads, who made the summit a businesslike gathering, bringing back those colleagues gently to earth when their flights of fancy made them abandon ground reality, even on South Africa.

Rajiv Gandhi may not be remembered for the NAM and CHOGM Summits he attended. He will be remembered with gratitude for the Delhi declaration, which he signed with Mikhail Gorbachev in November 1986. This was a historic document, which gave new hope to humankind. Here was the leader of the Communist Party of the Soviet Union putting his signature on a document extolling non-violence. Nothing even remotely similar had happened in the history of Communism. At the Vancouver CHOGM in October 1987, Rajiv Gandhi again played a primary role. He got a unanimous approval of the Commonwealth for the Indo-Sri Lanka Agreement.

1988 was his best year. In June, he presented his Action Plan for ushering in a 'Nuclear Weapon Free and Non-Violent World' to the UN at New York. This was in fact a charter for peace. Unfortunately, it did not suit the Superpowers to let India take the lead in this field and the plan remained a passionate exhortation. In December 1988, Rajiv Gandhi paid his trail blazing visit to China. The first by an Indian Prime Minister in thirty-four years. We worked on the visit for almost eighteen months, preparing the country, parliament and the opposition for it. When he embarked on his passage to Peking, he had the country behind him. After his talks with Deng Xiap Ping, a breakthrough was achieved. A message went round that the confrontational phase was giving place to a period of co-operation and reconciliation. No concessions were made by either side. The border question was not skirted. The charged atmosphere was no small achievement. The border issue remains unresolved, but both countries have accepted that a final settlement will be a negotiated one.

He took special interest in our relations with Pakistan. Had President Zia-ul-Haq not died in an air crash in 1988, he and the Indian Prime Minister would have reached an agreement on Siachin. His visit to Islamabad in December 1988, the first by an Indian Prime Minister in twenty-eight years, and did much to reduce tension between the two countries. Rajiv Gandhi believed that India had a distinctive role to play in world affairs. We would only do so if we were economically strong, technologically up-to-date and politically cohesive. He repeatedly asserted that the region extending from Pamirs to the Mekong was of special relevance to India. It is one of the great tragedies of our times that his life was cut short when India and the world were in sore need of his services.

Foreign policy between 1990 and 1996 received low priority in our national agenda. The government of V.P. Singh and Chandra Shekhar had inbuilt limitations and were too short-lived to make any impact. Narsimha Rao in his five years travelled much, spoke frequently, but the results were not spectacular. For almost four years of his tenure, he did not deem it necessary to have a full-time Foreign Minister. The collapse of the Soviet Union in 1991 removed from the map of the world a staunch friend and benefactor of India. No deep analysis was attempted to analyse this profound, world shaking development and the security implications that India faced with the USSR no longer there.

The Cabinet never discussed foreign policy, the Cabinet Committee on Foreign Affairs never met. Worst of all Kashmir was allowed to be internationalised and low-level functionalities of the US State Department were fawned upon and feted by the Rao government. Narsimha Rao did, however, dramatically improve India's economic standing by his liberalisation policy. At NAM and the UN, India appeared as an absentee. It must in fairness be noted that Rao carried forward Rajiv Gandhi's China policy. In 1993, India and China signed a Sino-Indian Agreement on maintaining peace and tranquility along the Line of Actual Control and reducing military forces in the border areas pending a final solution.

Successive governments of United Front and NDA could produce nothing remarkable on the front of foreign policy – so the time era of 1995-2004 was more or less confined with the repetition of ineffective policies.

Americans are adept at producing well packaged formulas (quick fixes if you wish to be colloquial). These they promote with messianic fervour or evangelical zeal, even when the authors have Jewish names. After being ardently isolationist for one hundred and twenty five years, the Unites States have for the past fifty been crusading interventionists. No less a guru than George Kennan has written with compelling candour about his great country's foreign policy assumptions and presumptions in his bestselling book, Around The Cragged Hill thus:

> 'I should make it clear that I am wholly and emphatically rejecting any and all Messianic concepts of America's role in the world: rejecting the illusion of unique and superior virtue on our part, the prattle about Manifest Destiny or the "American Century...And if there were any qualities that lie within our ability to cultivate that might set us off from the rest of the world, these would be the virtues of modesty and humility; and of these we have never exhibited any exceptional abundance...'

We Indians are long suffering, but also cussed. We do not like being pushed around. We do not seek confrontation or conflict. At the same time, India will accept no one's hegemony. The world needs Pax Planeta, not Pax Americana.

We are all ignorant about the future. Yet, each one of us has a vital stake in it, for the simple reason that we are all going to spend our lives there. Ignorance of the future, however, does not relieve us from the responsibility of chartering a path of action. Life compels us to plan for the future. Nations are doomed if they do not resort to contingency planning. Certain trends, some straws in the wind, past precedents, the lessons of history act as guides and warnings. The choice so often, as Nehru said, is not between good or evil, it is between the lesser and the greater evil, between one-fourth good and the rest three-fourths between bad and worse. There is no blueprint for the future. After thousands of years, we are still groping.

We now have several studies about organising the world order of the next century. Paul Kennedy gave us his book, *Preparing for the Twenty First Century in 1993.* In more recent times, three important reports have appeared. "Uncommon Opportunities", an agenda for Peace and

Equitable Development was prepared by the International Commission on Peace and Food, which was chaired by Dr M.S. Swaminathan. This was followed by "Our Global Neighbourhood", the report of the Commission on Global Governance, headed by Ingvar Carlson of Sweden and Shridath Ramphal, former Secretary General of the Commonwealth. In 1966 appeared, "Caring for the Future", the report of the Independent Commission on Population and the Quality of Life. This was chaired by Maria de Lourdes Pintasilgo of Portugal. All list the challenges and offer choices. These can be broadly identified as:

Preserving peace, reforming democracy and the United Nations, ensuring economic growth accompanied by equity and social justice, in other words a just world order committed to just means. Environment and ecology, science and technology should be used to uplift humanity, not exploit or expropriate. Population control is of paramount importance in China, India, Brazil, Africa. Finally, the need is to emphasise that any new order must have an ethical underpinning so that ends do not justify the means. Also fundamentalism and immigration from the poor South to the rich North.

This is the global scenario. Now we come to India. In the post-Cold War era, the USA is pre-eminent but not supreme. We do not live in a unipolar world. With the break-up of the Soviet Union, an alternative point of view has disappeared. There is much talk of a homogenised world. This India must resist. Our diversity is our strength. Our variety exudes our glory. India is perhaps the only country which can act as bridge between the industrialised West (G-7) and the developing world.

There is growing dissatisfaction with the functioning of NAM, and since December 1989, India's passive role has invited adverse comment. Much is heard of the irrelevance of non-alignment. Why do we need NAM? One might ask why do we need NATO? It must, nevertheless, be conceded that NAM has performed poorly on several issues—the Iran-Iraq War, PLO-Israeli issues (Norway, not NAM, took the lead to find solutions) Yugoslavia, Afghanistan, Bosnia, N.P.T, C.T.B.T, W.T.O. The movement showed lack of solidarity on all these issues. Also on the reform of the U.N, it is imperative that India shows more interest in NAM and comes out with new ideas. If the movement could speak with one voice on colonialism, racialism, disarmament, then why it cannot do so on environment, terrorism, drugs, etc. Narsimha Rao was right when he said in Tokyo in 1992, 'That the pursuit of a non-aligned foreign policy is even more relevant in the post-cold war period than ever before…regardless of the bloc phenomenon, the chimera of hegemonism must not be pursued.'

That the movement is relevant is proved by its growing membership. Russia, China and Germany obtained Observer status. NAM needs blood transfusion, it needs energising. India must reassert itself and tell fellow members that self-reliance is more realistic than running after the industrialised world, where growth is down, unemployment up (12 per cent in Germany). We should think carefully before tying up our economic and foreign policies to an area which is showing weakness. NAM countries are being pushed around by the new international Maharajas—the IMF and the World Bank. We are being manipulated by multinationals. This is not to suggest that we give up liberalisation of our economy. Our macro management had been wrong and, therefore, what Manmohan Singh did in 1991, was necessary. But the market philosophy is not the whole answer. In ASEAN countries, growth and development was spearheaded by the State, not the shop-floor. The market can never be a substitute for the State. Given our pluralistic, humanistic democracy, we and so many non-aligned states cannot abandon the role of the State. The market has not offered any evidence that it is capable by itself of responding to fundamental human needs. One billion people live on a dollar a day. What is the market doing for them?

What should our foreign policy/diplomatic priorities be? Our voice will carry greater weight if there is an improvement in our relations with Pakistan. Since 1947, the two countries have spent astronomical amounts on defence, on arms race in the Indian subcontinent. In today's world it is a luxury we cannot afford. Within the five principles of Panchsheel and the Simla Agreement, we should start a sustained peace process and lower tensions. We must stop apportioning blame, but work for constructive co-operation. Don't we see what is happening in the rest of the world? Agreed that no two situations are identical or similar, we cannot run away from the fact that yesterday's enemies are today's friends—USA and Japan, France and Germany, Russia and America, China and Russia, China and Japan, the PLO and Israel, America and Vietnam. Mandela has produced a near miracle in South Africa. I am not being starry-eyed, sentimental or unrealistic when I ask–cannot the land of the Buddha, Ashok and Gandhi give the lead in diffusing permanent turbulence and tensions in our sub-continent? The Gowda and Gujral governments deserved support for their foreign policy initiatives. Once the message goes around that India and Pakistan are genuinely seeking peaceful solutions, other things will begin to fall in place. Let us dare to think the unthinkable, make the impossible happen. War is not the answer. Acceptable compromise is beginning serious negotiations with Pakistan on all issues.

Next, India should make SAARC the pivot of her foreign policy. We should aim at the establishment of a SAARC Common Market. The economic potential of SAARC is greater than that of ASEAN. Even India's GNP will be twice that of ASEAN, once we will be able to maintain eight per cent plus growth rate.

With China, we should have even closer relations. Our economies are similar and so are our needs. I am aware of the hurdles we face while trading with China. These can be overcome. In the past, some people talked of an India-Soviet axis opposed to the Peking-Pakistan-Pentagon axis. This is outmoded thinking.

The State visit to India of China's President Jiang Zemin was the first ever by the Head of State and party. The agreement signed in New Delhi on 29 November 1996 by the two countries 'on confidence building measures in the military field along the Line of Actual Control in the India-China border areas', is a significant positive step forward in maintaining peace and tranquility on the India-China border. The agreement accords with the fundamental interests of the two peoples and will also contribute to the ultimate solution of the boundary question. Despite minor irritants, both the countries now believe that stable friendly relations, not confrontation, will be mutually advantageous to them.

We should not alter our principled stand either on N.P.T. or the C.T.B.T unless the treaties take into account our concerns and make these documents truly democratic. Efforts will be made to pressurise us.

These must be resisted. Similarly, we should make no concessions on our nuclear program and policy. We should make it clear that India is in no way influenced by what Pakistan does on the nuclear question. It really is extraordinary that the Permanent Five in the Security Council should preach nuclear disarmament to the world, having violated every single rule in the book themselves. They have no moral right to do so. Their hands are not clean. We should never dilute the intensity of our position to such double standards.

The Charter of the United Nations is one of this century's noblest and high-minded documents in many respects. But now, it is in urgent need of revision. The fiftieth anniversary of U.N in 1995 provided a good opportunity for having a fresh look at the inadequacies of the Charter. This opportunity was allowed to pass without any serious effort to reform, renovate, and restructure the U.N. System. The veto power bestowed on the five Permanent Members of the Security Council is an affront to all other members. It was insisted upon by the U.S.A in 1995.

The 1995 euphoria led a generally unenthusiastic man like Cordell Hull, the U.S. Secretary of State at that time, to make the following astounding observations:

> 'There will no longer be need for spheres of influence, for alliances, balances of power, or any other special arrangements through which, in the unhappy past, the nations strove to safeguard their security or to promote their interests.'

Subsequent events have shown how misplaced was Hull's optimism.

In the 1930s, Britain and France all but killed the League of Nations by condoning the aggressions of Japan, Italy and Germany. Today, the U.S. is busy strangulating the U.N. by starving it financially. Today that body inspires neither confidence nor hope. It evokes derision. It has become a graveyard of new ideas. The Security Council is the most undemocratic body in the world. It needs drastic reform. India cannot turn its back on the U.N., but we should not invest too much in such a body till the Charter is revised. It was monumental folly to have contested the non-permanent seat against Japan in 1996.

With the U.S.A., Western Europe, the U.K. (still an influential country), Japan, Russia, we should expand and enlarge our relations in all areas. We should modernise, not westernise. We should be among the winners, and not losers, in this game. The Arab world, Africa and Latin America have been our traditional friends. These ties need renewal and restructuring.

If India has a message, and I believe she has, it is the message of Gandhi as spelt out in the Delhi Declaration by Rajiv Gandhi and Mikhail Gorbachev. The fundamental question is—can the new century encourage an appreciation of the revolutionary potential of Gandhi's creed of non-violence? Humankind needs a non-violent approach to international security and disarmament. The traditional mindset has to be discarded. The much touted globalisation must work from below and not be imposed from above. The information highways should provide space for ethical roadways too. Knowledge and information must be tempered by wisdom.

India can play a creative part in making and shaping the twenty-first century, provided we have unity, stability and cohesion. We are good at reconciling contradictions in society, adept at converting our diversities into assets. For the political, economic and social transformations of our polity, we need faithful agents (Gandhi's phrase) and strong institutions. Both are in short supply. Democracy is being degraded in several states of the Union. This needs immediate and effective correctives.

For sixty years there existed a broad national consensus on foreign policy. Ours is an independent non aligned policy. Manmohan Singh has all but destroyed that asset. He is falling backwords to placate the U.S.A. That he is a good man is neither here nor there. He presides over an outfit which does not govern. Postponement of action is not the solution. It verges on disaster.

One of the pillars of our foreign policy was Non-alignment. It is being thoughtlessly abandoned. Non-alignment is not a dogma, nor a doctrine. It is a state of mind. It needs reinvention. Not rejection. The anti-non-alignment argument is—non-alignment is out of date. The Soviet Union has disappeared. The Warsaw Pact has packed up. Who are we non-aligned against? Well! Here is the counter argument. Why is NATO relevant? The Soviet Union is history. So is the Warsaw Pact. Who is the enemy? NATO is looking for one. It has not succeeded in finding one. Yet, NATO is extended to the borders of Russia. Is Iraq the enemy? The U.S.A. has destroyed a secular, non-aligned country. Afghanistan! After failing to do anything constructive for a decade, the Americans want to run and quit.

India is passing through difficult times. There seems to be a debilitating absence of direction, governance and purpose. One could go on and on. History will not forgive these men and woman who sit and do not serve, make excuses and practise escapism. The souls of Gandhi, Nehru and Indira Gandhi must be squirming.

I am a short term pessimist and long term optimist. The best is yet to be. There is a lot going for us. A mood of gloom and doom is unworthy of us. Let us never forget the words of Iqbal:

Yunano Misr Ruma Sab Mit Gaya Jahan Se,
Abtak Magar Hai Baqi Namo Nishan Hamara.
Kuchh Baat Hai Hati Miti Nahin Hamari,
Sadiyon Raha Hai Dushman Daure-Zamana Hamara.

Ancient Greece, Egypt and Rome have all lost their traces. But India survives as an entity. There is something about our country that though for centuries we have been besieged by enemies, we still retain our identity.

Politics and the Indian Middle-Class

—*Shashi Tharoor*

As I reflect on India since 1947, I am conscious that, before I entered politics myself, one of my more frequent laments had been about the abdication by the Indian educated classes of our political responsibility for our own destiny.

My generation grew up in an India where a vast gulf separated those who went into the professions or the civil services, and those who entered politics. The latter, at the risk of simplifying things a bit, were either at the very top or the very bottom: either maharajahs or big *zamindar*s with a feudal hold on the allegiances of the voters in their districts, or semi-literate 'lumpens' with little to lose who got into politics as their only means of self-advancement. If you belonged to neither category, you studied hard, took your exams, and made a success of your life on merit—and you steered clear of politics as an activity for those 'other people'.

But the problem with that approach—while completely understandable in a highly-competitive society where the salaried middle-class rarely enjoyed the luxury of being able to take the kind of risks that a political life implied—was that it left out of Indian politics the very group of people that are the mainstay of politics in other democracies. Around the world, the educated taxpaying middle-classes are normally the ones who bring values and convictions to a country's politics, and who have the most direct stake in questions of what government can and cannot do. Across Europe, for instance, it's people from the middle-class who set the political agenda: they make up the bulk of the activists, voters and candidates for political office. In most Western democracies, politics is essentially a middle-class pursuit.

But in India, our middle-class has neither the time for activism (they're too busy doing professional jobs to make ends meet) nor the money or the votes to count in politics. The money flows at the top, and the votes, in our stratified society, lie at the bottom, where the numbers are. So members of the educated middle-class abstain from the process, and all too often look at it with disdain. They don't show up to vote in large numbers; whereas, in the US, the turnout in poor black Harlem in most Presidential elections (barring Obama's) barely exceeds twenty per cent, in India the poor turnout en masse to vote, spending hours in the hot sun to cast their ballots. They believe, rightly, that their votes make a difference, whereas the middle-class disempowers itself by its disdain. No wonder there is so much disenchantment amongst ordinary middle-class people with the processes of our democracy, such cynicism about the lack of principle amongst our politicians, and such surprise in learning of an honest politician (because we routinely expect the opposite).

This is easily apparent in the public attitudes of middle-class Indians to politics and politicians. Growing up in India, I was used to a double standard: most Indians accept, indeed assume, conduct on the part of politicians that we would never condone in our neighbours. Traditional middle-class morality required arranged marriages, marital fidelity, scrupulous honesty and adherence to the law at all times, whereas politicians were expected to be different from the rest of us, and therefore exempt from these norms. As larger-than-life figures, they enjoyed a societal carte blanche to lie, cheat, dissemble, and commit large-scale duplicity, adultery and tax fraud; only murder was a little more difficult, though even there a handful of major politicians have been released from jail in India after allegations of offenses that might have earned lesser mortals fates worse than death.

So it was with some astonishment that I first went to America and discovered the opposite double-standard in operation: Americans expected, indeed required, conduct on the part of their politicians that they would never have presumed to demand of their neighbours. Middle-class Americans, for the most part, lived in an environment of pre-and extra-marital sex, divorce and adultery, and lapped up soap operas and television talk-shows where these were the staple fare. But they expected their politicians to be models of moral rectitude, their CVs punctuated by the standard long-lasting faithful marriage and 2.5 clean-cut children. At least it meant that they idealised their political leaders; in India, we routinely disparaged them.

The result is that whereas 10 of the last 12 American Presidential nominees of the two major US political parties were graduates of either Harvard or Yale, the products of our best educational institutions rarely venture into politics. In America, the commentator Michael Medved wrote that the skills and determination required to get into Harvard or Yale are in themselves indicators of suitability for high office—'the driven, ferociously focused kids willing to expend the energy and make the sacrifices to conquer our most exclusive universities are among those most likely to enjoy similar success in the even more fiercely fought free-for-all of presidential politics.' In India, the kids who 'conquer our most exclusive universities' would for the most part consider it beneath themselves to step into the muck and mire of our country's politics. The attitude of most Indians is that if you're smart enough to get into a good university, you can make something better of your life in a 'real' profession. Politics, it is generally muttered amongst the middle-class, is for those who aren't able to do anything else. And the skills required to thrive in the world of Indian politics have nothing to do with the talents honed by a first-class education. Can this state of affairs continue indefinitely? No—and it probably won't. My vision for India in 2020 is of a country growing economically, whose economic transformation brings more and more people into the middle-class—and by 2020, this process may have begun to reach the point where the numbers of the middle-class will indeed begin to matter in elections.

We already have, in the current Parliament, several educated and bright young professionals of the kind of background that for many years previously would not have been found in politics—people with good degrees, a national vision, international experience, intelligent ideas and the capacity to articulate them. It doesn't matter that a significant proportion of them are the sons of politicians: the fact that they are in Parliament brings a different standard to bear on the quality of our politics. As they change the public's expectations of what a politician should be like, they should be joined by 2020 by many others of similar qualifications but with no political background. In that, eventually, will lie our democracy's salvation.

So my message to young middle-class Indians who actually have principles and ideals is this: when you think about the future of India, think also of getting involved in politics. The nation needs you.

The Nobel laureate Archbishop Desmond Tutu, speaking of South Africa, once said he hoped his country would get leaders the people could look up to, 'not people we have to keep finding excuses for'. If well-educated, middle-class Indians—the kind of people who are the mainstay of our professions—want a return to an era when our country's political leadership was full of people whom the nation admired, they will have to enter the fray themselves. Otherwise, all too often, we will have to pay allegiance to people we need to find excuses for. My hope is that, by 2020, there will be many more educated, professional middle-class Indians in politics—and that they will do better than I have managed to do so far!

Kashmir: Past, Present and Future

—Jagmohan

Life and History are organic entities. They do not admit to sharp dividing lines. Past, present and future are, in fact, inextricably enmeshed. As T.S. Eliot puts it:

Time present and time past
Are both present in time future;
And time future in time past.

As we look at where the Kashmir problem stands at present, it would be instructive to survey the past, identify the fundamental forces of mind and matter that have so far determined the course of events, and consider how these forces should be reoriented to fashion out a better and fruitful future for Kashmir. Winston Churchill was right when he observed:

The further backward you look, the further forward you can see.

Mind and Soul Relationship

It is only when we go into the deeper layers of Kashmir's past that we can discover its true place in the Indian vision. At present, hardly any one realises that Kashmir's relationship with the rest of India is rooted in potent and enduring forces whom neither the turbulent tornadoes of the past nor the negativism and nihilism of the present-day politics can really destroy. It is a relationship of mind and soul that has existed from the time immemorial and found ample expression in common avenues of the intellect and emotions, poetry and literature, philosophy and outlook. Every green pasture that you walk around in Kashmir, every silvery peak that you watch from pleasurable distance, every stream that sings its song by our side, every enchanting lake that you come across now and then and every little town and city that you visit, has some signpost or the other of this deep and abiding relationship.

To understand in depth Kashmir's relationship with the rest of India, it is necessary to address ourselves a few basic questions. What do the various landmarks on the route from Pahalgam to the Cave of Amarnath—Chandanwari, Pishu Ghati, Seshnag, Panchtarni—stand for? What, in moments of poetic intensity, made Kalidasa see the 'laughter of Shiva' in the Himalayas and Subramania Bharati think of Kashmir as the Crown of Mother India?

The answer to all these questions is one and only one: Kashmir, for thousands of years, has been a part of the Indian vision—a silent and serene, yet an integral and inseparable part. Even when Islam came to Kashmir, it did not alter the ethos of the common folk. Most of the Islamic teachings were just grafted on Vedantic beliefs and thoughts. The central message of Kashmir's patron saint and founder of the Rishi Order, Sheikh Nooruddin Noorani, was:

There is one God/But with a hundred names.
There is not a single blade of grass/which does not worship Him.

Position on the Eve of Indian Independence

At the time of the Indian Independence Act, 1947 the political stage of Kashmir was crowded with a variety of actors. There was the National Conference, headed by Sheikh Mohammad Abdullah. It dominated the Valley but had a limited influence in Jammu and Ladakh. It had developed close rapport with the leaders of the Indian National Congress, particularly Jawaharlal Nehru, but its equation with the Muslim League was marked by hostility. Then, there was the Muslim Conference which had little following in the Valley but had acquired rapid strength amongst the Muslims of the Jammu region during the last two years on account of its ideological affinity with Jinnah's Muslim League. The Maharaja was yet another force. The Dogra Rajputs of

Jammu considered him their own kith and kin. The relations between him on the one hand and Sheikh Abdullah and Pandit Nehru on the other were marked by mutual distrust and dislike.

Tragedies and Triumphs

All these actors were soon to play their part in the first act of the tragic Kashmir drama. The Maharaja was indecisive. Jinnah was impatient. Pandit Nehru was caught in between his idealism and the stark realities of the situation. Sheikh Abdullah, with streaks of megalomania and duplicity embedded deep in the layers of his mind, was nursing secret ambitions to carve out a virtual Sheikhdom for himself and his coterie. Each one of these actors was pushed on the stage with their personal illusions and believed that the drama would end the way he desired. Consequently, there was confusion and inconsistency on the stage. Mistakes after mistakes were made. And Kashmir soon found itself in the whirlpool of national and international controversy and conflict.

The first grave mistake was made when Maharaja Hari Singh flirted with the idea of independence. Pakistan's leaders, having attained their goal of a separate state by way of 'direct action' and other questionable means, were in an aggressive frame of mind. They crafted an unusual plan to seize the state of Jammu and Kashmir by force. On October 22, a full scale tribal invasion, backed by Pakistan's regulars, was launched. The tribesmen were all operating under the overall command of Akbar Khan, a Major General in the Pakistani army, who was given the code name of 'General Tariq'. They easily captured the border town of Darhi and Dommel and also Muzaffarabad.

In the developments from October 22 onwards, time was of prime importance. Every minute mattered. The State forces under the command of Brigadier Rajinder Singh fought to the 'last man and last bullet' at Uri, delaying the advance of the main horde of raiders for two crucial days. Brigadier Rajinder Singh died like a hero and made an invaluable contribution in saving the State. Baramulla fell into the hands of the raiders on October 24-26. Overtaken by their wild habits, they indulged in large-scale looting, burning, raping and killing. They hardly realised that the time spent by them in committing their abominable crimes would turn out to be their punishment, as it enabled the Indian forces to land at Srinagar airport, on October 27.

Maharaja Hari Singh, in his letter of October 26, asked for accession and 'attached the instrument of accession for acceptance by the Government of India'. In his reply of October 27, Mountbatten accepted the accession but added: 'It is my Government's wish that, as soon as law and order have been restored in Kashmir and her soil cleared of the invaders, the question of the State's accession should be settled by a reference to the people.' This addition was the second major mistake.

On October 27, a few planes of the Indian Air Force hovered over Srinagar airport carrying the first batch of Indian troops under the command of Lt. Colonel Ranjit Rai. It was not certain whether the airport was safe. After landing, Lt. Colonel Rai led the small contingent of the troops towards Baramulla. He lost his life in this bold venture.

In another bold move, Major Som Nath Sharma engaged the raiders at Badgam as they had reached very near the airport (November 3). He was outnumbered seven to one. But he showed unbounded courage and inflicted heavy casualties on the enemy. He, too, lost his life.

When the raiders were on the outskirts of Srinagar and Lt. Colonel Ranjit Rai and Major Som Nath Sharma of the Indian Army had been killed, Sardar Patel, accompanied by Defence Minister Baldev Singh, flew to the State capital, assessed the situation and on return to New Delhi ordered stoppage of all airline services and diversion of all planes for flying troops to Srinagar. The timely arrival of reinforcements enabled Brig. Sen to lure the raiders in the nest of Indian forces, near Shaltang, and attack them on November 5 from three sides. The raiders were routed.

As one looks at the events that happened about sixty-five years ago, one gets saddened to note that the nation has practically forgotten all its heroes on account of whose supreme sacrifices, Kashmir could be saved for India. Along with the triumphs, unfortunately tragedies too continued. On October 28, the words, 'Plebiscite under the UN auspices', were included in Nehru's radio broadcast. Another major mistake was committed when, on 1 January 1948, India took the case to the UN.

Abdullah's Power Game

Of all the mistakes made in handling the Kashmir issue, at its initial stage, the most serious was the failure to sense Sheikh Abdullah's hidden ambition. Nehru placed too great a reliance upon him, but he proved incapable of rising above his ambition. The moment Nehru declared that plebiscite would be held in the State; Sheikh Abdullah calculated that India could not do without his support. He exploited the position to extract one concession after another.

For Sheikh Abdullah, it was his power game that got precedence over everything else. What suited him at a particular moment was all that mattered. When it suited him, he kept proclaiming that accession of Kashmir to India was based on fundamental principles and was irrevocable. At the same time, he was sounding various quarters for support to the idea of having an independent 'Sheikhdom'. As early as 28 January 1948, he discussed the subject of independence with American officials. This is evident from the note of the same date sent by Warren Austin to the State Department after an interview with Sheikh Abdullah. The report (September 1950) of Loy Henderson, the US Ambassador to India, noted: 'In discussing future-Kashmir, Abdullah was vigorous that it should be independent.' On 3 May 1953, Adlai Stevenson came to Srinagar and had a long meeting with Sheikh Abdullah. All these events and pronouncements, taken together, should leave nobody in doubt that Sheikh Abdullah was dreaming of becoming an independent ruler of Kashmir and the Anglo-US bloc was encouraging him.

It was Sheikh Abdullah's excessive ambition and virtual conspiracy to carve out an independent state that led to his arrest in August 1953. After his removal from the scene, both Bakshi Ghulam Mohammad and G.M. Sadiq adopted a constructive attitude and helped in establishing a smooth constitutional relationship between the State and the Union. However, Article 370 of the Indian Constitution, with elements of separatism inbuilt in it, remained.

The Indian leadership showed similar lack of understanding with regard to Z.A. Bhutto at the Simla Conference, 1972. At that time, India held all the cards in her hands. The advisers of Mrs Indira Gandhi failed to read the mind of Pakistan's Prime Minister. The way Bhutto's mind was actually working at that time comes out clearly in his letter of 23 June 1972, to General Tikka Khan: 'So neither a few years of arranged peace, nor the present situation can possibly permit us to ignore the reality that there must inevitably, sooner or later, bring another war...every invasion from this side has defeated India...And we ourselves have ruled them for eight centuries.'

Pakistan was in a state of disarray and its potential for any mischief had been crippled. But, unfortunately, the habit of relying solely upon personalities persisted. Sheikh Mohammad Abdullah was brought back to the helm of affairs through the Kashmir Accord (February, 1975). It was not even ensured that he would not revert to his old game of whipping up insular and parochial forces to build up his own nest of power.

The central leadership, apart from its failure to size up Sheikh Abdullah's personality correctly, has shown little understanding of the forces of fundamentalism and fanaticism that have been operating in Kashmir and shaping the course of social and political events on the ground. For this lapse, the country has paid, and is still paying, a heavy price.

Fundamentalisation of Kashmiri Islam

Till the beginning of the second half of the last century, Kashmir's Islamic ethos was shaped by the liberal order of Sufis and Rishis. Unfortunately, this liberal order was gradually undermined, first by the selfish politics of Sheikh Abdullah and his political party, National Conference, and then by the forces let loose by Jama'at-i-Islami and other fundamentalist organisations.

Because of the Jama'at-i-Islami's operation at social, educational and cultural levels in Jammu and Kashmir and growing number of its workers, it had always more strength beneath the surface than above it. Its electoral performances of the past are no indication of its real hold on the mindscape of the Muslims. Moreover, in the 1977 and 1983 elections, the National Conference, by its very communal, parochial and pro-Pak stance virtually displaced the appeal of the Jama'at-i-Islami. It did exactly what the Jama'a-i-Islami was intending to do.

It was in these circumstances that Sheikh Abdullah government enacted a new law—Resettlement Act, 1982. The ostensible objective of this law was to provide for the resettlement of Kashmiris who had migrated to Pakistan-Occupied Kashmir or Pakistan itself. But its real purpose was to present Sheikh Abdullah and the National Conference as champions of Kashmiri identity.

Fall-outs

By the time Sheikh Abdullah passed away in September 1982, the adverse fallout of unsound decisions taken in the post-1972 period had spread far and wide both in the Valley and abroad. If any proof of this phenomenon was needed, it was forthcoming in the form of virulent anti-India demonstration at the time of the India-West Indies cricket match, held at Srinagar in October, 1983, and the kidnapping and killing of Indian diplomat, Ravinder Mahatre, by the Jammu and Kashmir Liberation Front, at Birmingham in February, 1984. The separatist forces were further fuelled by the manner in which National Conference fought the State Assembly elections in June 1983 and the Lok Sabha elections of December 1984. It was extensively publicised that the 'Kashmiri nation' was in chains and the 'hands that had put these chains' had to be cut, implying thereby that the elements in favour of the Union had to be destroyed.

When I took over as Governor of the State in April 1984, I found the State in the grip of subversive and fundamentalist forces. Violence and terrorism were creeping in fast and presenting a formidable challenge to the security of the State and integrity of the Union. How this challenge was successfully met during April 1984-June 1989 need not be gone into here. Suffice to say, the history of this period shows that if the administration is committed to materialisation of principled governance, if political parties are subjected to healthy fear and made to believe that they could not advance their personal agenda by misusing religion and playing to the tune of fundamentalists, and if firmness, fairness and development-work remain the guiding stars of the government, the forces of subversion could be beaten back. I relinquished charge in early 1989.

The moment the aforesaid approach ceased and old permissive attitudes returned in mid-1989, subversion reappeared. Inexcusably, no action was taken even when prominent leaders of Pandit community—political leader Tikka Lal Taploo, Judge M.K. Gangoo and journalist P.N. Bhatt etc—were killed, Rubaiya Sayeed, daughter of the Union Home Minister, kidnapped and highly subversive literature, couched in militant terminology, distributed on a large scale.

Around this period, Afghanistan War (1979-89) was near its end. This war had the effect of making ISI one of the most dangerous and powerful intelligence organisations in the world. The United States had placed in its hand huge resources. Besides vast sums of money, it got a massive stock of sophisticated weapons and communication equipment.

All these resources were given to the ISI to train and motivate Afghan Mujahideens to wage a furious and fanatical war against the troops of 'Godless Soviet Union'. But the ISI, clever and crafty as it has always been, sliced off a good part of the finances and equipment. According to a report of US Congress, as much as 60 per cent of equipment was directly or indirectly, kept by the ISI for its own purposes.

Collapse and Retrieval

This entire wherewithal—finances, equipment, experience and motivation and trained manpower—enabled the ISI to spin an extensive network of subversion and terrorism in Kashmir. By the time, I landed at Srinagar for my second term on 19 January, 1990; the state had virtually ceased to exist. The reports of almost all the reputed national dailies bear testimony to this fact.

From these hopeless conditions, the State was retrieved by a series of innovative and determined measures. The success of retrieval action was acknowledged in Parliament by the Union Home Minister, when, on 25 April, 1990, he said: 'Governor had to function in a vacuum, in a situation where there was no respect for the law or the authority of the State Government. He braved terrorists, instilled courage in government officials who had almost given up the situation as a lost case.'

Negative Polity

But the negative politics of the country, rooted as it is in national ethos of superficiality, softness and short-termism, came back with a vengeance and brought a resolute action to a sudden end. The result is for everybody to see—twenty-one years of bloody turmoil causing about 50,000 fatalities and draining billions of rupees from the state and national exchequers.

The peace-initiative and track II diplomacy, undertaken by the government of National Democratic Alliance and carried forward by government of United Progressive Alliance, did not make any significant impact at the ground level. In fact, during this process, besides causing a war in Kargil (1999), Pakistan and terrorist outfits sponsored by its ISI have carried out some of the most lethal and savage terrorist attacks in Kashmir and the rest of India, including the attack on the Indian Parliament on 13 December 2001 and on Mumbai on 26 November 2008.

For the last two years or so, owing to extremely tense relations between Pakistan and United States and heavy preoccupation of the ISI and its Jihadi outfits with the Afghanistan imbroglio, pressure of terrorists on Kashmir and the rest of India have eased. But this is only a temporary phase.

Future Course

From the above analysis of events of the past and forces that are operating in Kashmir at present, it should be clear that if Kashmir has to be put on the road to lasting peace and progress, a fundamental transformation in the attitude of the decision-makers in Delhi has to come about. In this respect, I have seven suggestions to make.

First, let us not remain under any delusion that India can solve its chronic problems, much less a problem with as acute a criticality as Kashmir's, without its polity and system of governance being subjected to a strong impulse of reforms and renovation. A new set of values, positive and elevating, would have to be generated in the state and society.

Secondly, Kashmir's true place in the Indian vision, the nature of which has been elaborated by me earlier, should be strongly projected. At present, all that is spoken of or written about is the special relationship, the need to continue and strengthen Article 370, and of giving more and more autonomy—'anything short of *Azadi*'—promoting thereby a separatist psyche and according a tacit approval to the 'two nations' or 'three nations' theory. What could be more unfortunate than the fact that the Kashmiri Pandits have become refugees in their own country?

Thirdly, it should be made clear to all concerned that India has never accepted the two-nation theory. The Partition came about when India was not a master of its own destiny. Now that it is a sovereign, secular and democratic republic, providing constitutional protection to rights of minorities and their religion and culture, it cannot allow any part of its territory to secede merely on the ground that it has a majority of Muslims. Even otherwise, could India accept a position that seven or eight million Muslims of Kashmir cannot live in the Indian Union, while about 150 million Muslims can do so in its other parts?

Fourthly, the phoney nature of the ideas floated by the former President of Pakistan, Pervez Musharraf, in respect of 'self-governance', 'joint management', 'demilitarisation' etc should be rejected outright. They are not only impractical but also have a huge potential for mischief in future.

Fifthly, India should make it clear to Pakistan that the 'peace-talk' with it would continue only if Pakistan ensures that none of its agencies, official or non-official, serves directly or indirectly, as an instrument of causing terrorism-related activities in India.

Sixthly, instead of going on with the current pattern of dialogue which is not likely to bring durable peace and prosperity to both the countries, India should take a new initiative and offer new proposals to Pakistan on the lines of suggestions made by Jawaharlal Nehru to Ayub Khan in 1964. A broad framework of a loose federation amongst the three units of united India could be worked out. While each of the three federating units—India, Pakistan and Bangladesh—would be an independent sovereign state, they could form a joint economic community and also have a broad understanding on matters of defence and foreign relations. Such an arrangement could be the fore-runner of having a union similar to the European Union.

Seventhly, India must ensure that the terrorists are not able to dictate terms to the local population. If government continues to appease and the terrorists continue to terrorise, no negotiations with any functionary of the recalcitrant groups, can fructify. Nor can any new proposal to bring durable peace and prosperity to the region be accepted.

So far, unfortunately, the 'spirit of Munich' has determined the attitude of the Indian decision makers. A vague hope has been entertained: Tomorrow it will be all right. But it will never be all right. The logic of history is against it.

Revisiting Public Service Broadcasting

—*B.G. Verghese*

I decided to write on 'Public Service Broadcasting', though I am not a broadcaster but, rather, a print person. However, broadcasting is a very large and important part of the media scene today and has assumed greater salience because of the communications revolution that has made radio and T.V. and other forms of electronic communication both instant and global so that we live in a virtual world. You can reach the entire world in real time, even as things are happening. This has created an extraordinary new situation, which has greatly enhanced the power of the media. Not that the print media has become obsolete for that reason. But the headlines have been stolen by the broadcast media because it operates round the clock, day and night, with visuals, commentaries and crawlers.

Even so, the print media not merely fills out sound-bytes but plays a vital role by providing interpretation, analysis, background and perspective which TV most often lacks. Instant commentary is often shallow. Radio flourished in India quite early, growing steadily after Independence; but television was slow in coming. When the Constitution was being debated in the Constituent Assembly in 1948, the Prime Minister, Jawaharlal Nehru declared, he would like broadcasting in India to be autonomous. That was with reference to All India Radio because there was no Doordarshan or any other TV channel at the time. He hoped that in due course this would happen and that AIR would become autonomous 'on the lines of the BBC'.

Nothing happened thereafter. The Government continued to run All India Radio and it produced some good programmes, though there was no competition to it at that time. Then in the late-1950s, or early-1960s, TV came to India in a small way and Doordarshan was established. It is interesting to note that television in India was initially promoted not so much by the Ministry of Information & Broadcasting, but by the Indian Space Research Organisation and Vikram Sarabhai, because they saw the potential of satellite communication. *Krishi Darshan* was started and run by ISRO behind a Doordarshan nameboard. We had later a very successful Satellite Instructional Television Experiment or SITE programme, based on an American satellite that was drifted over the Indian Ocean. Programmes were beamed to the satellite from a clutch of ground stations and broadcast directly to clusters of four hundred villages in six to eight paired states in Kannada, Odia, Tamil, Marathi, Gujarati, Bengali and Hindi. This was one of the earliest direct satellite-to-home broadcast services anywhere in the world with the required technology for ground reception and transmission being developed by ISRO.

An ISRO control centre was located in the Ahmedabad Doordarshan Station to operate SITE under a Space Applications Centre team overseen by Prof Yash Pal and others like Kiran Karnik. These men and women went on to develop educational and extension broadcasting and demonstrate the power of satellite TV to reach remote viewers in village *chaupal*s.

Doordarshan subsequently came into its own and got 'Plan Funding' on the plea that it would promote rural broadcasting as an extension tool to push forward the incipient Green Revolution by visually demonstrating the value of improved seeds, fertilisers and the new green technology package in farmers' fields. This, it was argued, would be more effective than radio as people would visually see experiments being laid out and the ensuing results. Consequently, a number of relay stations were set up to create an extensive transmission network.

Unfortunately, this was to become the bane of Doordarshan, in particular insofar as it led to a pattern of hardware-led TV development, with a lot of relay stations and engineers but with little or no funding for software production and programme staff. So we got a lop-sided, hardware-cum-engineer led public broadcast system. The engineers are not to blame, but balance was lost. As television grew—and there was a great spurt in 1982, with colour TV being introduced during the Asian Games in Delhi—the software-hardware gap widened.

The only way to reach people in remote locations in the early years of Independence was through radio, and All India Radio therefore, became a vital, even strategic, means of communication. However, the perils of monopoly state control over broadcasting were starkly exposed in 1962 during the India-China border conflict in the Himalayas and Ladakh. On 19 November 1962, the Chinese broke through our ranks at Se La and rolled down to the foothills. But the next morning, All India Radio announced that fierce fighting continued, when the fact was that the Chinese had declared a unilateral cease-fire at midnight and said that they would stop at the foothills and, in fact, withdraw to the Line of Actual Control, which they defined as they willed, near the McMahon Line, provided Indian forces remained south of the foothills.

This happened because no one, not even the Minister or the Secretary I&B, let alone the Director General of Broadcasting, dared to make such a momentous announcement without the permission of the Prime Minister, and Nehru could not be disturbed till 8 o'clock in the morning. So, according to AIR's main morning news bulletins on 20 November, Indian jawans were still bravely repelling the Chinese when the war was over. The only two Indian journalists at Tezpur, of which this writer was one, were amazed by this complete travesty. Even earlier, everyone from the GOC in C IV Corps down to the jawans, the DC and tea garden labourers, had tuned into Radio Peking to find out what was happening. This sorry episode suddenly brought home to people the vital importance of communication and autonomy for Radio. Now the enemy was telling us what was going on in our own country! That shock did not shake the policy makers. AIR and, later, Doordarshan, remained chained to the government.

Nehru passed away in 1964. Lal Bahadur Shastri took office. Indira Gandhi who became Information & Broadcasting Minister was not satisfied with the structuring and running of the Ministry. So she set up a Committee under A.K. Chanda to look into the matter, department by department. Among its several reports was one on All India Radio. This was largely descriptive but for one single paragraph which said that AIR should be given autonomy in keeping with the promise of

1948. Nothing happened. Emergency imposed in 1975-76, when the primary instrument of control by Indira Gandhi and her colleagues was censorship. Everything was censored: Parliament, the courts, the media of course, the State governments. Anything that meant something to people was subject to censorship. Truth was the greatest casualty.

Censorship was the prime lever of control and went to the extent that even when the censorship guidelines were struck down by the Gujarat High court as *ultra-vires* and illegal, the judgement itself was totally censored. This, despite forewarnings by the plaintiffs who had requested the Court to please ensure that the judgement was not censored! Indeed, among the first casualties of the Emergency was the AIR Code, the do's and dont's of broadcasting, which was abrogated. When asked about it by the then Director General, Indira Gandhi's lofty response was 'AIR Code? What code? We are the Government'! That summed up the official attitude. So when the Janata Government was elected, having tasted the bitter fruit of State control it decided that broadcasting must be liberated from government. A committee with which I was associated was thereupon set up to go into the question of autonomy for AIR, still far the bigger partner, and Doordarshan.

The Committee produced a report titled 'Akashvani, A National Broadcast Trust'. This laid out the charter, structure and priorities for broadcasting and suggested what needed to be done. We also appended a draft bill so that there should be no delay in implementing the report. However, the new I&B Minister, L.K. Advani, ominously remarked that a committee set up to confer autonomy on AIR/DD, had instead 'granted it independence'. The opportunity was lost. A more constrained Prasar Bharati Bill was drafted but the Janata government fell apart and nothing happened. By 1982, television had grown and colour was introduced. The next milestone came in 1995-96 with signs of competition to DD through private video channels like News Track and Business News which portrayed the previous week's highlights with some commentary.

There were as yet no private radio or TV channels although the 1977 autonomy committee had recommended licensing cultural, educational and other approved bodies. There had been applications from IIT Kanpur, which taught television and had an in-campus television station, Pune University, the Ludhiana Agricultural University and certain cultural bodies. The Committee had opined that entities such as the Bharatiya Vidya Bhavan or Kalakshetra, IITs and others be franchised by a licensing committee as such stations would introduce an element of competition and diversity in both TV and radio. This again was not to be. After the fall of the Janata Government, Indira Gandhi continued with government control of the airwaves.

In 1995, a case came up before the Supreme Court pertaining to freedom of expression on account of denial of broadcast uplinking rights for a cricket fixture abroad. The West Bengal Cricket Association challenged the consequent nullification of the broadcast rights it had purchased. The case was heard and judgment delivered by Justices Sawant and Jeevan Reddy. This held that the Government could manage and allocate the electro-magnetic spectrum, a finite natural resource, but was not entitled to a monopoly of the airwaves. The spectrum must be licensed to private players as well. The Airwaves judgement was notionally implemented in 1990 by the National Front Government under V.P. Singh. A new Prasar Bharati Bill was drafted and faced many vicissitudes because the Government did not enjoy a majority in the Upper House. Bargains were struck and the end result was an unhappy compromise. Nonetheless it was enacted but the Bill was to come into force only on a date to be notified. The Congress came back to power again and it was only in 1997 under Inder Gujral that the Prasar Bharati Bill was finally notified with further compromises.

Whatever it was, some kind of autonomy had finally been statutorily granted to Prasar Bharati. Unfortunately, few other than the Prime Minister and Jaipal Reddy, the Minister of Information & Broadcasting, were for autonomy for broadcasting. To this day, neither Parliament nor any Government or political party truly favours autonomous public service broadcasting. The same seems largely true of the media, advertisers and general public. This is partly because none of them seem to understand broadcasting, let alone public service broadcasting and why Prasar Bharati should be autonomous. The Act specifically provided that the assets of AIR-DD system, one of the largest networks in the world, would be transferred to Prasar Bharati to vest it with financial autonomy. Of course, it would have to put up its demands to Parliament and they would need to be voted; but it could also levy certain charges. The Government was also authorised to consider levying broadcast receiver licenses, as in the UK, the proceeds of which would go to Prasar Bharati. These provisions have alas not been brought into play as the levy of broadcast license fees is considered tantamount to taxation.

The other major stipulation concerned personnel. Apart from the engineering and administrative staff, the programme staff consisted of two categories, permanent government cadres and casual artists of various kinds. The Act provided that all existing staff would be given the option of either joining the new Prasar Bharati cadre on its terms and conditions or retaining their current scales of pay and pension as government servants until retirement. However, all new entrants would be recruited as employees of Prasar Bharati. The idea was that government servants should be replaced or they faded away over time. Those who opted for the new system and new recruits would be on the rolls of Prasar Bharati and not of the Government. There was thus to be a transition of personnel from government service to corporate employees. Prasar Bharati was to set up its own selection boards and set the process of corporatisation of personnel in motion. This was not done.

Then for various reasons, the Government decided that the five permanent Board members, the CEO, the two Directors-General of AIR and DD and the Directors of Finance and Personnel, or the core group responsible for day to day administration, would be selected from the ranks of the bureaucracy. Somehow there seems to be a strange notion that ultimate wisdom in all matters essentially resides in the government. There are certainly many good people in government. But a lot of wisdom and experience resides elsewhere too. The Achilles heel inherent in this decision was revealed some years later when Prasar Bharat made its first autonomous selection, through its own Selection Board, and appointed S.Y. Quraishi, the present Chief Election Commission as Director General, Doordarshan. Lo and behold some years later, apropos of nothing, the Government suddenly discovered or decided that the government would fall or India would collapse unless Quraishi was immediately relieved of his services in Prasar Bharati and restored to active government service.

So without any reference to Quraishi or to the Chairman or Members of the Board, or to the CEO, he was overnight relieved of his duties in Prasar Bharati. All that was vouchsafed to the Board was that the Prime Minister and Deputy Prime Minister had agreed. When asked for an explanation, the I&B Minister Ravi Shankar Prasad, merely repeated that Quraishi must go. The best but totally unconvincing explanation was that as an IAS officer on deputation, the cadre controlling authority, the Department of Personnel, could recall him at any time. Thus Quraishi, a fine, creative officer and a man of integrity, was arbitrarily removed overnight. He then had to cool his heels for some time before being placed in the Steel Ministry. The Chairman of Prasar Bharati is appointed by an independent non-government panel of high functionaries. This is a good system—when it works. Unfortunately, Prasar Bharati's first Chairman, Nikhil Chakravartty took ill soon after being inducted. Within a few months, he was bed-ridden and tragically passed away a few months later. Prasar Bharati was left headless. No new nomination took place and it had to make do with an acting chairman by rotation!

At the next level, the Government felt that at the initial stage the CEO should be a bureaucrat who might enjoy at least a five-year term. Therefore, a senior Joint Secretary or a young Additional Secretary would have to be selected. But, mindful of the financial and personnel pitfalls of the transition period, it thought fit to have a more senior candidate. So, the CEO's retirement age was raised from 60 to 62 and S.S. Gill, a dynamic figure and who had been Secretary in the Ministry of Information & Broadcasting earlier, was brought in to fill the post by amending the Act. The new Board members—Romila Thapar, Rajinder Yadav, Abid Hussein, U.R. Rao, Verghese and Gill were nick-named Fogeys, an acronym of 'Friends of Gujaral'! The first 'fogey' to fall was Gill, when the Government changed. The NDA ousted Gill because it felt the rules had been bent to get him in. Again, for whatever reason, the selection panel did not meet and we had an acting CEO, a senior officer seconded from the Ministry of I&B.

Then one of the Director Generals completed his term. So we had an acting Director-General, Doordarshan and, later, acting Director-General of AIR. There was no Director of Personnel. Someone from the government would come and sit there and the staff selection process was simply not set in motion. The budget was virtually framed in the I&B Ministry as Prasar Bharati had no Finance Director. So everything was controlled by the Government. The PB Board of Governors displayed a signboard, but in truth there was no real Board. Later, when we agitated the matter about the Selection Board not meeting, it was decided that two full time DGs should be appointed. But if a ranking officer was inducted from the Government, we were told he must be allotted a house as he would have to give up his official residence! The alternative was that he be compensated with a higher salary. But it was unthinkable that a DG-AIR or DD be given a Rupee more than his colleague of equivalent rank in some Ministry! So we said Prasar Bharati would foot the extra salary or provide appropriate housing. But that was also considered infeasible. So PB soldiered on with acting DGs, an acting CEO and an acting Chairman and without a Finance or Personnel Director. It was a bizarre situation.

I&B Ministers kept changing. At one point of time, Pramod Mahajan happened to be the minister when the engineering staff of AIR went on strike because of some Pay Commission problem. They have been denied some benefit given to others. This threatened to bring AIR-Delhi at least to a standstill. Thereupon some of us on the Board intervened and found the engineers willing to settle. So we went with a formula to the Minister. He was very courteous and gave us tea and sympathy saying, 'I must tell you gentlemen that you have no locus standii. These are all government servants, so you cannot mediate or arbitrate.' We were virtually told to go home. The Minister was honest enough to say that the idea of autonomy for broadcasting was completely unreal. As some private channels were by now on the air and the print media was privately held, the government needed a trumpet of its own. This was a totally false argument. Apart from being a dubious principle in a democratic society, the government has never had a communications policy to this day. There is also another fallacy. If broadcasting was to be a government monopoly, what constitutes 'government'? The Central Government is 'the government' and broadcasting is on the Union List. Yet the State governments and grass-root level Panchayati bodies and Nagarpalikas also constitute governments. Why cannot they also be permitted to broadcast? However, Public Service Broadcasting has remained a Central Government monopoly.

This apart, Prasar Bharati has not devolved power to its regional and local units sufficiently. Around year 2000, the so-called local/rural broadcasting station of AIR at Bijnor, for instance, was controlled from Lucknow because there were no programme personnel available for posting there. Yet every relay station and every transmitter had an engineer. So Bijnor programming in those days was filled with recorded music. There was nothing else. It was pathetic and the whole process of broadcasting was completely lost. The same story repeated itself on a larger scale in Jammu & Kashmir. More transmitters were sanctioned. But when the Kargil War happened, though some Rs 400 crore had been sanctioned for the Kashmir channel and the infrastructure was in place, programme personnel were missing and no Balti speaker was available. There was no Station Director in Kargil and the man in Leh had to do double duty. The domination of Doordarshan has led to the decline of AIR which has been treated as a poor relative though radio is very versatile and cost-effective. AIR's External Service hangs a board but offers little service. It has been neglected. AIR's Monitoring Service, once shared with the Home Ministry to monitor foreign broadcasts for intelligence gathering and re-broadcast purposes, has all but disappeared. The school broadcasting service of All India Radio has been wound down and so too over Doordarshan. DD International was started but it faded away.

The licensing of private channels then saw some of DD's best talent migrating to these newer pastures. Altogether, it has been a tragic story. There still are good people in AIR and Doordarshan, but many in the organisation fear autonomy and accountability. Autonomy can be legislated, but it is never given. It has to be grasped. Many ask why Prasar Bharati matters since the private channels are there. The public service broadcaster is required to serve all the many 'publics' that make up the nation—young and old, rich and poor, men, women and children, the differently-abled, urban and rural audiences, sportsmen, academics, learners of every kind. And this in every language. The 'service' has to be comprehensive and constant, not selective and fitful. It must empower and promote creativity and culture and fulfil the many promises of the Constitution. This is a duty enjoined upon it as a public trust and hence its right to support from the exchequer.

Private broadcasters are commercially driven and seek 'ratings' to ensure high value advertising. Nothing is wrong in that except that advertisers are interested in 'viable' markets which exclude millions of poor and disadvantaged. About half or more of the people in India live on or below the poverty line. Many of them do not figure in the advertisers' 'market' as they do not have the disposable income to buy the goods advertised. Therefore, programming has to attract up-market advertising. None can blame the private channels. They too perform a valuable service and do a bit of public service broadcasting on the side. While the private broadcaster primarily caters to the consumer to earn its keep, the public service broadcaster must cater to the citizen. Now every consumer is a citizen, but not every citizen is a consumer. So, that means commercial broadcasting automatically excludes 40 to 60 per cent of the population—people who need relevant broadcasting as a powerful means of information, knowledge and empowerment.

With millions of people graduating from traditional 'Bharat' to modernising India year after year, we need to engage them in conversation and make them feel they are participants in governance and decision making and partners in whatever is going on. Their views must be heard and they must have the opportunity to listen to others and say 'hold on; have you considered this, that and the other?' That opportunity has been denied them. Community and local broadcasting have not been promoted as vigorously as they should. The rules and guidelines for them are overly stringent. Broadcasting has to mean more than cricket, cinema, political gossip and sensation. Therefore, we need to recognise the importance of public service broadcasting especially in this era of 'paid news' and 'private treaties' by well-heeled broadcasters in an era of convergence and multi-media. The communications revolution has made the media instant and exceedingly powerful. Everyone fears the media, but the media does not cater to the people nor necessarily match its power with responsibility. Public service broadcasting can and must set standards for 'Shining India' while serving 'Suffering India' as well. Distance learning can be a great aid.

The argument that he who pays the piper plays the tune is fallacious. Prasar Bharati is not funded by the government but by the public exchequer. The exchequer also funds Parliament, the Courts, the Election Commission, the UPSC, et al. Does it then mean that the government must or does control all these institutions? The proposition is absurd. So, things must change. It is necessary that we rethink this matter of broadcasting and communication and compel our masters to recognise that public service broadcasting is essential. The enormous potential of AIR and Doordarshan must be unleashed. Based on a technical study commissioned by it, the Board recommended that Prasar Bharati's engineering wing be hived off and made a transmission company, a subsidiary and separate profit centre to earn additional revenues. Prasar Bharati's vast transmission network would thereby no longer remain under-utilised, as is largely the case in many sectors. However, this measure too was never addressed as a means of ensuring cost-effectiveness and strengthening the sinews of public broadcasting.

Look globally; recall what a power CNN became during the first Iraq War with Peter Arnott covering it live from Baghdad. Likewise, with reference to the current West Asian ferment for democracy and change, one factor more than any other responsible for the Arab spring was the Qatar-based Al-Jazeera television because it gave the news to the people as it is. The Arab street could no longer be fooled by the Sheikh of this and the King of that who maintained broadcasting channels only to sing their praises, or by Islamic ideologues or anybody else. Al-Jazeera's advertising was stopped. They were threatened. For some time Qatar almost had no diplomatic relations with Saudi Arabia, but the Sultan of Qatar said he had allowed Al Jazeera the freedom to broadcast and they could do so. And so they continued.

The power and versatility of broadcasting is enormous. Therefore, we must mend our approach. Information is power and people do not want to lose power. That is the problem. Notwithstanding any of that, it is time for public service broadcasting to come into its own. Lok Sabha TV and the newer Rajya Sabha TV, also public service broadcasters, are steps in the right direction. Prasar Bharati too matters.

Note: As this piece goes to press, word comes that the Government has accorded full freedom to Prasar Bharati to broadcast news bulletins without any kind of direct or indirect official overseeing from 8 to 10 p.m daily with effect from 14 January, 2013. Jai Hind!

India's Polity: Crisis of Governance

—Bimal Jalan

Over the past several decades, the society has made multifold contributions to promoting India's cultural, social, democratic and secular heritage for the benefit of all irrespective of religion, caste, creed and regional considerations. I have chosen to concentrate the present topic for this anthology, as I believe that, as we look deeper and wider in the functioning of our polity, we have to recognise that we are at crossroads. Unless we tackle some of the emerging problems, the process of national integration, which is a hallmark of India's democratic heritage, may itself be at stake. Already 170 districts in India (out of 560), according to official sources, are ungovernable. Some years ago, the Prime Minister himself referred to Naxalism as the 'single biggest internal security challenge faced by our country'.

On the prevailing crisis of governance, it would be worthwhile emphasising that what makes the present situation much more alarming than during earlier decades is that it is no longer 'episodic', that is, confined to some outrageous event now and then. Over the years, it has become 'systemic' and spreads across practically all segments of the society, including governments at centre and states, public institutions, corporate sector, sections of the media, and so on. There is widespread deterioration in administrative and public accountability, prevalence of corruption, income disparities among various sections of the people, rising power of criminals in politics, and the emergence of small parties as primary factors in determining the survival of multiple-party coalitions in power.

Many of the recent developments in the working of the vital institutions of the state were not visualised at the time of the framing of our Constitution. Some of these have substantially reduced the responsibility and accountability of multi-party governments for what they do, or for that matter, what they do not do. A fundamental 'systemic' change, which dominates the working of India's politics today—unlike the first four decades after Independence is the emergence of coalitions as a 'regular' form of government since 1989. India has had as many as nine governments during past twenty-one years—with an average life of less than two and a half years. Of these, three multi-party coalitions survived their five-year terms with occasional setbacks and shifts in the composition of parties supporting them from inside or outside. Excluding these three and the present government in office, the average term of five governments with enormous powers to allocate resources, control public enterprises and decide inter-state allocation of investments was less than a year.

It does not take a political genius to recognise that if he or she is in politics and gets elected to Parliament or a State Legislature, his or her life expectancy in office is likely to be 'short' and entirely dependent on the party leader—unless, of course, he or she happens to be that leader, or a direct descendant of that leader. The crucial point here is that at the time of formation of a multi-party coalition government, general expectation of small and regional parties is that enormous powers that their nominees, as ministers, enjoy may not last very long—or that it may change if a more powerful leader of one or two large parties in coalition so decides.

Under the present Constitutional provisions, following the amendments carried out in 1985 and again in 2003 to prevent defections, now there is also a built-in incentive for fragmentation of political parties at the time of election. This is because smaller a party, the greater the power of an individual legislator to defect to another party in search of political power without having to relinquish his or her seat in Parliament or State Assembly. On the other hand, a member elected from a large national party has very little discretion to defect without the support of a substantial number of other members, who also wish to defect. Thus, the smaller a party the easier it is for a few of its members or all of them to switch from one coalition to another, and maximise their political capital. The same is true of so-called 'independent' members, who are supported by some political parties during elections. In a situation where multi-party coalitions are the norm, all regional or caste leaders naturally have a much greater incentive to form their own separate parties.

In addition to fragmentation of parties and short life expectancy of coalition government at birth, in recent years, there has also been a subtle change in the role of Parliament, and the accountability of executive to Parliament. Parliament now has multiple centres of power (in addition to the party leading the government, and the party leading the opposition). An important consequence of the emergence of multiple centres of power is that what Parliament does or does not do depends on 'behind the scene' agreements among different sets of party leaders within and outside the government. As long as the government has the backing of sufficient number of leaders, it is supreme and it can get Parliament to do what it wishes. As Eric Hobsbawm, the noted historian and political analyst, has pointed out in another context, when important national decisions are taken among small groups of people in private in a democracy, the position is not very different from the way they would have been taken in non-democratic countries.

Unfortunately, over the past two decades in particular, politics has also become a career of choice by persons with criminal records. The investigative and prosecution machinery for suspected criminal activities is under direct control of departments of the government. There is a natural reluctance to speed up investigations and the prosecution of persons who are leaders of political parties and/or members of the cabinet. According to the statistical survey of elections to the Lok Sabha in recent elections, it has been found that nearly 20 per cent of the candidates surveyed, cutting across party lines (excluding independent candidates) had criminal antecedents. In the present Lok Sabha which has 543 seats in all, well over 100 members had criminal cases pending against them. No wonder that physical scuffles and assaults among some members on the floor of state assemblies, and even Parliament, is not an uncommon sight when tempers rise because of charges of corruption and wrongdoing by leaders of one political party or another.

Further, unlike other democracies, in addition to major industries like oil, gas and steel, public sector enterprises in India are dominant in the financial field (particularly banking and insurance) and transport (particularly railways, ports and airports). Award of contracts as well as operational priorities, in addition to appointments, are subject to ministerial discretion without sufficient accountability. Recently, there has been widespread public outrage about corrupt ministers at the centre and states about scams relating to allocations of public resources, such as, land, mines and gas. Some ministers have also been sent to jail by the Supreme Court and High Courts because of involvement in bribery and other illicit practices. To see our so-called Hon'ble ministers in jail is a sad commentary about the functioning of India's democracy. But let us also ask ourselves—how is it that these Hon'ble ministers had the opportunity and such enormous discretionary powers to accept massive bribes from corrupt corporates? Who gave them this opportunity? Was it the intention of our Constitution to confer such powers on elected representatives of the people?

A fundamental principle laid down in our Constitution in Article 75(3) is that '*The Council of Ministers shall be collectively responsible to the House of the People.*' However, recent history is full of instances where important policy decisions, leading to considerable revenue losses to the government and/or unwarranted allocation of public resources for personal gain by political leaders, were taken without individual and/or 'collective responsibility'. A striking example, which still dominates media headlines, is in respect of allocation of 2G Spectrum. Heads of ministries, which were involved in the process of allocation, have been 'passing the buck', as it were, to some other ministry or to their own civil servants on the ground that they merely concurred in the decision taken by someone else. It has also been claimed that in any case, the final decision was approved by the Cabinet. If this was indeed the case, then the question arises: what does the 'collective responsibility' of the Cabinet mean?

Another development, which has gathered further momentum in recent years, is the politicisation of India's bureaucracy. In theory, under the Indian system of executive responsibility, there is supposed to be a clear division of roles between the permanent civil service and the political leadership. Government's policy priorities and its work program are set by politicians. However, bureaucracy is supposed to ensure that implementation of the approved program is done according to the laws and procedures in force, without fear or favour, for the benefit of all the people regardless of their political affiliations. Over the years, slowly but surely, the role of the bureaucracy has been seriously compromised. Any party which comes to power and joins a multi-party coalition, is inclined to appoint favored bureaucrats in sensitive positions who, in turn, are expected to carry out the wishes of its party leaders, irrespective of their merits or legality.

As emphasised by several former cabinet secretaries and other high level officials in their memoirs, most of the administrative powers which earlier rested in the hands of the civil servants have now been taken over by political masters at the ministerial level who have no direct or indirect experience of administration. As politics has become more combative and personalised, and coalition governments have become less secure about their tenure in office, transfers of civil servants have also become very frequent. Some years ago in U.P, for example, where two parties resolved to have six-monthly tenure in government, there were as many as one thousand transfers within a year amongst members of the IAS and the IPS. The first head of government transferred senior officers at an average rate of seven per day. The second head of government, who took office after the expiry of six-month period, decided to beat this record and transferred officials at the rate of sixteen per day!

As a result of frequent transfers, administration has naturally become weak. What is even worse is that civil servants, instead of being independent of political leaders or parties in power, have now become sub-servient to them. Bureaucratic corruption has also become rampant, both to avoid transfers as well as to secure remunerative postings. India perhaps also has the largest number of programs, launched by the government, to provide subsidised food, primary education, housing and improved rural infrastructure for the benefit of the poor. Yet, the absolute number of persons below the poverty line has been rising rather than declining. Assuming that as many as 200 or 250 million people are currently benefiting from the high rates of growth in manufacturing and services in the private sector, more than 800 million persons in India would still continue to be at the periphery of the circles of prosperity for quite some time. This paradox can only be explained by the poor state of governance and rising incidence of corruption in the public delivery system.

A good example of substantial diversion of subsidies and budgetary resources to unintended beneficiaries under an important poverty alleviation program is that of the Targeted Public Distribution System (TPDS). Under this program, in order to provide food security, certain quantity of foodgrains are provided under the Public Distribution System (PDS) at highly subsidised prices to households with incomes Below the Poverty Line (BPL). The objectives of this program are indeed laudable and are supported by all sections across the political spectrum. However, an evaluation study covering sixty districts and 3600 households, undertaken by the Planning Commission a few years ago, found widespread diversion of grain from genuinely poor families to other households. Among its findings, the following are particularly disturbing:

- Sixteen large states covered under the study were issued fourteen million tonnes of food from the central pool for distribution to BPL families. Of this, less than six million tonnes (or only about 40 per cent) were delivered to the BPL families, and the rest never reached them;
- Thus, for every kilogram of foodgrain delivered to the poor, Government of India had to issue 2.4 kg of subsidised grain;
- Out of the consumer subsidy disbursed by the centre to these sixteen states as much as 60 per cent did not reach BPL households;
- The Government spent Rs.3.65 through budgetary food subsidies to transfer Re.1 to the poor.

There could not be a more serious indictment of the governance system in India than the above findings of the Planning Commission. There are multiple reasons for failure of administration to deliver services to the poor, or for that matter, improve public infrastructure. The most important reason, in addition to some of the political factors mentioned above, for this state of affairs is the proliferation of ministries and offices of government over time. There is no item of government business for which a single ministry can be held responsible, except perhaps taxation or the budget-making. The number of ministries has shot up from 18 in 1947 to 75 or more now and there has been a sharp increase in the number of cabinet ministers, independent ministers of state in charge of separate ministries, and large number of ministers of state who report to cabinet ministers. Many of these ministries have very little to do. All ministries also have more than one department and several sub-ordinate agencies. The rigid hierarchy in the delivery and decision making process further ensures that horizontally as well as vertically, a dozen or more offices are likely to be involved from different ministries, including Planning Commission, even when there is no policy to be decided, such as, say, provision of drinking water or electricity to rural areas.

In addition to the Centre, there is similar proliferation of governmental organisations at the state and district level. It has become a routine matter for policy to be announced by the central government, but implementation to be in the hands of state government and their subsidiary organisations. The central government blames state governments, and the latter blame the central government for rigidity in the provisions of the scheme or inadequate allocation of funds. Within the central government, it is now common for one department or ministry to blame another department for any drawback in either policy formulation or policy implementation.

The proliferation of multiple government agencies involved in the decision making process, without any individual or collective responsibility, combined with complexity of administrative rules and regulations has had the inevitable result of increasing both the demand and supply of corruption in India. Thus, according to the widely quoted Transparency International's corruption index (EPI), India was ranked as having one of the highest levels of corruption in the world. India's rank was higher than non-democratic countries like China. It was also substantially higher than other East Asian countries like Japan, Malaysia and South Korea.

In addition to wide acceptance of corruption as a necessary evil, another area of grave concern is the interlocking or 'vertical integration' of corruption at various levels of the government hierarchy—elected politicians, higher bureaucracy and lower bureaucracy. Along with vertical integration, there is also horizontal spread of corruption to other public institutions, large corporates, parts of judiciary, media as well as independent professions. This has made the prevention and control of corruption even more difficult. As if all this were not enough, another unfortunate development has been the politicisation of corruption. Increasingly, cases of corruption are being given a political colour without any serious intent to tackle the problem. This has facilitated the entry into politics of persons with a track record of corruption. The public no longer knows whom to trust—the accuser or the accused.

Corruption is now a major hurdle in growth, development and poverty alleviation in India, as indeed in several other countries. Research has established that in the long run corruption reduces productivity, lowers investment, causes fiscal drain and has a debilitating effect on efficiency. Unfortunately, these adverse effects of corruption are not generally appreciated by India's political and legal institutions or its public. It is abundantly clear that unless Indian authorities take some measures to improve governance and reduce the 'demand and supply' of corruption in the economy, there is simply no way in which India can reduce the rising disparity (and despair) among the bulk of its people. Given the current political scenario of multiple-party coalitions with no shared agenda, dramatic reforms or 'hard' measures to improve administrative efficiency may not be feasible in the near future. However, hopefully, with the emerging pressure from the Civil Society, over the next few years it should be possible to evolve a consensus on introducing a package of reforms which are relatively benign and are likely to be in the overall interest of the country as a whole.

An important priority is to redefine the primary role of government in the economy. At the macro-economic level, the political (i.e. ministerial) role of the government should be to ensure a stable and competitive environment with a strong external sector and a transparent domestic financial system. While the macro-economic priorities (for example, the so-called trade-off between growth and inflation) may be decided by the government, the instrumentalities for achieving these objectives must be left to autonomous regulatory and promotional agencies. Similarly, government's direct role in economic areas should be re-set in favor of ensuring the availability of public goods (such as roads and water) and essential services (such as health and education) to the people. In these areas, the government's role must expand substantially. At the same time, its role in managing commercial enterprises deserves to be correspondingly reduced. The latter objective should be achieved without in any way affecting the financial and other benefits of those who are presently employed.

Similarly, it is necessary to simplify administrative procedures and reduce the number of agencies, at different levels, involved in providing clearances for undertaking any activity. For example, at least thirty different clearances involving several agencies at the Centre and the states are required for setting up even a modest-sized industrial factory. Except in selected areas, it is desirable to cut through the elaborate red tape and rely primarily on 'self-certification'. The government can lay down standards and norms (for example, in respect of environmental impact or safety), and the entity concerned may be required to 'self-certify' at the highest levels of management that these have been complied with as per the notified procedures. Government agencies can make random checks and in case there are violations, appropriate penal action can be taken. Similarly, the present complexity in regulations should be reduced drastically. Such simplification has been tried out in some areas with success (for example, foreign exchange transactions).

A related area is transparency in the decision-making process within the government. A major step in this respect has been taken with the enactment of the Right To Information Act, 2005. The beneficial impact of this legislation in making the government accountable and citizen-friendly is already visible. A further step in this direction is to make it mandatory for all ministries and departments of the government to voluntarily make information on the decisions taken by them available to the public (excluding security-related subjects). It may be clarified that information should be released by the ministries themselves without the need for any member of the public to ask for it. If this is done, the free media and civil society institutions will constitute an effective instrument for enforcing accountability in the decision-making process itself.

Case studies of international experience in the management of public services show that the objective of such programs can be achieved better, and at less cost, if a distinction is made between the ownership of these services (by the government) and the delivery of such services (by non-governmental organisations and local enterprises). In such cases, the public authorities retain the responsibility for regulating and monitoring the activities, providing subsidies where necessary, and laying down distribution guidelines. In India, two noteworthy examples of public-private collaboration in the area of public services are: the public call offices (PCOs), which revolutionalised the availability of telephone services all over the country in the 1990s, and the Sulabh Sauchalayas, which, despite some problems, are estimated to have provided sanitation facilities to ten million people at very low cost.

In addition to administrative reforms and improving the functioning of governments in power, it is also necessary to introduce some political reforms to reduce corruption, power of small parties to destabilise multi-party coalitions, and attractiveness of politics as a career for persons with criminal antecedents. I have dealt with these and other political issues which require urgent attention in some detail elsewhere. Let me just mention three urgent political reforms which require to be undertaken as early as possible.

First, the anti-defection law should be made applicable to small parties and independent members who choose to join the government. In other words, those who join the government cannot defect (as has happened in several states of India in the past few years) without having to seek re-election. At present, as mentioned above, there is a built-in incentive for fragmentation of political parties at the time of elections as the anti-defection law applies only to members of a particular political party irrespective of their numbers in Parliament or Legislatures. This has had the unintended consequences of providing an incentive for formation of small parties, and reducing the personal autonomy of elected legislators belonging to a large party.

Second, highest priority should be given by Courts to hearing cases of elected leaders with criminal antecedents. Their cases should be mandatorily decided within six months after their election. Such a procedure would effectively 'reverse' the incentive for criminals to choose politics in order to delay investigation of their cases and possible conviction. In fact, they may choose not to contest elections so that they are in a position to delay hearings through normal legal procedures!

Finally, in view of the high cost of periodic elections, governance cannot be improved without reducing the compulsion of political parties to raise funds through illicit means. This is one of the primary causes of political corruption, and state funding of elections is essential to help those—however few they may be—who wish to remain in politics without having to indulge in corrupt practices. Contrary to popular impression, the budgetary cost of funding elections by the state is unlikely to exceed 0.3 to 0.4 per cent of the total expenditure of Rs.600,000 crores or more in the current fiscal year. Part of such expenditure could also be covered, if necessary, by diverting funds being allocated to MPs and MLAs for financing projects in their constituencies (the so-called MP/MLA Local Area Development funds), which suffer from several deficiencies. For equitable distribution of budget funds among large and small political parties, as elaborated elsewhere, a simple formula can be put in place without much problem.

In conclusion, let me just add that notwithstanding our past performance, I am sanguine about India's economic potential and our ability to achieve high growth with financial stability. The reason for this confidence is that, despite problems in governance, the innate ability of our people is immense and has been demonstrated beyond reasonable doubt. The open, participative and democratic system ensures that a change, where necessary can be delayed, but it cannot be avoided altogether.

Recently, for example, the power of the people to bring about positive changes in the accountability of state institutions through peaceful democratic means was abundantly made clear in the formulation of the Lokpal bill. To begin with, as all of us are aware, there was considerable resistance by government to respond to suggestions made by Anna Hazare, and the movement launched by him to improve the bill. Later, however, the government had to agree to move a new bill in Parliament which met people's aspirations. Similarly, to curb political corruption and reduce discretionary powers of ministers in the allocation of public resources, government has announced its intention to take necessary legislative and administrative action. Much more, of course, remains to be done. While there would no doubt be resistance and delays, I am sure; ultimately 'people's will' shall prevail. India is a relatively young and vibrant democracy. I am sure that, given the will, India will achieve its full potential in the years to come, and India's poverty would have become a distant memory.

Putting Growth in its Place*

—*Jean Drèze, Amartya Sen*

It has to be but a means to development, not an end in itself.

Is India doing marvellously well, or is it failing terribly? Depending on whom you speak to, you could pick up either of those answers with some frequency. One story, very popular among a minority but a large enough group—of Indians who are doing very well (and among the media that cater largely to them)—runs something like this. 'After decades of mediocrity and stagnation under "Nehruvian Socialism", the Indian economy achieved a spectacular take-off during the last two decades. This take-off, which led to unprecedented improvements in income per head, was driven largely by market initiatives. It involves a significant increase in inequality, but this is a common phenomenon in periods of rapid growth. With enough time, the benefits of fast economic growth will surely reach even the poorest people, and we are firmly on the way to that.' Despite the conceptual confusion involved in bestowing the term 'socialism' to a collectivity of grossly statist policies of 'License Raj' and neglect of the state's responsibilities for school education and healthcare, the story just told has much plausibility, within its confined domain.

But looking at contemporary India from another angle, one could equally tell the following—more critical and more censorious—story: 'The progress of living standards for common people, as opposed to a favoured minority, has been dreadfully slow—so slow that India's social indicators are still abysmal.' For instance, according to World Bank data, only *five* countries outside Africa (Afghanistan, Bhutan, Pakistan, Papua New Guinea and Yemen) have a lower 'youth female literacy rate' than India (*World Development Indicators 2011,* online). To take some other

* This piece was earlier published in *Outlook*, dated 14 November 2011, and is being published here with the permission of the authors.

examples, only *five* countries (Afghanistan, Cambodia, Haiti, Myanmar and Pakistan) do worse than India in child mortality rate; only *three* have lower levels of 'access to improved sanitation' (Bolivia, Cambodia and Haiti); and *none* (anywhere—not even in Africa) have a higher proportion of underweight children. Almost any composite index of these and related indicators of health, education and nutrition would place India very close to the bottom in a ranking of all countries outside Africa.

Growth and Development

So which of the two stories—unprecedented success or extraordinary failure—is correct? The answer is both, for they are both valid, and they are entirely compatible with each other. This may initially seem like a bit of a mystery, but that initial thought would only reflect a failure to understand the demands of development that go well beyond economic growth. Indeed, economic growth is not constitutively the same thing as development, in the sense of a general improvement in living standards and enhancement of people's well-being and freedom. Growth, of course, can be very helpful in achieving development, but this requires active public policies to ensure that the fruits of economic growth are widely shared, and also requires—and this is very important—making good use of the public revenue generated by fast economic growth for social services, especially for public healthcare and public education.

We referred to this process as 'growth-mediated' development in our 1989 book, *Hunger and Public Action.* This can indeed be an effective route to a very important part of development; but we must be clear about what can be achieved by fast economic growth on its own, and what it cannot do without appropriate social supplementation. Sustainable economic growth can be a huge force not only for raising incomes but also for enhancing people's living standards and the quality of life, and it can also work very effectively for many other objectives, such as reducing public deficits and the burden of public debt. These growth connections do deserve emphasis, not only in Asia, Africa and Latin America, but also very much in Europe today, where there has been a remarkable lack of understanding of the role of growth in solving problems of debt and deficit. There is a tendency to concentrate only on draconian restrictive policies to cut down public expenditure, no matter how essential and no matter how these policies kill the goose that lays the golden egg of economic growth. There is a neglect of the role of economic growth in economic and financial stability in the European debate, with its focus only on cutting public expenditure to satisfy the market and to obey the orders of credit rating agencies.

Yet it is also important to recognise that the impact of economic growth on living standards is crucially dependent on the nature of the growth process (for instance, its sectoral composition and employment intensity) as well as of the public policies—particularly relating to basic education and healthcare—that are used to enable common people to share in the process of growth. There is also, in India, an urgent need for greater attention to the destructive aspects of growth, including environmental plunder (e.g. through razing of forests, indiscriminate mining, depletion of groundwater, drying of rivers and massacre of fauna) and involuntary displacement of communities—particularly adivasi communities—that have strong roots in a particular ecosystem.

India's growth achievements are indeed quite remarkable. According to official data, per capita income has grown at a compound rate of close to five per cent per year in real terms between 1990-91 and 2009-10. The more recent rates of expansion are faster still: according to Planning Commission estimates, the growth rate of GDP was 7.8 per cent in the Tenth Plan period (2002-03 to 2006-07) and is likely to be around 8 per cent in the Eleventh Plan period (2007-08 to 2011-12). The "advance estimate" for 2010-11 is 8.6 per cent. These are, no doubt, exceptional growth rates—the second-highest in the world, next to China. These dazzling figures are, understandably, causing some excitement, and were even described as 'magic numbers' by no less than Lord Meghnad Desai, who argued, not without irony, that whatever else happens, 'the government can still sit back and say 8.6 per cent'.

India does need rapid economic growth, if only because average incomes are so low that they cannot sustain anything like reasonable living standards, even with extensive income redistribution. Indeed, even today, after 20 years of rapid growth, India is still one of the poorest countries in the world, something that is often lost sight of, especially by those who enjoy world-class living standards thanks to the inequalities in the income distribution. According to *World Development Indicators 2011*, only sixteen countries outside Africa had a lower 'gross national income per capita' than India in 2010: Afghanistan, Bangladesh, Cambodia, Haiti, Iraq, Kyrgyzstan, Lao, Moldova, Nepal, Nicaragua, Pakistan, Papua New Guinea, Tajikistan, Uzbekistan, Vietnam and Yemen. This is not exactly a club of economic superpowers.

Having said this, it would be a mistake to 'sit back' and rely on economic growth per se to transform the living conditions of the unprivileged. Along with our discussion of 'growth-mediated' development, in an earlier book, we also drew attention to the pitfalls of 'unaimed opulence'—the indiscriminate pursuit of economic expansion, without paying much attention to how it is shared or how it affects people's lives. A good example, at that time (in the late 1980s), was Brazil, where rapid growth went hand in hand with the persistence of massive deprivation. Contrasting this with a more equitable growth pattern in South Korea, we wrote 'India stands in some danger of going Brazil's way, rather than South Korea's'. Recent experience vindicates this apprehension. Interestingly, in the meantime, Brazil has substantially changed course, and adopted far more active social policies, including a constitutional guarantee of free and universal healthcare as well as bold programmes of social security and economic redistribution (such as Bolsa Familia). This is one reason why Brazil is now doing quite well, with, for instance, an infant mortality rate of only 9 per 1,000 (compared with 48 in India), 99 per cent literacy among women aged 15-24 years (74 per cent in India), and only 2.2 per cent of children below five being underweight (compared with a staggering 44 per cent in India). While India has much to learn from earlier experiences of growth-mediated development elsewhere in the world, it must avoid unaimed opulence—an undependable, wasteful way of improving the living standards of the poor.

India's Decline in South Asia

One indication that something is not quite right with India's development strategy is the fact that India has started falling behind every other South Asian country (with the partial exception of Pakistan) in terms of social indicators, even as it is doing so well in terms of per capita income (see table below).

Table 1

India's Slipping Social Report Card in the Neighbourhood

South Asia: Selected Indicators (1990 and latest)

		SOUTH ASIA						
		INDIA	BANGLADESH	BHUTAN	NEPAL	PAKISTAN	SRI LANKA	CHINA
GNI per capita (PPP, current int. $	1990*	877	543	1,280	513	1,210	1,420	813
	2010	3,560	1,800	4,950	1,200	2,780	4,980	7,570
Life expectancy at birth (years)	1990	58	54	52	54	61	69	68
	2010	64	67	67	67	67	74	73
Infant mortality rate (per 1,000 live births)	1990*	81	99	96	97	96	26	38
	2010	48	38	44	41	70	14	16
under-5 mortality rate	1990*	115	143	139	141	124	32	48
	2010	63	48	56	50	87	17	18
Maternal Mortality Ratio	1990	570	870	940	870	490	91	110
	2008	230	340	200	380	260	39	38
Total fertility rate (children per woman)	1990*	3.9	4.5	5.7	5.2	6.0	2.5	2.3
	2009	2.7	2.3	2.5	2.8	3.5	2.3	1.6
Access to improved sanitation(%)	1990	18	39	-	11	28	70	41
	2008	31	53	65	31	45	91	55
Infant immunisation (DPT, %)	1990*	59	64	88	44	48	86	95
	2008*	66	94	96	82	80	98	96
Infant immunisation (measles, %)	1990*	47	62	87	57	50	78	95
	2008*	71	98	97	80	82	97	94
Mean years of Schooling	1990	3.0	2.9	-	2.0	2.3	6.9	4.9
	2010	4.4	4.8	-	3.2	4.9	8.2	7.6
Female literacy rate, age 15-24 years (%)	1991[a]	49	38	-	33	-	93	91
	2009[b]	74	77	68	77	61	99	99
Proportion (%) of underweight children	1990[c]	59.5	61.5	34	-	39	29	13
	2007[d]	43.5	41.3	12	38.8	-	21.6	4.5

*Three-year average centred on the reference year (e.g. 1989-91 average when the reference year is 1990). [a]1990 for China; the Sri Lanka figure is an interpolation between 1981 and 2001 figures. [b]2006 for India, 2005 for Bhutan, 2008 for Pakistan and Sri Lanka, 2009 for other countries (latest World Bank estimates). [c]1988 for Bhutan, 1991 for Pakistan, 1987 for Sri Lanka. [d]2005 for China, 2006 for India and Nepal, 2007 for Bangladesh, 2008 forBhutan, 2009 for Sri Lanka (latest World Bank estimates).

Sources: Mean years of schooling and life expectancy from Human Development Report 2010, online (http://hdr.undp.org); other indicators from World Development Indicators, online (www.data.worldbank.org). Some of the country-specific figures for1990 are subject to a significant margin of error; the focus is best kept on broad patterns rather than exact numbers.

The comparison between Bangladesh and India is a good place to start. During the last 20 years or so, India has grown much richer than Bangladesh: per capita income was estimated to be 60 per cent higher in India than in Bangladesh in 1990, and 98 per cent higher (about double) in 2010. But during the same period, Bangladesh has *overtaken* India in terms of a wide range of basic social indicators: life expectancy, child survival, fertility rates, immunisation rates, and even some (not all) schooling indicators such as estimated 'mean years of schooling'. For instance, life expectancy was estimated to be four years longer in India than in Bangladesh in 1990, but it had become three years *shorter* by 2008. Similarly, the child mortality rate was estimated to be about 24 per cent higher in Bangladesh than in India in 1990, but it was 24 per cent lower in Bangladesh in 2009. Most social indicators now look better in Bangladesh than in India, despite Bangladesh having barely half of India's per capita income.

No less intriguing is that Nepal also seems to be catching up rapidly with India, and even overtaking India in some respects. Around 1990, Nepal was way behind India in terms of almost every development indicator. Today, social indicators for both countries are much the same (sometimes a little better in India still, sometimes the reverse), in spite of per capita income in India being about *three times as high* as in Nepal.

To look at the same issue from another angle, Table 2 displays India's 'rank' among South Asia's six major countries (excluding tiny Maldives), around 1990 as well as today (more precisely, in the latest year for which comparable international data are available). As expected, in terms of per capita income, India's rank has improved—from fourth (after Bhutan, Pakistan and Sri Lanka) to third (after Bhutan and Sri Lanka). But in most other respects, India's rank has worsened, in fact, quite sharply in many cases. Overall, India had the best social indicators in South Asia in 1990, next to Sri Lanka, but now looks *second-worst,* ahead of only Pakistan. Looking at their South Asian neighbours, the Indian poor are entitled to wonder what they have gained—at least so far—from the acceleration of economic growth.

Table 2

Mirror, Mirror...How India Ranks in South Asia

India's Rank Among Six South Asian Countries (Top = 1, Bottom = 6)

	IN 1990	AROUND 2009
GNI per capita	4	3
Life expectancy	3	6
Infant mortality rate	2	5
Under-5 mortality rate	2	5
Maternal mortality ratio	3	3
Total fertility rate	2	4
Access to improved sanitation	4-5[a]	5-6[a]
Child immunisation (DPT)	4	6
Child immunisation (Measles)	6	6
Mean years of schooling	2-3[a]	4.5[a]
Female literacy rate, age 15-24	2-3[a]	4
Proportion of underweight children	4-5[a]	6

[a]Ambiguous rank due to missing data for Bhutan (or Nepal, in the case of "underweight children"). Source: See Table 1. The six countries considered here are Bangladesh, Bhutan, India, Nepal, Pakistan and Sri Lanka.

India and China

One of the requirements of successful growth-mediated development is the skilful use of the opportunities provided by increasing public revenue. There are interesting and important contrasts in the policies followed by different countries in this respect. Since China is often cited by advocates of a single-minded focus on economic growth, it is interesting to compare what China does with what India has been doing. China makes much better use of the opportunities offered by high economic growth to expand public resources for development purposes.

For example, government expenditure on healthcare in China is nearly four times that in India (after adjusting for 'purchasing power parity'—the gap is even larger otherwise). China does, of course, have a larger population and a higher per capita income than India, but even as a ratio of GDP, public expenditure on health is much higher in China (about 2.3 per cent) than in India (around 1.4 per cent).

As Table 1 illustrates, China has much higher values of most social indicators of living standards, such as life expectancy (73 years in China and 64 years in India), infant mortality rate (16 per thousand in China and 48 in India), mean years of schooling (estimated to be 7.6 years in China, compared with only 4.4 years in India), or the coverage of immunisation (very close to universal in China but only around two-thirds in India, for DPT and measles). While India has nearly caught up with China in terms of the rate of economic growth, it seems quite far behind China in terms of the use of public resources for social support, and correspondingly, it has not done nearly as well in translating growth into rapid progress of social indicators. While there are also, undoubtedly, other factors behind the China-India contrast, the differing use of the fruits of growth for social support would seem to be an important influence in this contrasting picture.

It is not at all our purpose to argue that India should learn from China in every respect. India has reasons to value its democratic institutions. Even with all their limitations, these institutions allow for a wide variety of voices to be heard, and facilitate significant opportunities for various forms of public participation in governance. There are, of course, many failings of Indian democracy (which we have discussed in our writings), but there are big democratic achievements as well, and also the hindrances can be addressed through democratic battles to remove them. If China officially executes more people in a week than India has done since Independence (and this is true of a shockingly large number of weeks every year in China), this comparison, like many others involving legal and human rights of citizens, is not to India's disadvantage. If there is something to learn from China, especially about how to ensure that the fruits of economic growth are more widely shared, then that is a case for learning from what there is to learn, not a case for blind imitation.

The China-India contrast does, however, raise another interesting question: could it be that India's democratic system is a barrier to using the fruits of economic growth for the purpose of enhancing health, education and other aspects of 'social development'? In addressing this question, there is some possibility of a sense of nostalgia. When India had a very low rate of economic growth, a common argument coming from the critics of democracy was that democracy was hostile to fast economic growth. It was hard, at that time, to convince the anti-democratic advocates that fast economic growth depends on the friendliness of the economic climate, rather than on the fierceness of political systems. That debate on the alleged contradiction between democracy and economic growth has now ended (not least because of the high economic growth rates of democratic India), but a similar skepticism about democracy seems to be now emerging, suggesting an alleged inability of democratic systems to pursue public health, public education and other socially supportive arrangements.

It is important in this context to understand how democratic decisions emerge and how policies get adopted. What a democratic system achieves depends greatly on the issues that are politicised, which contributes to their advancement. Some issues are extremely easy to politicise, such as the calamity of a famine—and as a result famines tend to stop abruptly with the establishment of a democratic political system. But other issues—less spectacular and less immediate—present a much harder challenge. Using democratic means for remedying inadequate coverage of public healthcare, non-extreme undernourishment, or inadequate opportunities for school education demands more from democratic practice—more vigour and much more range.

Authoritarian systems can change their policies very quickly, when the leaders want that, and it is to the credit of the Chinese political leaders that they have focused so much on social interventions in education, healthcare and other supportive mechanisms to advance the quality of life of the Chinese people. But authoritarianism does not, of course, provide any kind of guarantee that the social commitments will emerge (they clearly have not in North Korea or Burma), or that they would invariably be stable and non-fragile (there have been sharp variations in the past even in China, including its having the largest famine in world history during the failure of the Great Leap Forward initiative).

Even China's commitment to broad-based public healthcare has had ups and downs, and came close to being undone: the coverage of the rural cooperative medical system crashed from 90 per cent to 10 per cent between 1976 and 1983 (when market-oriented reforms were initiated), and stayed around 10 per cent for a full 20 years. During this period of abdication of state responsibility for healthcare in China, the progress of health-related indicators (such as life expectancy and child survival) slowed down sharply. This led eventually to another U-turn, around 2004-2005, when the rural cooperative medical system was rebuilt, with the coverage rising again to 90 per cent or so within three years (Shaoguang Wang, *'Double Movement in China', Economic and Political Weekly,* 27 December, 2008).

There is, in fact, no real barrier in India in combining multi-party democratic governance with active social intervention. But what would be needed is much greater public engagement with the central demands of justice and development through more vigorous democratic practice. The development of the welfare state in Europe has many lessons to offer here. As it happens, public debate is quite powerful in India, but the range of engagement has often been quite limited. The India-China comparisons tend to concentrate mostly on the horse race of relative rates of overall economic growth rather than the variations in mediation for development. Underlying this dialogic narrowness, there is a social picture. A big part of the Indian population—a fairly small minority but still quite large in absolute numbers—has been doing very well indeed, through the process of high growth alone; they do not depend on social mediation. In contrast, more vigorous mediation would be very important for other Indians—many more, in fact—whose lives are affected by ill health, undernourishment, lack of healthcare and other deprivations.

Power Imbalances, Old and New

The neglect of elementary education, healthcare, social security and related matters in Indian planning fits into a general pattern of pervasive imbalance of political and economic power that leads to a massive neglect of the interests of the unprivileged. Other glaring manifestations of this pattern include disregard for agriculture and rural development, environmental plunder for private gain with huge social losses, large-scale displacement of rural communities without adequate compensation, and the odd tolerance of human rights violations when the victims come from the underdogs of society.

None of this is entirely new, and much of it reflects good old inequalities of class, caste and gender that have been around for a long time. For instance, the fact that not even one of the 315 editors and other leading members of the printed and electronic media in Delhi surveyed recently by the Centre for the Study of Developing Societies belonged to a scheduled caste or scheduled tribe, and that at the other end, 90 per cent belonged to a small coterie of upper castes that make up only 16 per cent of the population, obviously does not help to ensure that the concerns of Dalits and adivasis are adequately represented in public debates. Nor is India's male-dominated Lok Sabha (where the proportion of women has never crossed 10 per cent so far) well placed to address the concerns of women—not only gender issues, but also other social issues in which women may have a strong stake. A similar point applies to rural-urban disparities: a recent study found that rural issues get only two per cent of the total news coverage in national dailies.

Some of these inequalities are diminishing, making it easier for disadvantaged groups to gain a voice in the system (even the proportion of women in the Lok Sabha, abysmally low as it is, is about three times as high today as it was fifty years ago). However, new or rising inequalities are also reinforcing the vicious circle of disempowerment and deprivation. For instance, the last twenty years have seen a massive growth of corporate power in India, a force that is largely driven—with some honourable exceptions—by unrestrained search for profits. The growing influence of corporate interests on public policy and democratic institutions does not particularly facilitate the reorientation of policy priorities towards the needs of the unprivileged.

It is important to recognise the influence of elements of the corporate sector on the balance of public policies, but it would be wrong to take that to be something like an irresistible natural force. India's democratic system offers ways and means of resisting the new biases that may emanate from the pressure of business firms. One instructive example both of a naked attempt to denude an established public service and of the possibility of defeating such an attempt is the long saga of attempted takeover of India's school meal programme by biscuit-making firms. The 'midday meal' programme, which provides hot cooked meals prepared by local women to some 120 million children, with a substantial impact on both nutrition and school attendance, had been eyed for many years by food manufacturers, especially the biscuits industry.

A few years ago, a 'Biscuit Manufacturers' Association' (BMA) launched a massive campaign for the replacement of cooked school meals with branded biscuit packets. The BMA wrote to all members of Parliament, asking them to plead the case for biscuits with the minister concerned and assisting them in this task with a neat pseudo-scientific precis of the wonders of manufactured biscuits. Dozens of MPs, across most of the political parties, promptly obliged by writing to the minister and rehashing the BMA's bogus claims. According to one senior official, the ministry was 'flooded' with such letters, twenty-nine of which were obtained later under the Right To Information Act. Fortunately, the proposal was firmly shot down by the ministry after being referred to state governments and nutrition experts, and public vigilance exposed what was going on. The minister, in fact, wrote to a chief minister who sympathised with the biscuit lobby: 'We are, indeed, dismayed at the growing requests for introduction of pre-cooked foods, emanating largely from suppliers/marketers of packaged foods, and aimed essentially at penetrating and deepening the market for such foods.' (*Hindustan Times,* 14 April 2008)

The bigger battle is still on. The BMA itself did not give up after being rebuked by the Union minister for human resource development. It proceeded to write to the Union minister for women and child development, with a similar proposal for supplying biscuits to children below the age of six years under the Integrated Child Development Services (ICDS). Other food manufacturers are also on the job, and despite much vigilance and resistance from activist quarters (and the Supreme Court), they seem to have made significant inroads into child feeding programmes in several states.

Similar concerns apply in other fields of social policy. For instance, the prospects of building a public healthcare system in India are unlikely to be helped by the growing influence of commercial insurance companies, very active in the field of health. India's health system is already one of the most privatised in the world, with predictable consequences—high expenditure, low achievements and massive inequalities. Yet, there is much pressure to embrace this 'American model' of healthcare provision, despite the international recognition in the health community of its comparatively low achievement and significantly high cost.

However, recent events have also shown the possibility of fighting back, not just in terms of winning isolated battles against inappropriate corporate influence, as happened with the biscuits lobby, but also in terms of building institutional safeguards against abuses of corporate power. The Right To Information Act, for instance, though not directly applicable to information held by private corporations, is a powerful means of watching and containing the state-corporate nexus, as the biscuits story illustrates. Regulations and legislations pertaining to corporate funding of political parties, corporate social responsibility, financial transparency, environmental standards, and workers' rights also have an important role to play in disciplining the corporate sector.

The Case for a Comprehensive Approach

The need for growth-mediated development has not been completely ignored in Indian policy debates. The official goal of 'inclusive growth' could even claim to have much the same connotation. However, the rhetoric of inclusive growth has gone hand in hand with elitist policies that often end up promoting a two-track society whereby superior ('world-class') facilities are being created for the privileged, while the unprivileged receive second-rate treatment, or are left to their own devices, or even become the target of active repression—as happens, for instance, in cases of forcible displacement without compensation, with a little help from the police. Social policies, for their part, remain quite restrictive (despite some significant, hard-won initiatives such as the National Rural Employment Guarantee Act), and are increasingly steered towards quick fixes such as conditional cash transfers. Their coverage, in many cases, is also sought to be confined to Below

Poverty Line (BPL) families, a narrowly defined category that tends to shrink over time as per capita incomes increase, which may even look like a convenient way of ensuring that social welfare programmes are 'self-liquidating'.

Cash transfers are increasingly seen as a potential cornerstone of social policy in India, often based on a distorted reading of the Latin American experience in this respect. There are, of course, strong arguments for cash transfers (conditional or unconditional) in some circumstances, just as there are good arguments for transfers in kind (such as midday meals for school children). What is remarkably dangerous, however, is the illusion that cash transfers (more precisely, 'conditional cash transfers') can replace public services by inducing recipients to buy health and education services from private providers. This is not only hard to substantiate on the basis of realistic empirical reading; it is, in fact, entirely contrary to the historical experience of Europe, America, Japan and East Asia in their respective transformation of living standards. Also, it is not how conditional cash transfers work in Brazil or Mexico or other successful cases today.

In Latin America, conditional cash transfers usually act as a complement, not a substitute, for public provision of health, education and other basic services. The incentives work for their supplementing purpose because the basic public services are there in the first place. In Brazil, for instance, basic health services such as immunisation, antenatal care and skilled attendance at birth are virtually universal. The state has done its homework—almost half of all health expenditure in Brazil is public expenditure, compared with barely one quarter (of a much lower total of health expenditure) in India. In this situation, providing incentives to complete the universalisation of healthcare may be quite sensible. In India, however, these basic services are still largely missing, and conditional cash transfers cannot fill the gap.

The pitfalls of 'BPL targeting' have become increasingly clear in recent years. First, there is no reliable way of identifying poor households, and the exclusion errors are enormous: at least three national surveys indicate that, around 2004-05, about half of all poor households in rural India did not have a 'BPL card'. Second, India's poverty line is abysmally low, so that even if all the BPL cards were correctly and infallibly allocated to poor households, large numbers of people who are in dire need of social support would remain excluded from the system. In 2009-10, for instance, the official poverty line in Delhi was around Rs 30 per person per day. This is just about enough to buy one kilogram of rice and a one-way bus ticket that would take you three stops down the road. Third, BPL targeting is extremely divisive, and undermines the unity and strength of public demand for functional social services, making a collaborative right into a divisive privilege.

The power of comprehensiveness in social policy is evident not only from international and historical experience, but also from contemporary experience in India itself. In at least three Indian states, universal provision of essential services has become an accepted norm. Kerala has a long history of comprehensive social policies, particularly in the field of elementary education—the principle of universal education at public expense was an explicit objective of state policy in Travancore as early as 1817. Early universalisation of elementary education is the cornerstone of Kerala's wide-ranging social achievements.

Less well known, but no less significant, is the gradual emergence and consolidation of universalistic social policies in Tamil Nadu (see '*Understanding Public Services in Tamil Nadu*' by Vivek S., PhD thesis, 2010, Syracuse University, and the literature cited there). Tamil Nadu was the first state to introduce free and universal midday meals in primary schools. This initiative, much derided at that time as a 'populist' programme, later became a model for India's national midday meal programme, widely regarded today as one of the best 'centrally sponsored schemes'. The state's pioneering efforts in the field of early child care, under the ICDS, has made great strides towards the provision of functional Anganwadis (child care centres), accessible to all, in every habitation. Tamil Nadu, unlike most other states, also has an extensive network of lively and effective healthcare centres, where people from all social backgrounds can get reasonably good healthcare, free of cost. NREGA, another example of universalistic social programme, is also doing well in Tamil Nadu: employment levels are high (with about 80 per cent of the work going to women), wages are usually paid on time and leakages are relatively small. Last but not the least, Tamil Nadu has a universal Public Distribution System (PDS), in both rural and urban areas. Tamil Nadu's PDS supplies not only foodgrains but also oil, pulses and other food commodities, with astonishing regularity and minimal leakages.

Himachal Pradesh began this journey much later than Kerala and Tamil Nadu, but is catching up very quickly. This is most evident in the field of elementary education: starting from literacy levels similar to the dismal figures for Bihar or Uttar Pradesh around the time of India's Independence, Himachal Pradesh caught up with the highest-performing Kerala within a few decades. This 'schooling revolution' was based almost entirely on a policy of universal provision of government schools, and even today, elementary education in Himachal Pradesh is overwhelmingly in the public sector. Like Tamil Nadu, Himachal Pradesh has a well-functioning PDS, providing not only foodgrains but also pulses and oil and covering both Below Poverty Line (BPL) and Above Poverty Line (APL) families. Himachal Pradesh has also followed comprehensive principles not only in the provision of essential social services (including schooling facilities, healthcare and child care) but also in the provision of basic amenities such as roads, electricity, drinking water and public transport. For instance, in spite of adverse topography and scattered settlements, 98 per cent of *Himachali* households had electricity in 2005-06.

It is perhaps not an accident that Kerala, Tamil Nadu and Himachal Pradesh also tend to have the best social indicators among all major Indian states. For instance, a simple index of children's health, education and nutrition achievements clearly places these three states at the top (Drèze, R. Khera, S. Narayanan, 2007, *'Early Childhood in India: Facing the Facts', Indian Journal of Human Development,* 1(2), Jul-Dec 2007). Despite wide historical, cultural and political differences, they have converged towards a similar approach to social policy, and the results are much the same too. There is a crucial lesson here for other Indian states, and indeed for the country as a whole.

A Concluding Remark

We hope that the puzzle with which we began is a little clearer now. India's recent development experience includes both spectacular success as well as massive failure. The growth record is very impressive, and provides an important basis for all-round development, not least by generating more public revenue (about four times as much today, in real terms, as in 1990). But there has also been a failure to ensure that rapid growth translates into better living conditions for the Indian people. It is not that they have not improved at all, but the pace of improvement has been very slow—even slower than in Bangladesh or Nepal. There is probably no other example in the history of world development of an economy growing so fast for so long with such limited results in terms of broad-based social progress.

There is no mystery in this contrast, or in the limited reach of India's development efforts. Both reflect the nature of policy priorities in this period. But as we have argued, these priorities can change through democratic engagement—as has already happened to some extent in specific states. However, this requires a radical broadening of public discussion in India to development-related matters—rather than keeping it confined to simple comparisons of the growth of the GNP, and naive admiration (implicit or explicit) of the high living standards of a relatively small part of the population. An exaggerated concentration on the lives of the minority of the better-off, fed strongly by media interest, gives an unreal picture of the rosiness of what is happening to Indians in general, and stifles public dialogue of other issues. Imaginative democratic practice, we have argued, is essential for broadening and enhancing India's development achievements.

K.L. Saigal's Legacy

—Pran Nevile

K.L Saigal was more than an icon of music, because in his varying roles, he not only shaped the modern Indian music but reached beyond its structural construct to give a sound and progressive impression to the newly born nation, India. His year of death and India's independence co-incidentally came in the same year, though the journey didn't stop here. His musical composition and legacy rather proved more remarkable and inspiring in independent India, when a growing India was in need to shape her on modern lines. Music was certainly not an area of exception—then or now. Since 1947, India has travelled too far, so recalling the contribution of a great legacy would be apt here with this present essay.

Remembered as the greatest singer of the twentieth century, K.L. Saigal (1904-47) was a musical genius who brought music to the masses. Earlier, the enjoyment of music was in the domain of a privileged few who had access to the *baithaks* of aristocracy and the princes or the salons of the *bais,* highly talented singers trained by the accomplished masters. His formative years were much influenced by his association with Sufi Salamat Yusuf a *Dervesh* at whose *Dera* music was a daily activity. Here Saigal practised his singing and held discussions with other musicians and devotees.

With his gifted voice and inimitable style, Saigal gave a totally new dimension to the music of his time. For him singing was as natural as breathing beyond the usual limit of skill and style. Without any formal training in music or a torchbearer of any *gharana*, Saigal was an acknowledged master of his art in every element that makes music mighty. The elemental force of his music stunned the great music maestros of his time like Fayaz Khan, Adbul Karim Khan, Bal Gandharbh, Pandit Omkar Nath and others who were amazed at his instinctive understanding of the *ragas* and his regal resonant voice which had a touch of the divine.

That Saigal himself was a poet and composer is little known to his admirers and fans. The only recording of his poetry which he composed himself is *Mein Baithi Thi Phulwari Mein,* a remarkable devotional poem which reveals his spiritual leanings and *sufiana* approach to life. A great artist, a great man, Saigal has bequeathed to us a great treasure of timeless melodies which continue to haunt and delight millions of his fans all over the world and have now become a part of our heritage. No other artist as yet has been able to surpass or even equal his popularity and fame in the Indian music world.

The founding father of Indian film music, K.L. Saigal was also the last luminary superstar of the fading gramophone era. His very first record '*Jhulna Jhulao*' had created history by selling over 500,000 pieces. Saigal's foremost legacy is the introduction and popularity of film songs among the music crazy masses of India. Until his heavenly voice appeared on the music scene, the film songs, largely lifted from the stage dramas had a limited appeal and were not even released on gramophone records.

The Gramophone Company HMV, in early 1930s, after the advent of talkies did not consider it viable to produce records of film songs. Then the leading film producer 'Madan Theatres' exploited the innovation of sound and converted in quick succession its popular theatrical stage dramas. The themes were mainly stories from mythology and famous Persian love tales like *Shirin Faryad, Laila Majnoon, Inder Sabha, Raja Harishchandra, Shakuntala, Bilwa Mangal,* etc. Madan's leading singing stars Master Nissar and Miss Kajjan could not make much impact on the music lovers and soon faded away. Same was the fate of other singer-actors with theatrical background. The 'Talkies' brought in a change in people's taste who looked for more appealing and melodious songs.

K. L. Saigal had already established his reputation as a gramophone celebrity and his songs in New Theatres' *Puran Bhagat* in 1933 were a great hit and this heralded the dawn of a new era in film music, which was destined to attain the supreme status of 'People's Music' in the coming years. Then followed some other box office hits like *Yahudi Ki Ladki*, *Chandi Das*, *President*, *Street Singer*, *Zindagi*, in which Saigal's songs created a sensation and Saigal became a national icon. This even prompted the New Theatres Calcutta to release gramophone records of film songs under its own label.

Thereafter, each and every song of Saigal's was separately recorded and had unprecedented sales all over the country. The H.M.V. which had earlier ignored film songs now recognised the popular demand and began recording every film song and even produced records of earlier popular hits. K.L. Saigal therefore could rightfully be acclaimed as the founder of this new market for film music records which benefitted his other contemporary actor-singers as well like K.C. Dey, Pahadi Sanyal, Kanan Bala, Surendra Nath, Shanta Apte and others.

The most noteworthy legacy of Saigal is 'Devdas', an all time classic of Indian cinema. An epoch-making landmark, 'Devdas' marked the blossoming of Indian cinema and cinematic music, and almost revolutionised the entire concept of filmmaking by bringing the film closer to life with all its feelings and emotions. Based on the renowned Bengali writer Sarat Chandra Chatterjee's popular novel of the same name, which he wrote at the age of seventeen, it was first filmed in the silent period by Naresh Mitra in 1928. P.C. Barua, a creative genius of his days, best remembered for directing 'Devdas', raised the level of his film to a solemn tragedy.

He introduced a totally new style of acting, natural and unaffected, a departure from the current theatrical mode and also adopted a simple easy-to-follow dialogue without any literary nuances. Barua played the title role in the Bengali version and K.L. Saigal in the Hindi one and both of them became cult figures. It was a film that touched many sensitive hearts and virtually a whole generation is said to have cried over it.

Both Bengali and Hindi versions of the film were released in 1935. Though K.L. Saigal was no match for Barua's attractive appearance and charm, he more than made it up with his enchanting melodies. Apart from his sterling performance which made him the Indian Cinema's first superstar, Saigal also had a sensational walk-on part in the Bengali version as one of the visitors to Chandramukhi's *kotha* and sang two Bengali songs '*Kahare je jodathey chai*' and '*Golab huey uthuk phutey*'.

It was noted in some quarters that the tragic ending of the story did not fall in line with the Indian classical tradition which required only happy endings. In Sanskrit dramas there was no room for tragedy since the Hindu mind treated life itself only as a transitional state. But in the nineteenth century, the western influence had its impact on Bengali literature and drama and the element of a tragic ending was already introduced before *Devdas*. Many literary stalwarts and critics consider the tragedy and its portrayal saturated with agony and anguish to be a far greater literary achievement than comedy.

The greatest asset of the film was the golden voice of Saigal who was the first artiste to sing in a relaxed, naturalistic and intimate style and his songs were essentially dialogue in the musical form. The camera work was done by Bimal Roy, a genius in his own right. The songs like '*Balam aao baso mere man mein*' were on everyone's lips throughout the country and Saigal became a household name and a virtual legend in his own lifetime.

Saigal is the only singer-actor who has bequeathed to us a valuable treasure of non-film music of bhajans and ghazals. In the course of time millions of his fans pined to hear his voice and whatever he sang became a popular hit. He has inspired both amateur and professional singers of later generations to take to ghazal singing. Saigal selected and composed the ghazals and contributed in no small way in bringing name and fame to some forgotten poets whose verses he sang in his original and unique style which cast a spell on the listeners.

Saigal's legacy is most evident in his choice of Ghalib's ghazals which continue to be all time favourites for every ghazal singer. The ghazal queen Begum Akhtar has observed that so many singers have sung Ghalib but no one has ever been able to surpass K.L. Saigal. This estimation has been supported by many other eminent artists including Malka-e-Tarannum Noor Jahan and Iqbal Bano.

The playback era in film music gathered strength only after the demise of K.L. Saigal. The succeeding generation of playback singers like C.H. Atma, Mukesh, Talat, Mohommad, Rafi and Kishore Kumar were deeply influenced by Saigal's singing style and struggled to model themselves after him. For them Saigal was an institution in himself and a role model for every aspiring singer. C.H. Atma from his childhood was a devotee of Saigal and whatever he sang during his brief career carried a flavour of Saigal's style. His very first record *Pritam Aan Milo* recorded in 1945 shows him trying to imitate Saigal. Later his film song *Ro-oon Mein Sagar Ke Kinare* after Saigal's demise echoed Saigal's expression and at once reminded the audience of Saigal.

In the same way Mukesh's first hit song *Dil Jalta Hai to Jalne De* in *Pehli Nazar* set to music by Anil Biswas reminded one of Saigal's diction and playing with words. In fact Biswas had worked on Mukesh for a long time to produce that pathos and pain characteristic of Saigal whom Mukesh had idolised from his childhood. Talat Mehmood had candidly admitted that it was the Ghazal King K.L. Saigal who inspired him to take to ghazal singing. His first recorded song *Sab Dil Ek Samaan Nahi* shows his trying to emulate Saigal. Mohommad Rafi, who got his first break by singing a few lines in chorus in Shah Jahan fondly remembered all his life with pride of his association with Saigal, the icon who inspired him throughout his career.

Coming to Kishore Kumar, who struggled for nearly twenty years to emerge as a successful playback singer, he was a consistent fan and follower of Saigal. A jester as he was in his boyhood, he used to sing for his friends and charge an *anna* per song, but when he was asked to sing Saigal's song, he demanded four *annas* per song. When Kishore was given his first break—in film *Ziddi* he sang *Marne Ki Duaein Kyon Maangoon* and copied Saigal's style. Even Saigal's contemporary Surendra Nath who made his debut in the 1936 *Deccan Queen* tried to emulate Saigal which is evident when one listens to his vintage song *Yaad Na Kar Dil-e-Hajin.*

It was difficult for the new generation of singers during 1950s to depart from Saigal's spell and hypnosis and his unique way of rendering lyrics. Saigal's persona and voice had gripped the nation, even the renowned music directors and maestros of classical music were amazed at Saigal's spontaneous response to words and sound based on traditional ragas. Such was the magical spell of Saigal's voice that even an ordinary man felt as if he himself was singing.

No wonder that melody composers were also influenced by Saigal's mode and manner of rendering songs in his mellow voice. It would also not be out of place to mention that the first generation of song writers such as Kidar Sharma, Shailendra, Pandit Indra, D.N. Madhok and others were greatly influenced by Saigal's diction and expression and his inimitable way of playing with words.

Saigal was the first music superstar whose aura and charisma still survives after a lapse of over sixty years. He set such perfect standards that are nearly impossible to improve and so remain unsurpassed until now. There were many singers who tried to imitate him but Saigal's clones did not last long while others had to change their mode and style in order to succeed as playback singers, Saigal was so permanently etched in people's minds that no one could replace him and no one has been able to do so until now. In fact the music directors had to advise strongly even talented playback singers to avoid aping Saigal and evolve their own style.

Saigal's influence is also visible on the recent successful ghazal singers like Jagjit Singh, Mehdi Hasan, Amanat Ali, Salim Raza, Ghulam Ali and some others. These non-film personalities, having Saigal as a role model, created their own style which appealed to the listeners even when they sang some favourite numbers already sung by K.L. Saigal. In the post-Saigal period there have been many technical innovations and sophisticated means of recording voice and also introduction of several new musical instruments which were not in vogue earlier.

K.L. Saigal is the only singer in the world to be heard at a particular time 7:57 am to 8:00 am from Radio Ceylon for the last over fifty years. It was during mid-1950s the Radio started its Hindi service under the supervision of Vijay Kishore Dubey who introduced a program of old hit songs in the morning. He hailed Saigal's voice as the voice of the century in the subcontinent and decided to have one of Saigal's songs at the end of the daily program. Since then this practice has continued. Legends like Saigal forever remain original and their magic never withers with time. He has been acclaimed as Tansen of the modern period who surpassed Akbar's royal singer in popularity since Akbar's Tansen enchanted the Mughal ruling elite and nobility and was not accessible to the masses.

Hailed as the *Shehenshah-e-Mausiqi* (Emperor of Melody), Saigal's recorded music continues to have a ready market not only in the sub-continent but also abroad. Beginning with 78 rpm records, Saigal's songs continue to be released along with the development in recording technology, first in extended play form (45 rpm) followed by the LP records (33rpm) and cassettes and now they are available in CDs.

To conclude, I would like to quote Babu Rao Patel, the legendary editor of *Filmindia* who observed, 'People didn't merely love Saigal, they revered his glorious voice and called it divine. Saigal tuned music into a simple emotional poetry of the soul—he can't be forgotten so easily, not till this music loving nation suddenly goes deaf.' Also I would like to add here the eminent music director Naushad's poetic tribute to Saigal:

'Mere Dil Ko Yakin Hai Ye Mukammal,
Naghmon Ki Kasam Aaj Bhi Zinda Hai Wo Saigal,
Saigal Ko Faramosh Koi Kar Nahi Sakta,
Wo Aisa Amar Hai Ke Kabhi Mar Nahi Sakta'

Naushad swears by his lyrics and proclaims with total confidence that Saigal is very much alive; no one can ignore or forget him as he is among those who defy death and are immortal.

The Time Ahead for Indian Economy

—Bibek Debroy

The first BRIC (Brazil, Russia, India, China) paper by Goldman Sachs was partly responsible for popularising the idea of India's explosive income and consumption growth potential.[1] It is useful to remember India's track record of annual average real GNP growth. The Eighth Plan (1992-97) produced 6.6 per cent, while the Ninth Plan (1997-2002) produced 5.5 per cent.[2] However, the Tenth Plan (2002-07) produced 7.9 per cent. More importantly, the period from 2003-04 to 2007-08, that is, before the recent global financial crisis, produced annual rates of growth of 8.5 per cent in 2003-04, 7.5 per cent in 2004-05, 9.5 per cent in 2005-06, 9.5 per cent in 2006-07 and 9.8 per cent in 2007-08. This suggested a break in the historical growth trajectory from 2003, and once the global financial crisis was out of the way and the global economy recovered, a possible increase in the growth rate to 9 per cent and more. For example, the Eleventh Plan (2007-12) envisaged growth of 10 per cent during the Twelfth Plan (2012-17).

For the moment, one should note two points. First, the bullish projections one reads about do not involve such high rates of GDP growth. This becomes clear from Table 1, where unlike internal projections that talk about real GDP growth rates of 9 per cent and more, external projections rarely exceed 6 or 6.5 per cent, notwithstanding India's higher growth rates from 2003. There is a curious element in this. While short-term projections often assume growth rates more than 8 per cent, there is an inherent assumption that these growth rates will slow down over the medium-term. Second, high levels of consumption and income occur not by 2025, but beyond. This is the nature of the exponential function. All projections involve factoring in labour and capital inputs into a production function and allowing for total factor productivity growth. This leaves issues of how one addresses inflation and exchange rate appreciation. For the most part, projections avoid the inflation issue by expressing numbers in today's US dollars.

In this paper, no attempt is made to undertake projections for the other economies in the world. The projections are limited to India. Therefore, just so that one has a sense of the comparative perspective, some figures are cited from the Third BRIC paper[3] for the largest economies in the world in 2025. In constant US dollars, the largest economies in the world are projected to be United States (USD 20.1 trillion), China (USD 18.4 trillion), Japan (USD 5.6 trillion) and India (USD 4.3 trillion).

Table 1

Some Existing Projections till 2025

	Real GDP growth (%)	GDP constant trillion USD, 2015	GDP constant trillion USD, 2025	Per capita GDP (USD), 2015	Per capita GDP (USD), 2025
1st BRIC paper[4]	5.7%[5]	1.4	3.2	1,149	2,331
2nd BRIC paper[6]	5.5%[7]	1.7	3.6	1,369	2,656
3rd BRIC paper[8]	5.95%[9]	1.9	4.4	1,502	3,005
1st PWC projections[10]	5.2%[11]				
DB Research[12]	6%[13]				5,000[14]
HSBC Global Research[15]	5.65%[16]				
McKinsey[17]	5.9%				
ADB[18]	9.5%				6,050[19]
Arvind Virmani[20]	7%				

Sources of Growth and Reforms

What will it take to achieve annual real rates of GDP growth of 9 per cent and more? At one level, per capita GDP is nothing but the average productivity of India's inhabitants.[21] World Economic Forum's Global Competitiveness Index (GCI) analyses competitiveness on the basis of twelve pillars:

1. institutions;
2. infrastructure;
3. macroeconomic environment;
4. health and primary education;
5. higher education and training;
6. goods market efficiency;
7. labour market efficiency;
8. financial market development;
9. technological readiness;
10. market size;
11. business sophistication; and
12. innovation.[22]

As one moves up the development ladder, successive pillars become increasingly important. At India's levels of development, capital and labour inputs are key drivers behind high GDP growth. If question marks are raised about this growth reaching a plateau, that's because one assumes this input-based growth reaches a frontier and therefore, begins to slow down.

But before talking about this, a digression on reforms is useful. India's present cycle of economic reforms was triggered in 1991 by an external sector balance of payments (bop) crisis. There was an earlier cycle of reforms that has been described as reforms by stealth.[23] This dates to the second half of the 1970s and involved trade liberalisation, as well as elements of industrial deregulation. However, this first cycle was more piece-meal and ad hoc and was not as comprehensive as the second cycle, introduced in 1991. One should begin by asking what one means by economic reforms. Sometimes expressions like first generation and second generation are also used, suggesting that first generation reforms were introduced in the first post-1991 flush and that the second generation is what awaits us now. Unfortunately, the expressions 'first generation' and 'second generation' are never very precisely defined. However, two overlapping interpretations are possible. First, 'first generation' refers to reforms that concern the external sector—elimination of Quantitative Restrictions (QRs) on exports, rationalisation and elimination of export subsidies and their replacement by a system of export incentives[24], reduction in import duties, a market-determined exchange rate with a convertible rupee, a liberal policy on foreign institutional investments and opening up to Foreign Direct Investments (FDI). On each of these, reforms have already been introduced, or there is a time-frame for their further introduction, although external sector reforms are also linked to negotiations, multilateral, regional or bilateral. They cannot always be introduced unilaterally. In contrast, second generation reforms concern the domestic economy, although a neat water-tight compartmentalisation between the domestic and the external isn't always possible. Understandably, political economy considerations and vested interests are stronger in domestic economic reforms, compared to the external. Second, one can also interpret the 'first generation' as reforms that concerned and were under the purview primarily of the Centre, or the Union government. In contrast, in a federal setup, second generation concerns reforms that have to be introduced at the State-government level.[25] Thanks to the first generation having been implemented, the focus of policy change has thus shifted from the Centre to the States. The cutting, and the blunting edge, of reforms thus lies at the level of the States and different States have reacted differently to liberalisation. What is also of note is that most product market policies are with the Centre, while most factor market (labour, land) policies are with the States. Having said this, the major reform issues are the following.

The Demographic Dividend or Deficit: When one contrasts the Indian growth story with that of China, attention is often drawn to China's success in manufacturing. The etymology of the word 'manufacture' isn't certain. But it seems to have a link with the Latin *manu factum*, meaning 'made by hand'. Irrespective of ingredients of technology, capital (plant and machinery), entrepreneurship, and perhaps even land, entering as inputs or factors into production processes, labour remains a core input. And there is no denying that India possesses, or should possess, a comparative advantage in labour. As with every other developing country, that has always been the case. Labour is relatively more abundant than capital. In a completely integrated and globalised world, national boundaries should make no difference. But that ideal never happens. Even if cross-border movements of technology and capital are relatively free, there will be restrictions on cross-border movements of labour. Integration of labour markets will only happen in niches, in selected segments. Therefore, India should be in a position to exploit its cost advantage in labour, and in natural resources, to push manufacturing growth. Nor should one forget India's strengths in science and technology and in education. These reinforce the labour cost advantage. To this traditional labour cost advantage has been added what is called the demographic dividend. With aging populations in developed countries, and even in countries like Russia and China, there has been talk of India's demographic dividend.[26] That the demographic dividend argument works, is known. For East Asia, several studies suggest that between 25 to 40 per cent of the East Asian miracle was due to the demographic dividend.[27] Other than East Asia, it has worked in Japan in the 1950s, China in the 1980s and Ireland in the 1980s and the 1990s. Several factors explain the demographic dividend.[28] First, there is the obvious increase in working-age populations, with a reduction in dependency ratios, and the direct impact of a larger quantity of labour input. To take but one dramatic number, between 2001 and 2026, India's total population is estimated to increase by 371 million and 83% of the increase will occur in the age-group of 15-59 years.[29] Second, the quality of the labour input can increase and this is reflected in what economists call Total Factor Productivity (TFP) growth, measured after netting out the contribution of increased labour and capital inputs.[30] Third, when dependency ratios decline, savings rates increase, leading to increases in investment rates and higher rates of GDP growth. Fourth, if the decline in dependency ratios is at the lower end of the age spectrum as a result of fertility declines, female work participation rates increase.

The present population projections till 2026 do not yet factor in the results of the 2011 Census. In the aggregate, the preliminary figures available for Census 2011 do not suggest any dramatic changes in these projections. The key points in the present projections are the following. The population will increase to 1.4 billion in 2026, an annual increase of 1.2 per cent between 2001 and 2026. Between 2001 and 2026, because of declining fertility, the proportion of under-15 population will decline from 35.4 to 23.4 per cent. The proportion of population in the working age-group of 15-59 years will increase from 57.7 to 64.3 per cent in 2026 and the share of old people will increase from 6.9 to 12.4 per cent. The average age will increase from 23 years in 2001 to 31 in 2026, suggesting that beyond 2035, the effects of the demographic dividend will begin to wear off. The urban population will be 38 per cent in 2026 and urban growth will account for 67 per cent of the population increase. States with low rates of population growth will be Tamil Nadu and Kerala. Out of the 371 million increase in population between 2001 and 2026, 187 million will be in the States of Bihar, Chhattisgarh, Jharkhand, Madhya Pradesh, Rajasthan, Uttar Pradesh and Uttarakhand. Table 2 indicates these inter-State variations in population growth within the working age-groups, illustrating geographical areas where the burden of employment generation will be concentrated.[31]

Table 2

Annualised Growth in 20–60 Working age-groups, 2001 to 2020

State	2001 population (million)	2020 population (million)	Annualised growth rate (%)
Andhra Pradesh	38.1	56.4	2.1
Assam	11.4	19.4	2.8
Bihar	30.2	53.8	3.1
Delhi	5.0	9.0	3.1
Goa	0.7	1.0	1.7
Gujarat	22.8	34.4	2.2
Haryana	8.9	15.4	2.9
Himachal Pradesh	3.2	4.5	1.8
Jammu & Kashmir	4.4	6.2	1.8
Karnataka	25.0	37.3	2.1
Kerala	14.4	19.6	1.6
Madhya Pradesh	27.3	45.4	2.7

Maharashtra	44.0	67.4	2.3
Odisha	16.4	24.5	2.1
Punjab	10.2	15.7	2.3
Rajasthan	25.0	44.6	3.1
Tamil Nadu	31.8	42.1	1.5
Uttar Pradesh	59.1	104.2	3.0
West Bengal	37.8	58.5	2.3
India	447.4	715.9	2.5

The point is the following. There is nothing automatic about a demographic dividend materialising. Among other things, that is a function of health and education outcomes. More specifically, there is question of skills. The overall skills deficit has often been flagged. For instance, in 2002, the S.P. Gupta Special Group[32] constituted by the Planning Commission stated, 'It should be noted, however, that on the average the skilled labour force at present is hardly around 6-8 per cent of the total, compared to more than 60 per cent in most of the developed and emerging developing countries.' In 2001, the Montek Singh Ahluwalia Task Force[33], again constituted by the Planning Commission, stated, 'Only 5 per cent of the Indian labour force in this age category[34] has vocational skills.' While the numbers are marginally different, the Eleventh Five Year Plan document adds the following.[35] 'The NSS 61st Round results show that among persons of age 15-29 years, only about 2 per cent are reported to have received formal vocational training and another 8 per cent reported to have received non-formal vocational training indicating that very few young persons actually enter the world of work with any kind of formal vocational training.' If more numbers are needed, the following drive home the point.[36] 80 per cent of new entrants into the work force have no opportunities for development of skills. While there are 12.8 million new entrants into the work force every year, the existing training capacity is 3.1 million per year. In both rural and urban India, and for both males and females, attendance rates in educational institutions drop by around 50 per cent in the age group of 15-19 years.[37] Simultaneously, labour force participation rates begin to increase in the age group of 15-19 years and by the time it comes to the age group of 25-29 years, it is 95 per cent for rural males and 94.4 per cent for urban males. The figures for females are lower at 36.5 per cent in rural India and 22.1 per cent in urban India. The 15-29 age-groups can be used as an illustration. Since post-educational institution training opportunities are limited, 87.8 per cent of the population in this bracket has had no vocational training.[38] Of the 11.3 per cent who received vocational training, only 1.3 per cent received formal vocational training.[39] 'The said results also reflect that 38.8 per cent of the Indian labour force is illiterate, 24.9 per cent of the labour force has had schooling up to the primary level and the balance 36.3 per cent has had schooling up to the middle and higher level. They also reveal that about 80 per cent of the workforce in rural and urban areas does not possess any identifiable marketable skills.'[40] Among the youth, most of those with formal training are in Kerala, Maharashtra, Tamil Nadu, Himachal Pradesh and Gujarat.[41] Not surprisingly, Bihar's share is the lowest but things are changing now under the improved performances by the State government. A better indicator of the State's performance is the share of the young population that has some variety of formal training. In this, Maharashtra, Kerala, Tamil Nadu, Gujarat and Andhra Pradesh perform well. Is this because there is better training capacity and infrastructure? Is it because industrial activity exists in these States? Is it because there is a positive correlation between some minimum level of educational attainment and acquisition of formal training? The answer is probably a combination of various factors.

Inter-State Differences in Human Development: Since inter-State differences in skills have been mentioned in the context of the demographic dividend, it is worth flagging the broader issue of divergences across States. Specifically on human development, one can either use poverty ratios or broader MDG (Millennium Development Goal) indicators. Until recently, the internationally accepted poverty line used to be 1 US $ per day, at constant PPP (purchasing power parity) prices. PPP transformations typically increase incomes in developing countries and lower them in developed countries, since prices are lower in the former. Recently, the World Bank has recalibrated the poverty line to 1.25 US $ per day, because prices were being under-estimated in several developing countries. This is different from India's own indigenous poverty line, but that is irrelevant for present purposes. Irrespective of which indicator is used, head-count or poverty ratios are very high in parts of rural India. However, this is expenditure or income poverty and poverty has broader dimensions too, such as access to health and education. These are captured in the MDGs. There is also a multi-dimensional poverty index (MDPI), devised by the Oxford Poverty and Human Development Initiative.[42]

There are different ways to look at the economic geography of a country, depending on the administrative division one has in mind. State administrative boundaries are natural dividing lines to use. Academic work and popular impression have often used the BIMARU (Bihar, Madhya Pradesh, Rajasthan, Uttar Pradesh) nomenclature, with a pun on the word *bimar*, meaning ill or sick. While this is still useful as a starting-off point, the states of Bihar, Madhya Pradesh and Uttar Pradesh have now been sub-divided and Odisha is often worse than some of these four traditional BIMARU States. BIMARU thus becomes BIMAROU, not to speak of deprivation, according to some indicators, in Jammu & Kashmir and the North-East. Although undivided Madhya Pradesh and Rajasthan are no longer as deprived and backward as Bihar and the eastern parts of Uttar Pradesh, and Uttarakhand is better off than Uttar Pradesh, many of these traditionally backward areas tend to be concentrated in the North. In understanding India's development, especially after the 1991 reforms, one thus tends to often use a North-South framework. Two simple explanations are often used to explain this phenomenon. First, in the pre-1991 era, when licensing and proximity to the centre that granted licenses was important, the North performed relatively better. With licensing having disappeared, at least for manufacturing, this relative advantage has vanished and the South has come into its own. Second, given the inadequacy of internal transport infrastructure, coastal regions, where this inadequacy is less manifest, tend to flourish. While both these arguments have a grain of truth, and property rights that govern land are also important, this North-South dichotomy is a trifle too simplistic, as is the East-West dichotomy, with a dividing line vertically drawn between Kanpur and Chennai, regions to the West of this line performing better than regions to the right.

Indeed, the use of State boundaries to facilitate our understanding is itself somewhat flawed, since development and deprivation do not follow such administrative distinctions. However, there is an in-built bias in favour of using States, since data problems are easier to handle then. Data problems become more difficult to overcome if one thinks of India's regions, or even districts and villages. Most backward districts, identified by any criterion, are geographically contiguous and are also associated with violent movements. If one considers these backward districts, one notices that these are generally concentrated in Central India, extending eastwards, and going all the way up to the North-East, thus reinforcing the earlier impression. India cannot prosper if significant sections of India continue to be bypassed and marginalised. The Institute for Conflict Management has a map of conflict in South Asia, through its South Asia Terrorism Portal.[43] This map shows an obvious correlation between deprived districts and intensity of terrorism or violence, at least at the all-India level. Apart from Jammu & Kashmir, which belongs to a special category, this correlation is obvious for the central parts of India, extending eastwards.

The policy issue can be stated in the following way. For those who are able-bodied, there can be institutional constraints in accessing market-based opportunities. These can be in the form of inadequate access to health, education, skills, technology, information, financial products, land, physical infrastructure (roads, electricity, water) and law and order. Are all these necessarily public goods, in the classic sense? Beyond law and order, it is not obvious that these are public goods. They are often collective private goods. As a follow-up question, are there demonstrated instances of market failure in these segments? One must remember that thanks to possibilities of unbundling and advent of technology, what used to be regarded as an example of market failure in the 1950s is no longer pertinent. Therefore, there are possibilities of private sector provisioning, even if this is backed by public sector financing. Hence, have entry regulations been sufficiently relaxed for private sector entry? To the extent that there are market failures and public sector provisioning is important, how does one improve the efficiency of public expenditure? Other than this, there is the question of direct anti-poverty measures through subsidies. Food, petroleum products, fertilisers, roads and power are instances. However, poverty is an individual characteristic. By equating it with collective categories like gender, caste, religion and ethnicity, one makes a double mistake. There is an error of commission, through including non-poor, simply because they are members of that particular category. There is also an error of omission, through non-including poor, simply because they are not members of that particular collective category. It is because this problem hasn't been addressed head on that there continue to be controversies about identification of Below the Poverty Line (BPL) households, though since the Ninth Plan, and more so since the Tenth Plan, the Planning Commission has been advocating decentralised and household-based identification of BPL. The unique national identity numbers (Aadhaar) may make it easier to eliminate multiplicity. But per se, they don't solve the policy question.

Unorganised versus Organised: The Indian labour market is segmented. In a recent study, the World Bank stated, 'Of the 413 million prime-aged persons in the Indian labour force in 2004-05, the overwhelming majority, about 90 per cent, are employed in low productivity informal sector jobs.'[44] The reference is to 2004-05, the 61st round of NSS (National Sample Survey), because NSS large-samples are held at infrequent intervals, with an average gap of five years in between. The results of the next large-sample (66th round, 2009-10) have not been released. Consequently, most data-based work is still based on 2004-05 numbers. The National Commission for Enterprises in the Unorganised Sector (NCEUS) was set up in 2004 and one of its reports had a very good discussion of definitional and statistical issues in analysing India's informal economy.[45] For purposes of this paper, let us use the terms organised and formal synonymously, just as the terms unorganised and informal are used synonymously. In contrast with developed economies, and also in contrast with several developing economies, a large chunk of employment occurs in the rural sector. In 2004-05, India's labour force was 420 million. The work force was 385 million.[46] 35 million were therefore unemployed, though it is impossible to figure out whether they were unemployed voluntarily or involuntarily. Out of the labour force of 420 million,

303 million was in rural India and 116 million was in urban India.[47] Out of the work force of 385 million, 278 million was in rural India and 107 million was in urban India. Out of the rural labour force of roughly 300 million, 72.7% earned a living from agriculture.[48] But some comments are in order about such figures. First, these refer to usual principal and subsidiary status, implying that there may be a secondary occupation outside agriculture. Indeed, with the seasonal nature of the bulk of India's agriculture, that is invariably the case. Second, there are variations across states. Third, the pace of decline, as opposite to the base figures, also varies quite a lot across states. Fourth, there are gender differences. The farm to non-farm transition happens first for males and a feminisation of the agricultural work force occurs. Fifth, out of those who are in agriculture, roughly two-thirds (64 per cent) describe themselves as self-employed, that is, they are farmers. The remaining roughly one-third (36 per cent) are wage workers, almost invariably on casual basis. There are labour market issues connected with transforming low-productivity and subsistence-level agriculture and creating off-farm employment opportunities. We will turn to that later.

Outside of agriculture, informality can be defined in one of three different ways. First, there is a definition in terms of exemptions from paying indirect taxes. Second, there is a definition in terms of small-scale industry (SSI), which again is defined in terms of threshold levels of investment in plant and machinery. Third, there is a definition in terms of labour laws. That is, an enterprise is unorganised if it uses power and employs fewer than 10 people or does not use power and employs fewer than 20 people.[49] The last definition is the one that is used most often and according to this, in 2004-05, 92.4 per cent of employment was in the unorganised sector.[50] That is, 92.4 per cent of the labour force employed in the unorganised sector has no labour rights worth the name. Protective legislation is absent, be it in the form of safety, minimum wages or social security. Another important point should be flagged. Unorganised labour (wage labour without contracts) can also exist within the organised sector. The aforementioned NCEUS report estimated that there were 52.9 million wage workers in the unorganised sector (excluding agriculture). However, if one includes unorganised or informal sector workers within the organised sector, the number increases to 76.7 million.[51] This is a figure for wage employment, excluding self-employment. While the standard definition of organised/formal is in terms of labour laws, with unorganised/informal being defined as a residual category, it must be remembered that all informal non-agricultural employment isn't based on an employer-employee relationship. Other than wage employment, there is self-employment too. An ILO study found that between 50 and 75 per cent of non-agricultural employment in the developing world is informal.[52] Informal employment includes both self-employment in informal (small and unregistered) enterprises and wage employment in informal jobs (without labour contracts, worker benefits and protection). The figure is higher for India. Subject to data problems, 83 per cent of India's non-agricultural employment was estimated by ILO to be informal.[53] Self-employment constituted 52 per cent of non-agricultural informal employment.

The segmented and heterogeneous labour market thus represents a dichotomy. Labour laws create rigidities in the organised segment, while minimal labour rights are non-existent in the unorganised segment. To the extent that the labour rights exist *de jure*, they are not enforced *de facto*. Reforms should break down this segmentation and bring the two kinds of markets closer to one another. In the reform discourse on labour markets, one also witnesses what is a bit like a dichotomy. There is one line of argument that focuses on lack of rights in the unorganised sector, NCEUS being a case in instance. This is also true of UN documents, such as Human Development Reports (HDRs).

A digression on self-employment is necessary. In 2004-05, 56.5 per cent of the work force reported itself as being self-employed. In the non-agricultural work force, 62.8 per cent of workers reported themselves as self-employed.[54] There are also wide inter-state variations. For instance, more than 65 per cent of non-agricultural workers reported themselves as self-employed in Andhra Pradesh (65.2 per cent), Assam (65.6 per cent), Bihar (80.8 per cent), Jammu & Kashmir (73.7 per cent), Madhya Pradesh (65.5 per cent), Odisha (70.3 per cent), Uttar Pradesh (68.1 per cent), West Bengal (68.2 per cent) and Uttarakhand (67.2 per cent). In contrast, the figure was lower than 50 per cent in Himachal Pradesh

(48.4 per cent) and Kerala (47.9 per cent). The higher the degree of self-employment, the lower seems to be the prosperity of the State. This suggests that self-employment is not a viable occupational category at all. It is a subsistence-level occupation because people cannot afford to remain unemployed. Outside of agriculture, the total self-employed population was 92.1 million. Some of these were in relatively high income occupations, like independent professionals (doctors, lawyers, artists, and accountants), shop owners in urban areas, rice-mill owners, workshop owners, commission agents, real estate and housing brokers and owners of small hotels and restaurants. But others were in relatively low income occupations, like handloom weavers (mostly women), *chikan* workers (mostly women), street vendors, food processors, rickshaw pullers, rag-pickers, *beedi* rollers (mostly working out of home), *agarbatti* makers (mostly women), potters and bamboo product makers.[55] The self-employment category is extremely heterogeneous. But some of the self-employed workers in the relatively low income categories would be better off in wage employment were that to be possible.

Typically, own account enterprises aren't registered. In 2004-05, 84.9 per cent of own account enterprises were not registered and this needs to be flagged, because registration also brings attendant benefits, such as access to credit or government subsidies on marketing and technology. Why aren't own account enterprises registered? The answer isn't entirely lack of information. Opting out of registration is probably a conscious decision, because the benefits from registration are not commensurate with the costs. Not only are procedures connected with registration complicated and tiresome, registration brings with it the attendant problem of bribery and rent-seeking from the government machinery. For instance, for rickshaw pullers and street-vendors, studies in many parts of urban India have documented harassment and bribery by municipal authorities and police.[56] The non-registration issue spills over into the existence of the unorganised sector in general. It is often presumed that rigid labour laws in the organised sector encourage informality. But this is a partial explanation. There are other reasons behind informality—avoidance of taxes, complicated transaction costs associated with registration, rent-seeking and few perceived benefits from formalisation. The last Small Scale Industry (SSI) Census was held in 2001 and found that 16.89 per cent of unregistered units were in Uttar Pradesh, with a large number of unregistered SSI units in Andhra Pradesh, West Bengal, Maharashtra, Madhya Pradesh, Tamil Nadu, Karnataka, Bihar, Rajasthan and Gujarat too. When asked about the reasons for non-registration, 53.13 per cent said that they weren't aware of the provisions, while another 39.8 per cent said that they 'were not interested'.[57]

Turning now to the organised labour market, there are several cross-country governance surveys that explicitly seek to measure and gauge the nature of the labour market and flag the Indian rigidity. This is not to deny that there are problems with such governance surveys.[58] Some of these problems are the following. First, some indicators depend on *de jure* international commitments made by countries and these may have no relation with what actually obtains *de facto*. These are indicators based on ratification of standards, codes or treaties, but monitoring implementation is close to impossible, the point made earlier. Second, measurement should be based on tangible improvements in outcomes or performance. However, governance is a process and quite apart from the problem of differing perceptions about what should be included and what should be excluded, objective data are impossible to obtain. Hence, one relies on subjective responses to questionnaires administered to respondents. Having said this, what are the various surveys that seek to rank the Indian labour market? The first one to be mentioned should be the Fraser Institute's *Economic Freedom of the World* (EFW). The structure of the EFW index involves aggregation across five heads of (1) size of government (expenditure, taxes and enterprises); (2) legal structure and security of property rights; (3) access to sound money; (4) freedom to trade internationally; and (5) regulation of credit, labour and business. Given the focus on labour market reforms, what is of interest is the fifth head, especially labour market regulations and the variables included in this sub-head encompass minimum wages, hiring and firing regulations, centralised collective bargaining, mandated costs of hiring and mandated costs of worker dismissal. In the 2010 rankings, the Indian score was 7.9.[59] What is of greater interest is the inter-temporal movement. While India's labour market score has improved over time, it continues to be low for hiring and firing regulations and mandated cost of worker dismissal. Heritage Foundation and Wall Street Journal's Index of Economic Freedom is almost a parallel exercise to EFW and is based on ten broad factors of economic freedom. One of these is labour freedom, interpreted as government restrictions on wages, hours of work and so on. Under this head, in the 2011 rankings, India scored 67.2. While there has been improvement over time, 'The non-salary cost of employing a worker is moderate, but dismissing an employee is costly.'[60] There is also the World Bank's 'Doing Business' set of indicators, now ranked across 183 economies. One of these is on employing workers and focuses on problems associated with redundancy.[61] The simple point thus is that there is a focus on firing problems.

The official *Economic Survey* is often interpreted as setting out the government's reform agenda. Barring one instance, *Economic Survey* has rarely been forthright about the labour market reform agenda, though it has often been mentioned in passing. Consequently, this section, from *Economic Survey, 2005-06*, deserves to be quoted at length.[62]

> 'Indian labour market is characterized by a sharp dichotomy. A large number of establishments in the unorganized sector remain outside any regulation, while the organized sector has been regulated fairly stringently. It can be reasonably argued that the organized sector has provided too much of job-security for too long, while the unorganized sector has provided too little to too many. Various studies indicate that Indian labour laws are highly protective of labour, and labour markets are relatively inflexible. These laws apply only to the organized sector. Consequently, these laws have restricted labour mobility, have led to capital-intensive methods in the organized sector and adversely affected the sector's long-run demand for labour. Labour being a subject in the concurrent list, State-level labour regulations are also an important determinant of industrial performance. Evidence suggests that States, which have enacted more pro-worker regulations, have lost out on industrial production in general. Perhaps there are lessons to be learnt from China

> in the area of labour reforms. China, with a history of extreme employment security, has drastically reformed its labour relations and created a new labour market, in which workers are highly mobile. Although there have been mass layoffs and open unemployment, high rates of industrial growth especially in the coastal regions helped their redeployment. In spite of hardship, workers in China seem to have benefited from wage growth, additional job creation and new opportunities for self employment.'

The intention is not to get into a detailed discussion of labour laws. As has been mentioned, labour laws are not the only reason behind informality. In the process of transition, India must encourage informal to become formal and self-employment to move to more productive wage employment.

The Farm to non-Farm Transition: In the earlier section, a comment was made about labour movements from the agricultural to non-agricultural sectors. This involves commercialisation and diversification of agriculture, as well as the creation of off-farm employment opportunities. Hence, there is an agricultural reform agenda and there is a rural reform agenda that goes beyond agriculture. Within the agriculture set, there are issues like allowing corporate sector involvement in agriculture, removal of government imposed restrictions on production, marketing and distribution[63], refocus of public expenditure away from input subsidies to infrastructure[64] and extension services[65], dis-intermediation of distribution chains, forward markets, contract farming, revamping credit and insurance, and freeing up of land markets[66]. All these are linked to encouraging commercialisation and diversification. There is also an issue of encouraging off-farm employment and this is where rural sector reforms kick in, through provision of physical and social infrastructure.

Governance: Governance has become a bit of a buzzword and there are quite a few cross-country governance surveys. As has been mentioned, there are problems with these surveys that one tends to gloss over. The point is not to denigrate the use of governance surveys. After all, one is trying to capture something that is difficult to measure. However, most governance surveys tend to gloss over these problems and suggest robustness in governance estimation that simply does not exist. Having said this, the most commonly cited governance surveys are (1) Transparency International's[67] Corruption Perceptions Index; (2) The World Bank Institute's Governance Matters set of indicators[68], with governance measured under six aggregate heads or clusters—voice and accountability, political stability and absence of violence, government effectiveness, regulatory quality, rule of law and corruption; (3) World Economic Forum's Growth Competitiveness Index[69], based on three components of economic growth—a technology index, a public institutions index and a macroeconomic environment index; (4) Heritage Foundation and *Wall Street Journal*'s Index of Economic Freedom[70], based on ten broad factors of economic freedom—trade policy, fiscal burden of government, government intervention in the economy, monetary policy, capital flows and foreign investment, banking and finance, wages and prices, property rights, regulation and informal market activity; (5) Fraser Institute's Economic Freedom of the World[71], based on five heads of size of government, legal structure and security of property rights, access to sound money, freedom to trade internationally and regulation of credit, labour and business; and (6) The World Bank's Doing Business Indicators[72], based on starting a business, dealing with construction permits, employing workers, registering property, getting credit, protecting investors, paying taxes, trading across borders, enforcing contracts and closing a business. This is by no means a comprehensive list of all governance surveys, but these are certainly the more important ones. There is subjectivity in each of these surveys, on responses to questionnaires, attaching weights, converting ordinal ranks into cardinal scores and methods of aggregation. Consequently, not too much weight need be attached to any particular survey. However, taken together, the surveys do show robustness and underline institutional problems in India.

If one distils out the essence of these governance surveys, one finds that one is fundamentally talking about law reform, including reform of administrative law. Quite often, the more important problem is about procedures, not about law, legislation or policy *per se*. This is the broad area of administrative law reform and if India doesn't perform well on "Doing Business"-type indicators that is because of these procedural problems, also important for labour law. Administrative law means the subordinate legislation in the form of rules, regulations, orders and instructions from ministries and government departments and these can be at State-level, as well as Central. Often, constraints to efficient decision-making come about through administrative law, rather than through statutory law and discretion, bribery and rent-seeking are fallouts. Unfortunately, administrative law is not readily available and this is especially true at State-level. Administrative law reforms are often interpreted as civil service reforms, although they should be much more than civil service reform. The broader agenda of administrative law reform involves two kinds of relationships that can overlap—dealings between the citizen and the government and dealings between an enterprise and the government. The latter can again be divided into three phases of an enterprise's existence—entry, functioning and exit. On the entrepreneurial side, countervailing pressure, highlighting constraints to efficient decision-making through discretionary subordinate legislation, have been highlighted in reports brought out by larger chambers of commerce and industry like FICCI, CII and ASSOCHAM.[73] But one should not form the impression that big business alone is the issue. Since transaction costs have economies of scale and scope, they have a distributional angle and hurt the small entrepreneur more. In 2000, the Prime Minister's Council on Trade and Industry also submitted a report on administrative and legal simplifications.[74] Understandably, this had an industry focus and listed the following as industry concerns. "Large number of clearances/permissions required; Complex regulation governing day to day functioning; Multiple agencies regulating operations functioning independently; Lack of co-ordination between various governing agencies; Frequent changes in policies/procedures/tariff structures; Unpredictability of changes; Lack of clarity on issues between Centre and States; Transaction oriented approach of the system instead of a corporate approach, leading to increased costs and delays; Lack of openness and transparency in communication and providing information." It is not that procedures have not improved anywhere, but the success greatly varies from State to State.

One should add to that the problem of legal reform, including dispute resolution. Within statutory law reform, there are issues of rationalisation and harmonisation across statutes that have been enacted at various points in time, eliminating old laws that serve no purpose, junking unnecessary State intervention in many of these statutes and even introducing new legislation where none exists. On faster dispute resolution, a new Arbitration Act has been in place since 1996, but conciliation/mediation is still not credible. Within the court system, there is an estimated backlog of 30 million cases stuck in courts, not including those that are stuck in quasi-judicial forums. There have been faster clearances in the Supreme Court, but not yet in High Courts and Lower Courts, with understandable variations across States. About two-thirds of pending cases are criminal ones. With amendments to the Civil Procedure Code in 2001 and 2002, dispute resolution should become faster for civil cases and there is some evidence of this having happened. But this is not yet true of criminal law.

Urbanisation: Globally, economic development has been correlated with urbanisation. The 2001 Census showed that 74.27% of India's population lives in rural India, while 25.73% lives in urban India. There are 384 rural agglomerations, 5161 towns, 27 million-plus cities and 35 million-plus urban agglomerations. An urban agglomeration is a continuous urban spread with a city, and its adjoining urban growth. There are some areas that are classified as towns in a statutory way, in the sense that a municipality, corporation, Cantonment Board or notified town area committee exists. More generally, the Census defines "urban" as an area with a minimum population of 5000, with at least 75% of the male working-age population engaged in non-agricultural pursuits and a population density of at least 400 per sq km. More to the point, there are 638,365 villages, some of which are uninhabited. More relevant is the number of inhabited villages in 2001, at 593,643. Should one plan for people to stay in rural India or should one plan for an urban India, remembering that urbanisation is slower in India than in many parts of the developing world? Not only is urbanisation lower in India than in developed countries, and even in several developing countries, it has also slowed over the decades. For instance, between 1971 and 1981 the annual average rate of urbanisation was 3.79%, but declined to 3.09% between 1981 and 1991 and to 2.73% between 1991 and 2001.[75] There are several reasons why villages disappear. Thanks to migration and improved connectivity, some disappear. Others become mainstreamed into urban agglomerations. Still others are reclassified as urban as development proceeds. All these are desirable developments. The average population in an Indian village is 1,161 and this doesn't make the village viable, to provide physical or social infrastructure. 91,555 of India's villages have population sizes less than 200 and 12,644 of them are in Odisha, with other large numbers in Himachal, Uttaranchal, Rajasthan, UP, Jharkhand and MP. Another 127,515 of villages have population sizes less than 499; 14,806 have population sizes more than 5000; and 3,962 have population sizes more than 10,000. The idea is not to have a quota on the number of villages. Instead, the argument is that if urban planning is properly undertaken, more than 200,000 of India's villages will disappear, as they should, and there will be larger villages or towns with populations upwards of 10,000 and approaching and even crossing 100,000.

There are three kinds of resistance articulated against this rural to urban transition. The first is a sentimental kind of association with some notion of a rural Arcadia. It is also worth mentioning that several studies have documented the pro-urban bias in subsidy delivery systems. The second kind of argument is based on the premise that with this transition, India will no longer be able to feed its increasing population. This fails to appreciate the low productivity levels Indian agriculture possesses, not only in comparison with the rest of the world, but also in comparison between India's irrigated and non-irrigated areas, with irrigation having so far benefited only 45% of the cultivated area. If required agricultural reforms are introduced, India will have no problems in feeding double its present population. The third argument is directed against the kind of urban life that is delivered, with pressures on urban infrastructure like water supply, sewage clearance and drainage, waste disposal, transportation, power, housing, law and order and environmental pollution issues. After all, the slum population in 2001 was estimated to be 61.82 million, with 640 towns reporting slum populations.[76] This is less an argument against urbanisation and is more of an argument against the kind of urbanisation that has taken place. 68.9% of the urban population is in Category I cities and 37% of the urban population lives in the 35 million-plus cities. Indeed, urbanisation has been occurring in these mega cities.[77] The point is that both push and pull factors are distorted. They are distorted in terms of preventing urbanisation and creating disincentives against rural to urban migration. And they are also distorted in terms of creating the wrong kind of urbanisation.

If these policy-induced distortions are removed, the right kind of rural to urban transition will occur. For instance, State-government policies prevent creation of rural land markets and work against acquisition of agricultural land and its conversion to non-agricultural usage. Understandably, this is linked to issues of compensation, resettlement and rehabilitation and devising alternative rural or urban livelihoods, a controversy witnessed in recent SEZ (special economic zone) and non-SEZ debates. States are reluctant to notify rural settlements as towns, because many subsidies and grants from the Centre are geared towards retaining rural status. Urban land markets are also distorted through State intervention. Most land is publicly owned and does not come on to the market. This creates artificial shortages and housing and real estate shortages are compounded by dysfunctional building (and tenancy) laws. For instance, even for the slums, it is possible to unbundle ownership and create rights for the poor, so that incentives are created for improvement, including loans and the offering of collateral. Urbanisation should also lead to formalisation and employment in the organised sector.

Infrastructure: Infrastructure means several different things and there can be no quarrel with the proposition that inadequate infrastructure holds up Indian GDP growth. As a generalisation, the infrastructure area where there have been visible improvements is telecom, with roads perhaps following as a somewhat distant second. The contours of unbundling, user charges and regulatory agencies are known. The issue is simply one of getting infrastructure reforms implemented and some areas of physical infrastructure are State subjects. The issues are twofold. First, given scarce government resources, where are these best deployed? Second, again given scarce government resources, what is the scope for private sector involvement? The Eleventh Plan document states, "Good quality infrastructure is the most critical physical requirement for attaining faster growth in a competitive world and also for ensuring investment in backward regions. This includes all-weather roads; round-the-clock availability of power at a stable voltage and frequency; water for irrigation; railways that are not overcrowded, which run on time and do not overcharge for freight; ports with low turnaround time to reduce costs of imports and exports; airports to handle the growing traffic; air services that provide connectivity to all parts of the country; and telecommunications and broadband connectivity to provide the benefits of the Internet to people all over the country."[78] It is impossible to disagree with this objective, or with the intention of increasing investment on infrastructure from 5.43% of GDP in 2006-07 to 9.34% in 2011-12, a target that is certain to be missed.

In 1994, the World Bank's World Development Report (WDR) had the theme of infrastructure for development.[79] Later WDRs have also tangentially touched upon the subject. A few pointers from the 1994 WDR are useful. First, economic infrastructure includes public utilities (power, telecommunications, piped water supply, sanitation, sewerage, solid waste collection and disposal, piped gas), public works (roads, dams, canals) and other transport (urban transport, railways, ports, waterways, airports), what economists often refer to as social overhead capital. Economic infrastructure and social overhead capital are both umbrella terms and share technical features (like economies of scale) and externalities (spillovers from users to non-users). Second, because of natural monopolies and market failures, one has often tended to assume that infrastructure is a public good and must be provided by the public sector. That's no longer necessarily true and there are opportunities for unbundling, facilitated by advances in technology. Second, using cross-country estimates, a 1% increase in the stock of infrastructure is associated with a 1% increase in GDP. Third, "Major investments have been made in infrastructure stocks, but in too many developing countries these assets are not generating the quantity or the quality of services demanded....The causes of past poor performance, and the source of improved performance, lies in the incentives facing producers. Fourth, even among the poor, there is a willingness to pay higher user charges, provided that quality of service is ensured. Fifth, efficiency can increase through private sector involvement in management, financing and ownership. "Competition can be introduced directly, by liberalizing entry into activities that have no technological barriers, and indirectly, through competitive bidding for the right to provide exclusive service where natural monopoly conditions exist and by liberalizing the supply of service substitutes." In addition, though WDR did not mention it directly, there are competition policy instruments, such as through the Competition Commission of India (CCI). Sixth, even when there are privatisation options, the government will have a role in financing and regulation.

Volume 3 of the Eleventh Five Year Plan document included physical infrastructure, specifically transport, energy, urban infrastructure, housing, basic services and communication and information technology.[80] Subsequently, there has been the mid-term appraisal for the Eleventh Plan.[81] This tells us the following. Investment in physical infrastructure was expected to increase from 5% of GDP during the Tenth Plan to 9% of GDP by 2011-12, the terminal year of the Eleventh Plan. This meant that investment would have to increase from 218 billion US dollars during the Tenth Plan to 514 billion US dollars during the Eleventh Plan. 30% of investments during the Eleventh Plan were expected to be from the private sector. During the first two years of the Eleventh Plan investments from the private sector have actually amounted to 34.32% and 33.73% respectively, higher than what was expected.[82] We now have infrastructure investment figures of 7.18% of GDP in 2008-09, 8.37% in 2011-12 and 7.55% for the Eleventh Plan as a whole. However, there are several sector variations. Compared to expectations, private investments in electricity have been higher, but public investments have been lower. Roads have flagged. But there is a target of 20 km of roads per day under NHDP (National Highway Development Programme) and PMGSY (Pradhan Mantri Gram Sadak Yojana) might also pick up. Railways have under-performed, including on award of PPP (public private partnership) contracts. The performance of the telecom sector has been phenomenal. With the exception of private sector minor ports, sea-ports have performed below par. But airports have done well and so has oil and gas. Water supply, irrigation and even Bharat Nirman are cause for concern. For the Twelfth Plan, infrastructure investments are expected to increase from 8.37% of GDP in 2011-12 to 10.07% in 2016-17, with an average of 9.95% for the Twelfth Plan as a whole.

The background is several initiatives on infrastructure. Under the Chairmanship of the Prime Minister, a Committee on Infrastructure (COI) was constituted in August 2004 to ensure time-bound completion of infrastructure projects, including in the PPP mode. A Cabinet Committee on Infrastructure (CCI), also chaired by the Prime Minister, was established in July 2009. With Department of Economic Affairs and Planning Commission representation, there is a Public Private Partnership Appraisal Committee (PPAC). A viability gap funding scheme was announced in 2006, to provide 20% as grant to infrastructure projects undertaken through the PPP mode. There is an Inter-Ministerial Empowered Committee for viability gap funding projects. The India Infrastructure Finance Company Limited (IIFCL) was set up to fund long-term infrastructure projects. There are model concession agreements for PPP projects for national highways and state highways, operation and maintenance of highways, urban rail transit systems, non-metro airports, Greenfield airports, port terminals, operation of container trains, re-development of railway stations, procurement and maintenance agreements for locomotives and transmission of electricity. There are model bidding agreements and guidelines and manuals. There have been several reports. As the list below shows, it is not quite the case that there have been no successes in PPP.[83] However, it is also the case that success has fallen short of expectations.

Some Illustrative PPP Projects

1. Bangalore International Airport, Karnataka
2. Rajiv Gandhi International Airport, Hyderabad
3. Indira Gandhi International Airport, New Delhi
4. Chhatrapati Shivaji International Airport, Mumbai
5. 6 Laning of Jaipur–Kishangarh National Highway
6. 8/6 Laning of Delhi–Gurgaon Expressway

7. Hyderabad–Vijaywada National Highway
8. Offshore Container Berths, Mumbai Harbour
9. Deep Draft Iron Ore Berth, Paradip Port
10. Mega Container Terminal, Chennai
11. Multi-purpose Cargo Berths, Kandla
12. Hyderabad Metro Rail Project, Hyderabad
13. Colaba Bandra Metro Corridor Line-III, Mumbai
14. Jhajjar Power Transmission Project, Haryana
15. Mundra Port, Gujarat
16. Pipavav Port, Gujarat
17. Gangavaram Port, Andhra Pradesh
18. Krishnapuram Port, Andhra Pradesh
19. Vadodara–Bharuch State Highway, Gujarat
20. Indore-Edelabad State Highway, Madhya Pradesh
21. Yedshi–Latur–Nanded State Highway, Maharashtra
22. Jaipur–Bhilwara State Highway, Rajasthan
23. Delhi Western Peripheral Expressway (KMP Expressway), Haryana
24. Bridge across River Godavari between Yanam–Edurulanka, Andhra Pradesh.

Earlier, mention has been made of the World Development Report, which suggests that 1% increase in infrastructure stock can increase GDP by 1%. The Indian figures that float around are higher. For instance, the National Manufacturing Competitiveness Council formulated a National Strategy for Manufacturing, where it argued that adequate infrastructure can improve GDP growth by a factor of 1.5%, with 1% accounted for by the power sector alone. That National Strategy said the following. "Among infrastructure sub-sectors there has been visible improvement in telecom, with roads sector following as a somewhat distant second. The contours of unbundling, user charges and regulatory agencies are known and the issue is simply one of getting infrastructure reforms implemented to stimulate private sector investments and public sector viability. From the manufacturing perspective, perhaps the most important infrastructure areas where reforms are to be speeded up are power, ports and railways, followed by roads....It is estimated that power shortage alone contributed to a production loss of at least one per cent of GDP."[84] In some recent speeches, the Finance Minister has jacked up incremental GDP estimates from 1.5% to 2%. That thus, is the opportunity cost of lost GDP growth.

Other than telecom, why has infrastructure development flagged? The Planning Commission identifies part of the problem as the following. "In a federal country like India, participation and support of the State Governments is essential for development of world class infrastructure. The State Governments' support in maintenance of law and order, land acquisition, rehabilitation and settlement of displaced persons, shifting of utilities and obtaining environmental clearances is necessary for the projects undertaken by the Central Government or the private sector."[85] Land and environment are major issues and there are several other issues that have often been discussed in detail.[86] But let us also mention a few other points that are often not talked about. "However, structural and regulatory barriers that impede the flow of domestic capital into infrastructure—asset liability mismatch and exposure limit issues for banks; the high pre-emption of funds from the banking system; investment restrictions on long-term savings mobilisers, namely insurance, pension and provident funds; the shallowness of the bond market; and constrained supply of External Commercial Borrowings (ECB)–will hamper funding to the sector. Further, the global economic slowdown and rising interest rates make project funding for infrastructure more expensive and financial closure more difficult."[87] "India does not compare favourably with other countries in executing projects. Data from government and industry suggest that on average, each project suffers from 20 to 25 per cent time and cost over-runs, while in some sectors this is as high as over 50 per cent…Indian providers (engineering, procurement and construction or EP&C companies) often fail to tap significant opportunities to reduce time and cost."[88] This report flags items that are often not recognised. Quality of planning and engineering design is poor. It is common to tender unviable PPP projects. Inappropriate contracts are used. The pre-tendering approval process is centralised and slow. Dispute resolution processes are ineffective. Performance management is weak. There is insufficient availability of skilled and semi-skilled manpower. There are weak risk management skills. Design and engineering skills are below par. Procurement practices are not the best. Lean construction practices are not used.

One should also recognise that India is a large and heterogeneous country and there are considerable differences among States and even within States. There have been attempts to compute infrastructure indices for States. For example, Finance Commissions have been concerned with vertical equity (Centre versus State issues) and also horizontal equity (allocations among States). Horizontal equity and horizontal transfers have been made a function of a State's backwardness and physical infrastructure is one of the indicators used in determining backwardness. Whenever such an infrastructure index is constructed, the values depend on the variables included, the weights attached to them and the aggregation formula. Consequently, different indices can show differing results. The Twelfth Finance Commission grouped States into five categories, on the basis of an infrastructure index constructed by IDFC.[89] Goa, Maharashtra and Punjab were "high". Gujarat, Haryana, Kerala and Tamil Nadu were "high middle". Andhra Pradesh and Karnataka were "middle". Himachal Pradesh, Madhya Pradesh, Odisha, Uttar Pradesh, Uttarakhand and West Bengal were "lower middle". And Arunachal Pradesh, Manipur, Meghalaya, Jharkhand, Mizoram, Nagaland, Assam, Chhattisgarh, Sikkim, Tripura, Jammu & Kashmir, Bihar and Rajasthan were "low".

Taxation: This has both a direct and an indirect tax angle and the directions for reform are known, involving standardisation, harmonisation and removal of exemptions, with reduction in compliance costs.[90] There are still several exemptions, leading to distortions in resource allocation and varying the incidence across sectors. Without elimination of discretionary exemptions, it is also difficult to reduce collection, enforcement and compliance costs. The broad shape of indirect tax reform is also clear. There should be a combined goods and service tax (GST), with service sector taxation integrated into the VAT framework instead of being a tax on turnover. This will be accompanied by a withdrawal of all other taxes like central excise, central sales tax, octroi, State-level sales tax, entry tax, stamp duties, transportation taxes and so on. The problems with the earlier indirect tax structure are known. First, the tax base is fragmented between Centre and States. Second, services are not taxed properly and not integrated into a VAT (value added tax) framework. Third, there are cascading effects and multi-point and multiple (tax on tax) taxation exist. Fourth, discretion and exemption lead to distortions in resource allocation and tax revenue is disproportionately dependent on a few items. Fifth, tax administration is also complicated and there is no harmonisation of classification and valuation. Sixth, tax rates varied from one State to another, leading to tax arbitrage and rate wars among States. A VAT, with unification of State-level sales tax, was introduced between 2003 and 2006, with most States coming on board from April 2005. Uttar Pradesh was the last State to switch in January 2008. But this was never a complete VAT. It was no more than unification of State-level sales tax and there were problems there too, since the rates varied from State to State. It is by no means obvious that the proposed unified goods and services tax (GST) will remove exemptions or whether it will lead to the elimination of all other indirect taxes. In a similar vein, it is by no means obvious that the proposed DTC (Direct Taxes Code) will remove all exemptions. If one includes State-level taxes, the present tax/GDP ratio is 17%. With the removal of all exemptions, direct as well as indirect, the tax/ GDP ratio can increase to 23%.

Efficiency in Public Expenditure: The question of efficiency in public expenditure has already been touched upon. Therefore, only a few minor points will suffice. This has a Centre, State and even local body aspect. Although the importance of each element is a function of the level of government that one has in mind, a substantial chunk of public expenditure is on interest payments, wages and salaries and pensions. In the short-run, this expenditure is inflexible, although in the long run, one can borrow less, employ fewer people and enter into new pension arrangements with new entrants into the civil service. On reforming civil services in India, several recommendations have been made. The issues of downsizing, identifying surplus manpower, retraining, voluntary retirement schemes (VRS), contractual appointments, lateral entry and evaluation and vertical mobility keep recurring and the reform agenda is also known. However, they haven't been implemented. In addition to borrowing and expenditure on the administrative machinery of the government, public expenditure also includes public services. Such expenditure is never linked to tangible improvement in outcomes and administrative costs of delivery are extremely high. Other than changes in budgetary and accounting procedures, there are issues of transfers to States and devolution within States, scrapping discretionary transfers through the Planning Commission.

In concluding this section on the pending reform agenda, a few back-of-the-envelope kinds of numbers should be flagged. Whatever be the baseline trend of GDP growth, adequate infrastructure services will provide an increment of 1.5% to GDP, of which, 1% is on account of the power sector alone. Legal reform can add another increment of 1%. Improved morbidity, mortality, skills and higher work participation rates can add another 1.5%. Satisfactory delivery of public services can add another increment of 1%. This is in the realm of the potential.

The Projections Till 2025

While all these reforms are unlikely to happen in their entirety, there is enough slack in the system for a few reforms to ensure growth rates of 9% and more in the years leading up to 2025. The assumptions behind the projections are the following:

- A base GDP of US $ 1.99 trillion in 2011-12.[91]
- An increase in the savings rate to 37% of GDP. In 2009-10, household sector savings were 23.5% of GDP. Indeed, household sector savings in India compare quite favourably with those in China, the difference is accounted for by corporate and public savings. The factors that have driven the increase in household sector savings are certain to continue. However, public savings are contingent on government's adhering to fiscal consolidation targets. For example, there is a target of reducing the fiscal deficit to 3% of GDP by 2014-15. With capital inflows, one therefore should have an investment rate of 40% of GDP. But in addition to fiscal consolidation, financial sector reforms have to ensure more efficient usage of capital. With an incremental capital/output ratio of 4, and this can also be driven down through competition, this suggests a trend rate of growth of 10%.

- A decline in agriculture's share in GDP by about 0.5 percentage points a year. By 2015, agriculture's share in GDP should be around 13% and this should decline to around 9% by 2025. There will be a corresponding increase in the shares of services and industry, more the former. Agriculture and allied activities are unlikely to grow by more than 4% a year, the point being that this shift in the structure of national income itself fuels GDP growth, since industry and services will grow faster than agriculture.
- An increase in the labour force by 2% a year, with the demographic dividend contributing 1% to GDP growth. This can be higher, with better health and education outcomes and increased work participation rates.
- In Cobb-Douglas production functions, growth shows up as a function of labour and capital inputs. Everything else shows up as total factor productivity (TFP) growth, including infrastructure improvements, more efficient usage of natural resources and the phenomenon of backward States catching up. An annual 1.5% growth is assumed in TFP.
- An annual exchange rate appreciation of 1.5%.
- A GDP-deflator based inflation of 5%.
- Some degree of global recovery and a negative impact of 0.3% on GDP growth of every increase in oil prices by US $ a barrel.

If all of these are factored in, one gets a real GDP rate of growth of 8.5% till 2015, accelerating to 9.5% between 2015 and 2020, before slowing to 8.5% between 2015 and 2025. As an average, one can assume a real rate of GDP growth of 9%. This is contingent on some reforms occurring and is a likely scenario, not a best-case one. However, as a worst-case scenario, projections are also given of a real GDP growth rate of 7.5%. We do not get into questions of when India's rate of growth will overtake the Chinese, or when the size of India's economy will overtake that of any specific country. Those are peripheral questions for the purposes of this paper. In passing, 2020 will roughly be the year when India will move into the high development category.[92] By 2025, the poverty ratio, assuming an unchanged poverty line, will be around 7% if the Planning Commission poverty line is used and just over 10% if the $ 1.25 poverty line is used. This is because income (or expenditure) distributions are not symmetric and are log normal and substantial drops in poverty are possible when the thick part of the distribution moves above the poverty line. The adult literacy rate will be around 90% and the infant mortality rate will be around 35 per thousand. While India will still remain a poor country, and there will be significant inter-regional variations, the nature of poverty will be vastly transformed. Table 3 shows the kinds of results one obtains with these projections.

Table 3

Projections, 2015 and 2025

	2015 (7.5%)	2025 (7.5%)	2015 (9%)	2025 (9%)
GDP current Rs trillion	144	468	151	563
GDP, today's36 dollars, trillion (Rs 45 to 1 US $)	2.7	5.5	2.8	6.7
Per capita GDP, today's dollars	2076	4074	2154	4963
GDP, today's dollars, with exchange rate appreciation	2.8	6.4	3.0	7.8
Per capita GDP, today's dollars, with exchange rate appreciation	2203	4278	2286	5760

Growth also provides additional resources for public expenditure in absolute terms, though not necessarily as shares of GDP. In talking about public expenditure, one needs to differentiate between the Centre and the States. Let us stick to the Central government. Net of State shares, the Central government's tax revenue is around 7% of GDP. With exemptions removed, an unlikely prospect, the Central government's tax revenue should increase to around 10% of GDP. Since this is unlikely, one should stick to a figure of around 7%, with non-tax revenue adding another 2% of GDP. With capital receipts included, but with borrowing excluded, one has around 12% of GDP to play around with, assuming disinvestments are increased. Of this, at least 5% should be in the nature of capital expenditure, though admittedly, differences between Plan and non-Plan and revenue and capital can be artificial. About 3.5% of GDP is on interest payments, while another 2% is on subsidies. Of these, interest payments are cast in stone. And if subsidies are properly targeted and delivered to all the poor, they are unlikely to decline. That leaves only about 1.5% of GDP, including wages, salaries and pensions. It is a different matter that capital expenditure hasn't usually exceeded 2% of GDP and deficits have been financed through borrowing. The point of this is that without dramatically reforming public expenditure, government budgetary and accounting processes and transfers to States, there are few degrees of freedom. There are competing claims, such as increasing public expenditure on education to 6% of GDP and increasing public expenditure on health to 4% of GDP. Of course, this includes State-level expenditure too. Indeed, beyond defence, interest payments and subsidies, most public expenditure is social sector in nature and should be delivered by States, with further decentralisation within States. The elimination of several layers (Ministries/departments) in the delivery mechanism, will double the amount that reaches the target beneficiary. While a target of 3% of GDP for defence expenditure is often mentioned, this includes both capital and revenue expenditure. Revenue expenditure on defence has typically been between 1 and 1.5% of GDP and questions can legitimately be asked about whether this form of defence expenditure legitimately serves India's strategic interests. Having said that, 3% is a doable figure, because there is plenty of slack in the system. However, anything beyond that requires a revamp of revenue (tax exemptions, disinvestment) or expenditure.

Endnotes:

1. *Dreaming with BRICs: The Path to 2050,* Dominic Wilson and Roopa Purushothaman, Global Economics Paper No.99, Goldman Sachs, 1 October 2003.
2. These figures are from *Economic Survey 2010-11,* Department of Economic Affairs, Ministry of Finance, Government of India.
3. *BRICs and Beyond,* Jim O'Neill, Goldman Sachs, 23rd November 2007.
4. *Dreaming with BRICs: The Path to 2050,* Dominic Wilson and Roopa Purushothaman, Global Economics Paper No.99, Goldman Sachs, 1 October 2003. For BRIC countries as a whole, an annual exchange rate appreciation of 2.5% is assumed.
5. 5.9% for 2010-15 and 5.7% from 2015-2025.
6. *How Solid are the BRICS?,* Jim O'Neill, Dominic Wilson, Roopa Purushothaman and Anna Stupnytska, Global Economics Paper No.134, Goldman Sachs, 1st December 2005.
7. 5.7% for 2010-15, 5.5% for 2015-20 and 5.4% for 2020-25.
8. *BRICs and Beyond,* Jim O'Neill, Goldman Sachs, 23rd November 2007.
9. 6.0% for 2015-20 and 5.9% for 2020-25.
10. *The World in 2050, How big will the major emerging market economies get and how can the OECD compete?,* John Hawsworth, Price Waterhouse Coopers, March 2006. This has projections for 2050, but not for the intervening years of 2015 and 2025. There were subsequent revisions to this in March 2008 and January 2011. But we are ignoring those, because they continue to relate to 2011. However, the 7.6% growth (with exchange rate appreciation) was increased to 8.1% in January 2011.
11. 7.6% with exchange rate appreciation.
12. *India Rising: A Medium-Term Perspective,* Jennifer Asuncion-Mund, Deutsche Bank Research, May 2005.
13. 7.5% with substantial reforms.
14. This is a PPP (purchasing power parity) figure and is for 2020, not 2025.
15. *The World in 2050, Quantifying the Shift in the Global Economy,* HSBC Global Research, January 2011. This also has projections for 2050, but not for the intervening years of 2015 and 2025.
16. 5.7% between 2010 and 2020 and 5.6% between 2020 and 2030.
17. *The Bird of Gold: The Rise of India's Consumer Market,* McKinsey Global Institute, May 2007.
18. *India 2039, An Affluent Society in One Generation,* ADB and Emerging Markets Forum, 2009.
19. 2024, not 2025.
20. *A Tripolar Century: USA, China and India,* Arvind Virmani, ICRIER Working Paper No. 160, March 2005.
21. Since per capita GDP is GDP divided by population (and not just the working-age population), per capita GDP is more accurately the average productivity of India's working-age population.
22. http://gcr.weforum.org/gcr2010/
23. See, for example, *India: The Emerging Giant,* Arvind Panagariya, Oxford University Press, 2008.
24. Export incentives are WTO-compatible. Even when WTO-compatible, trading partners can subject export subsidies to countervailing duties.
25. The Seventh Schedule to the Indian Constitution sets out a Union List, a State List and a Concurrent List.

26. "India: On the Growth Turnpike," Vijay Kelkar, 2004 K.R. Narayanan Oration, Australian National University, reprinted in Raghbendra Jha edited, *The First Ten K.R. Narayanan Orations,* ANU Press, 2006; *Can India grow without Bharata?,* Shankar Acharya, Academic Foundation, 2007; "The Indina Model," Gurcharan Das, *Foreign Affairs,* July/August 2006; *India rising; a medium term perspective,* Deutsche Bank Research, May 2005; "Growing Old the Hard Way: China, Russia, India," Nicholas Eberstadt, *Policy Review,* Hoover Institution, April/May 2006; and "Dreaming with BRICs: The Path to 2050," Dominic Wilson and Roopa Purushothaman, *Global Economics Paper No. 99,* Goldman Sachs, October 2003, are some instances.
27. See, David E. Bloom, David Canning and Jaypee Sevilla, "Economic Growth and the Demographic Transition," *NBER Working Paper 8685,* December 2001.
28. The empirical and theoretical literature is reviewed in *World Economic Outlook, The Global Demographic Transition,* IMF, September 2004.
29. *Population Projections for India and States 2001-2026, Report of the Technical Group on Population Projections Constituted by the National Commission on Population,* Office of the Registrar General and Census Commissioner, May 2006.
30. Some skepticism of TFP estimation is warranted. However, one study that contrasted India and China in two sub-periods, 1989-1995 and 1995-2003, is worth mentioning, since it found that the labour contribution to India's growth was driven more by quantity than quality. See, Dale Jorgenson and Vu Khunog, "Information Technology and the World Economy," Scandinavian Journal of Economics, Vol. 107, No. 4, 2005.
31. Adapted from *India Labour Report 2008,* TeamLease and Indicus Analytics.
32. *Report of the Special Group on Targeting Ten Million Employment Opportunities per year over the Tenth Plan Period,* Planning Commission, May 2002, http://planningcommission.nic.in/aboutus/committee/tsk_sg10m.pdf
33. *Report of the Task Force on Employment Opportunities,* Planning Commission, July 2001, http://planningcommission.nic.in/aboutus/taskforce/tk_empopp.pdf
34. 20-24 age-group.
35. *Eleventh Five Year Plan, 2007-2012, Vol. I, ibid..*
36. *Ibid.* These numbers are based on the 61st round (2004-05) of the NSS.
37. The drop is sharper for rural females and is higher in rural than in urban India.
38. 85.5% for males and 90.2% for females. Understandably, the numbers without training are higher in rural areas.
39. The number is higher for males and higher in urban than in rural areas.
40. *Ibid.*
41. *Skill Formation and Employment Assurance in the Unorganized Sector,* NCEUS, August 2008.
42. www.ophi.org.uk
43. http://www.satp.org/satporgtp/icm/index.html
44. *India's Employment Challenge, Creating Jobs, Helping Workers,* The World Bank and Oxford University Press, 2010.
45. *Report on Conditions of Work and Promotion of Livelihoods in the Unorganized Sector,* NCEUS, 2007, http://nceuis.nic.in/Condition_of_workers_sep_2007.pdf
46. There are statistical issues we are glossing over. The working age is defined as between 15 and 59 years, though a little over one million children are also estimated to be in the labour force/work force and the figures given include this child labour component.

Employment is defined in one of three different ways – usually employed, principal and subsidiary status (UPSS), weekly status and current daily status (CDS). The first is over a 365-day period. The cited figures are for CDS. For UPSS in the same year, the labour force was 471 million and the work force was 460 million.

47. The numbers don't add up because of rounding approximations.
48. NCEUS, *ibid.*
49. Strictly speaking, this is a Factories Act definition.
50. One should also mention that more than two-thirds of the employment in the organised sector was in the public sector.
51. NCEUS, Ibid.
52. ILO, *Women and Men in the Informal Economy: A statistical picture,* Geneva, (2002).
53. Ibid.
54. More accurately, they reported themselves as own account workers.
55. NCEUS, *Ibid.*
56. Manushi's work is but one example. See, Madhu Purnima Kishwar, *Deepening Democracy, Challenges of Governance and Globalization in India,* Oxford University Press, 2005.
57. http://dcmsme.gov.in/ssiindia/census/highlights.htm
58. See Sudders, M. and Nahem, J (2004), *Governance Indicators: A Users' Guide,* UNDP, Oslo, for a comprehensive discussion.
59. http://www.freetheworld.com/2010/reports/world/EFW2010_BOOK.pdf. The higher the number, the better, the maximum score being 10.
60. http://www.heritage.org/Index/Country/India#labor-freedom
61. http://www.doingbusiness.org/data/exploreeconomies/india/employing-workers/
62. *Economic Survey* 2005-06, Department of Economic Affairs and Ministry of Finance, Chapter 10.
63. For instance, the Agricultural Produce Marketing and Control (APMC) Acts and orders under the Essential Commodities Act.
64. Plus decentralisation in the management of rural infrastructure.
65. There is also a research and development agenda, but it is not necessarily obvious why this has to be public sector driven. Extension services will have to be largely public sector driven.
66. There are two distinct issues of ownership laws and tenancy laws here. The former is contentious, the latter less so.
67. www.transparency.org/surveys.
68. www.worldbank.org/wbi/governance.
69. www.weforum.org
70. www.heritage.org/research.
71. www.freetheworld.com
72. http://www.doingbusiness.org
73. Many such studies suggest that transaction costs add around 20% to costs of doing business. However, these studies also tend to include infrastructure costs in transaction costs. That is, transaction costs are not procedural costs alone.
74. This was chaired by Kumar Mangalam Birla.
75. There was an earlier period of decline between 1951 and 1961, but that was because some towns were declassified.
76. Census 2001 figures.
77. One should recognise that there is a reclassification effect here too. But this only

explains part of the phenomenon. Indian censuses classify urban areas by size class of towns – I (more than 100,000), II (50,000 to 100,000), III (20,000 to 50,000), IV (10,000 to 20,000), V (5,000 to 10,000) and VI (less than 5,000).

78. *Vol. I, ibid.*

79. *World Development Report 1994, Infrastructure for Development,* World Bank and Oxford University Press, 1994.

80. *Eleventh Five Year Plan (2007-2012),* Vol.III, Planning Commission and Oxford University Press, 2008. Other elements of infrastructure were covered elsewhere in the Plan document.

81. *Mid-Term Appraisal for Eleventh Five Year Plan 2007-2012,* Planning Commission, 2010, http://planningcommission.gov.in/plans/mta/11th_mta/MTA.html

82. Data are not yet available for subsequent years.

83. *Ibid.*

84. *National Strategy for Manufacturing,* National Manufacturing Competitiveness Council, March 2006.

85. *Ibid.*

86. See, for example, *India Infrastructure Report 2008, Business Models of the Future,* Infrastructure Development Finance Company, Indian Institute of Management (Ahmedabad), Indian Institute of Technology (Kanpur) and Oxford University Press, 2008.

87. *Building India, Financing and Investing in Infrastructure,* McKinsey and Company, http://www.mckinsey.com/locations/india/mckinseyonindia/pdf/Building_India_Executive_Summary_web.pdf.

88. *Building India, Accelerating Infrastructure Projects,* McKinsey and Company, http://www.mckinsey.com/locations/india/mckinseyonindia/pdf/Building_India_Executive_Summary_Media_120809.pdf

89. *Report of the Twelfth Finance Commission (2005-2010),* Ministry of Finance, November 2004.

90. *Implementation of the Fiscal Responsibility and Budget Management Act, 2003, Report of the Task Force,* July 2004, summarises both direct and indirect tax reform intentions succinctly.

91. This is the figure given in the Prime Minister's Economic Advisory Council report, dated February 2011. This has a current dollar per capita income figure of $ 1,662.

92. This is based on UNDP's HDI (human development index). HDI is computed on the basis of PPP per capita income, education (gross enrolment, literacy) and health (life expectancy), with a HDI value more than 0.80 classified as high human development.

93. 2011-12.

The Decade of Environmentalism of the Poor

—*Sunita Narain*

In this last decade, India's environmental movement had a rebirth. It was first born in the decade of the 1970s, when the industrialised world was seeing the impact of growth on its environment. In that decade, air and rivers of London, Tokyo or New York were full of toxins and bad health. The world was learning the pain of pollution. The world's first major conference on environment—the Stockholm meet—was held to find ways to deal with this growing scourge. India's key environmental legislations were enacted in this period—the Water Pollution Act 1974 and then the Air Pollution Act 1980. But we were innocents in the world of pollution. We had not yet witnessed the intensification of growth that would in turn destroy our environment.

It was also in the 1970s that the second challenge of environment—issues of access and sustainable management of natural resources—had taken root. High in the remote Himalayas, the women had pushed out the timber merchants from cutting their forest. But their fight was not to protect the forest. Their fight was to assert their right to the resources of the forest. It was a battle over the right to resources. It was an environmental movement because the women of this village in Chamoli district knew that they had to protect the forest to protect their livelihood. It was a call to redefine development and growth.

But it is only in this decade of 2000 that these two sides of the environmental challenge have truly come home to India. Importantly, this is the decade, where environmental issues became centre-stage in the country. It is talked about extensively, considered in policy; frankly, nobody today would dare to say they aren't environment friendly.

Car companies sell their products for luxury and sustainability; real estate giants boast about rainwater harvesting systems; Bollywood stars dance their fondness for all things green. And governments say they want low-carbon economies for the future. Being green is the 'in-thing'.

But still matters are going from bad to worse. The pollution in our rivers is worse today than three decades ago. The garbage in cities in growing by the day, even as governments scramble to find ways of reducing plastic and hiding the rest in landfills in far-off places. Air pollution in cities is worse and toxins hurt our bodies, damage our lungs.

This, in spite of efforts to contain the problem. We have invested in building sewage treatment plants to deal with water pollution. We have improved the quality of fuel that runs our vehicles; changed emission standards and set up institutions to regulate industrial emissions. But still we find we cannot catch up in this game of growth and its toxic fallout.

In this decade as well, the struggles for the control over resources have intensified. In every nook and corner of the country where land is acquired, or water sourced, for industry, people are fighting even to death.

In Sikkim, bowing to local protests, the government cancelled eleven hydro-electric projects. In Arunachal Pradesh dam projects cleared at breakneck are not being contested by downstream Assam. In Himachal Pradesh, dams are so controversial that elections were won where candidates said they would not allow these to be built. In Narendra Modi's Gujarat, it is said that his party in the recent local elections only lost where farmers have opposed industrial projects. The South Korean giant POSCO's iron ore mine, steel plant and port are under fire. In Maharashtra, mango growers are up in arms against the proposed thermal power station in Ratnagiri.

This decade has seen a million pollution mutinies. The fact is, in India vast numbers—and it is vast numbers—depend on the land, the forests and the water they have in their vicinity for their livelihood. They know that once these resources are gone or degraded, they have no way ahead.

This is the environmental movement of the very poor. Here, there are no quick-fix techno solutions in which the real problems can be fobbed off for later. In this environmentalism, there is only one answer: changing the way we do business, with them and with their environment. It will demand we reduce our need and increase our efficiency for every inch of land we need, every tonne of mineral we dig and every drop of water we use. It will demand new arrangements to share benefits with local communities so that they are persuaded to part with their resources for a common development.

If we can listen and learn, maybe this environmentalism of the poor may teach not just us, but the entire world, how to walk lightly on earth. Maybe. Just maybe.

These are the same choices the environmental movement of the rich countries asked their countries to make, some two generations ago. They failed. This is why the challenge of climate change remains a challenge. Today, these societies are rich; they have cleaned up their streams and their black smoke. But their economic growth and their lifestyle is putting the entire world at risk because of climate change. They have no real answers to the future because they want to keep tinkering with the present. They are looking to find small solutions to the massive problem of increased emissions, linked to growth.

The western environmental movement also has a different history to ours. It began after these societies had acquired wealth. So, the movement was a response to the garbage, the toxic air or the polluted water, resulting from the growth of their economies. They had the money to invest in cleaning and they did. But because they never looked for big solutions, they always stayed behind the problem—local air pollution is still a problem in most western cities, even if the air is not as black as ours. It is just that the toxin is smaller, more difficult to find or to smell. They keep spending. Keep investing in technology to deal with the present. As such, the rich world's environmentalists are garbage managers, nothing more.

We want to emulate them, with much lesser resources and much more inequity and poverty. The fact is we cannot find answers in the same half solutions they invested in. This is the challenge of our next decade.

Sadhya, Sadhan aur Sadhna

—*Anupam Mishra*

At the very outset I must confess that these three Hindi words are difficult to translate. They represent the ends, the means and a kind of penance. I did not choose that title to score a point or satisfy my ego. I chose it because all NGOs, their coordinators, workers, generous funding agencies—whether *desi* or foreign—and people's movements, regardless of size and reach, should ponder over these words. A debate rages over the question of funding, it gets particularly stormy when it comes to foreign funding, invariably the debate centres on the ends and the means. Perhaps there would be some clarity if we stopped for a moment to consider *sadhna* or penance as well. For only penance will tell us what the people really want. And, when we know that and direct our energies at achieving it, the means and the ends will fall in place.

In my opinion, the source of funding is not very important. The money can be raised from the local village, mohalla or city. It could be sent across continents. There can be divergent opinions on the best sources of funding. What is more important is the outcome. The end result must be what we the people want. Apart from a few exceptions we don't have a clear idea of what we wish to achieve. NGOs or civil society movements keep shifting their focus. Most of us will recall at one time social forestry fetched a high price on the environment stock market. Funding came from the four corners of the globe and we rounded up a few million dollars. The best among us started implementing social forestry projects without first debating what precisely 'unsocial forestry' was.

And then suddenly this flag was brought down. In its place, one fine morning, the brand new flag of wasteland development was unfurled. This time too, nobody cared to define wastelands. A lot of money, energy and time were spent by eminent members of society in the wasteland development venture. Initially, a small department in the central government handled the idea. It was replaced by a new ministry. Lots of NGOs, from Kashmir to Kanyakumari, started wasteland development. But like the previous avatar, wasteland development died in its infancy. There were no condolence meetings to mourn the death of this 'marvellous' scheme and we soon started celebrating the birth of a new movement called watershed development.

This programme has been translated and adapted into various languages. In Hindi-speaking states, watershed development is called 'Jalagam Vikas'. In Maharashtra, it is termed 'Panlot' and elsewhere it is called 'Pandhal'. Despite the *desi* badge, the programme does not touch our hearts. For the moment, our best NGOs are putting their most talented people from urban and rural areas, into developing a few watersheds here and there. Nobody knows when we will begin shedding tears over this programme. Running neck to neck with watershed development is Joint Forest Management (JFM). Here too, some NGOs are ahead of the rest in providing a *desi* touch. So JFM is called 'Sanyukt Van Prabandh' in some regional dialects. Grassroot NGOs, who object to the Sanskritised word *sanyukt*, opt for the more colloquial *sanjha*. But essentially JFM is a programme and its end result has been dictated by the World Bank or some other multilateral institutions with western dominance.

I do not wish to narrate all this to make fun. These are indeed serious matters. If our society really needed the JFM programme, we should have first seriously reflected on the administration of forests by individual agencies and their managers. Who were they? How long did their authority last? Whom did they snatch these forests from? How did the country's forest cover dwindle to 10 per cent when it should have been 33 per cent? We have paid a price for deforestation. Floods in Bihar, Odisha, Chhattisgarh and drought in eighteen states are the net outcome. The people who mismanaged these forests and the political leadership which protected them should have apologised publicly before JFM was launched. We must also remember who the true managers of the forests were, how they were dispossessed by the British and looted of their green gold.

It is much the same story with programmes in areas other than the environment. Numerous plans exist on women's empowerment, child rights, reproductive health and formation of self-help groups. Every NGO implements the same programmes, regardless of political ideology. The leftists, the rightists, the Gandhians, the missionaries, even the RSS display a rare consensus. The monoculture of ideas is alarming. It seems there is an invisible mint somewhere in the West, which constantly coins new terms for us to fill our pockets with. So should we believe everybody has sold out? No, there are some heroes who have bravely fought the idea of monoculture. After the emergency in the 1970s, a few drove out Coca-Cola and IBM. To commemorate this great victory, a cold drink called Double Seven was introduced. But Coca-Cola re-emerged, in the garb of our heroes, drowning Double Seven and our original champions. This is a beautiful example of co-existence.

So this debate on ends and means, funds from here and there, will lead us nowhere. The answer is to find a good mission and for that to happen we have to look within. Once we have our own ends, the means will follow. A small example can be narrated from a village near Jaipur. In this drought prone area a routine NGO constructed a tank to harvest water. It invested some 30,000 rupees in the project. The tank narrowed the distance between the NGO and the community. At one of the meetings an elderly person suggested constructing a small temple and a *chhatri* on the embankment of the tank. But the cost of constructing the *chhatri* and the temple was not in the NGO's budget. The NGO explained that it could get a grant for the tank but not for the *chhatri*. But the elderly person politely replied that the village was not asking for money from the NGO. Within a month the villagers collected the amount and the *chhatri* was constructed.

Most of our NGO friends will consider the money spent as wasteful expenditure, but for the villagers, this is the difference between a house and a home. They need water structures that belong to them. And when they own something they protect and maintain it. Otherwise it's a kind of PWD structure. We should not forget in this land of 500,000 villagers and few thousand towns there were two million water structures before the British came. There was no water mission, no watershed development programmes. Society created these structures using its own resources. There was no Zilla Bank or World Bank at that time, but only the Village Bank. There was an invisible and invincible structure to carry out this job in a country that has a Cherrapunji as well as a Jaisalmer. Now we talk about people's participation and Participatory Research Appraisal (PRA). We get funds from within and outside, but our aims and ends do not represent the needs of the people. We keep on pushing a different agenda. If we were to invest half our energy in understanding our society, we would generate enough means from within. But that requires a kind of penance.

Looking Back: 64 Years of Independence

—*Rakhshanda Jalil*

I am a child of the sixties. I grew up in a country that still had vestiges of Nehruvian idealism and traces of the self-sufficient self-assurance that helped win its freedom. Universities and colleges were deemed temples of modern India. Thrift and industry were laudable qualities as was self-reliance and economy. Parents believed education, not religion, was the great leveller. A handful of Lohiawadis still lurked and socialism expressed itself in ways both spartan and sudden. The economy was sheltered and the Great Indian Middle Class was waiting to take wing and emerge chrysalis-like as the Big Spenders of the twenty-first century.

Independent India is only sixteen years older than I am. You can say we grew up together or, at the very least, I have some fond memories of a still-young, gauche country, still marked by simplicity, still touched by the bloom of innocence. While I missed the first flush of exuberant nation-building of the fifties, the stories of great courage and strength of the first generation of pioneering men and women were brought vividly alive when narrated by parents and older relatives. I was old enough, however, to get infected by the spirit of the times captured brilliantly on film by some idealistic Hindi film makers and brought liltingly to life by 'progressive' film lyricists such as Sahir Ludhianvi and Kaifi Azmi. The radio, blaring from every *panwadi* and *kirana* store, played songs from the popular cinema eulogising all that was best about a sovereign, socialist, secular republic: *Saathi haath badhana, Tu Hindu banega na Musalman banega, Bachon tum taqdeer ho kal ke Hindustan kii, Jinhe naaz hai Hind par woh kahan hain*, and countless others. I can recall just as well the black and white documentaries produced by the Films Division of India which portrayed the nation's history-in-the-making in drab monochrome through de rigueur screenings in every big and small cinema hall in every big and small Indian town.

I can also recall the thrift and economy of my childhood. You shut the tap while brushing your teeth because there were people who trekked miles to fetch a pot of water in places not too far from our home in New Delhi, we were told sternly. You switched off the lights and fan before leaving a room because, as our parents never failed to remind us, there were villages that had no electricity where people spent their evenings in lamp light. And you always, no matter what, finished what was on your plate because there was someone going hungry in some part of the country, virtually as one spoke.

If you went looking for toothpaste, you could choose from one of maybe three brands. So also with soaps, shampoos, shoes, and most other commodities. There was no rationing or shortages, except during the wars, in 1965 (which I don't remember) and 1971 (which I do remember for the austerity drives practised in middle-class Indian homes behind the recycled brown paper pasted on window panes for fear of air strikes). Most goods were plentifully available, though there were fewer brands and even less brand consciousness. And everything was 'Made in India'. On the roads of Delhi, the city I came to live in when I was four years old, one saw the lumbering Ambassador or the marginally niftier Fiats, the broad-bellied DTC buses carrying advertisements for Nirodh on their rear and telling us that a small family was a happy family, and *phat-phatiyas* mounted on World War II vintage mobikes driven by burly Sardars. And, of course, there were the *tongas*, *ekkas*, *bail-gadis*, cycle-rickshaws and bicycles which far-outnumbered the four-wheel drives. One saw them everywhere, even in Connaught Place which seemed intimidatingly modern back then.

It is of these years, the good old days as one would call them, that I am reminded as yet another Independence Day approaches and India celebrates its sixty-fourth year of independence. The country that began its tryst with destiny as a sovereign, socialist, secular democratic republic has come a long, long way. The shiny optimism of the early days soon gave way to a hard-eyed realism as we coped with excess in every imaginable sphere—escalating population, rising inflation, and ever-widening rift between the haves and have-nots. A slew of legislatures were introduced over the years to address pressing issues of food scarcity, hunger, poverty, unemployment and graft as also land use, rights of minorities, tribals and Dalits. While several government schemes have been designed with the express purpose of generating livelihoods, such as the Mahatama Gandhi National Rural Employment Generation Scheme (MGREGA), the lot of the rural poor remains a cause for national shame and the numbers for those living Below the Poverty Line (BPL) continue to be horrifically large.

The great pity, to my mind, seems to be that even after six decades of independence we have still not bridged the chasm between the Two Indias: the urban and the rural India, the rich and the poor India, the developed and the under-developed India, the affluent and the marginalised India. In fact, it is shocking the way urban Indians have ceased to care about the less-affluent, those who occupy the bottom rungs of the socio-economic pyramid or those who are so disempowered and disenfranchised as to be rendered practically invisible. The blithe spirit of market economics is so blasé that a great majority of the urban middle class now thinks it is best not to acknowledge the dark under belly of Shining India.

Socialism—once such a pillar of the Nehruvian era—began to leach out from the fabric of Indian life and polity during the early days of License Raj; the privatisation of the seventies and the opening up of the economy in the eighties simply drove the last nail in its coffin. The secularism survives, frayed and patched from time to time though it is but serviceable nonetheless, and if not exactly a role model then certainly better than the template adopted by, say, France or Turkey or Algeria. Moreover, the checks and balances enshrined in our Constitution ensure that our secular fabric is periodically repaired, its rents stitched up and its holes darned and plugged. The sovereignty, however, remains—unblemished, unchallenged and largely unexamined. It is this singular quality of nationhood that I believe we need to celebrate today on the eve of the sixty-fourth Independence Day.

Incarcerated in the trumped-up Rawalpindi Conspiracy Case, Faiz Ahmed Faiz had voiced the angst of an entire generation—and not confined to his side of the border—when he had written the following lines from inside his prison cell in 1953:

Yeh daagh-daagh ujala yeh shab-gazida seher
Yeh woh seher to nahi tha intezar jiska

While it is true that the night-bitten dawn that came after the long night of Partition was indeed not the dawn that many, like Faiz, had dreamt of, it is also true that India and Pakistan chose to chart different trajectories in that moment of patchy light. We in India chose to set off on a path of constitutional democracy while our neighbour and conjoined twin ran aground in the muddy waters of self-determination. Sixty-four years later we in India have still not redeemed our pledge when India awoke to freedom in full or ample measure, but we can say with some satisfaction that we have indeed been true to the notion of sovereignty. We have tested it again and again and found it not fool's gold but the real thing. The absoluteness that comes from sovereignty has been our touchstone.

There have always been groups within the larger Indian polity that have understood and interpreted sovereignty in different ways. While the Sangh Parivar has viewed the *rashtra* or nation through the prism of Hindu nationalism, the left parties have claimed the right of self-determination to be the only true principle of sovereignty. But the only definition of sovereignty that has survived sixty-four tumultuous years of nationhood has been the one that acknowledges that sovereign power rests with the people, individually and collectively. For all our hits and misses, gains and losses, bugbears and blots, possibly the only reason to cheer as yet another 15th of August dawns, is the continuing survival of democracy in our part of the world.

Another India: Voices from the Periphery

—Udaya Narayana Singh

The title I have chosen does not allow me to entertain any doubt whether we are justified in talking of the dichotomy of 'centre' vs. 'periphery'. But I guess one could still open with an argument that in a plural space such as South Asia, each political entity will have, at any given point of time, many centres—depending on which way one decides to assign values to one or the other cultural parameter. But then there are also differences of opinion in respect of those who look at such plurality from outside, and those who live in such spaces.

Which India shall I talk about? The space that gets to be seen in the words woven by our writers who happen to write or rewrite in English may appear to be a conundrum to the reading public from this part of the world—a universe plotted as a pastiche on a canvas which looks remote and diverse at the same time.

But for those of us who think and write in—let me use the much maligned word, 'vernacular languages'—those that stand on the other side of the lamp that is sustained on an English wicker, it is evident that rather than illuminating the concept or the space we would like to call India, Indian English writing allows a large part of India to perpetually remain outside the focus. What is in focus suddenly becomes the centre, even if it is a dormant Kantapura, or a sloppy town in Kerala. But what is outside this written world remains in the periphery for the Anglophone Indian, no matter how interesting Labtolia or Purnea may be in Bibhutibhushan or Renu's unforgettable stories.

There is yet another India, often not understood by the readership of mainstream Indian literatures. I am talking about the stories of Chandayana in Rajasthan or Raja Salhes in Mithila, or the Manteswami episode of the Tulus in Karnataka which typically lie outside our known worlds. What is happening in Kurmali, Bodo, Adi-Galong or Bhojpuri is none of 'their' concern. They become newsworthy only when there is a caste war or when they throw up a tainted political figure.

There are other Indias, too—where speakers of the same language are scattered over a vast space so disjointedly that they can hardly communicate with or read each other. The speakers of Urdu in Punjab or Lucknow would not know what a Hyderabadi Dakkhani Urdu speaker says, or what an Urdu speaker from Hubli would surmise. The language occupies an official position in a state (Jammu & Kashmir) where almost all speak a different mother-tongue—Kashmiri, Ladakhi or Dogri, and yet is not even recognised as an associate official language in the state (Uttar Pradesh) where a large percentage of people speak it as mother tongue.

Then there is the situation of diagraphia about which International Journal of Sociology of Language has devoted an entire issue this year: We have Konkani which is written in Roman, Deva-nagari, Kannada and Malayalam scripts—the same language with different literate zones. There is Punjabi in Gurumukhi, Deva-nagari and Perso-Arabic script, with Sindhi in the last two writing systems. Alternatively, there may be the same culture but many mutually almost unintelligible expression systems, as in Nagaland with thirteen different varieties, many of which are rich in music and expressions. Can we forget the Shompens and the Jarwas in the Andaman Islands with speakers whose numbers do not cross a few hundred? Now with public interest litigations or interventions made by different NGOs, they may occupy limelight, and come to centre-stage.

So, let me return to my original question: Which India could I talk about to my fellow '*Indianists*'? A country which talks in 1,576 'rationalised' mother tongues and in 1,796 'other mother-tongues'? (Believe me—these are not the terms that are invented for this presentation. They are taken straight from the Census documents.) Even if I restrict the number of languages in India by the number of speakers—10,000 or more, we still have 114 languages with a speech community as large as 338 million (as in case of Hindi) to 10,144 speakers of languages like Maram (in Manipur). It is a space where 146 speech varieties are beamed through radio network, sixty-nine are used in schools, and newspapers are brought out in thirty-five.

- India has always been a space which could be characterised as multi-centric. It was one nation and many at the same time. (Therefore, no wonder if there are question marks about its boundaries.)
- India has had one culture and many—seemingly contradictory but nevertheless true. (Hence the talk of multiple identities—that too structured at different layers—Indian vs. Gujarati or Bengali; Aryan vs. Dravidian; Brahmin vs. Baniya; the 'twice-born' vs. the scheduled castes; the 'forward' vs. the 'backward' communities; the Hill people vs. the plains-men; these and many other formations—each term demanding a footnote for the uninitiated readers. But each term must be understood in relation to other terms.)
- The plural linguistic scene that India depicts—whether we look at Census documents or linguistic surveys (such as the one conducted by Grierson during 1888-1902), in spite of all diversities, the pressure of living together for thousands of years has created 'India as a linguistic area'—something that was proposed by Emeneau (1958) and supported by further evidence by many, including Colin Masica (1985), Peter Hook (1988), K.V. Subbarao (1984) and Anvita Abbi (1991, 1994 and 2006) but something that was latent in the research findings of Suniti Kumar Chatterji from his ODBL-days (1926: Origin and Development of the Bengali Language), evidenced later in Chatterji (1951). Therefore, linguistically, too, India is one and many at the same time.

What happens to a seemingly contradictory configuration such as India with many centres—each one with its own peripheries, when English is introduced as a medium of modern expressions and learning? That should be an interesting question. But for a scholar of English or large nation-states with ingrained singularity such as Germany or France, one may wonder how does one manage to live in a plural world!

My answer to the above questions will have to begin with further questions: Isn't it wonderful to live in a plural world? Yes, it is. But let us ask ourselves: What kind of world is this? Is it a world of hope, or a world full of despair? Is it a world in which only rivers flow or is it a place where the mountain blows its conch loud and clear? Can there be a place for both, the stationary and the hyper-mobile, the young and the old, or the aged and the agile? But why do you ask, you might say. Didn't our poets say:

'The river runs swift with a song, breaking through all barriers. But the mountain stays and remembers, and follows her with his love.' [1]

Even when we talk of streams, and claim to be in the mainstream, or at least, swear by it, where are the other streams—those numerous torrents and tributaries? Do the edges, the periphery, have a story to tell? Those who have by now got into a habit of staying only in their cocoons, can they narrate a tale of places far and wide?

Let me further ask: Do we live in a world where the alphabet begins with an 'I' and end with another? Or, say, begins with an 'a' (for *ahaM*) and ends with another 'a' (*asmaakaM*)—where there is no scope for othering? Or, is there a scope for you? Are we forgetting the fact that the creative moment comes only when the I and the you—the *ahaM* and the *tvam*—begin to mould each other? The poet admits,

'When I thought I would mould you, an image from my life for men to worship, I brought my dust and desires and all my coloured delusions and dreams.

When I asked you to mould with my life an image from your heart for you to love, you brought your fire and force, and truth, loveliness and peace.'[2]

Let I and you merge into a 'we'. Talking about us, in India, we have had a rich and long experience of living together. Those who ruled at the regional as well as supra-regional levels have also had interesting experiences in managing our multilingualism. No doubt there have been both tamed and wicked problems of managing this plural space. While tamed and tameable problems have had their resolutions, there are many wicked problems that are still dodging any attempt to solve, however well-meaning the attempts may be. Coupled with that, there has been interesting interplay of different formations. The politics of planning and execution of policies have been as interesting as the socio-political forces that any effort of this gigantic size has to learn to deal with.

Many other developing nations are now trying to learn from the Indian experience in managing our pluricultural and multilingual scenario. The time has now come to document many of these problems in the area of language management as well as consider situations across our spaces which pose problems for social engineers. However, any attempt to prepare an archaeology of living traditions of these large number of languages in the developing and under-developed world has to remember the enormity of this task and the interesting theoretical challenges they throw up for our disciplines.

The last five decades in the life of our nation has seen numerous language problems in different parts of the country and different solutions offered to them. Some problems have arisen from denial of basic language rights to minor and minority speech communities while others sprang up from control over scarce resources in a situation where different linguistic groups lived together. While some communities have been linguistically tolerant to others, some have demonstrated what seems to be puzzling prejudice towards others. Studies have revealed interesting linguistic attitudes that a given sub-group has towards others within a speech community. To summarise—linguistic fanaticism has been on the rise.

Compare this scenario with a recent prediction by a bio-mathematician called Pagel that, out of 6,000 odd distinct human languages spoken all over the world, only 10 per cent will survive the first half of this new century. Given that the developing and under-developed countries house close to 90 per cent of this stupendous figure, it portrays a bleak picture for many of our languages and their speakers. With these languages, their rich cultural heritage—as much as they are preserved through their speech behaviour—will also disappear. I need to know, whether it is multiple norms of standard formation spread over a large space as in the case of Marathi or Konkani, or the question of multiple socially determined stylistic standards (such as *saadhu* and *calit* in Bengali, or the *graanthika-vyaavahaarika* distinction in Bengali), or the question of graphemic plurality (as mentioned earlier in respect of Sindhi, Punjabi and Kashmiri), India seems to be full of these fluctuating centres. Even in fields such as mass media—say, in the case of newspaper penetration and distribution, or in television channels and their popularity ratings, domination of any one or two languages may seem to be ruled out.

Although there are other parameters such as flow of translation traffic, viewership of films as well as their distribution network, market value of anchors, actors and tele-personalities as well as the relative price of books, and their print-run, often tell us conflicting stories on this aspect of what kind of space a given language occupies. Further, since most of our major languages have both static and dynamic speech areas (e.g. Gujarati is spoken largely in Gujarat but is also spread over in Maharashtra, Rajasthan, Madhya Pradesh, and even in Tamil Nadu), and as each one is used as a link language to build bridges, it will be difficult to imagine that either English or Hindi in India will occupy the central place it would have in less pluralistic nation-states. It is not just the plurality of languages (which may be the case in Indonesia, for instance where over 300 speech varieties are spoken, and yet where the language planners have been able to implement a planned domination of the Bahasa Indonesia) which is responsible for this state of affairs, but the dynamics of languages in India that are in the periphery. In fact, there are both centripetal and centrifugal forces in operation in India in the context of politics of language. It is often the case that the displaced speakers of one language community live like a diasporic group in another part of India for a certain period, and then become a part of the local scene. The Saurashtri weavers in Tamil Nadu or Bengali diamond cutters in Surat are both enmeshed in the local fabric of Tamil and Gujarati speech communities, respectively because of such interplay of interesting forces.

The picture, of late, gets further complicated because of the emergence of numerous literary languages from what once was considered to be 'periphery'. Their variety and vitality—despite the attempted dominance of a neighbouring language locally, and the two national official languages—are both refreshing and new developments. There is no doubt about the literary potential of languages from 'another' India, and the activities in Bhojpuri, Bodo, Garo, Khasi, Kurmali, Lushai, Magahi, Maithili, Nepali, and Santali, etc, and the reference and connections they make with the mainstream media of literary expression can be easily pointed out. It is not surprising to see them write this way:

I don't mind being drenched in sweat!
At least I don't have to please others!
True, I get to eat only half as much as I can,

Get to wear half of what I need, or eat half as much!
But I don't have to be under the pressure of a king!
May have to repair shoes or polish them
But at least I don't have to put the shoes on Sahib's legs!
Let me not even touch apples, or eat grapes
But at least I don't have to call tamarinds 'mangoes'!
Let me speak with eyes and breathe through the skin,
But let me not be forced to speak up
Only to tell you—
in a foreign language, 'I love you!'[3]

When we talk of the dynamics of centripetal and centrifugal forces in operation in India, we find that the problem of what occupies the centre-stage becomes a real problem on more than one count. We know of only the written mode of expression as all other media that draw our attention today (films, television and newspaper included) discuss mainly those who *can* and *do* write. But India has a vast reservoir of the 'Spoken world' which has only one focus: the centrality of the spoken word. They know that all the poetry that gets formed...all the songs that get sung are the products of the teeming millions of illiterate people (who in our definition will be called 'uneducated'). Consider what another unknown poet from Bhojpuri says:

I am looking for poetry!
My belly is full,
And I have dressed up well
With a shirt of the latest design,
As I sit in a new house!
But there's this man
In dire hunger
Whose back n' belly look alike;
On whose head will burst
The sky above – crashing down,
And from under whose legs
Will flee the ground,
Realities–

That's where sits the poem,
That's where![4]

When we talk of the 'spoken world', which lies far away from the centre of 'literary stage', we need to appreciate a few concerns that the inhabitants of such worlds have. The written words are defined by 'text', but how do we look at the author of spoken texts? Are they similar or definable in the same way? Perhaps not. When we talk about the ethics of speech, and the violence that are often to be withstood by those on the margin, are we concerned with the relationships that obtain among the majority and the minority speech communities? Or, are we defining the relationship between these authors of two different kinds, and their words? Or, between their words and the real world?

Where does today's author stand in all these? Is the author standing on a one-way street? Is it a path where none is allowed to get 'lost'—everyone has a pre-ordained trajectory to follow? Do we have pre-defined 'imperatives', or can we 'impure' our interlocutors in as many ways as we can think about? If we are free, how free are we? What awaits the author of written texts in the next crossroad—a surprise? Or, a direction board? Or, a set of icons the meanings of which are to be discovered if one were to move further? How different are authors of the spoken texts? All these factors of speech pose a strange paradox before us:

- *The author*, as we all know, complains of the tyranny of words. But the authors of the spoken world love and respect words...which are more important than anything scribbled on a piece of paper.
- I suppose, *the words* too must have their own set of complaints. But where would they turn to—to let them be known? *The critics* are unable to reopen the body of a word to know about the shame it has had to bear with, the vices it had committed or the virtues it had itself been unaware of. In short, a word is often unwilling to reveal herself before a critical eye—before someone who lacks empathy.
- *The readers* of written texts are often unwilling to travel halfway through to meet the authors, and hence are unable to grasp the import of numerous words and usages. In comparison, the listeners

of the spoken texts empathise with those who sing them out...they often interchange their roles, and it becomes a communication.

- *The commentators, interpreters,* and *translators* of written words have this dilemma of being twice removed from the text—first, in terms of medium or language, and secondly, in terms of creativity. (It is a different matter that for all that this community has done in the few thousand years of the history of civilisation, the translators are more misunderstood and underrated than anyone else.)

As linguists, we are often tied by this paradox that we have to deal with, namely, the urge of being committed to the primacy of speech over writing, and yet be concerned with written texts like true philologists. Then there is this urge of trying to track down and image the internalised rules of the mental grammar of an ever elusive 'native speaker', and yet be aware that language keeps on changing from one moment to the next, and Saussurean 'synchrony' is, therefore, a mirage. I guess what we need is a different kind of linguistics to appreciate the world of spoken languages and their own mechanics.

Even though a sociolinguist would say that a community would get the grammar it deserves, the statement is useful only in the context of writing communities who occupy the centre-stage. What does the grammar do to words there? First, grammars define the texts and their contexts. Grammars also author patterns that weave newer and newer expressions—constructs that are possible but are not normally available. They also demarcate the boundary that authors are expected to confine to. Any form of grammatical violation—purposeful or otherwise—is considered to be a deviation from the norm—a challenge our authors like to accept so as to redefine these norms. But such challenges are often projected as defiance against the tyranny of linguistics, because literature (which is often equated with 'written' literature) is generally viewed as a liberating force.

Does it mean that literary studies will only look at the centre, leaving the periphery to linguistics and anthropology to explore? Here comes the other kind of diversity we need to tackle. Knowledge in the twentieth century has been specialised into a tremendous set of semi-autonomous sub-disciplines, each trying to outsmart the other and occupy the centre-stage of our intellectual tradition, at the cost of even severing its relationship with others. We love to imagine that physics and psychology have nothing in common, just as many think—erroneously though, that linguistics and logic are miles apart.

Further, there has somehow emerged a naive belief that it is the sciences that occupy the centre and all other softer disciplines the periphery. It must be the sciences that should aim at providing conceptual tools to grasp this world of differences, changes, emergent processes and somehow present a coherent picture in which crucial differences between physical, biological, psychological and sociological processes can all be seen within a single ontology.[5]

But recall that in the tradition of Charles Sanders Peirce's semiotics, as stated by the early twentieth century, when sciences were less fragmented than today, one could see an attempt being made to bridge the gap between specialised disciplines, and to investigate what might be called the evolutionary semiotics of energy. Peirce (1892) in his essay "Man's Glassy Essence" from *The Monist* (vol.3, p.1-22), writes about matter as something not completely dead, but rather mind hidebound with habits:

> 'Hence, it would be a mistake to conceive of the psychical and the physical aspects of matter as two aspects absolutely distinct. Viewing a thing from the outside, considering its relation of action and reaction with other things, it appears as matter. Viewing it from the inside, looking at its immediate character as feeling, it appears as consciousness. These two views are combined when we remember that mechanical laws are nothing but acquired habits, like all the regularities of mind, including the tendency to take habits, itself; and that this action of habit is nothing but generalization, and generalization is nothing but spreading of feelings.'[6]

It is hard for us even today to understand all aspects of Peirce's position, which may sound like a peculiar form of objective idealism. Without digressing too much on this yet another kind of debate on centre and periphery, let me say that we need to bring down the disciplinary boundaries that have arisen of late, mostly due to our ignorance, between language and literature, between literature and fine arts, or between 'static' and 'performing' arts, if we were to appreciate the creativity that emerges from the margin.

I am reminded of the interesting allegory that Tagore, the artist, performer, literary person and linguistician—all rolled into one, narrates in the following lines:[7]

> 'The lofty building lies in the dust and all is scattered and broken.
>
> Mind looked about. But what was there to see?
>
> Only the morning star and the lily washed in dew.
>
> And what else? A child running laughing from its mother's arms into the open light.
>
> 'Was it only for this day that they said it was the day of the coming?'
>
> 'Yes, this was why they said there was music in the air and light in the sky.'
>
> 'And did they claim all the earth only for this?'
>
> 'Yes', came the answer, 'Mind, you build walls to imprison yourself. Your servants toil to enslave themselves; but the whole earth and infinite space are for the child and for the new life.'
>
> 'What does the child bring you?'
>
> 'Hope for all the world and its joy.'
>
> Mind asked me, 'Poet, do you understand?'
>
> 'I lay my work aside,' I said, 'for I must have time to understand.'

I guess time has come for all of us to try and understand each other. Understand what living is like, in the plural world.

Endnotes

1. Tagore, Rabindranath, 1913. The Gift, in The Crescent Moon, In Das, S.K., ed. *The English Writings of Rabindranath Tagore, vol 1: Poems*. 1994: 153.
2. ibid, 1916. Fruit gathering 33, pp 168.
3. From Ashtabhuja Shukla 2000 'But' published in *'Paatii', Indian Literature* tr. from Bhojpuri by Udaya Narayana Singh.
4. From Brij Bhushan Mishra 2000 'The Poem', *Indian Literature* tr. from Bhojpuri by Udaya Narayana Singh.
5. Emmeche et al. 1997.
6. CP 6.268.
7. Cf. The Fugitive, ibid., 1921, pp. 259-260.

India adrift: Great Power Aspiration Without Grand Strategy

—Ninad D Sheth

The story of India's search for a strategy that defines its security needs and serves its national interest is one of incoherence and disconnect. For Liddle Hart, strategy is a '...purposeful employment of all instruments of power available to a security community'.

The Indian state has failed to either articulate a strategy or demonstrate strategic intent in the conduct of its policy. The result is a country failing time and again to match capability with intention and translating military heft into diplomatic outcome. Facile grandstanding and incomprehension has replaced achievable results in the pursuit of national interest.

Some of the reasons for this failure are well known. A Hindu way of looking at time where planning has no real meaning and everything is transient means India neither records history well nor plans for the future in any substantial manner. A cocooned sense of sub continental security derived from geography especially—the Himalayan mountain range is another factor that has influenced absence of strategy in India's security and external affairs.

While these aspects certainly hinder a 'security system' that serve as building blocks of strategy they are not by themselves enough to explain the glaring inadequacy of a country that has been unable to secure either its citizen or frontier.

The real reasons for the Indian elephant seemingly lost in a hostile forest lie elsewhere. These can be located in three primary aspects. The first is an emasculated approach to diplomacy. The second is its colonial legacy and post colonial experience, where non violence was the starting point and democratic institutions dominated the military. The third is a lack of understanding of the world as it really is. An idealist approach based on a false sense of the 'self' has contributed to a security posture that looks self-righteous at best and absurd at worse.

In the absence of any strategy, India has seen an approach to security affairs that is delusional and reactive. When confronted with choices and pressed for action this approach has repeatedly allowed the adversary the advantage of initiative and resulted in a sort of 'reverse strategy' where India has had to adjust to developments in its littoral and beyond rather than pushing for its own security agenda.

Emasculated Diplomacy

Without strategy you have only bluff and bluster. For India, alas this cocktail has had disastrous results. India has ceded too much and gained too little, not in the field of battle, but the small print emerging from the diplomatic table. It is as if when sitting across eyeball to eyeball Indians feel inadequate. Freud would have loved to put Indian negotiators including some Prime Ministers on the couch. What has been termed as strategic restrain in Indian diplomatic history has actually been amateurish and feeble statecraft.

The years since independence have given enough instances for those who are interested in diplomacy to ponder how India has crumbled when it came to taking any tough decision. It is an ugly picture when looked at in retrospect. The first test came early, when Nehru, who thought rather highly of himself as a statesman in the imperial mould, decided to go to the United Nations for a ceasefire even as Indian forces were winning the 1948 Kashmir War on the ground. Time was on India's side with its fast mobilising armed forces and the discovery by Pakistani tribal attackers that Kashmir was not in mutiny mould as they had hoped. Yet, an anxious and emasculated Nehru preferred to internationalise the Kashmir issue rather than fight it out on the ground. These were early signs of a confused nation unable to stand up and deliver where it really matters—on the battlefield and seeking outside help to get it out of hotspots.

India's quick and total acceptance of the Chinese occupation of Tibet also happened under Nehru's watch. Not just that, he also surrendered all of the inherited imperial trading privileges in Tibet. In one stroke, he did away with a critical aspect of Imperial strategy—the creation of buffers between powers.[1]

That strategic myopia is bi-partisan was reflected almost fifty years later when the then Prime Minister Atal Bihari Vajpayee, a great orator in parliament during the 1962 War, shifted India's position on the status of Tibet when visiting china in 1992. The joint declaration was pointed in saying that there is only one China of which Tibet is a part. Thus India shifted its long held position that Tibet is an autonomous region of China to recognising it as a part of China; the hope was that this will lead to a softening of the Chinese stand on the larger border issues. As subsequent events have shown the Chinese position has only hardened.

The third time India lost on the negotiation table what it won in war was even starker. After the 1965 war with Pakistan India gave up the Haji Pir Pass which was won with great courage and was of high tactical value at negotiations that followed the ceasefire in Tashkent. The hope was a moderation in Pakistan's behaviour which of course never happened.

The Simla Agreement is the most obvious example of India as the reluctant victor bereft of a strategy. The victory in 1971 left approximately 5,000 sq kilometers of territory and 93,000 prisoners of war in India's hand. Yet the Simla Agreement did not address a final peaceful solution for India and left the Kashmir question open.[2] Nietzsche's famous axiom 'freedom from what' and 'freedom for what' is at the heart of any strategy. Strategic freedom by itself is nothing.[3] It has to be married to long term objectives that require a thought out set of options on a grid that form the security superstructure. At Simla in 1972 India did not know what to do with its victory and how to protect its long term interests. Two fallouts from that debacle happened within half a decade—Pakistan launched a vigorous terror campaign in Kashmir to ensure it did not have to fight another head on war with India. It also started its quest for the nuclear bomb to bring strategic parity in the sub continent. The blitzkrieg like victory in 1971 was thus brought to a grinding halt by the Simla Agreement. There is no parallel of a war winner giving up so much for so little anywhere in history.

More recently, the complete absence of strategy was brought home by the war in Kargil. In India the Kargil War is celebrated as a victory. The truth is Pakistan lost little in the war. A major gain for Pakistan was that it tested India's nuclear restrain. Its strategic decision was proved to be correct that even a frontal assault in Kashmir will not provoke a nuclear reaction from India or for that matter even a conventional one beyond the confined theatre. This is a major strategic lesson that Pakistan learned from Kargil. It was evicted from the high mountains but India was unable to escalate the conflict there by validating Pakistan's viewpoint that the nuclear balance of terror will allow the Islamic republic tactical flexibility.

Thus post-Independence history of India's diplomacy underlines that India does not have leadership calibre, institutional capability or coherent strategy to pursue its national interest.

Colonial legacy and post colonial experience in diplomacy

India is unique in its self image, and to an extent experience, of having 'won' its independence through non-violent means. This experience has contributed to its inability to employ a strategy that can peruse coercion as a means to secure national interest.

The Indian National Congress moved away from armed resistance as an option under the leadership of the Mahatma. This ensured that India achieved its freedom without resorting to arms. For Indian foreign policy this non-violent struggle left three important legacies. Firstly persuasion replaced hard power. Mahatma Gandhi's work in South Africa and his anti-colonial legacy translated in an Indian 'voice' across the Third World a rhetorical streak unique among developing nations replacing appreciation of self interest.

Lastly, pacifism dictated a subordinate role for the Indian military in public affairs. In fact till the massive defeat in the 1962 War it was not uncommon for Indian defence production factories to churn out consumer goods like coffee grinders instead of their original job of producing weapons. In Indian higher defence decision making the Armed Forces have very little direct involvement. Chiefs of the Armed Forces are not even present in critical cabinet committee on security deliberation and this ensures that unlike in China and Pakistan the Armed Forces are one step away from decision making even in times of war. This hinders both operational conducts in war time and strategic planning in peace.

The Indian attempt at creating space in foreign affairs through its policy of Non-alignment also has its origin in the freedom struggle. The policy of not aligning with either the USA or the USSR did little good for India. A non-aligned India did not amount for much till the late sixties simply because India had little influence of substance in world affairs. Non-alignment was shorn of its utility within twenty years of independent India—though it continued as the dominant rhetoric for many more decades and has lately resurfaced as a policy option![4] The first break from Non-alignment came in the mid-1960s when India's third way was exposed in the most humiliating of circumstances. The country had to seek massive food aid from the United States under the PL 480 program to avoid mass starvation. This signalled to the world that India's room for independent diplomacy was limited.

A few years later, in 1971, with the prospect of a war with Pakistan, India did the second significant U turn from its cherished goal of an autonomous foreign policy by securing a 'friendship' treaty with the USSR. The treaty assured India of top end weapons from the Soviet Union as well as significant diplomatic support in international avenues such as the UN Security Council.

One of the great mysteries of Indian foreign policy has been the long freeze in India's relations with the United States. Given the role that the US played during and just after the World War in nudging the UK to grant India independence, this is all the more surprising. President Roosevelt was determined to cut the British Empire to size by the middle of the Second World War. What better place to start than taking the jewel of the imperial crown, India, out. Although Churchill avoided the 'Independence' option for as long as he could, the fact that the balance of sterling payments had turned against the United Kingdom and diplomatic efforts from Washington were as much of a contributing factor for India's independence—if not more—as the struggle led by the Mahatma.

In Indian public discourse very little attention focuses on to the three international developments that were as critical as the non-violent struggle that led to India's independence. The success of Nazi Germany in weakening Britain to the point of exhaustion was the first. The second was borrowing in sterling from India to finance the British war effort. Lastly American moves that were aimed at reducing the scope of the British Empire.[5]

This is easily explained by the fact that the Indian National Congress could hardly give foreigners credit for India's Independence. Sadly for the formulation of a strategy, these foreign influences found relegation to the dominant myth of India winning freedom through non violence. India has failed its countrymen by relegating the full impact of international relations and the Second World War in securing even if by default, her freedom to footnotes. This was replaced by the myth of a non-violent freedom struggle as the dominant narrative. The result is a strongly held conviction that India attained her freedom in a vacuum almost as if the non-violent struggle for independence forced Britain's hand. Contemporary historians shy away from taking note of the role played by circumstances that led to India's freedom. The connection between Dunkirk in 1941 leading up to India's tryst with destiny in 1947 awaits academic reconstruction. Had the foreign circumstances been given their due, India could have learned an early lesson of cooperating with bigger powers through alignment rather than vainly attempting to create space for itself within the superstructure which at that point in history would have afforded much larger diplomatic leeway.

The world is what it is—India as a status quo power

The good thing about strategy is that a nation determined to pursue its self interest can find it to be a very simple exercise. Over the near term horizon, India has very clear security imperatives.

The first security imperative is to sustain its relatively rapid economic growth; the second is to manage the fallout from a nuclear armed Pakistan that still considers pursuit of terror as State policy. Pakistan is also complicated because structural pressures within the Islamic Republic could spiral out of control and will need management. The third major challenge to India comes from the People's Republic of China with the unresolved border being the major cause for a possible outbreak of hostilities.

The imperial Indian ambition of a zone of influence from Aden to Singapore has not been translated into a strategic capability that can influence this natural geographic span. India has shrunk as an inspirational power in the absence of a grand strategy. The country recessed into a strategy by default—this is to ensure status quo; this far and no further is India's current security bottom-line. This is a narrow parameter and by itself this is no strategy. On all vital requirements a status quo approach to power will lead to poor diplomatic choices, especially one which is not already a part of a system—like the permanent members of the Security Council. For instance on Siachen, India cannot negotiate if it wants to convert the Line Of Control into actual border that by definition will need to include all of Jammu & Kashmir.

Status quo mindset also has bearing on the dangerous nuclear weapon equilibrium in South Asia. Foreign experts watching India's nuclear posture have come to the conclusion that India has a weapons posture that is not only minimal but also far from ready for operation at short notice; thus nuclear weapons are seen as political rather than military in scope.[6]

In nuclear deterrence it is unclear how India's no first use option and the so called minimum deterrence helps. It cannot deter Pakistan with a threat of an overwhelming second strike for the simple reason that Pakistan's strategy of a nuclear first strike is rooted not in nuclear weapons asymmetry with India but instead in its shortcoming in standing up to a conventional armed attack from India.

Besides any decision maker from Pakistan will consider nuclear capability not a declaration of intent to determine response. Thus instead of helping reduce nuclear danger, the declaration of no first use of nuclear weapon actually increases it. The declaration maybe rooted in India's long held approach to nuclear weapons but has clearly outlasted its utility.

The credibility of a no first use of nuclear weapons pledge vis a vis China is also unlikely to work given China's massive lead in nuclear strike capability. China will assume that it makes strategic sense for India to strike first should the Chinese be winning in a conventional war or to avoid nuclear annihilation of a Chinese first strike.

No first use is also politically amoral in a democracy. It exposes the citizens who elect a government to possible nuclear annihilation. This amounts to abdicating the safety of the citizens, the sacred duty of any elected government. To say that in the face of a nuclear aggressor we will wait for an annihilating crippling strike that could kill millions and only strike later is untenable morally as well as politically in a democratic setup. Should this ever become an election issue one can be sure that the nuclear no first use will be abandoned by the politicians.

India has also done a recent puzzling strategic miscalculation by announcing a ballistic missile defence shield as part of its nuclear weapons strategy. By so doing India is signalling to the world that it does not mind raising the nuclear stakes. The missile shield is not only a largely untested scheme, it will act as a turbo charger for a nuclear arms race with Pakistan in particular feeling the need for a greater number of nuclear weapons. No first use doctrine when coupled with a ballistic defence shield increases the likelihood of the sub-continent having many more nuclear weapons which will defeat the purpose of India's so called minimum nuclear deterrent.

Recalibrating Strategy: Towards an alliance of maritime democracies

India's current security needs are not being met by the drift in strategic thinking. India needs nothing short of a strategic revolution. The redrawing of strategic parameters call for a complete overhaul of long held presumptions of security, if India is to address its defence concerns and strategic priorities.

With a belligerent and totalitarian China to the northwest and a Jihad terror oriented nuclear powered Pakistan to the east, India is clearly in the most dangerous neighbourhood in the world.

Four options need to be debated and developed for securing Indian interests. The foremost is a strategic alignment with maritime democracies around the world led by the United States to replace any Non-alignment that India may have fancied in international relations.

Secondly India needs to shift its military emphasis from a continental approach to a maritime one.

Thirdly, India needs to consolidate and develop an indigenous military industrial complex that can over time wean it away from its dependence on foreign vendors for its arsenal.

Fourthly, the Indian military needs to be accommodated in apex strategic decision making.

This reorientation in strategic outlook will create space for India to execute its national interest priorities. They will also come with new risks particularly vis a vis the likely Chinese reaction. One thing is certain—the old ways of being a constrained status quo conscious power are over. The world has changed and the old approach could lead to disastrous errors of judgment in international relations and constrain the space for making a viable choice for securing India.

That there is very little new thinking in foreign policy is obvious from a recently discussed report called 'Non Alignment 2.0'. The report stressed wrongly that India must continue with a fiercely independent streak in foreign policy and not align with either China or the USA in the emerging world order. This is not going to workt for the simple reason that India does not have strategic capability, military ability or economic power to go it alone. The space that India craves for independence is nonexistent.

India will do much better to forge an alliance of maritime democracies across the world led by America. As things stand India's historic nuclear pact with the USA was a step forward however from intelligence sharing on terrorism to sharing of dual use technology to sticking points like Iran there is a trust deficit between the two great democracies. For India there is the additional issue of the US approach to Pakistan. For any India-US alignment to really take off, Washington will have to press Pakistan harder on its use of terrorism as state policy against India. Some commentators have blithely written that the US should simply ignore India's concern vis a vis Pakistan.[7]

Fortunately, US policy is slowly moving in the other direction as the full scope of a duplicitous Pakistan emerges. This is especially so because the same groups that began by threatening India—such as the Lashkar-e-Taiba—now directly threatens US homeland security. The greatest challenge for both countries is to evolve this critical engagement to a full scale alignment of interests in International affairs through a committed bilateral partnership that can in time evolve into a multilateral security institution. A lot of political capital was accumulated to make the India-US nuclear treaty a reality and it ought to be compounded with new security alignments to give the relationship lasting depth.

The traditional impediments for better relations between the USA and India are slowly giving way. Largely on account of economic cooperation, anti Americanism is a thing of the past. India is already a large recipient of US weaponry and is cooperating in nuclear as well as civilian fields.[8]

However, within civil society in India, knee, jerk anti Americanism is still very much alive. Similarly, many thinktanks in Washington DC beltway and beyond still see India as an unreliable ally and occasionally demonstrate patronising attitudes ill suited when dealing with a nuclear weapon state that is a $1.7 trillion economy, growing at more than 6 per cent per year.

Genuine sticking points like India's approach on Iran makes it obvious that a closer and more meaningful alignment with the USA is a prospect with formidable diplomatic obstacles.

Strategy, by its nature requires the exercise of choice. It also calls for compromise between competing options. It evolves to adjust to new realties when an able leadership is determined to steer a new course to overcome challenges. In today's world the need for a greater convergence in diplomatic postures of the USA and India is the self evident big story of international relations. Writing this story will need statesmanship, it will need risk taking and most of all it will need a flexible approach that can over time lead to greater trust. These are hard tasks. Will both countries look beyond old structures; will they have the wherewithal to develop capacities in their respective societies? History is illustrative of many such alliances—one between Japan and the USA being a prime example. However, in that great engagement one was a victor and the other vanquished. No such situation exists between these two great democracies. For the lack of a better paradigm the need is to overcome narrow self righteousness and turn diplomatic efforts to focus on shared concerns. Time for this grand project in international relations—always so critical in strategy choices—is running out.

The second pillar of a new strategy could however mitigate some of these obstacles. There is a rare concurrence of interests between maritime democracies around the world. They look at the rise of China with suspicion and face a common goal of keeping globalised free trade running in the face of worldwide economic crisis. These countries also face the threat of radical Islamic extremism.

Both in geography and the capability parameter, the Navies of these countries have assets that could hinder China's new maritime ambitions. They could in addition influence events in the Arabian Sea littoral thereby ensuring that land locked Afghanistan does not get too belligerent. The architecture of this new maritime way will include the US fifth fleet in Bahrain, the seventh fleet in Diego Garcia, the Indian Navy, the Navies of Singapore, Thailand and the Philippine flanked by Australia and Japan.

This new alliance in whatever form that it can be nurtured will provide a strategic counter envelop for India to cope with the encirclement threat that India perceives from China. If the US is serious about its commitment to Asia this 'new NATO' will be the flagship.

India has very little to lose from such an engagement. With the relative decline of US power on the world stage India can play an important regional role, which will allow it to exert over time the imperial legacy of influencing a region from Aden to Singapore albeit within a cooperative superstructure. For this to happen, India will have to overcome its sea blindness. Ever since independence India has had a continental mindset. Its military emphasis has been on land warfare as reflected in a million plus manpower. The new strategic paradigm calls for exerting presence far beyond India's borders and the Indian Navy is ideally suited for this role. Although it has been slow, the maritime orientation in Indian defence is fast gaining in prominence. This is also in tune with India's need for a credible triad—submarine based nuclear strike capability.

Over the next decade India has ordered about forty ships of different sizes and four hundred aircrafts for its naval fleet. The acquisition of aircraft carriers from Russia as well as the leasing of a nuclear powered submarine added to the new P8i reconnaissance aircraft will give India vital elements of littoral sea control. What is most interesting about Indian Naval development is that while still dependent vastly on foreign vendors it is more indigenous in content when compared to its counterparts in the Army and the Air Force.

Cost and capability of two marquee programmers—the indigenously built nuclear submarine and an indigenous air craft carrier will go a long way in determining the scope, effect and range of India's new fondness for maritime assets.

The fourth pillar of the strategy to develop an Indian military industrial complex will also be critical. India is the world's largest importer of weapons.[9] Two thirds of all Indian defence equipment is procured from abroad. The procurements are often tangled in corruption allegations and are indefinitely delayed. For a country that has an 8000 range ballistic missile built in-house, it is embarrassing that everything from coffins to socks and bullets needs a global tender. India has a long record of reserving defence production for the public sector. This policy is now universally recognised as a massive failure. Instead of self reliance it has fostered a crippling dependence on foreigners for armaments. Some change is happening with India insisting on offsets for projects in excess of $300 million; however the offset policy demands too much too soon and as a result is gaining in too little. Some large Indian firms such as Larsen and Toubro, the Mahindras, the Tatas and Reliance are taking tentative steps towards entering defence production. Similarly smaller companies such as Samtel Electronics are also making a mark. India will need a realistic offset clause and a focused national level push to incentivise private firms to enter weapons production. Without an indigenous weapon making capability it will be difficult for India to evolve a truly independent defence policy.

The final critical aspect of building a new strategy will involve accommodating the Armed Forces in the top decision making structure of Indian security system. As things stand the top military brass is not a part of decision making and is rarely invited to the cabinet committee on security; the Apex decision making body. What is more India has a curious diarchy where the party president has more power than even the prime minister of the day. In Pakistan, the army runs defence policy; in China, the PLA is integrated with the politburo—India is alone in a situation where the Armed Forces have to carry out orders without the flexibility of giving input at the highest level. If this does not change—and fast—India will remain constrained in its command and execution of war plans.

As it looks to secure its future, India confronts difficult choices of formulating a strategy that will serve it in the new multi polar order. The ability to formulate this strategy will ultimately depend on its leadership calibre, economic growth and understanding of self interest. The time has come for a radical strategic reorientation. It remains to be seen if India can grasp the challenge. A strategic inertia could lead to a rude surprise akin to the loss in 1962 China War. It is surprising how little strategic options are discussed in the country's public domain. In an otherwise boisterous democracy, this silence bodes ill for the long term.

Endnotes

1 For a detailed account of how lack of strategy contributed to the 1962 war with China read *Aksai Chin and the Sino Indian Conflict* by John Lall, Allied Publishers, New Delhi 1989.

2 For a fascinating account of How India's negotiation strategy developed post 1971 war read P N Dhar *Indira Gandhi and the Emergency* Oxford University press 2001.

3 Twilight of the Idol Friedrich Nietzsche richer polt translator June 1997 Hackett publishing.(first published 1889).

4 Non alignment 2.0 a foreign and strategic policy for India in the twentieth century published by Centre for Policy Research New Delhi, 2012.

5 For a detailed analyses of the role played by international relations in speeding up India's independence read *Shameful Flight the Last Years of the British Empire in India* by Stanely Walport, Oxford University Press, October 2 2006.

6 This is the central point of a book by Ashly Tellis "*India's emerging nuclear posture.*" RAND corporation 2001.

7 This point is made by Stephen Cohen and Sunil Dasgupta in "Arming without aiming India's military modernization", The Brookings Institution 2010.

8 For a recent interesting take on India US relations read "Failure 2.0" by Sadanand Dhume, *Foreign Policy* March 16 2012.

9 Stockholm International Peace Research Institute 2011 yearbook.

In the Chicken's Neck

—Sumana Roy

'Chicken's neck' is a phrase that is bound to put vegetarians off. But for those who live inside it, as flies do in ears of cows, it is not a matter of choice; or ethics. Birds inside cages don't sing freedom songs. Honestly, they don't even care.

As we don't.

I live in the Chicken's Neck—the Siliguri Corridor—a stretch of land that connects India's north-eastern states to what is called its 'mainland'. It's a narrow strip of land, varying between twenty and forty kilometers in width, with the countries of Nepal and Bangladesh lying on either side of the Corridor. Like most children growing up in small towns, we were just happy to see our town live as a forgotten acne mark in the map of our country. Growing up increased its sense of importance—just as a parent gradually becomes a surname, my small town came to become a metaphor, on the map and otherwise. From dot, a prick of indifference, it became a 'Corridor', an architectural term for passageways, for barter and flight, a collapsing of all divisions. For corridors always connect. But 'Neck'? Necks are corridors too, but so often, things get stuck there, as do fish bones and people, when both transgress and become illegal immigrants in that space.

Growing up at a time when air travel had still not become inexpensive, plane journeys were rare picnics that stand out in our maps of childhood. Most often, we had to be content with watching planes take off from airports on television. One such occasion was an advert for the airline Cathay Pacific. I knew the words of the male voiceover by heart: 'Today people travel between countries as they once did between cities…' and so it went. I failed to understand why travelling to countries was considered more important than travelling to cities. I lived in a town where I could reach Bangladesh and Nepal in about ninety minutes. Calcutta, the nearest city, was six hundred kilometers away. Bhutan was four hours by car on a mountainous road, and China, always the eyebrow to the eye, never too far off, certainly not from a weekend's getaway to the neighbouring state of Sikkim, only a hundred kilometers by a road that runs parallel, for most of the journey, to the beautiful emerald river Teesta.

How, then, does it feel to live in a place—and 'corridor' is only a spatial euphemism—which is enclosed by *international* borders on all sides?

Here the border's water

The Indo-Nepal border is a bit of an oxymoron: there is, at least to the eye, no border. But borders everywhere are perhaps like that—they are marks that birds can't see, grazing cows can't sense, and which men hunt for only as symbols on their children's maps. The only things that can recognise borders are perhaps automobiles —like women in burqas who lift their veils only in familiar places, thus carrying two sets of faces, cars acquire new numbers—and number plates—at borders. At least, at the Indo-Nepal border.

As National Highway 31 wriggles itself out of the mess that is the city, it becomes shyer, losing girth at first and then, in the presence of yellowing green paddy and maize fields, and carpets of tea gardens on either side, it becomes almost adventurous. In no time, Naxalbari arrives, the place that gave its name to the violent Maoist uprising by labourers, first in Bengal, then in tribal pockets all over the country. When I first visit it, it's an unremarkable village town, where not a souvenir survives of that violent movement of the late nineteen seventies; a string of English medium schools, with names that can come only from taking a crash course in Christianity, lead us into town, and this is followed by an ageing officious looking building that announces itself as the police station. It's painted brick red and when my brother and I make a joke about the colour of the paint being the only survivor of that era, my father gives us an admonishing look. We wait for him to tell us about Charu Mazumdar, the revolutionary who started it all, but he doesn't. My mother is relieved: she's heard the story one time too many. I have too, without anyone telling. For when one of my favourite professors taught us E. M. Forster's *A Passage to India* in college, I sat there, half-listening to his lecture and thinking more about his father, the leader, now dead, allegedly killed in jail by the West Bengal police.

It is of *A Passage to India* that I think a little later, as we leave Naxalbari (my mother having lost any interest in the town for she, by her own admission, had come here looking for some 'museum of blood' as a memory of that bloody revolution) and its oldest school building that warns, 'Stick no bill', without, of course, in the style of all bureaucracy, specifying the punishment. Old abandoned mills and railway tracks, both complaining of neglect, are soon washed out of our sight as the car takes turns, in what seems to me a method in arbitrariness, and a signpost arrives. And we are relieved—for a few moments away from the written word scares us, this generation and its reliance on crutches of information.

Galgalia 20, Panitanki 5: it announces. Distances have begun to decrease, and as these names of places, the first onomatopoeic, mimicking the flow of water, and the other with the Nepali word for 'water' in it (*Pani*; a tank to hold water would be the literal meaning), arrive; the expectation's been abetted without our realising it. The border therefore arrives like poetry—sensed from afar, like the sound of water, its lost-world shine in the darkening afternoon, it is the fruition of anticipation. For we knew, without really knowing, that there was and always will be a border.

Aberration in the ritual of welcome in the age of paper verification: we need no passports for India's border with Nepal is 'porous', the men in uniform look at our faces and then at the colour of our car, and deeming both fit enough to cross into the neighbouring country, they show their assent by slapping our driver on the back. It is not a friendly pat. The poor fellow is startled, but he only asks, in the driver's cryptic, 'Ours or Theirs?'

'Ours, ours,' begins my mother without knowing. Then, as if further convincing was necessary, she points to their uniform in the rear view mirror, 'that's *our* uniform, can't you see?'

The confusion with binaries continues for this border's a coin with two faces: what was 'Security Check Post', we discover by looking back from the other side, is also *Swagat Dwar* (Welcome Gate). In the meantime, our car's acquired a new number plate for fifty rupees: the first three letters standing for Mechi in the Devanagiri script, followed by the number 1068. It's white on a square green plate, and for a reason that I will never understand, it seems to make our driver happy. The border, and all talk of it, is only optical rhetoric, my mother concludes, until we come to the Mechi.

Mechikhola: the sight of the unremarkable river, one that divides or joins, depending on one's late perspective, makes my brother throw an eraser he was carrying in his pocket into it. It's a bit like a child's sacralia but my mother lets him off with a half-hearted scolding. And the Kali Bridge: unremarkable except for its name, which usually supplies the prefix to the name of a temple. We would have forgotten it altogether had not our driver taken his hands off the steering wheel and folded his hands into a prayer.

For after the intimidating signboards of the 'Department of Immigration, Kakarvita, Jhapa, Nepal', the conglomeration of polysyllabic words scaring us like obese dictionaries, and a casual survey of shops titled 'Impex' in Dhulabari (literally the house of dust), we buy only a packet of a candy called 'White Rabbit'. My brother and I chew it hard to see whether it tastes any different from candies in our country, and whether it really is the sweetmeat of Nepali rabbits, my parents fight a little as they usually do, whenever they are in a new place.

I have visited the Indo-Nepal border in Kakarvita many times since. I know that Indians who have chosen to live in Nepal are called *dhoti* while those who think of themselves as the *original* inhabitants of Nepal call themselves *topi* (the hat), thereby elevating their status through this clever sartorial symbolism. I have eaten many White Rabbits since too. I know that India is perhaps the only country in the world that has a regiment dedicated exclusively to a foreign country and that Nepali soldiers defend Indian borders against Pakistan.

And this, perhaps, is one of those rare instances where a border is a bridge, and a bridge a border.

Only I will never quite understand why there should be borders between the two countries. Perhaps like the white chalk-like academic marks on a Brahmin's forehead, they are necessary—a country's caste marks.

Here the border's land

My father's family came from Bangladesh to India in 1947. My father was born in August, just five days before independence. He likes to believe that he scared the British away. He has, expectedly, no memory of the place where he was born in but it is other things he 'remembers'. These are, of course, late acquisitions, like going through one's 'baby book' in adulthood, but these acquisitions are, in no way, innocent. They have made my father the person he is today.

First, a few of my father's *stories*: Bangladesh was then East Pakistan. My grandparents, young, almost illiterate, a child hanging from each of their necks, became 'Indians' overnight. They would never understand its significance, or even if they did, it was way too insignificant compared to what they thought they had lost. And that, by their account, was a lot—land, love, and lives. But they were not the only ones: this forced migration of people from one part of the sub-continent to another, all because a line would be drawn through farms and fields that had been theirs till yesterday, affected thousands like them. All their life, they tried to do what was expected of them—to forget, and in it, they failed miserably.

I grew up on stories of relatives being raped by neighbours who overnight, because of that accident of history, became 'Pakistanis', of gold being smuggled inside underwear, of houses burnt or occupied and taken by force. And yet, in spite of all this, my grandparents never ceased to believe that had they stayed on in what would later become Bangladesh, they would have been happier.

It irritated us, their stories, their attachment to something abstract and invisible, their indifferent acceptance of this new country's customs, and most of all, their lack of enthusiasm for the political systems here. They treated their ration cards with contempt, they paid taxes on their property unwillingly, and they reserved their praise for India (though I cannot remember them ever using the name; it was always 'this country'), however qualified it might have been, for another life.

It would have been a mixture of curiosity and contempt that made me ask my uncle to take me to Bangladesh. I must have been a child of nine or ten then, small enough to be carried, along with my brother, on a bicycle. We had no idea about passports and visas—the only paper we had any use for at that time in our lives were our annual report cards. And memories of those we left behind when we visited our grandparents in Hili, the tiny frontier village-town at the Indo-Bangladesh border.

It was supposed to be a secret, this visit to Bangladesh, a promise made to uncle. We combed our hair neatly and wore our best holiday dresses, not knowing all the while that a visit to Bangladesh would change us forever, that we would come back as different people. We were even scared, though it was only a joyous nervousness, that our parents might not be able to recognise us when we returned.

We didn't go too far. We couldn't go too far

After uncle had shown us houses where the border had divided the kitchen, so that the rice was cooked in Bangladesh but eaten in India, and 'Indian' cows grazing on Bangladesh land, an Indian husband with a Bangladeshi wife, jewellery shops selling Bangladeshi gold ornaments, things which might have interested adults but about which we felt not the slightest curiosity, he took us to the abandoned railway station. I still remember two rail tracks running parallel to each other, and the three of us holding hands and walking on it, until we came to another station. Two signposts, black on yellow, a few feet away from each other: Hili (India), Hili (Bangladesh).

Just as there are two Hilis, I like to believe that I had two sets of paternal grandparents, one I shall never meet, the people my Indian grandparents would have been had I been Bangladeshi. I do not think about it too often, but when I do, a few of my grandmother's afternoon stories come back to me. The stories haven't survived, only the fear that her ghosts from Bangladesh brought into my Indian summers still do. And her words, her joy at torturing her 'Indian' born grandchildren, 'In no country in the world would you find as many ghosts as you do in Bangladesh. And what their varieties…'

It was perhaps these ghosts that I wanted to see when I pleaded with my father to take me to the Indo-Bangladesh border one evening many years later. The Indo-Bangladesh border is less than an hour by road from where I live. Leaving the peak of the Kanchenjunga shining behind us in the November sun, my father drove through Fulbari (a suburb whose name literally means 'a house of flowers'), we took a road that we had never taken. In a few minutes, we had reached the border.

In Hili, I had seen and met Bangladeshi policemen who had shaken hands with me, I had seen Bangladeshi trains puffing dark smoke like old smokers, and I had met an old woman, hunched and toothless, whose words I did not understand, who my uncle said spent her day in India and night in Bangladesh. In Tinbatti, I saw nothing. I saw no one. The sky grew dark, then heavier. I waited. Even the ghosts didn't keep their appointment. My father switched on the headlights of the car and stood still. And yet, nothing happened. Nothing moved. That is my strongest memory of the Indo-Bangladesh border.

A dark and brooding silence. And a waiting for ghosts.

Here the border's a gate

Bhutan is one of the happiest countries in the world. I think I discovered this on television, in one of those rare moments when there was a temporary pause in the reporting and documentation of bloodletting on screen. It must have been a breather, something like the weather report, but what I remember having carried from that evening was the discovery—or was it creation?—of a new memory. Like a child doing a match-the-column exercise, I tried to excavate smiling Bhutanese faces, equating, as I had been taught, by whom I did not know, happiness with smiles and laughter. I made myself stand outside the beautiful open gate outside the Bhutanese city of Phuntsholing, its Buddhist designs of flowers and animals in white and blue and yellow on a red background. It is the only time I have seen a border as gate—perhaps it is this Zen-like indifference to entry and exit that explains the happiness of the people of this country. Or perhaps the concluding plea of their national anthem has been granted—May the people shine like the sun of peace and happiness!

Phuntsholing was an expensive city, and my father, a banker in a nationalised bank before economic liberalisation, could only afford to buy us pencils and sharpeners and water bottles, all three moulded in the childhood shapes of dolls and mice and generic animals. I have no memory of eating any meal in Phuntsholing, and I do not understand why that absence continues to occupy such a significant position in my memories about the country. Rolling the Buddhist prayer wheels, sitting on the lawns of its temples (an unfamiliar experience for a small town Hindu child like myself, who had never seen a temple with a lawn or garden—all these invisible spaces in Hindu worship, left vacant for playful gods!), waiting beside a queue while my father paid bills and bought tickets, and not for once being pushed or scolded by strangers as I would have been in India.

Pets, I have often heard being told, are like children, only they are children who never grow up. The relation between India and Bhutan has long been the relation between a pet and a child. One has grown up while the other has, like a pet, become more used to the domesticity of a life of dependence. Signs of this relationship survive in the names of places that took me from the Chicken's Neck to Bhutan.

Jaigaon is the last proper town on the Indian side of the border. Like all frontier towns, it is unremarkable, drawing as little attention to itself as ticket counters do in theatres. My father often came here on work, and the name of the town had thus gradually become a part of the family's consciousness. When I first learnt to sing the national anthem, and I must admit that I learnt it much later than children do these days, I began to think of it as the place from where the poetry and the song had emerged. Children's epiphanies are difficult to explain but its sincere corruptions are retrospective delights.

When I stood outside the Bhutan gate, as it is called, I held my brother's hand and burst into the anthem:

Jana Gana Mana Adhinayaka Jaya He

My parents, caught between confusion and fun, let me sing the entire song, and when, at last I arrived at the climax that I'd been waiting for, the crescendo of *Jaya He, Jaya He, Jaya He,* I began looking in two opposite directions, at what was in front of me—the Bhutan Gate—

and what lay behind, Jaigaon. There was a reason behind this: Jaigaon, I'd broken up into two parts—*Jai* and *gaon*. *Jai* means victory and *gaon* stands for village, together it is 'the village of victory'. The *Jaya He* of the national anthem, celebrating the conglomeration of states that India would become (for Rabindranath Tagore died before the British *idea* of India could become a reality), was an anticipatory and prophetic hailing of the United States of India, and the *jaya* in it was a felicitation and celebration of that idea. Goaded by mishearing, I had allowed Jaigaon, that town whose biography was to be a footstool to its country, to become a place from where these sounds of victory would erupt. *Jaya He, Jaya He*. But all around it, as if gagging those conch shells in the voice, was the kingdom of silence, the quietest country in the world. That is my most definitive memory of the Indo-Bhutan border, of leaving Bhutan and its border as I had found it—intact and unchanged. The people of the kingdom of Druk, because television was banned in that country then, had probably never even heard the national anthem of any other country besides theirs. While theirs celebrated their 'precious sovereign', ours did the 'Jana Gana'—the King of Druk versus the *janagana*, the public.

When I sat beside the window on a bus that would carry us back to the Chicken's Neck, I began to wish that I had brought a broom with which I could have swept away my footsteps and the trinket sounds of *Jaya He* back through the gate. And I learnt that open gates need not always signify openness. Gates, especially those that do not support hinges, are museums in their own right. They embalm divisions; they are living corpses of separateness. The Bhutan gate is, in that sense, the strictest border—it will allow no converts. No *Jaya He* for Buddha and Druk.

Here the border's a wall

Maps of India are Made-in-China. And both countries know that. And no one seems to mind. And...there could be a series of 'ands' after that, but like 'ands' which hold so much in balance, which link without dissolving, like straws and necks, the Chicken's Neck in the map of India looks less like a staircase and more like a temporary makeshift podium that could crumble and collapse during a stampede. And, like most 'ands', it has its double, its mirror opposite, as it were. For far away to its left, to its west, is the Pakistan Akhni Chicken's Neck, also called the Akhnoor Dagger, a narrow strip of Pakistani territory that extends into India, in the state of Jammu and Kashmir, the de-facto Indo-Pakistani border on the west side over which India now has control. Necks, therefore, are geographical metaphors that give the English expression 'stiff-necked' a completely new meaning.

For there's China

Gangtok, its name meaning a 'hilltop', is the capital of the Indian state of Sikkim. I have no memory of my first visit to the town. And even if I do, it's a pattern of repetition, as of spotting clouds in the sky so that one is never sure which cloud one began counting first. I did not know the meaning of *Gangtok* then. My brother and I, in a way that is common to children, broke up a word into possible Bengali components and looked for some hidden meaning in it. *Gang* we conveniently took to be the English word, that suffixed by *tok*, meaning 'sour' in Bengali. A rowdy violent group was fine, but how they could be 'sour' was difficult to explain, and so like children who had lost use for their toys just before falling asleep, gave up ownership of such an interpretation.

We found no gangs in Gangtok, and that was more disappointment than relief. So when the tourist guide told us that he would take us on, what he called a 'Seven Point' sightseeing tour, my brother and I took no time to conjure up an unfinished version of Enid Blyton's *Secret Seven gang*. Our dream had come true—the gang would at last be found. Whether it was sweet or sour was inconsequential.

Gangtok was—and is—a city-town. It is a city only in its ambition, in every other respect, it is like a small town schoolboy who thinks that kicking a ball into the goal makes him the best footballer in the world. One road runs through the town like a river, giving its buildings a social gradient and throwing into its sky a ribbon of afternoon conversation. This road is called M. G. Road, modern India's friendly colloquial for Mahatma Gandhi, the Father of the Nation, who, like Dhritarashtra, the father of a hundred sons in the epic *Mahabharata*, has given birth to a thousand streets and alleys and roads in the nation. Much later, when I would visit Gangtok again, in my early twenties, I would wonder how this tiny state, which was only as Indian in time as I was (both of us having been born as Indians in the mid 1970s), had chosen Gandhi to keep guard over the capital. Gandhi had been dead for more than a quarter of a century and the country, then trying hard to adjust to new ecosystems of power and a violent Naxalism, both of which were completely non-Gandhian, had turned the Mahatma into a mantra. Saying the word—the name—made the Indian feel powerful, even though it necessarily didn't. The M. G. Road in Gangtok must have found its name in the same spirit of self-fashioning.

It was, in many ways, ironic that we rode on Gandhi's back to see the Chinese border. What could we have expected to see? I cannot remember. I do remember what I felt years later when recording a voiceover for an Indian Air force video. Sweating in a tiny recording studio (the air-conditioner had stopped working and the whirring of fans would disturb the soundtrack), I'd watched the snow covered peaks of the Himalayas and learnt the names of a hundred different 'passes' that only men in uniform can spot. The blinding whiteness of snow and the absence of any human in the frame, except, of course, the invisible cameraman in the helicopter from where the film was being shot, had, for an instant, made me eager to spot what they technically called an 'infiltrator'. A Chinese infiltrator: I was curious for the sound of the word in the frame, it rhymed with traitor and I wanted to use it. I didn't get the chance to, for miles and miles of snow hid men and the boundaries of their land from themselves and from me. Nathu La Pass: the name of that pass, one of the legitimate entry points in the Sino-Indian border, so French and foreign, stayed with me. The 'La' and its fashionable twang, added to the allure of border crossings.

When my father raised his children on his shoulders, the twin rounded peaks of our heads the mouth of periscopes eager to swallow all sights in view, the three of us and my short mother standing on her toes looking in the direction advised by the tourist guide, what did we really expect to see? Where? Where? The air was nervous with tourists' queries—where really was the border? The mist gathered over our heads, our earlobes stung from the sharp scratching cold wind, but we stood there clinging to wet straws of hope.

'Where's the border?' someone asked again.

'Neil Armstrong saw it from the moon, and you can't see it ten feet away,' coaxed the guide.

'Oh, it was visible from the moon, and not from India?' My mother asked.

That evening, a group of Bengali tourists searched for the Great Wall of China with torchlights and searchlights, even with matchsticks and cigarette lighters. But they didn't find it.

That was where China began and India ended: the border story.

But it's one we could never begin reading.

India: Underlined in Red!

—Atul Kumar Thakur

The purpose of this essay is not to enter into theoretical polemics linked to the concept of radicalism or Naxal movement, but to bring out the truth about the conflict between the state and the downtrodden tribal in India. All the major tribes of India are actually peasant societies existing within the broad political economy of the state. Their existence and motion can only be understood in terms of a class analysis of the societies and the articulation of the different modes of production within their structures. In post-Independence India, the principle contradiction in the agrarian economy started appearing fairly early and clear. The primary contradiction was that between the mass of the working peasantry and labourers on the one hand, and on the other hand the minority of landlords, traders and money lenders who monopolised controls over land and capital, thereby exploiting the peasantry through different exorbitant means.

Though this dialectic status was not unprecedented, as such equation had been part of the general contradiction between the Indians as a unit and British colonial rule in the past; but in independent India, it came to the fore and strengthened the immediate agenda of the democratic struggle by the bursts of hope with Nehruvian idealism in late 1960s, which practically grew in 1970s for a long programming. The principle contradiction was no longer as static as earlier, now local comprador allies of new imperialism design were playing the monopolising control over the crucial resources and strategies. But under this objectionable design, the volatility and instability represented by the enormous bulk of erratically flowing capital without any effective regulation and with great destructive capacity capable of overthrowing national economies and governments within few hours cannot be simply overlooked So it is true that the vertiginous separation of speculative capital from the real productive base as an expression of the parasitic state of capitalism has its limitations.

Marx had warned long ago that the structure of international economic relations is the objective process of capitalism. The unrestricted cross-border flow of capital—one of its definitive features—facilitated the establishment of a world system as one of the aspects of capitalist domination, the first of its kind in the history of mankind. This very commercial international mobility assisted by the mammoth scientific and technological advancements and shadowy conducive policies framed by the slavishly polarised multilateral and bilateral engagements have resulted in an extremely high level of internationalisation of capital. But perhaps, as it is insistently proposed, does globalisation signify the universal and definitive triumph of capitalism or the abolition of contradictions between social classes or between countries or regions, or the elimination of the crisis of the system or the cancellation of revolutionary upheavals or the inevitable adoption, in the manner of uniformity of a certain code of conduct by all countries in their internal and external policy?

As far as India is concerned, it was at one time a completely subjugated colony of an imperialist power while China was to never fall from grace in the same manner. At its worst, it remained a semi-colony. The Japanese attempt to colonise it completely not only failed miserably, but ended up leaving the revolutionary forces in the high influence within the Chinese society. So cases of India and China appear with high differences while comparing the relations of their mass and state. The disdain for politics, contempt for the political process, is what characterises substantial sections of the middle class in India today. The rise of messianic moralism is a part of the same popular trend, which leads to nothing else but a process of 'death of politics'. Middle class moralism at best upholds causes, not programmes for the rational outcome. It roves through those circles with no clear intention of finding a way out. And it apotheosises the absence of systematic political alliances. One may call it a bit 'post-modern politics', but eventually it amounts to a negation of politics.

This trend is extremely dangerous, as this same Indian middle class has been benefitted most through the liberalisation of Indian economy since 1991. Its foundation could be looked back to the Green Revolution, which brought in new class contradictions and sharpening of the old contradictions in the hinterlands, owing to violent spates of small tenant evictions with the conversion of erstwhile feudal renters to capitalist landlords, resulting in the class of rural labourers growing as a share of rural population, and large-scale migration of low-wage labour to higher wage areas. The minority of well-to-do peasant farmers, having obtained some benefits from initial land reforms stalled and sabotaged further reforms to benefit the landless and really land-poor, except in a few states especially where committed left governments ensured registration and security of occupation as well as flow of institutional credit to the disadvantaged.

Cutting subsidies on food, health and education which benefit the masses is essentially a firm part of the neo-liberal theology, and goes hand-in-hand with their advocacy of giving more spending money to the already well-to-do by way of lower taxes on them and making the latest luxuries available to them. Shifting incomes, however unequal they already might be, even more towards the well-to-do is part of the largely successful global political strategy of the Bretton Woods institutions for winning the support of local elites in third world countries for running 'austerity' measures, viz. policies of reducing state development spending and cutting social expenditures. Their policies may be lucidly summed up as austerity for the poor and more spending money for the well-to-do.

The tribals of India's mainland live in rich forests, filled with precious mineral resources that lead to trouble for the local population. Adivasis were frequently displaced from their age-old habitat when the state once endowed with the commanding heights of the economy and its biased commercial interest started colliding with the poorest of the poor. Plights of displacement and dispossession of natural livelihood rights grew even more acute under the auspices of breathless liberalisation and globalisation that made India's new state 'a one man player' for its chosen section of beneficiaries. The opening of the Indian economy has had superlative outcomes in parts of the country where the availability of an educated workforce allows ideal ground of cheap service outsourcing to the global markets. On the other side, its tantamount are much brutal with increasing exploitation of unexplored raw materials, and by keeping aside the original inhabitants at the grim periphery.

Over the decades, the Government of India has defied its own constitutional guarantee in practice to provide the Adivasis with opportunities for social and economic development. More harshly, policies of the different governments have invariably dispossessed Adivasis of their traditional means of life and livelihood by undermining the historically proven truth that uniting force of the Adivasis is not their cultural or other community specific distinctiveness, but their economic concern. The colonial phase is full with rebellions in tribal areas, noticeable among them are—Kol and Bhumj revolts of the early 19th century, the Santhal hool of 1855, the Birsa Munda-led ulugulan in the 1890s, the uprising in Bastar in 1911, the protests in Gudem-Rampa in the 1920s, and the Warli Revolt of 1945-46. Most of the protests were placed against the violation of land and forests rights under the oppressive British rule. India's policy establishment has failed in post Independence phase to act differently than the colonial rulers in framing the right set of conditions to all its citizens including the tribals. Instead, the wrong corporate forces with extraordinary plundering powers of resources were given the extra edge in actual formulation.

The name, 'Naxalite' draws its antecedence from the movement that emerged in 1967 at the Naxalbari area of Darjeeling district in West Bengal. The term comes from Naxalbari, a small village in West Bengal, where a section of the Communist Party of India-Marxist (CPI-M) under the leadership of Charu Mazumdar, Kanu Sanyal and Jangal Santhal led a violent uprising in 1967, trying to develop a 'revolutionary opposition' in opposition to the CPI-M leadership. The insurrection started on 24 May 1967 in Naxalbari village when a peasant was attacked by hired hands over a land dispute. Local peasants retaliated by attacking the landlords and the violence escalated on a massive scale. Chief Naxal ideologue, Charu Mazumdar greatly admired Mao Zedong of China and mandated Indian peasants and lower classes to follow his revolutionary ideas and overthrow the existing political system and bourgeois classes. Further, however, he brought down the Naxalite movement with his slavishly China-centric writings with complete distorted vision for locally-rooted problems, the most famous was the 'Historic Eight Documents' which formed the basis of the Naxalite ideology. Not surprising, the conditionally exuberant Communist Party of China hailed the movement as the 'Spring Thunder of India'—temporarily they were in gain-gain situation.

It is normally believed that the objective of the new movement was 'seizure of power' through an agrarian revolution. Though the real strategy was closer to the elimination of the oppressive feudal/ ethnic order in the countryside to free the poor from the clutches of oppressive landlords and replace the old order with an alternative one that would implement land reforms effectively. The tactics to achieve it was through guerrilla warfare by the peasants to eliminate the landlords and build resistance against the State police force or allies. Consequently, ethnic antagonism got sharply consolidated among the tribal Adhiars as they felt discriminated by the Rajbansi Jotedars as compared to the Rajbansi Adhiars who enjoyed close social ties with their masters and carried out many of the social activities like marriage and religious rituals together. While the Rajbansi Jotedars and the Rajbansi Adhiars could share water from the same well, the migrant tribal Adhiars were discriminately debarred. Thus it makes it difficult to accept the Naxalbari episode only as a class war or an agrarian movement as proclaimed by the Naxalites. The so-called class enemies annihilated were mostly Rajbansi landowners. It rather led to a kind of ethnocide. This inherent lacuna mainly resulted in an early exit of the movement. Even the local tribals later realised about the fallacy of the Naxalite leaders who were trying to take advantage of their hideouts. Naturally the movement could not sustain genuine mass participation by the tribals with a sense of solidarity.

The distinctive characteristic of the Naxalite groups since their formation has been their exhibited allegiance to Mao Zedong's thought and the essence of Marxism-Leninism of modern epoch. Except for the pro-Albania groups that denounced Mao Zedong thought, all groups continue to swear allegiance. However, their perceptions of its content and role differ and each accuses the other of distorting or revising

Maoist ideology. Naxalite tactics had been characterised by a dogmatic and sole reliance on armed struggle in its first phases. This was based on the sectarian 'people's war' thesis put forward by Lin Biao at the ninth congress of the Chinese Communist Party (CPC). In India this brand of adventurism was reinterpreted by Charu Mazumdar to be the tactic of individual terrorism. After the debacle of this tactic in 1970-71 many groups split away condemning the 'annihilation theory'. However the pro-Charu groups have persisted in defending this 'revolutionary line' and continue to be practitioners of terrorism. The pro-Lin Biao groups in West Bengal, the Vinod Mishra group in Bhojpur, the People's War group in Andhra Pradesh and the Venu group in Kerala have all in some form or another continued to rely on the line of annihilation. The difference exists only in the level of emphasis.

Above and beyond these various protests, Maoist revolutionaries have been active in tribal areas. The village Naxalbari, which gave the 'Naxalites' their name, itself lies in a remote part of West Bengal which has a substantial tribal population with aloof geography. Another major centre of Naxalite activity in the late 1960s was the tribal districts of Andhra Pradesh. In the 1970s, the Maoists spread their operational influence in two main areas—the feudal terrains of central Bihar, and the tribal districts of the southern parts of the state (now Jharkhand). In recent decades, as the Maoist insurgencies have expanded, its major gains have been in tribal districts of Maharashtra, Jharkhand and Odisha but now most strongly in Chhattisgarh. Over the past four decades, the Adivasis of central India have often expressed their collective discontent with the policies and programmes of the State. Their protests have sometimes—in Bastar in 1966 or later in Jharkhand in the late 1970s—taken recourse to traditional means and traditional leaders. On other times in Maharashtra in the 1970s, or during the early days of Narmada Bachao Andolan, Adivasis have been mobilised by social and environmental activists from urban, educated middle-class background. But henceforth, idealism has been substituted by violence and tribal alienation has been wrongly manipulated by the armed Maoist revolutionaries.

Geographical remoteness is the major reason which encourages the presence of Naxalites in areas dominated by the Adivasis—the red belts in hills and deep forests of central India are well suited for the guerilla warfare. But the spread of Naxalism is not limited to the geographical reasons alone—looking at the modern Indian history it is also equally imperative to acknowledge how the Adivasis have gained the least and lost the most from sixty-five years of India's political independence. In fact, the problems and resistance are not separable here. State's impractical policy deliberations have caused for the neglect of local population in most of India's mineral rich areas that are making the State 'less than angel' among the Adivasis that know their plights but are unaware how to cope with them except willingly or unwillingly relying on the cynical leadership of alternative radical groups. The Naxalite movement gathered its lost force after the merger in 2004 of the PWG and the MCC. The new party emerged as the Communist Party of India (Maoist), its planned dualist abbreviation CPI (M) mimicked that of a mainstream Indian communist party that participates in the democratic process under the Indian Constitution. The new party has claims of being the real inheritors of the legacy of revolutionary Marxism, whereas they stressed the democratic left front which ruled Kerala, West Bengal and Tripura for long are merely a bunch of bourgeois reformists.

The new, unified party has been a mere eight years in existence, but in that time it has rapidly expanded its influence in the different states of India. The erstwhile MCC cadres have moved southwards into Jharkhand and east into the rural West Bengal. Those who were once with the PWG have penetrated towards Odisha and Chattisgarh. In Chattisgarh, Maoists have made the most miraculous influence. Large parts of the district of Dantewara, in particular, are under the siege. On one side of the river Indravati, the Indian state holds an uncertain control by day and hardly any control at night. On the other side of the river known as Abujmarh, the state has flatly no presence by day or by night—State is a nonexistent entity here. Dantewara forms part of a minerally rich forest belt which spreads over from Chattisgarh to Andhra Pradesh and Maharashtra. The region was known in mythical times as 'Dandakaranya', a name the Maoists have now adopted on their own line. Under the Special Zonal Committee for Dandakaranya operate several Divisional Committees which in turn have Range Committees reporting to them. The lowest level of organisation is at the village, where a committee of committed workers is known as a 'Sangam'...this is altogether a different world, might be an anti-thesis of the rest—consumption driven emerging India.

Tribal India is facing a double tragedy even in present times. The first tragedy is that the state has treated its Adivasi citizens with contempt and disdain. The second tragedy is that their presumed protectors, the Naxalites, offer no long term solution either. So how to believe, that the Communist Party of India (Maoist) would come to power in New Delhi through armed struggle? Never to forget, India is not Nepal—even though there too, Maoists rose to power and led the abolition of monarchy only after adopting the democratic means. In strategic terms, now China and India have different affluence in the new world order than what they earlier had in 1960s and till a few years back...on many counts, India has an open advantage over China through its multiple integration with the US and other western forces. So, at this point of time, Naxals spread from Pashupati/Kathmandu to Tirupati/Andhra Pradesh have to rethink on continuing with China's tenacious hold over their programme; what would be rather more pragmatic to be onerous in finding the localised solution of the localised maladies, for they have been fighting for a long time without reaching conquerable solution.

Irrespective of geographical or regional variations, radical movements are primarily targeting the feudal or industrial exploitation. Their ideology talks of uniformity in aim. The visible reason of conflict is the unlawful restriction on stakeholding for these disadvantaged sections in the dividend of farming or industrial productions despite the fact that these 'modern occupations' have been blossoming by altering the symbiotic relations between natural resources and their original successors. Industries have either no answer for redeeming the local affected population through their operation or have a monotonous and hypocritic solution, namely Corporate Social Responsibility. CSR, now which is itself a hugely profit making area where the new discipline of academics and R&D along with a full-fledged international stock exchange is giving the corporate ambition a wild mileage of flying high in its atrocities. Equally supported by a unique legitimacy and sustenance hitherto never seen anytime in the history of resource plundering!

The Indian Home Ministry now has a single prong strategy of talking through the gun with every dissent voice in its catchment, which opposes the lootings of resources and its inequitable distribution. Comrade Azad, a Maoist who was called for the peaceful talk from New Delhi was encountered midway...only few months before his encounter, Siddhartha Varadrajan of *The Hindu* carried a long interview with him, where he stressed on the need of change of strategy in radical programming. As a leader, he was dreaming to change the violent and illegal tactics of Maoist operation but here in the nation's capital, lawmakers were hardly in sync with the same proposition, so the constructive move failed and started another wave of mindless violence where thousands of ordinary soldiers and Maoist cadres lost their precious lives for fighting over the 'game of rights'. Loss of lives are painful for all sensible minds but unfortunately the Prime Minister could think only of the opposite side as the 'gravest internal threats of the nation' and never as the struggling and misled masses finding it impossible to walk with new India's growth which stands only for a section of its total population.

P. Chidambaram is a man of few words, while talking about internal security. However as a corporate lawyer, his affiliation with Vedanta was much more dynamic. He still upholds those old bonds of his foregone corporate career but for the national issues like Naxalism, normally he prefers 'passing the buck' at imagined tables of overgrown ghost bureaucracy. The mandate is coming clear that the state no longer has the patience or feels the need to take care of all its citizens; the silence of New Delhi over Hillary Clinton's recent visit to Kolkata (which was very objectionable, though found no opposition even from the opposition parties) and her lauding of Mamta Banerjee for overthrowing the Left Front is indicative of similar tendency.

It's not that India's highest powerholders have no understanding of ground level realities but their action never reciprocates the existing problems. Addressing a meeting of the standing committee of the Chief Ministers of the six Naxalite affected states on 13 April 2006, Prime Minister Manmohan Singh argued that factors such as exploitation, artificially depressed wages, iniquitous socio-political circumstances, inadequate employment opportunities, lack of access to resources, underdeveloped agriculture, geographical isolation and lack of land reforms contributed to the growth of the Naxalite movement (*The Hindu*, New Delhi, 14 April 2006). As anticipated, his preaching was over with no further action. With lobbyists' recommended ministers, expecting anything different than 'a full scale war' inside the country would be unrealistic. Even if put lightly, the last five years have turned India's home ministry under an undeserving home minister, mocking India's democracy and the beliefs of ordinary Indians. The sustained state violence on the masses and the growing impoverishment are not just by chance or some exception, but somewhere are the outcome of indifferent people holding big power in Delhi and the states!

The major achievement of the Naxalite movement, at least in some clusters is that it has empowered the oppressed classes by its effect, equations of power have changed in these regions. But the failures of Naxalites to understand the benefits of development have deterred the improvement of material life in villages where they have footprints. Shockingly, such forced hiatus in growth related activities is making the masses in the rural areas idle and causing blockade of positive atmosphere. Perhaps the Naxal movement couldn't gain the wider acceptance because of its consistent devoid to come to terms with people's wider interests—same can be said on the overall Left movement in India. Even those, who have been working in the mainstream democratic ways, have failed to look beyond the rigid terms of ideology and any fresh efforts from their side to work upon a unique 'India model' remains a distant dream. As for the rest, factionalism marred the Left movement and people left far in the corner instead being crucibles of 'growth agenda'—bad capital and cronyism permanently delved deep the agenda for a different route.

There is no reason however that the Maoists' confused action should be glorified. Their obstinate stand has immensely harmed the peoples' cause and it has derailed the core progressive democratic idea of 'equity within the system' to 'overthrowing the existing structure of state', which is untenable and outrageously wrong. Even in the present gloomiest phase, there should be no different view that Indian Constitution has all the strength needed to carry forward this diverse nation, though the enactment of good laws have always remained elusive in the past and still the condition is emphatically stasis. The potential of violence, commonplace in Maoist's camp or from the side of the mighty state would ultimately help no one; it is better if the realisation comes even at this stage. The blockade of constructive dialogue mechanism is underlining India with uncomfortable reds, which is not going to be healthy for it as a swiftly rising power—its end result would be as bad someday as would be the havoc generated from IPL cricket. India's industrialists can dream in billion dollars now, not through their entrepreneurial drive but with amazing participation in 'bad capital's celebrated cronyism'. Post 1991, India's new economic policy and political casualisation have embedded this hateful change and also the pauperisation of its lowest tier citizens.

Yet, the Planning Commission, which was once termed by Rajiv Gandhi as 'the resting place of a bunch of jokers' is adamant on pursuing a wrong economic planning model under the differently-trained economist, Montek Singh Ahluwalia who thinks that even on Rs. 22, a person can lead a decent life in a hyper-capitalist economy like India. Though even in frugality, his own foreign trip expenses gives a huge jerk to India's exchequer…only solace is, Ahluwalia is still way behind our ex-President, who spent more than 210 crore rupees on foreign trips alone for sightseeing and wining/dining, which often is also confused with the 'diplomacy of high order and low return'. Such deviation in state's core agendas leads to governance failure on large scale, which further gives birth to the resistance to the state; nomenclature could be many like, Maoism, Naxalism, etc, but in their belief, they have single aim to overthrow the exploitative state machinery. In 1966, Pravir Chandra Bhanj Rao was killed by police when he virtually revolted against the government for the rights of tribals in his erstwhile principality of Bastar. It's worth noticing that he was not violently brokering the movement, as it had been thoroughly carried out by the Naxals. Instead of calling this incident or many of the same type 'an error of judgement', it would be better if India's bureaucracy on a large scale could be seen as the puppet inheritor of British colonial bureaucratic model which ruled the subjects in India. Almost in a similar fashion India's modern bureaucracy is ruling its own vulnerable 'citizens'.

In the last six decades, India has witnessed a horrific destabilisation of the sovereignty of its forests, including flora, fauna and the tribals who have been the intrinsic part of that collective existence—it is not the advent of modernism but the biased policy dictates of the state that made tribals more the part of museum rather participants in good or bad direct outcome of industrial development. The mainstream Indian communist parties like CPI, CPI (Marxist) now believe that the ideology of communism needs some academic maturity to be understood but these tribals who are fighting under the Naxal leadership don't know the endgame of their struggle. They are fighting to survive, not for securing any plush arrangements in New Delhi or 'passing the buck' at the two edificial blocks of power centre in New Delhi, which is craving for moralistic overhaul now. From outside, only assessments are possible on the chronic conflict of state's interest and the genuine legitimate demands of disadvantaged sections being led by the selected few who are wrongly addicted to an ideological opium of Maoism for getting out from another theology which is mishandled and losing its shine.

Tribals and all those whose existence is at stake need their basic rights to be functional. The extra assertions of ideology or repression would do all the more harm than anticipated in the days to come. It's true that India's political parties including mainstream leftist parties have done most of their good work in rhetoric rather than in actuality but even as the worst form of the system, the prospects of representative democracy in India could not be undermined in the severe absence of any alternative. Though all who run the democracy have no understanding of how important this functional system is. So is true with the opponents who don't want to consider its merits. Despite the umpteen flaws imbibed with the functioning of Indian democracy, there is a chance of revival and better participation of all voices under its democratic mainframe. The wrongs of the past can be cured only by making the system more transparent, participative and socio-economically equitable. By simply abstaining from the mass platform that a democracy like India offers would bring more ills inside, in place of solving the old systemic disorders. Both the state and dissents have to be more responsive in reaching a common ground from where the broader issues could be properly oriented for an optimum way out.

On 13 December 1946, Jawaharlal Nehru moved the Objectives Resolution in the Constituent Assembly of India. This stated that India would be an 'Independent Sovereign Republic'. Its Constitution would guarantee citizens 'justice, social, economic and political; equality of status; of opportunity, and before the law; freedom of thought, expression, belief, faith, worship, vocation, association and action, subject to law and public morality.' Remarkably, the same day Jaipal Singh Munda, an Oxford educated tribal leader from then south Bihar (now Jharkhand), made clear the thousands of years of exploitative history that kept the tribals at the periphery throughout the long perpetual course of history. Jaipal Singh was also a great hockey player who had led India in Amsterdam Olympic—tribals' contributions were undermined then and still no changes are foreseeable with such an obstinate mental frame. After more than six decades, things have changed only symbolically, for e.g. getting a few tribals in good jobs and educational institutions but alarmingly downsizing the rest, which is entirely pitiless. Since 1947, India has indeed shaped itself as a 'nation' but not all its citizens are proud of it. It is the most naked reality and outcome of India's uproarious 'tryst with destiny' that involves more vertiginous feelings than hope, otherwise supposed to emanate from a democracy of the highest size and repute!

The Art in Modern India

—Benoy K Behl

Since ancient times, India has had one of the most highly developed traditions of art the world has seen. Therefore, art in modern India is deeply rooted in a continuing culture and has to be seen in relation to that. The aesthetic experience is considered to be of great value in Indian thought. It lifts the veils of illusion that hide the truth from our eyes. Our experience of beauty when we respond to a sunrise or to a great work of art is seen to be a moment when we perceive the grace which underlies the whole of creation. In that moment, the veils of illusion of the material nature of the world are lifted and we see beyond.

This moment of the aesthetic experience is stated in Indian thought to be 'akin to Brahmananda', or the final ecstasy of salvation itself. Therefore art has played a most important part in the life of the Indian sub-continent. What survives today of the early art of India is only a small fraction of what would have been created. Yet it consists of such vast numbers of monuments and sculpture that it staggers the mind. The corpus is gigantic and spread to every corner of the sub-continent.

The tradition of art in India was a strong and living force which continuously evolved over the centuries. However, in the eighteenth and nineteenth centuries, this tradition was fractured. In this period, there were fundamental changes in the political, economic and social life of India. European dominance was established in all aspects of life. Vastly different influences of culture and art came from far away shores and new examples were set to be emulated by the Indian people. For the making of vast numbers of drawings, paintings and prints, European artists took on Indian apprentices and assistants. They found what they considered to be basic flaws in the Indian ways of painting and drawing. Along with other educational institutions, art schools were set up to teach Indian artists the Western manner of painting. The style of academic realism of Western art became a norm to be appreciated and emulated in India.

From the 1920s, new strands began to appear in the tapestry of Indian art. Against the backdrop of India's ancient artistic legacy and the changing times, the Indian artists attempted to evolve their personal vision. A new national cultural identity was forged. One that was not based on the slavish imitation of past traditions, nor on Western norms; but one which derived sustenance and inspiration from a great legacy and looked forward dynamically into the future. In the 1940s in India there was an excitement in the air. The people's movement and struggle to gain independence from foreign rule had gained momentum and freedom was not very far away. The Bengal School had risen at the turn of the century, led by artists like Rabindranath Tagore. The work of these artists represented a harking back and a deep nostalgia for the great art of ancient and medieval India. They rejected the Western academic style of painting, which till then had been the norm in India in the early twentieth century.

After the Second World War, winds had begun to blow in from Europe and America, where existing philosophies and ideas in art were being dismantled. New norms were being created as artists struggled to come to terms with the chaos around them. New ways of looking at the world and new manners of expression were coming into being. The people of India were beginning to see themselves as a nation with a proud and long history stretching back to ancient times. Indian artists were also groping and rediscovering their roots in the soil of their ancient traditions. Traditions, which had been severed over the period of two hundred years.

In the 1940s, there emerged a group of artists in Bombay who wished to create a modern Indian identity. One that was based neither on a sentimental looking back to the past, as the Bengal School had done, nor on the following of Western traditions. The progressive Artists Group was established. There were six founding members: K.H. Ara, S.K. Bakre, H.A. Gade, M.F. Hussain, S.H. Raza, and F.N. Souza. They tried to break out from the established orthodoxies prevailing in Mumbai at that time.

The next institutional event that led to a major art school was in Baroda. The setting up of the M.S. University in Baroda brought together some of the finest artistic minds: N.S. Bendre, K.G. Subramanyam and Sankho Chaudhary. The Baroda School became a very important influence on the development of Modern Indian Art. From the 1960s, there has been much discussion about the double destiny of the Indian artist. We have a tradition which is thousands of years old, which could not be denied. At the same time, we are living in a world which is modern and you have influences coming from all over. Therefore, there has to be a synthesis.

The ancient Indian treatise on painting, the *Chitrasutra* of the *Vishnudharmottara Purana*, says that paintings are among the most valuable treasures of mankind. It states that paintings, which are made with an understanding of the harmony of the whole of creation, are extremely beneficial to the viewer. What the ancient or medieval Indian artist would have done is to affirm a life-giving worldview that was shared by the society at large. But since we have lost that worldview and we no longer have that coherent image of society in the cosmos, the artist's role has to change from an affirmative one to a critical one. The artist today searches for a universal expression, one which would be understood across the boundaries of nations and cultures. Traditions bring to us the distilled knowledge of the finest minds of the past. Roots in one's local soil help us to understand ourselves and our own culture. It is from this understanding that the artist can hope to have a meaningful expression, which is relevant for mankind.

Since Independence, it has been a very exciting time for the Indian artist. On the one hand, the artists have been conscious that they are the inheritors of one of the greatest traditions of art of the world. On the other hand, there has been a force of universalisation, under the umbrella of western culture. Indian artists have responded dynamically to these challenges and often created notable works of art, quite different from those produced in the west. Artists like S.H. Raza became conscious that our own traditions offered much more to him than did those developed in other cultures. His best work came from this understanding. An artist like M.F. Hussain was deeply rooted in the Indian idiom, yet able to express himself in a truly modern way.

Society everywhere today has lost the coherence and sublime balance which used to be there in early times. Therefore, it is not possible for the Indian artist today to produce the gentle and exquisite art which was made in ancient times. In fact, much of contemporary art has reflected the noise and confusion of modern times. Perhaps the time has come and Indian artists have matured enough, to integrate the life-giving and compassionate outlook of India with the needs of a universal art today. In that case, Indian art may be poised to contribute a great deal to the people and the art of the world.

One cannot write about the art of India without reference to the art of the tribal people of this sub-continent. There was a time when the waking of the sun and the call of the ecstatic bird ruled the lives of men and women. Amidst all the frantic clamour of the restless and modern world, the tribal communities in India still preserve a quieter and simpler way of life. These are men and women who still live closely with nature. Amid all the influences of the fast changing world, they continue an ancient legacy. They lead a life which is shaped by the changing seasons and the rising and setting of the sun and the moon. They know no days and hours of the modern world and their lives follow other rhythms.

They have a direct and intimate relationship with the many animals around them whom they see as their fellow creatures. The pains and joys of every hen and cow are as real as any of their own. The animals are beings which are a part of their lives, just like the trees which give them shelter and the flowers which provide the fragrance. These are not men and women struggling against the vicissitudes of a confusing and painful human existence. These are people living in the harmony of all of creation.

These men and women accept the collective understanding of their ancestors coming to them through their traditions. They accept the fact of the simple harmony of the world and that the human being is only one small part of the great dance of the cosmic creation. They do not always try to twist and turn and to dominate the forces of nature around them. They do not have the need to subjugate other forms of life to provide them more and more sustenance for an unlimited greed. The art of the tribals is an integral part of their lives. Through their paintings they create gods who protect and heal them. They continue the unchanging thoughts and the eternal themes of humankind.

The art of the tribals in India is the oldest continuing tradition of painting in our country. It brings to us images which are ever fresh, ever lively. These paintings are never copies, they are created each time afresh and we can relate to their directness and honesty every time. Year after year, they are made, lost and then made again upon the walls. There is no desire to possess these forever. These are not merely works of commercial art—these are the deities of the people who summon them. These paintings are an integral part of life. While we speak about the wonderful art of the many tribes across the Indian sub-continent, we must not lose sight of a great change which has been taking place, especially over the past forty years. The modern spirit of marketing and profit-making has taken this art of the tribals out of its context within their lives and upon their walls. Instead of it being an integral and essential part of their existence, it has become a commodity they produce to sell.

This is the paradox of the modern world. Art is gradually being removed from our lives as competitive marketing is taking over. A country with a tradition of art as comprehensive and as strong as we have had needs to reassess the importance of art in life. The science of life has to be revived again instead of just our focus on the science of how to gather more material goods. With our past traditions of aesthetics and also of the patronage of art, India should really be a world leader in this area. It should be one of our most important contributions to the modern world in times to come.

Litany of Lost Tongues

—Saugata Ghosh

If literature be a reflection of history, then the story of Indian literature in English translation is intimately linked with that of modern India—both its liberalised present and its colonial past. In this essay I have attempted to position Indian literature in translation in the context of both its colonial origins and post-colonial concerns, for an understanding of the latter is incomplete without an assessment of the former. In trying to measure the role that translation has to play in our multilingual, pluralistic society, still hopelessly divided along ethnic and linguistic fault-lines, to assess its relevance as a 'link literature' for modern India, I have also tried to situate it in the context of that other post-Independence literary phenomenon—the rise of Indo-Anglian writing, because both are post-colonial literary trends, though one has never really subsumed the other. The growing body of work related to translation studies since the 1970s has enabled me to quote authoritative sources wherever possible, though the conclusions arrived at are mostly my own. In piecing together this story of Indian literature in translation, I have tried to demonstrate the currency and relevance of the subject to the development of modern India, which is a mandate of this book and if I am even partially able to do so then I consider my efforts well-rewarded.

In Rana Dasgupta's Commonwealth Prize-winning *Solo*, a book written in English and set largely in Bulgaria, the protagonist reads a story in a magazine in which a group of explorers came upon a community of parrots speaking the language of a society that had been wiped out in a recent catastrophe. Astonished by their discovery, they put the parrots in cages and sent them home so that linguists could record what remained of the lost language. But the parrots, already traumatised by the devastation they had recently witnessed, died on the way. When the protagonist reads the story he feels a great affinity with those birds. He feels he carries, like them, a shredded inheritance.

Like many other traditions of the sub-continent, the etymology of written translation too is a venerable one, dating back to the fourteenth or fifteenth century when works of Sanskrit literature saw translation into different regional languages. These included the *BhagavadGita* and various (sub) versions of the *Ramayana* and the *Mahabharata*. Though in this sense the outflow from Sanskrit into regional languages was analogous to the movement in Europe from Latin into the vulgate, in the sub-continent the move also implied an attempt to free Sanskrit scriptures from 'the monopolist custody of Sanskrit pundits' (Susan Bassnet and Harish Trivedi, *Post-colonial Translation,* 1999). Therefore, as has been noted, these translations into vernacular were hardly passive cultural creations: an act of freedom was implicit in them and gradually they came to embody an alternative literature that told the same stories with subtle emphases to alternative audiences. Translations from and to Persian—the other dominant source as well as target language for translation also happened regularly during the period of Muslim rule in India and continued well into colonial times.

The roots of translation of Indian literature into English lie in the history of the colonisation of the subcontinent. G.N. Devy (*Indian Literature in English Translation: An Introduction*, 1993) has classified the initial as well as the subsequent, overlapping phases of this movement as

1. The Colonial Phase (1776-1910)
2. The Revivalist Phase (1876-1950)
3. The Nationalist Phase (1902-1929)
4. The Formalist Phase (1912-present).

Rita Kothari (*Translating India*, 2006) has pointed out that in the initial stages, translation of Indian texts into English went hand-in-hand with empire-building itself and translations initiated in the phase of British Orientalism 'provide an enduring account of the construction of knowledge and relationships integral to colonial rule' (Kothari, 2006). In the early days of colonial rule, Warren Hastings set about fashioning an 'Orientalist' administration, believing that the natives had to be ruled according to their own principles and institutions. Accordingly, there was an intense curiosity about studying the 'Hindoo' psyche and the ancient texts seemed to be an appropriate place to begin the enquiry. The first Indian text to be translated from Sanskrit to English (via Persian) was therefore *A Code of Gentoo Law* (1776) by Nathaniel Halhed, followed shortly by *The Ordinances of Manu,* a translation of the Sanskrit text *Manusmriti* by William Jones. These works were primarily works by Englishmen for other Englishmen, notably colonial administrators. However, the first translated work to have a far-reaching impact on the Indian audience was the landmark translation of *Gita* by Charles Wilkins, the first English scholar to translate directly from Sanskrit. The identification of the *Gita* for translation by the rulers and the primacy accorded to it had a profound impact on the ruled even though the translation was of far less practical value to the rulers than the *Code.* However, despite the persistence of a patronising attitude on the part of the colonial rulers towards native texts, the interest of the Orientalists in translating Sanskrit texts was already moving away from mere codification of native laws to a deeper exploration of Sanskrit literature. This trend culminated in the translation of Kalidasa's *Abhignanshakuntalam* by William Jones. This translation introduced the literary side of India to the West and touched a deep chord at home as well. It became a marker of India's cultural prestige and got translated into more than ten Indian languages in the nineteenth century itself.

The Orientalist interest in translating the sacred texts of India ebbed early in the nineteenth century. This was partly because of the decline of Romanticism in England (appreciation of Sanskrit literature had formed a part of this movement), the consolidation of the Empire through the efforts of Christian missionaries who naturally decried efforts at translation from Sanskrit as a near-heretical act of embracing a heathen culture and lastly, the reversal of roles from Sanskrit as a donor of ancient wisdom to English as the language of liberalism and science. While more and more works began to be translated from the language of the coloniser to those of the colonised, it actually fell upon the latter to revive the tradition of English translation from Sanskrit and Persian. In the early nineteenth century, the translation of Samkara's *Vedanta* by Raja Rammohun Roy was a significant move towards projecting through English and vernacular translations, the monotheistic and reformist version of Hinduism that the great social reformer was bringing about. Roy was well-versed in the traditions of both the East and the West and this gave his translation a standing and seriousness that rendered the question of 'fidelity', either to the source or the target language, peripheral. By and large, the translations by Indians in the revivalist phase followed in the footsteps of the Indologists. Translations from Sanskrit, ranging from well-known treatises to poetry and drama gained momentum in this period and were primarily targeted at erudite Indologists and discerning Indian scholars conversant in English, a primary aim being to reclaim India's past and confer dignity upon the colonial present. The translations of the Indian epics by R.C. Dutt, for instance, were meant to exhibit the similarity these epics bore to the *Iliad* and the *Odyssey*. The significant achievement of ILET (Indian Literature in English Translation) in the revivalist phase was, however, the rendering into English of the works of ancient theorists on poetry, drama and language. The fact that modern Indians can today talk about Panini, Bhartrihari, Abhinavagupta and others is due to the scholarly exposition of their works by R.C. Bhandarkar, Ananda Coomaraswamy and others.

It is interesting to note that while translations from Sanskrit into regional languages also continued vigorously in the nineteenth century (Kaliprasanna Sinha's monumental translation of the *Mahabharata* into Bengali prose was a milestone of the Bengali intellectual renaissance), translations from the vernacular into English were largely insignificant in the nineteenth century, a notable exception being the English translation of Dinabandhu Mitra's *Nildurpan*—a trenchant play of racial exploitation of Indians by European indigo planters. The translation coincided with a period when dissatisfaction with British rule was on the rise, soon to culminate in the Great Indian Mutiny of 1857. The publisher of the translation, Rev. James Long, was put on trial and penalised. In this sense, the translation of *Nildurpan*, purportedly by Michael Madhusudan Dutt, is significant in two respects—it was the first major translation into English from a regional Indian language (in this case Bengali) and it was a political act in tune with the growing nationalistic aspirations of the sub-continent.

It was in the third phase, however, that translations began to be aimed at a wider, general readership. This period began with Sri Aurobindo, a polyglot and prolific translator who translated, among other works, parts of the epics and Kalidasa's works, as well as Bankimchandra's *Anandamath* into English. It also included the serialised autobiography of Mahatma Gandhi, *The Story of My Experiments With Truth,* translated by Mahadev Desai. This was also a phase that saw the cultural hegemony of the English language being demonstrated in strange and unpredictable ways through 'translations of translations', notably the multiple translations into Hindi of Edward Fitzgerald's *Rubaiyat of Omar Khayyam,* the most well-known transcreation (to borrow a word from the late P Lal) of it being *Madhushala* (1935) by Harivansh Rai Bachchan. But the work in this phase that came to have the same impact on the Western reader as Jones' *Shakuntalam* was Rabindranath Tagore's *Gitanjali*, translated by the poet himself and published in 1912, the work that fetched an Indian author the Nobel Prize in literature for the first and, till date, only time.

The importance of the publication in English of *Gitanjali* to the cause of Indian Literature in English Translation (ILET) cannot be overstated even though post-colonial assessments of the text itself have drawn attention to the 'cavalier and accommodating' nature of the translation—'the constant adjustment to suit the poetics of the coloniser'. Be that as it may, the response to *Gitanjali* was unequivocal and overwhelming and through his translation Tagore was seen to personify not just his poetry and message but India itself, with its centuries' old spiritualism as opposed to the scientific rationalism of the West. While earlier translations by Indians (Roy, R.C. Dutt and others) had been rooted in revivalism and nationalism, the primary motive behind *Gitanjali* was to make the poet known to a bigger world and thus it marked a new and 'formalist' phase of translation, when translation itself became the primary motive. One can therefore, according to Devy, consider 1912 as the beginning of translation in India, for it is since then that Indian translators, following Tagore turned towards translating contemporary Indian authors. It also marked the first notable entry of ILET into the commercial publishing space when MacMillan purchased the publishing rights to *Gitanjali,* with the aim of turning it into a selling proposition.

If translation can be seen as 'an overarching metaphor for the unequal power relationship which defines the condition of the colonised, (Tejaswini Niranjana, 1992), the traditionally inferior status accorded to a translated work being a symbol of the colony, which was a 'copy' or translation of Europe, then in the post-colonial age, one way to get over this dilemma of the metaphor was, as Salman Rushdie has suggested, for the Empire to write back, in the language of its erstwhile masters. The phenomenon of Indo-Anglian writing can be traced to this, as it can be traced to the wave of national and international migration that took place in post-Independence India, a natural outcome of which was the adoption of a bilingual identity with English remaining in a position of equivalence with the mother tongue. In many respects the Indo-Anglican writer was 'a translated man', spatially if not culturally uprooted from home and the growth of this form of writing mirrored this. The growth of English translation of Indian literature went hand in hand with the rise of Indian Writing in English (IWE). This is not to say that the relationship between ILET and IWE has always been one of easy symbiosis. Practitioners of ILET have often resisted the attempt to categorise their work as a byproduct of IWE because the latter has received its fair share of criticism as the output of a *khichdi* language that uncomfortably straddles Western publishing norms in transmitting experiences that belong to India and the Indian diaspora. For instance, Rushdie's particular use of Urdu words in his English has been pointed out by critics who have refused to accept him as a truly bilingual author though, paradoxically, it is Rushdie's use of such words that authenticates him as a post-colonial writer. Despite the bones of contention, it can be stated that both ILET and IWE inhabit the bilingual space, the 'contact zone' (Bassnett and Trivedi, 1999), traditionally a place where cultures met on unequal terms, which is now redefining itself as a space of multiplicity, exchange, renegotiation and discontinuities with English serving as both the message and the medium. The slew of translations as well as Indo-Anglian writing coming out have fed the maturing English language publishing business in India and in the process each has benefited the other. Vikram Seth's initial endorsement of an English translation of the Bengali novel *Chowringhee*, which went towards giving the translation the critical and commercial success it received, is a case in point.

With the hegemony of English translation of Indian works now clearly evident, the question we would return to now is what social use translation can be put to in a pluralistic, multilingual society like modern India. Does translation have a higher purpose to serve beyond the admittedly laudable one of making well-known works of Indian literature available to a wider reading public? For instance, is there something that ILET can look to beyond what appears to be its predilection for more and more translations of the epics and the works of Tagore? It may be pertinent here to return to the lost tongue being uttered by the parrots in *Solo*.

More than eighty years after the first Linguistic Survey of India conducted by the British officer George Grierson, six volumes of the findings of the People's Linguistic Survey of India (PLSI), spearheaded by G.N. Devy were released on 7 January, 2012. The findings were, to say the least, startling. Of the 1652 languages listed as 'mother tongue' by the Census of 1961, 310 were on the verge of extinction, spoken by less than 1000 people and in some cases less than five. In other words, about a fifth of India's linguistic heritage was nearing an end. Very often, these languages died because entire communities, denied livelihood in one language undertook large scale migration in the course of which they began to speak another language altogether that helped them survive. Traces of the old language remained, in the form of stray words that lingered in the new vocabulary, much like the lost tongue the explorers heard being parroted in the jungle.

This 'loss' of language has been especially noticed with marginalised tribal societies whose literature often encompasses not just folk tales or song but more complex forms such as novels and drama, all of which are in danger of being lost forever unless serious efforts are undertaken to preserve them. Linguistic preservation is not the same as archeological preservation and the reluctant fundamentalist ought to yield ground here to the English language translator who undertakes the arduous task of acting as a curator for such marginalised literature, though individual passion has to be complemented here by institutional support for anything substantial to get done. The laudable efforts of bodies such as the Sahitya Akademi and the National Book Trust in undertaking such efforts from time to time would be further strengthened by the participation of commercial publishers. Tribal literature is not the easiest and most accessible material for translation and finally the translated work needs to have strong literary value to command wide readership. However, this is true of the style and aesthetics of all translations. Even the renowned translator A.K. Ramanujan despaired of translating from medieval Tamil to English. The two languages were so different that any 'literal rendering of the syntax' of one was impossible in the other. The issue of translatibility of an individual work and the process of translation are of course beyond the scope of this essay and will be left to the competence of the individual translator. But the fact remains that translation into the dominant language of discourse is perhaps the only way to preserve these dying languages and with that, perhaps, ways of life that are withering away.

The issue of 'language loss' today also extends to major Indian languages. With increased focus being placed on an English-language based education, it is not surprising that the younger generation is hardly conversant with 'mother tongues' such as Bengali, Marathi, Gujarati and has almost wholly lapsed into a dependence on English and in many cases Hindi. This trend points disturbingly in the same direction as the findings of the PLSI do and it seems logical that with English still the unofficial lingua franca of our country thanks to our colonial inheritance, the power of English language translation needs to be harnessed here as well to stem the rot. Sujit Mukherjee (*Translation As Discovery*, 1981) has pointed out how English translation can serve as a 'link literature' in the present scenario, given the great advantage that an English translation or an Indo-Anglian work enjoys over a British or American text in classrooms because the student has direct access to the culture surrounding the text. Mukherjee goes on further to elaborate on the utility of introducing English translations in middle or high school curricula in our country—first as a tool for learning English and thus reaching out to a global society and secondly as a means of accessing literary material from other Indian languages and even one's own mother tongue. I am not sure how far this thought of introducing English translation as a link literature has permeated the consciousness of our educators yet, but given the rising focus on English language training as a means of enhancing vocational employability of rural as well as urban youth, the cultural significance of using translations as an effective educational tool cannot be overlooked, not to mention the important role such translations have to play in preserving our heritage and passing it down the generations along with an idea of 'India'. It must also be mentioned that translation from one Indian language into another also has a similar, important role to play here. To the extent that each subculture of our country will continue to produce literature that mirrors its concerns and anxieties, dissemination of such literature through the medium of translation to make such concerns accessible to other regions is an important way to foster the unified, pluralistic society that our founding fathers dreamed of.

The act of translation as pointed out by George Steiner (*After Babel: Aspects of Language and Translation*, Steiner 1975) has variously been described as a Faustian pact, a heresy enacted against the Divine Majesty of God Who scattered the peoples of the Earth into different tongues after they presumed to rival Him by building the Tower of Babel. It has also been endowed with Kabbalistic mystique as the quest for *Ur-Sprache*, the primal source language from which all tongues originate. In the context of India, translation, we have seen, has had a profoundly social and political significance that continues to this day. It has at different times been the vehicle of domination and resistance, unity and discord. If all communication is but a form of translation, then surely it is in translation that the history of our land will be chronicled, to serve as a guide for posterity, for, as Jorge Luis Borges writes:

All things are words of some strange tongue, in thrall
To Someone, Something, who both day and night
Proceeds in endless gibberish to write
The history of the world. In that dark scrawl
Rome is set down, and Carthage, I, you, all,
And this my being which escapes me quite,
My anguished life that's cryptic, recondite,
And garbled as the tongues of Babel's fall.

A Woman Named Honour: the Good, the Bad and the Remembered

—Rafia Zakaria

I never met my mother's aunt but the memory of her lingered around the margins of my childhood. Perhaps it was inevitable that a person whose name meant 'Honour' would invoke a child's fascination and wonder, just as if she were named 'Truth' or 'Fortune'. But perhaps 'Honour' in particular meant more to me because I was a girl. The burden of upholding honour, the trickiness of maintaining it, and the strictures of respecting it defined my life and continued to grow as I got older.

My mother's aunt died before I was born, not long after my mother (one of four sisters) was married in the late seventies. She, her mother, and her sisters grew up on the suburban edges of Karachi, before those edges of the city were as populous or as accessible as they are now. In a modern bungalow in the sandy, almost-hilly recess of North Nazimabad, my mother and aunts learned life's lessons through the lives of the women around them. The story of Aunt Honour, unfolding before them, was a cautionary tale. She was all wrong for the new country made just for the sub-continent's Muslims; too friendly, too flirtatious, too eager for frivolity. She had come from Bombay a city with a cosmopolitan culture where she lived among an urbane set of Iranian émigrés and Zoroastrian socialites who saw theatre in the evenings and opera on the weekends.

Karachi was different—a city anxious and uncertain about what it meant to be Muslim and democratic and cosmopolitan and, of course, female and honourable. This was true even in the sixties and seventies; I had trouble imagining the theatre matinees and dance recitals of that era in the post-Islamisation Karachi of the late eighties and nineties. In this Karachi, Aunt Honour, with her Persian ancestry and her elegant Bombay society mien, stood out. From my mother's telling, it is difficult to extricate the lessons from the life. Her two sisters, including my grandmother, were better at reading and following the dictates of respectability in the new country, better at compromise, better at being female.

Aunt Honour, like her sisters, was married, but her union was shadowed with doubt from the start. With her characteristic impetuosity, she insisted on marrying on a day my superstitious great-grandmother believed was inauspicious on the Iranian calendar. She gathered her similarly rebellious friends, the eggers-on of the ill-fated, and married a man from a Sindhi family. He enjoyed a prominent post in the inland city of Hyderabad so the bride and groom set off for a new life. Aunt Honour would be the wife and the host, and it seemed all would be well.

But when Aunt Honour's expectations did not meet reality, she refused to follow the hushed tradition of saying nothing when nothing good can be said. It is said that her husband was abusive, that she returned again and again from the isolation of Hyderabad, beaten and bruised, emotionally if not visibly. She rebelled against her husband and her marriage at the same time that my mother passed through adolescence. In her sister's home, full of teenage girls brimming with aspirations and hope, Aunt Honour cast the bitterness of her own failure, her realisation of the violence and antagonism that relationships can be reduced to. Aunt Honour's disappointments came fast and furious and always at times that were supposed to be joyous—the two Eids, birthdays, weddings. She told stories of manipulation and exploitation, of accusations of infidelity, of beatings. With each one of them, she was diminished more and more from a bubbly, charming beauty to a washed out, morose, and hostile shadow. Her face hardened and lost its bloom. To kill the pain she began to take pills; to free herself from the pills, she took some more.

And then one day the fights were over forever. Aunt Honour left her husband, told my grandmother that she would not return again to the cruel man she had married. There was no room to weep for her tragedy; my mother and her sisters were to be married, and Aunt Honour's act jeopardised all of their futures. It was yet another episode of selfishness whose price would be paid by others. Aunt Honour's decline continued; she became mentally ill, attempted suicide, and was institutionalised, her life—a life that did not fit in the spaces available—gone awry. The family found Aunt Honour a room, rented from a respectable family, where she could live alone, hidden from the scrutiny of suitors awaiting another generation of women. In her seclusion, Aunt Honour rode the tides of paranoia and ostracism that were now her life. She never forgave her mother and sisters, whose concerns about respectability she laughed at in her lunacy.

My mother does not remember her Aunt Honour fondly; the acrimony of her end was too large and pressing, the lessons of her transgressions impressed too deeply on the girls that watched them unfold. There is an Aunt Honour in the lives of every Pakistani woman, indeed perhaps in the life of every woman. I tell her story—the story of this ancestor who was transformed from a woman to a lesson—to underscore a paradox that women everywhere are led to believe: that there are no good women without bad ones, enlightened women without ignorant ones, empowered women without weak ones, and free women without enslaved ones. The moral hues of Aunt Honour's name were clearly marked by the women who told it to me; but for me her story echoes also with a question both they and I continue to wrestle with decades after her death. Is the enlightened woman the one who follows fast and swallows easily the pallet of silences and manipulations that enable survival in a world made to fit men; or one like Aunt Honour who rebels regardless; and is left to endure the bleak punishments that come with that choice? I cannot answer for us all, but I can say that in doing what was different, Aunt Honour, so castigated in her present, is remembered and respected and loved in these words of a finally arrived future.

The world of women is a world of opposites where we locate ourselves and others firmly and only in terms of these contraries which elevate some, denigrate others. The story of Aunt Honour, a newly-wed Pakistani woman who lived and died in the remote recesses of a foreign land, is not only a story of a woman wronged by circumstances, of the vagaries of female existence in a patriarchal society. It is a story about this disastrous dance of opposites that divides and conquers and silences women, besetting them with hatreds and capturing them in boxes, so they become schooled in blaming only each other, remain convinced that the women who fall and fail will never, ever be them.

Recollected decades later, this story from the cusp of Partition, from the creation of a new country on the memory marked terrain of an old civilisation; presents the complicated truths of history that has been tampered and toyed with. Constructing the past is always a political project; but when it becomes singularly a political project, it becomes impoverished and ill equipped to guide the present. Aunt Honour was a free woman born in a free country; but liberty can create its own shackles when unaccompanied by the tempering of compassion, of empathy and a respect for those that choose paths that are not well-worn by the beliefs of the many, the comforting cadence of conformity.

Just as Aunt Honour's story remains poised between the binary of good and bad; the question of women and their honour haunts both Pakistan and India. In both and either, women are interpreted as markers not of their own lives and decisions but of a nation's image of itself. Carrying these loads on their shoulders; women's lives are cut up by the demands of tradition and legacy, even as they mediate the rapid incursions of urbanisation, economic disparity that come riding the hems of progress. Independence came a long time ago, but perhaps only for half of those who awaited it.

Gender Responsive Budgeting in India: What has Gone Wrong?*

—*Yamini Mishra, Navanita Sinha*

Abstract

The manner in which the Indian initiative on Gender Responsive Budgeting has panned out appears to be a classic case of putting the cart before the horse. This article analyses the two prime strategies adopted by the Government of India for institutionalising GRB, namely the Gender Budget Statement and Gender Budgeting Cells to highlight what has gone wrong, and what needs to be fixed. The authors also draw on experiences from other countries, to argue that GRB in India needs a completely different rhythm if it has to translate into better outcomes for the women of our country. With the formulation of the Twelfth Plan under way, the moment is opportune to push for groundbreaking changes in the policy discourse on GRB.

Gender Responsive Budgeting in India: What has gone wrong?

Globally Gender Responsive Budgeting (GRB) has come to light as an important tool in the ongoing struggle to make budgets and policies more gender responsive. From just one country in the mid-1980s to over 90 countries now—the last two decades have witnessed an overwhelming endorsement of GRB as a valuable tool for engendering budgets and policies all over the world.

In India too, GRB has drawn significant attention from policy makers. Both the Tenth and the Eleventh Five Year Plans made explicit mention of how GRB should be used. With the Approach Paper for the Twelfth Plan in the public domain, a lot of effort will now be invested in formulating the Twelfth Plan. The moment is

* This piece was earlier published in EPW dated 28 April 2012, and is being published here with the permission of the authors.

thus opportune to reflect on ground breaking changes that we want from the Twelfth Plan. This piece focuses on the experience of GRB in India—what has gone wrong and what needs to be fixed in the Twelfth Plan.

Trajectory of GRB in India

While much ground work had been done in the years preceding its introduction in 2004-05, it was arguably the Report of *the Expert Group of Classification of Government Expenditure,* which became instrumental in laying out the roadmap for GRB. One of the terms of references (ToRs) of the Expert Group was to look into and suggest means to integrate GRB in the budgetary processes of the Government of India by means of plausible institutional mechanisms. The expert group submitted its report in July 2004 and broadly prescribed the norms under which the ministries/departments would report their gender budget.

Following this, the Ministry of Women and Child Development (MWCD) adopted '*Budgeting for Gender Equity*' as a mission statement in 2004-05. A Strategic Framework of Activities to implement this mission was also framed and disseminated to all departments and ministries of the Government of India (GoI). That same year, the Ministry of Finance, initiated the process of creating an institutional mechanism for mainstreaming gender by mandating the setting up of Gender Budgeting Cells (GBCs) in all ministries/departments. These GBCs were envisaged as focal points for mainstreaming gender through GRB.

2005-06 became the landmark year for GRB in India,with the introduction of the Gender Budget Statement (GBS) in the Union Budget, to reflect the quantum of budgetary allocations for programmes/schemes that substantially benefit women.

Although the Indian government's experience of GRB is widely used as reference point for other GRB initiatives, there seems to be a visible gap in what was envisioned and what has been achieved under the rubric of GRB. In fact the government's own road map for gender budgeting as envisioned by the Ashok Lahiri committee was far more comprehensive[1]. With the preparation of the GBS, our energies seem to have stagnated on Step 1; and unfortunately no concerted efforts have been made to deepen GRB work beyond this stage. Furthermore, commentators have also drawn attention to several problems/weaknesses in the way in which GRB is being done, particularly the manner in which the GBS is prepared and the functioning of GBCs, etc. We will discuss these in detail in the next section.

Having reflected on both the policy endorsements as well as on its gaps of GRB work, one is left wondering whether these policy pronouncements have led to any tangible gains for the women of our country. Have budgets or policies of any select ministry/department of the Union or State government become more gender responsive? Have any of these efforts translated into more gender-responsive outlays and outcomes?

Although cognisant of the fact that translating policy commitments into tangible gains is invariably a long drawn process, the subject of our inquiry is this: can we construe the gap between what has been achieved and what could have been achieved by GRB in India, essentially as one of time lag? Or does GRB, require a different rhythm all together if we want tangible outcomes for women of India. In this piece, we argue that it is the latter. We develop our critique at two levels—at one level, we analyse the prime strategies adopted by the government for institutionalising GRB, namely the GBS and GBCs; and at another, we build on experiences from other countries, to map out certain alternative pathways for GRB in India.

The Gender Budget Statement: Inaccurate reporting or design flaw?
If one looks at the larger choice set of GRB tools available, GBS is the only tool that has been institutionalised in India. The Indian GBS (Statement 20, Expenditure Budget, Vol. 1) is a purely quantitative format. Currently 33 Demands for Grants out of a total of 106 disaggregate their allocations by sex and report in the GBS. The Statement comprises of two parts: Part A, which details schemes in which 100 per cent allocations are for women; and Part B, which reflects schemes where the allocations for women constitute at least 30 per cent of the provisions.

The GBS has been studied in great detail and both its strengths and limitations highlighted. On the positive side, the GBS in India is a definite step towards greater transparency. Prior to its introduction, there was no way of even estimating how much of the government's total expenditure was flowing to women. Now, with the production of the GBS as part of the Union Budget documents, an institutionalised effort is being made to answer this basic question. The other significant advantage of producing the GBS is that by asking line ministries to disaggregate allocations by sex, a thinking process is being initiated or a 'consciousness' so to say, being created, of at least beginning to assess and hence reflect on the impact of allocations of a particular ministry on women.

On the flip side, attention has been drawn to the limited scope of the exercise—from the low levels of allocations for women as revealed in the GBS, to the number of ministries/demands for grants covered in the scope of the GBS, as well as the various methodological inaccuracies that mar the current GBS (see Das and Mishra 2006a, 2006b; Jhamb and Mishra 2007).Despite several attempts at refinement and restructuring to ensure accurate reporting, the GBS remains fraught with huge methodological errors/flaws. Some of the main anomalies are listed below:

- Allocations for schemes reported in Part A of the Statement where clearly 100% of the beneficiaries are not women. For instance, *Indira Awas Yojana* continues to figure in Part A, despite the fact that 100 per cent of its allocations do not benefit women. In 2008-2009 for instance, of the 20.94 lakh houses constructed, only 17.16 lakh houses were allotted to women, the remaining were jointly allotted to men and women from the same household (Government of India 2010a).
- Allocations for schemes reported in Part B, wherein 100 per cent of the allocations are reported as opposed to reflecting the percentage that actually flows to women. For example, most schemes of Ministry of Minority Affairs, Ministry of Earth Sciences and Ministry of Labour and Employment report 100 per cent of their allocations in Part B, whereas they are clearly not meant exclusively for women.
- Allocations for schemes reported in Part B, where the reported percentage is less than 100% but there is no clarity on how the

ministry estimated the percentage flowing to women. For instance, under the Department of Higher Education, the budget line *National Council for Promotion of Urdu Language* shows approximately 33 per cent of its total allocations under the GBS. What was the basis of arriving at this figure?

As discussed above, there are glaring methodological inaccuracies in the GBS, and it is critical that all necessary steps be taken to correct the same. Equally important is the need to monitor the GBS. Presently no such monitoring or audit mechanism of the GBS is in place in India. Therefore there is no way to ascertain whether what has been promised in the GBS is actually being fulfilled or not. In this section our focus however is not on the inaccuracies of the GBS (whether the figures are correct; what was the basis of arriving at the figure, etc). Our critique is hinged on a different peg—we argue that the major weakness of GRB work in India pertains to the format of the GBS, which is purely quantitative. In this section, we discuss some of the major limitations of this format.

Disaggregation of allocations by sex of the beneficiary in the GBS is not very useful

The first major limitation of the quantitative format is that it disaggregates allocations by sex of the beneficiary. In other words, it breaks down the allocations by its incidence on who it falls on—men or women. The fundamental question that the GBS therefore answers is—what percentage of allocations fall on women? For instance, under Part A of the GBS for 2011-12 is the item '*Washing Drying/Women's Laundry*' (Demand no. 54 - Police, ITBP). This expenditure was (or will probably be) incurred on women police officers and is thus reflected in the GBS. Similarly, the line item '*Engaging women employees on a contract basis*' (Demand no. 52, Ministry of Home Affairs), women employees were (or will be) engaged on a contract basis and hence the money allocated for them is reflected in the GBS.

In both these examples, while the allocation reflected is meant for women, the question that escapes scrutiny here is whether these allocations, in any way, seek to redress gender imbalances. For instance in the second example, the women employed on a contract basis could actually be worse off in terms of the employment contract, than their corresponding women or men counterparts in permanent jobs for similar work. Does this expenditure then promote gender equality or women's empowerment in any way?

In contrast, consider for instance, a hypothetical expenditure: a training programme organised on gender sensitisation for male police officers. This expenditure clearly falls on men. Therefore, if one were to go strictly by the logic of our current GBS, it probably will not feature in the GBS. But looked closely, the expenditure in this case, is clearly meant to address a critical gender concern—the need to make service delivery more gender responsive. Such expenditure is therefore much more likely to promote gender equality than expenditure incurred on laundry of women officers' uniforms. Does our GBS format leave any space to ask these questions? The answer is a resounding 'No'!

What these examples demonstrate clearly is that there is an inherent drawback in disaggregating expenditure by the *sex of the beneficiary* rather than by the *objective of the expenditure*. Various GRB proponents have proposed categorisations reflecting the latter. The most famous perhaps is Rhonda Sharp's 3-way categorisation of expenditure wherein expenditure is divided into the following: (a) Gender-targeted expenditure; (b) Equal opportunity expenditure for civil servants; and (c) Mainstream expenditure (the rest) considered in terms of its gendered impact.

Another categorisation proposed by Nirmala Banerjee, appears more relevant for the Indian context. In her pioneering work on '*Gender and Fiscal Policies: The Case of West Bengal*' she proposes sub-categorising expenditures on public schemes for women, in the following manner (Banerjee and Roy 2004):

- Relief Policies, which are not aimed at solving any perennial or structural problems.
- Gender Reinforcing Assistance, which supports women but strictly for their needs in accepted gender roles.
- Empowering Schemes, which focus on removing gender-based disadvantages of women.

Though the format used is purely quantitative, the Nepalese GBS too presents an interesting alternative. It uses an interesting mix of disaggregating expenditure by both—its incidence (on men and women) as well as its objective. The indicators used in this case are (with an equal weight of 20 per cent each): (a) Women's capacity development; (b). Women's participation in programme formulation and implementation; (c). Benefit incidence of public expenditures on women; (d) Support to women's employment and income generation; (e) Positive impact on women's time use and care work.

We argue that an objective-based disaggregation is a much more useful way of disaggregating public expenditure. It is clearly more informative about the direction public policy ought to take to be more gender responsive.

More importantly, classifying allocations and expenditure by sex can be relevant only for specific ministries—specifically those that are "divisible" (i.e., where beneficiaries can be counted). For indivisible ministries where beneficiaries cannot be easily counted, one is bound to get stuck in a hair splitting exercise of how to arrive at the proportion flowing to women. Possibly this is one of the reasons why the number of ministries reporting in the GBS has stagnated over the years. This is also perhaps the reason why the basic question in GRB that has occupied the mind-space of most ministries is unfortunately, "how do we disaggregate allocations for our ministry". Instead, the more fundamental question that needs to be asked is this: "how can the policies and budgets of different ministries and departments be made more gender responsive"? Unfortunately, this question has not been centre-staged in the current GRB discourse.

A similar problem has been experienced with regard to the implementation of Scheduled Caste Sub Plan (SCSP) and Tribal Sub Plan (TSP). The Narendra Jadhav Task Force set up by the Planning Commission in 2010 to review and re-examine the SCSP and TSP guidelines suggested several progressive steps for better implementation of SCSP and TSP but made it non-obligatory for 43 ministries/departments to implement SCSP and TSP (Government of India 2010b). The important point to note here is that so long as one insists on disaggregating expenditures based on the identity of the beneficiary (whether based on gender or caste) and not on the objective of the expenditure, it is most likely that several ministries/departments will remain off the hook.

There is a further limitation as well, with significant implications about how we conceive of gender and its relationship to other forms of disadvantage. By having a format that insists on a binary disaggregation between men and women, there is a direct reinforcement of homogeneous conceptions of masculinity/femininity, and by extension an implicit invisibilisation of alternative sexual identities such as bisexual, transgender and intersex within public policy. Furthermore, the question of intersectionalities across other categories of discrimination or exclusion is not raised.

Current format of GBS does not inform policy making in the line ministries

The second major problem with this format of the GBS is that it neither serves as a tool that informs policy making nor does it enable policy makers to assess the additional steps needed to make the policy/scheme gender responsive.

Gender relations are complex, and any exercise which seeks to capture these complex relations through a number is evidently problematic. At times, what may be required to address key gender gaps may be resource intensive (such as constructing separate toilets for girls in schools), but at times they need not be resource intensive and may require certain modifications to operational guidelines, such as converting a room in a school into a crèche. The current format encourages ministries to report higher amounts/allocations flowing to women and puts a premium on higher amounts—something akin to a battle of numbers, but provides no fillip to officials to take small but critical steps towards engendering programmes, such as setting up crèches, creating sexual harassment committees, providing maternity leave, flexi-timings, etc.

Therefore, the second major limitation of a purely quantitative format is this: while it helps us answer the question how much is supposedly being allocated and spent on women, it does not in any which way facilitate gender responsive planning and budgeting. It would be far more useful if the GBS began with (a) identifying the pressing gender gaps in a particular sector/scheme, followed by (b) what steps the ministry/department will take, in the particular year, to address the gap and (c) then identifying the budgetary resources needed to address these pressing gender gaps and ensure that the requisite funds are made available and spent well. Unfortunately, the current format reduces GRB to merely a number crunching exercise, something that is done as an afterthought, and in no way seeks to inform policy making.

Take the example of Sarva Shiksha Abhiyan (SSA). Based on the enrolment ratio of boys and girls, the Department of School Education and Literacy shows 48 to 53 per cent of the funds in the GBS. Evidently thus the reporting of SSA in the GBS is based on a mechanical division of the total spending on boys versus girls on the basis of the available enrolment ratio. For the GBS to be used as a tool to engender policy making, the process would necessarily have to commence with the identification of the additional activity which the ministry would undertake that particular year to make a programme like SSA more gender responsive, and then follow it up with a more precise estimation of the resources required to implement the same, for instance, engendering curriculum, or engendering teacher training material, etc.

We argue that a format of the GBS that uses a mix of both qualitative and quantitative methodologies can address this gap. Countries such as Indonesia have experimented with formats that have an appropriate mix of the qualitative as well as quantitative. Although qualitative formats also differ with regard to the scope and depth of the exercise, most are drawn from the Five-Step Framework of GRB, one of the important contributions made by Debbie Budlender to the field (Budlender et al 2002).

With sectoral ministries being asked to report in the GBS, without an institutionalised process of either gender analysis of the situation or gender analysis of policies, we are essentially starting with Step-3 of Budlender's Five-Step Framework. The starting point of any good GRB work has to be a strong gender analysis of the situation or the issue at hand.

GBS is only suited for a few ministries; there is a need to engage with other GRB tools

It is important to look at the entire choice-set of GRB tools available and accordingly reflect on which tool is most appropriate to meet the larger objective of making policies and programmes of different ministries/departments more gender responsive. For instance, Sex Disaggregated Revenue Analysis, (in which one tries to assess how men and women are affected differently by the kind of revenues raised by government) is a tool that revenue-generating ministries (and only they) can use. Whereas sex-disaggregated analysis of impact of budget on time use, (which analyses the impact of government resource allocation on the amount and the way time is spent by men/boys and women/girls) is a tool that Ministry of Statistics might be best suited to use, although it should inform policy making by other line ministries as well.

Globally too, GBS is one of the most popular tools but there is a need to reflect more carefully on which tool is most appropriate in keeping with the specificities of the context and the sector.

There are few examples from the South Asian region itself, where governments have taken the lead in institutionalising other tools. In Pakistan, for instance, the GRB Initiative was introduced in 2005 at the federal level and in two pilot districts of the province of Punjab and the implementation strategy developed highlighted the priority areas and provided a road map to be followed. GRB tools used were—Gender Aware Policy Appraisals, conducted for the Education, Health and Population Welfare Sectors which became part of the gender related inputs for the sector review reports of the government; Gender-Aware Beneficiary Assessment survey, undertaken in the two districts of Punjab province; a nationwideTime Use Survey, which revealed the macro-economic implications of the unpaid care work of the family; and in 2006, a pilot Gender Budget Statement was prepared for the Education, Health and Population Welfare Sectors in Punjab (Mahbub and Budlender 2007; Government of Pakistan and UNDP 2008). In Bangladesh, on the other hand, the government allocated funds for undertaking gender disaggregated beneficiary assessment.

Gender Budget Cells: An effective institutional mechanism for GRB?

As mentioned earlier, in India the second major step taken by the GoI to institutionalise GRB was the creation of Gender Budget Cells (GBCs) in various ministries/departments. While the idea emerged from the recommendation of the Ashok Lahiri Committee, it was a charter issued by the Ministry of Finance (MoF) on March 8, 2007, which finally mandated the formation of GBCs. As per the Gender Budget Charter, GBCs were to be set up with the objective of:

> ...influencing and effecting a change in the Ministry's policies, programmes in a way that could tackle gender imbalances, promote gender equality and development and ensure that public resources through the Ministry budget are allocated and managed accordingly. (Government of India 2007a:64).

Much attention was paid to the composition of the GBCs as well. As per the Charter, the Gender Budget Cell should comprise a cohesive group of senior/ middle level officers from the Plan, Policy, Coordination, Budget and Accounts Division of the Ministry concerned. It should be headed by an officer not below the rank of Joint Secretary. The functions and working of the GBC may be reviewed at least once a quarter at the level of Secretary/Additional Secretary of the Department.

The functions listed were also a good start. Amongst others, three important tasks assigned to the GBCs were:

- Identifying a minimum of three and maximum of six largest programmes (in terms of budget allocation) implemented by the Ministry to analyse gender issues addressed by them.
- Conducting/Commissioning Performance audit (at the field level wherever possible) for reviewing the actual physical/financial targets of the programme, the constraints if any, in implementation, the need for strengthening delivery systems, infrastructure/capacity building etc.
- Organising meetings/discussions/consultations with GBCs of related departments within the Ministry, field level organisation/ civil society groups/NGOs working in the sector for exchanging ideas and getting feedback on the efficacy of sectoral policies and programmes.

The Eleventh Plan also noted that efforts will continue to create GBCs in all ministries and departments (Government of India 2007b). Going by the number of GBCs formed within various ministries and departments, (56 on last count), one would tend to assume that much work has been done on this front.

Unfortunately, the GBCs have not been able to execute the tasks assigned to them. Despite a commitment in the Eleventh Plan that 'data from these cells will be collated on a regular basis and made available in the public domain', not much is known about the functioning of these cells. Within policy circles, there seems to be a latent feeling that these cells have been largely ineffective and remained mostly on paper. What is even more disturbing is that no comprehensive review of these GBCs has been conducted by the government so far.

Our critique of the GBCs is not only based on the specifics of the Indian experience, but also draws on the experiences of similar gender architectures/machineries in other countries—to highlight what has worked, and what has not.

Low Priority given to the Gender Agenda

It must be mentioned that the non-functioning of GBCs is a problem not typical to India alone. Gender architecture/machineries (GRB architecture is a sub component of the larger gender architecture) in many countries have grappled with similar challenges and constraints that have adversely impacted their working. One such fundamental problem is that despite being articulated as a priority in policy circles, the gender agenda continues to be relegated to an "additional charge" status, and often times, falls on the lap of overworked officials who are unable to prioritise this, even if they consider gender to be a priority. This de-prioritisation of the gender agenda manifests in two peculiar syndromes.

The first is what we refer to as the 'too high up or too low below' syndrome and is related to the position of officials responsible for the gender agenda within the hierarchical bureaucratic order. In many countries the prime responsibility rests with officials who are too senior in the hierarchy, and are therefore unable to dedicate the time required for pushing the gender agenda.

The second is the "individual versus group" syndrome. Many countries have appointed Gender Focal Points in line ministries/ departments. These Gender Focal Points are mostly individual driven. Though they benefit from the energy or commitment that the individual brings in, there is a major weakness of this arrangement as well. Oftentimes, when these Focal Points are transferred/shifted, the work has to be initiated all over again. In contradistinction, some countries have set up Gender Mainstreaming Groups or Cells within ministries/departments. While these structures have the advantage of not being individual centred; it is often a challenge to get a group together in line ministries, where priorities are often not related to gender, but to sectoral concerns. Therefore, in this tussle between individuals and groups, unfortunately efforts to strengthen GRB get diluted. The underlying problem is that in most countries the focus has not been on developing the necessary institutional capabilities—but remained largely individual centric, and have therefore failed to bring about transformations at the level of institutions and systems. Since a lot of energy has been invested in conducting GRB trainings and capacity building exercises in several countries including India, it would be valuable at this stage perhaps, to take stock of all these efforts towards capacity building in GRB. For GRB to move forward now, it is important thus to reflect in a strategic way on whose capacities need to be built, what kind of capacities need to be built and what is the best way of building these capacities.

Lack of a Coordinating/Monitoring Mechanism

Since GRB by its very definition entails cross-sectoral work and requires coordination between various sectoral ministries, some institutional mechanism to facilitate the process is often required. Different countries have experimented with different structures—some have set up Committees and Task Forces, others have set up cells within line ministries and/or a secretariat to coordinate, among others.

Unfortunately in India, GRB efforts have been severely impeded due to the absence of such a coordinating mechanism for harmonising the work of Gender Budget Cells, across line ministries. Based on the experiences of other countries, it can be argued that a basic minimum in terms of an institutional mechanism is required to make GRB effective. Some of these criteria are outlined below:

It is imperative that the GRB machinery which involves the sectoral ministries (not just the Ministry of Women and Child Development and the Ministry of Finance) is robust and functional. This is critical because, it is the sectoral ministries which need to use GRB as a tool to make their policies and budgets more gender responsive.

It must be mentioned here that the need for a similar mechanism was highlighted in India by the Ashok Lahiri Committee, which recommended an Interdepartmental Steering Committee (ISC) on Gender Budgeting in addition to GBCs in individual departments/ ministries, for identifying and sharing 'the issues of gender budgeting which cut across departments, for instance, the issues of budgetary allocations related to domestic violence, microfinance, homelessness, etc.' (Government of India 2004: 12)

Since GRB is about budgets, the GRB architecture must also find legitimate space in the budget making cycle of the country. This is one of the most critical weaknesses of the GRB architecture (or the gender architecture that GRB uses) in many countries. In India, for instance the Ministry of Finance, issues circulars, Gender Budget Statements are produced by the sectoral ministries, but there is no space for the GRB machinery within the formal budget making process.

A rare model which Philippines has used is including the National Commission on the Role of Filipino Women (NCRFW) (which has taken the lead in GRB in Philippines) in all budget discussions conducted by the Ministry of Finance for sectoral ministries. To put it in context, since 1998 all agencies have been required to formulate Gender and Development (GAD) plans and submit these to the NCRFW for approval. The NCRFW Management Committee members sit in on the technical budget hearings conducted by the Department for Budget Management and also sit in on Congress meetings where agency officials defend their budgets (Budlender et al 2002).

The presence of the GRB machinery in the formal budget negotiations between the Ministry of Finance and the sectoral ministers will be critical for the following two reasons. Firstly, this will help ascertain the extent to which sectoral ministries have been able to fulfil their commitments for GRB (whether in the GBS or elsewhere) and secondly, it will assist the sectoral ministries in identifying ways in which their policies and budgets can be made more gender responsive. Creating such a space for the GRB machinery within the formal budgetary process would be pivotal for realising the objective of making budgetary outlays and outcomes, gender responsive.

It is important for certain ministries to act as key drivers for GRB. Given the nature of work, the Finance Ministry, Women's Ministry (in India, the Ministry of Women and Child Development) and the Planning Agency (Planning Commission for India and ministries of planning in other countries) are critical to this equation. In several countries one has witnessed this debate of where should the key responsibility for GRB be placed—within the Finance Ministries or within the Women's Ministries or the Planning Ministries. While there is no one mantra for this difficult question, what can be said with confidence is that the involvement of the Ministry of Finance is critical, since it is mandated with the important task of deciding the resource envelope for sectoral ministries.

GRB in India: Putting the cart before the horse?

The manner in which the Indian initiative on GRB has panned out appears to be a classic case of putting the cart before the horse. Beginning with the GBS and the GBCs, in the manner in which we did, was perhaps not the best way to begin. As the experience of GRB in other countries reveals, for GRB to have a meaningful start, it must necessarily begin with purposive gender planning for each scheme/sector—first by identifying the gender gaps in the sector and then delineating prioritised action points to address the gender gaps. Scrutinising budgets and ensuring good quantity and quality of budgetary spending should come in only after that. Instead as discussed in the previous sections, the current format of the GBS has reduced GRB to nothing but a number crunching exercise. With the formulation of the Twelfth Plan underway, there is a massive window of opportunity to redraft the format of the GBS and thereby chart a different course of action for GRB.

It will be timely to recommend the formation of a committee to review the format of the GBS and suggest a more appropriate one, which can concretely inform policy making.

It is equally critical that the Twelfth Plan reflects on the institutional architecture for GRB in our country. Clearly, the GBCs have remained an exercise on paper, and failed to propel the GRB agenda further. There is a pressing need thus to rethink and reinvigorate these GBCs. Without a robust institutional mechanism to support GRB across the various line ministries, India will not be able to harness the potential that GRB offers.

The Indian Novel in English and National Identity

—*Banibrata Mahanta*

As we look back in time from the vantage point of the second decade of the twenty-first century, the Indian novel in English seems to enjoy unprecedented visibility on the global bookshelf. The significant presence of the Indian novel in English is evident in its presence on almost every other course on postcolonial literature across the globe, the Booker Prize and Commonwealth Writers' Prize, astronomical pre-publication advances to both established and aspiring authors, sustained attention from internationally prominent critics, reviewers and publication houses and the ubiquitous and sustained presence of the genre in national and international literary journals, magazines and newspaper supplements of repute. The Indian novel in English is beyond doubt a literary and cultural phenomenon that needs to be examined in a broad radius that takes into account its complex originary antecedents, its subsequent evolutionary trajectory and its fissiparous character. Traversing, in the words of Balachandra Rajan, the shift from 'the old imperial tripod of commerce, conquest and conversion' to 'a new one built upon commerce, culture and consent', the Indian novel in English makes for an interesting engagement not just in the genre, but in the idea of the nation as it has evolved from the pre-colonial times to the age of globalisation and its (dis)contents, and also of its discursive parameters and practices (qtd. in Monkman). This essay is an attempt to chronicle these issues by charting the thematic and chronological trajectories of the Indian novel in English, with a focus on the paradigmatic aspects.

The Indian constitution recognises English as one of the official languages. However, the connection between the Indian novel in

English and the historical accident that brought the British to India is the cause of sustained and sentimentalised regional and nationalistic critique, locking novels in English and those written in the vernacular languages in an oppositional discourse that brings into play a range of factors from class and region to cultural nationalism and configurations of power structures. Outlining the contours of this debate Meenakshi Mukherjee, comments: 'No one would write a doctoral dissertation on the Indianness of a Marathi novel. But when it comes to English fiction originating in our country, not only does the issue of Indianness become a favourite essentialising obsession in academic writings and the book review circuit, the writers themselves do not seem unaffected by it, the complicating factor being that English is not just any language—it was the language of our colonial rulers and continues even now to be the language of power and privilege.'

The writer himself is not 'unaffected' by this linguistic and cultural double-bind, as borne out in Raja Rao's 'Preface' to *Kantapura*: 'The telling has not been easy. One has to convey in a language that is not one's own the spirit that is one's own. One has to convey the various shades and omissions of a certain thought movement that looks maltreated in an alien language. I use the word 'alien', yet English is not really an alien language to us. It is the language of our intellectual makeup, like Sanskrit or Persian were—but not of our emotional makeup.'

And it is not just the language. The nation itself has been the outcome of this historical accident. While ancient and medieval examples of territorial and cultural communities abounded in India, and we also have examples of more widely-encompassing ideas of community from those times, the idea of 'nation' and 'nationality' and its political implications are primarily 'modern' and Western and came to India with the British. Ironically, the country that the British initially unified through various developmental strategies consolidated itself further through oppositional positioning against the coloniser. This initial consolidation was subsequently complicated by the emergence of regional, and later, religious nationalism. The Indian novel in English is, therefore, not just the flagbearer of the national presence globally; it is a complex repository of the formation of and challenges to the nation. In this essay, I have attempted a broad survey of how the Indian novel in English progressed from its formative pre-national beginnings to the nationalist phase, manifesting the contradictions of consolidation and fragmentation of its 'national' character during the pre and post independence eras, and how the changed post-1980 global realities finally set it on a changed course.

The Beginning

The processual dynamics involved in the production of the first work in English by an Indian throws light on its complex nature. The title of this book, written by Dean Muhammad, prefigures many such complexities that were to govern the course of the Indian novel in English. *The Travels of Dean Mahomet, A Native of Patna in Bengal, Through Several Parts of India, While in the Service of The Honourable East India Company, Written by Himself, In a Series of Letters to a Friend* was published in 1794. Dean Muhammad was an Indian placed under the care of Ensign Godfrey Evan Baker from whom he learnt the English language. Later he converted to Christianity. When Dean Muhammad subsequently went to England, it was at Baker's estate that he worked for the major part of his stay in that country. He married an Irishwoman, Jane Daly. Dean Muhammad experienced a new language and culture through employment, marriage, conversion and friendship, which have been identified by Dharwadker as the four contact zones between the British and the Indians. In addition, he observes that the presence of mediating zones such as an English education and a journey to England provide the 'maximum points of contact and acculturation'. When Dean Muhammad planned his book, his social status in Ireland was sufficiently secure for 'a total of 320 people [to entrust] him with a deposit...long in advance of the book's delivery'. Dean Muhammad's choice of subject (India), his choice of form (epistolary travelogue), his consciousness of his readership (English/Irish), his handling of the publishing and marketing of the book are indicative of the pluralism and the socio-economic factors that would characterise the growth of the Indian novel in English.

The beginnings of the Indian novel in English are characterised by the issues mentioned above. Indian writers faced the complex task of negotiating the colonial matrices of power while writing indigenous experiences in the colonial form and tongue. The beginnings of the Indian novel in English are traced here through a study of six novelists—Bankimchandra Chattopadhyay, Lal Behari Dey, Kylash Chunder Dutt, Shoshee Chunder Dutt, Krupabai Satthianandan and A. Madhavaiah.

Rajmohun's Wife (1864) is an important text which deals with the problems faced by the Indian writer. Bankim's return to his mother-tongue after his maiden attempt at writing in English makes it, simultaneously, the first Indian novel in English and one which raises more questions than it resolves. In her foreword to a recent edition of the novel, Meenakshi Mukherjee wonders: Why did Bankim stop writing in English? Could he not identify his readership? Was it semantic and connotative hurdles that caused him to change track? This novel does underline some themes and issues though. It talks about the impact of urban education, the social status and sufferings of women and faith in colonial institutions and administrators.

In contrast Lal Behari Dey's *Govinda Samanta or the History of a Bengal Raiyat* (1874) attempts an untraversed path in its depiction of rural destitution. However, the vitality of description is offset by the author's painstaking attempts to simplify cultural nuances for his target readership, which is evidently British. The novels of Kylash Chunder Dutt and Shoshee Chunder Dutt offer interesting points of comparison. *A Journal of Forty-Eight Hours of the Year* 1945 (1835), written by the former, celebrates an urban resistance to the British. The latter's *The Republic of Odisha: A Page from the Annals of the 20th Century* (1845) talks of a tribal uprising against the British. However, his subsequent works exhibit an increasingly pro-colonial perspective.

Krupabai Satthianandan's novels *Kamala* (1894) and *Saguna* (1895) need to be analysed in the light of her personal circumstances. Krupabai was actively involved with women's reforms. Her parents were the first Brahmin converts to Christianity in the Bombay Presidency. Her autobiographical novel, *Saguna*, deals with the inter-related issues of Christianity, colonialism, the women's question and nationalism. The issue of the liberation of Hindu upper-caste women from repressive patriarchal familial ideologies lies at the heart of the novel. *Kamala* too deals with the issues of gender, caste and culture. But it is a landmark novel because it is the first Indian novel in English which represents untouchables and tribals as individuals, and India is depicted as a cultural rather than religious entity.

Although a servile and obsequious tone characterised A. Madhavaiah's *Thillai Govindan* (1908), it is the first Indian novel in English which portrays the dichotomies of the East-West encounter. On the one hand the encounter with the West provides greater individual freedom and relief from the straitjacketed regulations of an upper-caste Hindu existence. On the other, it is simultaneously perceived as a threat to the spiritual Hindu or Indian identity.

These early experiments in the Indian novel in English, taken together, manifest certain broad directions of movement. The generic template is decidedly borrowed from prevalent British novels of the times as, more often than not, are the themes. The anxiety about language is also in evidence. However, we can sense the nascent political imaginings of the people seeking shape, either in terms of identification or difference on racial terms, or in terms of transacting a group; community identity or a cultural ideal and working towards a cultural nationalism are also evidenced.

The First Phase of Nationalism

The next phase of the Indian novel in English coincides with and is propelled by important events in history which led to the emergence of new social and political thought. Concurrently, the novel also became a site of contention for the diverse ideologies that marked this turbulent period. The consolidation of the idea of India as a nation, the emergence of Gandhi, the upsurge of nationalist sentiment—all these factors combined to produce an event that was unique in the Indian Novel. The novelists of this period, by the circumstances of their education, experience or location, were influenced by the European intellectual tradition. When faced with the phenomenon of Gandhian nationalism and the iconic figure of Gandhi himself, these authors tried to resolve the contrasting and/or complementary claims of the 'home and the world' in the creative tension of their works. This creative tension can be observed in the discordance of nationalist discourse in the struggle between the modern, western ideology of Nehru pitted against the more traditional Gandhian philosophy as also in the dominance of the discursive framework and potential of Hinduism in the nationalist discourse. The uneasy coexistence of both is present as much in politics as in literature. Reflecting these issues, the novels of this period can be classified into three broad categories: the novels dealing with the issues of nation and nationalism, the novels dealing with the East-West encounter, and the novels dealing with the problematic issues of religion and pan-Indian identity.

In the first category are novels which depict Gandhian models of social, economic and political life. K.S. Venkataramani's *Murugan the Tiller* (1927) talks of the Gandhian model of village-based economy. His *Kandan, The Patriot: A Novel of New India in the Making* (1932) is a bildungsroman about the making of a local leader who bears more than an incidental likeness to Gandhi. If Venkataramani's novels talk of public service and self-abnegation, the two novels by K. Nagarajan—*Athavar House* (1937) and *Chronicles of Kedaram* (1961)—talk of the Gandhian ideas of nationalism and religious harmony respectively. Bhabani Bhattacharya's *So Many Hungers* (1947) talks of the Gandhian way of life. Mulk Raj Anand's *Untouchable* (1938) and K.A. Abbas's *Inquilab* (1955) deal with the redemptive qualities of Gandhi as a person, his voice and his touch changing the lives of Bakha and Anwar respectively. Anand's novel, *The Sword and the Sickle* (1942) attempts, through the character of Lal Singh, to position Gandhi and his ideology with respect to communism. Raja Rao's *Kantapura* (1938) shows how Gandhianism triumphs over the divisions of class, caste and gender, and ultimately over colonialism.

Although nation is posited as the ultimate ideal, many novels present Gandhi either as a quick-fix solution to the conflict at hand or in an unconvincing portrayal. This is due to novelistic expediency or unnecessary sentimentalisation. Such novels fail to present the genesis and the resolution of societal conflict in a logical manner, succumbing instead to a facile, but (in the context of the times) popular solution. A notable exception is *Kantapura* which displays an organic unity between the philosophic ideal and its social realisation. However, its evident egalitarianism is marred by the religious-casteist bias in conferring leadership on Moorthy and in the presentation of Bade Khan as an ally of the English.

The second category—the novels dealing with the East-West encounter focuses on the Indian response to immediate historical circumstance. The West becomes at once the repository of progressive values and a threat to the spiritual traditions of the East. *Kantapura*, apart from being a novel about Gandhianism, is also a novel about the encounter between the East and the West, between India and the world, and also between the storytelling tradition of India and the western genre chosen to express it. It is with *The Serpent and the Rope* (1960) that Raja Rao creates the paradigmatic text of the East-West encounter. This latter novel, though regarded as a classic, can be interrogated. The privileging of the Hindu-Brahmin hero, Ramaswamy, and of a cultural tradition that is Sanskritic, and by implication, upper-caste, is also complicated by the lack of sympathy in the portrayal of women characters.

The East-West encounter, in its earliest forms, varies from novel to novel. A number of novels beginning with Sarath Kumar Ghose's *The Prince of Destiny* (1909) have talked in various ways about the encounter between the traditional way of life and the one that came via colonialism. Beside Ghose and Raja Rao, Kamala Markandaya's *A Silence of Desire* (1960), *Possession* (1963) and R.K. Narayan's *The Vendor of Sweets* (1967) talk of incompatibilities. Anand's *Two Leaves and a Bud* (1937) and Markandaya's *The Coffer Dams* (1969) are dominated by stereotypical representations of English characters. There are other novels, as Meenakshi Mukherjee points out, where the East is pitted against the West: Santha Rama Rau's *Remember the House* (1956), Markandaya's *Some Inner Fury* (1957), Nayantara Sahgal's *A Time to be Happy* (1957), Balachandra Rajan's *The Dark Dancer* (1959) and Attia Hossain's *Sunlight on a Broken Column* (1961). Apart from *Some Inner Fury,* which shows that the schism between East and West cannot be bridged, the other novels show the triumph of Indian values. However, as in the case of the Gandhian novels, the conclusions are sometimes too pat or too reductive.

There is another category of novels of the East-West encounter where the narrative ends on a note of uneasy reconciliation between the two. The novels of Mulk Raj Anand, particularly *Untouchable* (1935), *Coolie* (1936) and *Two Leaves and a Bud* (1937) deal with this encounter at a complex level. Experimenting with social realism in a critical tone, he aims to portray the arrival of a casteless society. However, he also portrays the wide economic divide that is even harder to bridge. Bakha in *Untouchable*, Munoo in *Coolie*, Gangu in *Two Leaves and Bud* and a host of other characters struggle against the inequalities of society. The city, the industry and other such sites of development are shown to be as oppressive as traditional, caste-ridden rural societies. R. K. Narayan's novels—*Swami and Friends* (1935), *The Dark Room* (1938), *The Vendor of Sweets* (1967), *The Painter of Signs* (1977), to name a few—also fictionalise the East-West encounter against the backdrop of a small town, Malgudi. The influence of the modern West manifests itself in behaviour, attitudes, choices and circumstances, and becomes the immediate impetus to propel the story forward. The new world becomes a source of confusion, of bewilderment and of disappointment for the people who are unable to keep pace with the transition. A closer reading of Narayan shows that many of these characters are marginalised Brahmins whose security of existence in a caste-based society is threatened. A novel that stands by itself in this category is G.V. Desani's *All About H. Hatterr* (1948). It talks about the disillusionment of the protagonist with both Indian and Western culture. The novel is however considered a landmark in its unselfconscious handling of language.

The third category of novels that deals with the problems of a homogenising concept of the nation also needs to examined. These novels form a counter narrative to the euphoric nationalism of the first category of Indian novel in English and the more or less predetermined endings of many novels exploring the East-West encounter in both the first and second categories. As early as 1883, we see S.C. Dutt saying in *The Young Zemindar* that English rule was better than Islamic rule, thus pointing to an inherent problematic in the construction of the national ideal. The portrayal of Bade Khan in *Kantapura* is also part of the same problem. The optimism about Independence is also to be seen in the context of the fact that even in the nationalist novels of Muslim writers, like Aamir Ali's *Conflict* (1947) and K.A. Abbas's *Tomorrow is Ours: A Novel of the India of Today* (1943), the protagonists are Hindus. In 1940, Ahmed Ali's *Twilight in Delhi* clearly indicates that Indian nationalism had failed to enthuse and adequately appeal to the Muslim populace. Writers like Anand and Raja Rao are also uncomfortable or uncomfortably silent when it comes to dealing with Hindu-Muslim relations. It is, however, the novels depicting the events leading up to the Partition of India and the violence that followed in its wake, which offer a doppelganger of sorts to the euphoria of anti-colonial nationalism. Repeatedly, in novel after novel, we see the dark underside of the ecstasy of Independence. Khushwant Singh's *Train to Pakistan* (1956), Balachandra Rajan's *The Dark Dancer*, Manohar Malgonkar's *Distant Drum* (1960) and *A Bend in the Ganges* (1964), Chaman Nahal's *Azadi* (1975)—all depict the horrors of Partition and the cost of Independence.

Nationalism: The Second Phase

As the nation progressed from birth to maturity, the initial enthusiasm of the first phase of nationalism gave way to a sense of alienation caused by dissatisfaction with modern life and circumstances. With the nation having become independent, collective ideals were eventually supplanted by individual quests and responses. In the novelists of this period too—a diverse group in themselves—no clear trend can be discerned. Manohar Malgonkar wrote quite a few novels during this period. Apart from the two novels discussed previously, Malgonkar also wrote *The Princes* (1963). Malgonkar's response to the times he lived in was usually contempt for the Indian people and their attitudes, combined with a tendentious Anglophilia. Sudhin N. Ghose's *The Vermillion Boat* (1953) and *The Flame of The Forest* (1955) are important takes on the times they were written in. P.M. Nityanandan's *Long, Long Days* (1960) was the first campus novel in Indian English. Khushwant Singh's novels—*Train to Pakistan* (1956), *I Shall Not Hear The Nightingale* (1959) and *Delhi: A Novel* (1989)—offer varied perspectives on the historical circumstances of India and its people. The important novels of Arun Joshi are *The Foreigner* (1968), *The Apprentice* (1974), *The Last Labyrinth* (1981) and *The Strange Case of Billy Biswas* (1971). All these works are explorations into the workings of the minds of alienated individuals.

Women Novelists

The decades following Independence witnessed the emergence of a number of women novelists. The beginnings of this trend are marked by semi-autobiographical novels of self-discovery in which educated women with progressive views are in conflict with traditional social mores. Venu Chitale's *In Transit* (1951), Zeenuth Futehally's *Zohra* (1951), Mrinalini Sarabhai's *This Alone is True* (1952) and Attia Hossain's *Sunlight on A Broken Column* (1971) belong to this category. The same conflict can be observed in the novels of Nayantara Sahgal, although it is major political events of the country that form the backdrop to her novels. Tradition and modernity are seen to be negotiated in Kamala Markandaya's novels too. In some of her novels like *Nectar in a Sieve* (1954) and *A Handful of Rice* (1966) she attempts to portray the rural and urban poor. But she is not always successful or accurate in her attempts. Anita Desai's fiction is marked by an inward turn—apart from external circumstances she also probes the psychology of her characters. Ruth Prawer Jhabwala focuses on the urban Indian middle class in her fiction, but her point of view is, by her own admission, that of an outsider.

Diaspora

The changing economic and political scenario created opportunities for many Indians, including writers, to journey and settle abroad. For most of the earlier diaspora of India—from the *girmitiya*s to the moneyed-class to the emissaries of nationalism—the colonial encounter was the context of migration. The modern diaspora consisted of people who chose to go West for intellectual, creative, economic or entrepreneurial purposes. Writers belonging to the first category—Seepersad Naipaul, Harold Ladoo, Subramani, Cyril Dabydeen, David Babydeen, K.S. Maniam and Neil Bissondath—wrote mainly about displacement, alienation and angst, their tones ranging from the ironic to the acerbic. The reference to India, if any, is oblique. A writer who stands by himself in this category is V.S. Naipaul.

Menon Marath, Balachandra Rajan and Santha Rama Rau form a small group of novelists whose diasporic concerns are overtaken by nationalist considerations. Marath's *The Wound of Spring* (1960) and *An Island for Sale* (1968), Rajan's *The Dark Dancer* (1959) and *Too Long in the West* (1961), Rama Rau's *East of Home(1960)* and *Remember the House* (1956) deal with various aspects of the nation's history. The second category includes writers like Bharati Mukherjee, Farrukh Dhondy, Rohinton Mistry and also some women writers discussed earlier, like Kamala Markandaya, Anita Desai and Nayantara Sahgal. In present times though, the category of diaspora needs to be reframed, as many current writers divide their time between India and another country, and cannot be termed diaspora in the exact sense of the term.

Rushdie and Beyond

1980 was characterised by a lull in terms of the Indian novel in English. After the major authors of the nationalist phase were gradually becoming a spent force, the decade preceding the 1980s was characterised by sporadic activity. At the same time, English was becoming more popular as a language of communication. On a global level too, the 1980s was important in that the collapse of the USSR led to the world becoming unipolar. It was during these years that globalisation also became a significant phenomenon. India too was caught in the throes of a new world order waiting to be born.

As it sometimes happens, one particular event marks the culmination of diverse occurrences and becomes a signpost for subsequent changes. Salman Rushdie's *Midnight's Children* (1980) was one such instance. In retrospect, it became the point at which all the diverse trends prevailing in the Indian novel in English reached a point of culmination and also led to the charting of subsequent paths. *Midnight's Children* was unique not just on account of when it was published. As a novel too, it was important. The unselfconscious use of language struck a chord with the post-Independence generation, as did the fact that it did not take received versions of history uncritically. Destabilising established notions of the narrative of the nation, it focused on the issue of control; the narration was not objective, but fragmentary; the narrator was evidently fallible. Gossip, rumour and popular culture all combined to articulate a reality which both embodied problems and hinted at resolutions.

Post-*Midnight's Children*, we can see some common issues which concern Indian English novelists: an increasing concern with the burgeoning

Indian middle-class, an awareness of the changed realities of the world, more assurance in handling the form of the novel and ease in the language of expression. Amitav Ghosh's *The Circle of Reason* (1986), I. Allan Sealy's *The Trotter Nama* (1988), Mukul Kesavan's *Looking through Glass* (1995) and Vikram Chandra's *Red Earth and Pouring Rain* (1995) are evidently influenced by Rushdie's novel. Upamanyu Chatterjee's *English, August* (1988), *The Last Burden* (1993) and *Weight Loss* (2006) talk of alienation within national boundaries in their own unique idiom. Allan Sealy's *Hero* (1991), Shashi Tharoor's *Show Business* (1994), Ruchir Joshi's *The Last Jet-Engine Laugh* (2001) and Hari Kunzru's *Transmission* (2004) explore the domain of Bollywood either directly or tangentially. Shashi Deshpande's novels like *The Dark Holds No Terrors* (1980), *That Long Silence* (1988) and *Small Remedies* (2000) talk of urban middle-class women's lives.

The fissuring of the body politic started by Rushdie finds further expression in novels like Amitav Ghosh's *The Shadow Lines* (1988), Shauna Singh Baldwin's *What the Body Remembers* (1999) and Arundhati Roy's *The God of Small Things* (1997) among others, which address perceived representational deficiencies and interstices. Subsequently there has been a deluge of Indian novels in English: the award winning works by Aravind Adiga and Kiran Desai, the impressive works of established names like Salman Rushdie, Amitav Ghosh, Vikram Seth, Shashi Deshpande and Upamanyu Chatterjee, an impressive crop of new novelists as varied as Amit Chaudhuri and Kiran Nagarkar, Mohsin Hamid and Siddhartha Deb, and women novelists as diverse as Githa Hariharan, Temsula Ao, Anjum Hassan and Manju Kapur, and the massive output of popular fiction fuelled by the success of Chetan Bhagat.

The present survey is not comprehensive; in fact it does not aspire to be so. It is representative, and reflects an attempt to understand the impulses, inspirations and influences on the form perceived in terms of its evolution and current prominence. All history is a projection of narrative backwards from the present, and this survey is no exception. This paper too is an attempt to discern influences and trends in the Indian novel in English and show how the country is the overriding concern in the form, and the consolidation, interrogation and contestation of the nation, either directly or obliquely, are its primary impulses. In this way, it is a direct participant in the dialogue with the past and the present of the country and is thus a potent and hence popular and critically acclaimed participant in the discourse of the times. Now, as always, the novel continues to be shaped by the ideologies around us.

In Search of India's Destiny

—Bishal Thapa

Tryst with Destiny

As midnight beckoned on the eve of India's independence in 1947, Prime Minister Jawaharlal Nehru spoke of the country's *Tryst with Destiny*. The time had come, he said, 'to *redeem our pledge, not wholly, or in full measure, but substantially*.' After six and a half decades of independence, there is little doubt that India has inched closer to fully redeeming her pledge. Only one question has hauntingly remained: Exactly what sort of a destiny was meant to be redeemed?

I am one of India's direct beneficiaries. I studied in India through K-12. I survived the Indian board exams, which as it turned out, was enough to prime me for the world. I meandered off to distant lands in search of an education, a job, love and all of the glorious things that an eighteen year old might yearn for. But when I look back, I think that perhaps the decision to leave was nothing more than the yearning for a pair of really cool Levi jeans—the kind that were faded and ripped through in several places.

Through much of the 1980s when I was in boarding school in India, it was difficult and expensive to make a long distance call to my parents. We had to book the trunk-call days in advance. When we did finally get through, the person on the line sounded like a voice at the other end of a long tunnel. The scratchy sound and the frequent cross connections notwithstanding, a long distance conversation with our parents could still be had. A really cool pair of Levi jeans, faded and ripped through in several places, simply could not be had.

I arrived back in India in 2005 for the chance of a second wind in my professional career. Everybody was returning back, it seemed. It wasn't a sense of adventure or the longing to be home that made us return. It was the sense of calculated opportunity.

By the time I returned, the faded Levi jeans ripped through in several places had long lost its cool lustre. It could be bought for Rs. 500 from the local bazaar if you spent enough time in the sun rummaging through the pile of export rejects on the sidewalk. Or it could be bought for Rs. 5,000 from an air-conditioned glass front store in an expansive shopping mall.

These days, a clear phone connection with almost universal access to mobile phones is brandied as the symbol of an emerging India. But that image underestimates something equally important: the power of satiating an eighteen year old's unbridled yearning for a cool pair of faded Levi jeans ripped through in several places. Besides, what would an eighteen year old rather have? A clear phone connection on demand with their parents, or a really cool pair of faded Levi jeans ripped through in several places.

Maybe it has to be a bit of both. A really cool mobile phone sticking out of the back pocket of every faded Levi jeans ripped through in several places. Could that take India closer to redeeming her pledge in full?

Two decades of Indian liberalisation have presumably set off 1.2 billion dreams. Every Indian youngster believes that the cool faded Levi jeans, ripped through in several places, can be had. Every Indian realistically believes that a clear phone connection on their personal mobile can be instantly had.

Six and half decades after independence, three generations of Gandhi after Nehru, 13 prime-ministers and 12 presidents later, the aspirations of 1.2 billion Indians have finally been unshackled. Everyone finally has a destiny to redeem.

Make all the people of India what destiny intended them to be

India has been generous to me and many of my friends. In my first year back in 2005, the country gifted us a Valentine's Day present. The Sensex, the key stock market indicator, peaked on that day. Within the next three years, before the global financial crisis set in, the Sensex more than tripled from the high on Valentine's Day. Economic growth had been barrelling along at over 7 per cent annually. We were being swept along in the wave of economic prosperity. It felt like there would be no looking back. Once in a while, we did pause to glance around.

Occasionally, when I swiped my card, or purchased a toy that my son could have easily done without, I was mindful of the millions to whom India had been less generous. Those were the millions for whom the cool faded ripped jean or the shiny new mobile could be had in theory but was still realistically out of reach. On most days, this intense dichotomy of India didn't tug at my conscience. I made the purchase without a second thought. But occasionally, when I was in a meditative mood with enough spirits for reflection, it was hard not to wonder.

350 million Indians currently live under the official poverty line. As much as prosperity is easy to spot, poverty is difficult to count. India's official poverty statistics identifies only the poorest of the poor. Even at very low consumption levels, well short of the World Bank's typical metric of $1.25/day, 30 per cent of the country's population is classified as poor.

India's incidence of poverty is based on a revised methodology that was adopted after much criticism of India's previous approach. With the change in statistical method, the incidence of poverty in 2004-2005 increased from 28 to 42 per cent of the population. Over a 110 million more Indians were consequently classified as below the poverty level—a paradoxical mid-course correction for a country in the midst of one its unprecedented growth periods.

Though economic growth has had an impact, these poverty levels are staggeringly large. Between 2004-2005 and 2009-2010, the share of people under the poverty line declined from 37 to 30 per cent. Approximately 52 million Indians were lifted out of poverty in those 5 years. But these gains have not been uniform. Poverty actually worsened in several of the north-eastern states. The worst performing larger states made little progress. Poverty among minorities and other disadvantaged communities has been more persistent than the rest. Income disparity has widened significantly.

India's official poverty head count ratio has been caught in a fierce debate about the appropriateness of the poverty threshold. Some of the debate is mere political rhetoric—an effort to deride a government already in tatters. Some of it, though, has really to do with big policy questions. A higher poverty line could swell the number of poor. Policies aimed at providing the poor with benefits could become fiscally and administratively unmanageable. In an odd way, poverty estimates are a circular game, determined as much by the number of poor the country can officially afford to support as the science of counting them.

Also odd is the parallel between how the government, on the one hand, and me and my friends, on the other, think about India's poverty. The Government determines the incident of poverty by implicitly determining how many poor people it can support. My friends and I reflect on India's poverty based on how much of the tugging at our conscience we can absorb.

Either way, there is still a lot of poverty that the nation of India as well as the consciences of its economically fortunate inhabitants cannot support.

The depth of India's poverty is marked equally by the absence of a proportionately sizable middle class. An increase in the poverty line to just $2 a day, for instance, would more than double the incidence of poverty to over 800 million, close to two-thirds of the country's population.

India's storied middle class, the cohort powering the country's economic growth, is turning out to be much smaller than imagined. Birdsall, a researcher with the Centre for Global Development, defined the middle class as someone who earns more than $10 per day (enough to provide some savings) but are not in the top 5 per cent income group for the country. By that count, she estimated that India had no middle class.

Poverty is not new to India. Income and social inequality are not new to India. But widespread, perhaps even universal aspirations, 1.2 billion strong, are new to India. Economic growth, liberalisation and democracy have brought all of these aspirations into focus. A billion destinies are now lagging behind, anxiously waiting to be redeemed.

In his speech on the eve of independence, Nehru clearly was aiming at redeeming all of India's destinies. '...till we make all the people of India what destiny intended them to be,' he had said.

As the divide between India's rich and poor magnifies, as the multitude of destinies take shape and tug away in different directions, does India have what it takes to redeem on its billion destinies. 'Are we brave enough and wise enough to grasp this opportunity and accept the challenge of the future?' Nehru has asked. Six and a half decades later, we are all still on that very question.

Whither do we go and what shall be our endeavour?

A billion are a lot of destinies. I worry about my own future, my family's future, my son's future. Even that worry is sometimes more than I can comfortably handle. I can't imagine the weight of a billion destinies. Most days I try not to think about it. But there are times, when an old pair of faded jeans ripped through in several places, almost in shreds now, reminds me of the journey that has been. In those moments, I find reason both to be hopeful and to despair about the future.

Economic growth, military expansion and the population dividend have been the triumvirate underpinning India's emergence. Following the liberalisation of the nineties, India enjoyed two decades of sustained economic growth. It was a period marked by strong domestic demand, growing foreign direct investments, stable macro-economic fundamentals, stable government and a slow, but steady and continuous improvement in the investment climate. Despite the slowdown resulting from the global financial crisis, India continues to post growth well over its pre-boom era.

Economic growth has been accompanied by increased military spending. Emerging as the only possible regional counter-balance to China, India is conscious of its new role in the geo-political theatre. Although the country officially retains her policy of Non-alignment, the increased engagement with the US suggests that the line between Non-alignment and strategic alliance appears to be blurring.

At a time when developed countries are greying, India has the benefit of the largest population of young people in the world. All of those young people will be yearning for faded ripped jeans and a shiny new mobile phone. It is no wonder that India's unintended population dividend is regarded today as a key source of her growth.

India's emergence has opened up a new set of possibilities. She has gained in international stature. India is now a member of the UN Security Council, a key member of the G20 group of nations, founding member of the BASIC (Brazil, South Africa, India, China) bloc, a recognised nuclear state with dispensation for nuclear trade without having to sign the Non-Proliferation Treaty, and possesses the capacity to stall or forge international agreements.

India has rightfully gained a place in international affairs. Where will we go from here? Whose destinies will India represent?

The confusion about whether we are a confident rich country staking our claim in global affairs or a country still overburdened with the depth of poverty often defines how we act out.

India's foreign policy, particularly on international climate negotiations, is one area where the ambiguity of the country's identity is played out. For a long time, India had cast herself, much like the rest of the developing world, as a victim of climate change. Developed countries, it argued, had been the ones that were historically responsible for greenhouse emissions. Equity would demand every individual be accorded the same carbon space, irrespective of the starting position, implying that developed countries would be straddled with all the emissions reduction requirements. That position resonated with other developing and least developed countries. Even as international negotiations faltered, India held to this position suggesting that it had become a red line before which everything was non-negotiable.

That red line never fully held, or at least turned to be porous a lot more quickly than anyone had expected. Whether the change reflected the pressure of the faltering international negotiations or India's desire to globally express its new found confidence is hard to precisely determine. A leaked letter from the Indian Minister of Environment and Forests to the Indian Prime Minister prior to the UN climate change conference in Cancun suggested that the shift in India's position was inevitable.

The leaked letter argued that India's historic position on climate didn't align with her global projections. A country seeking a permanent seat on the UN Security-Council couldn't also be perceived as nothing more than a group leader for least developed countries. India pulled away sharply from the G-77, aligned itself with the BASIC and began to encourage examinations for alternate definitions of equity. India needed to be perceived as a pro-active leader on the global stage.

Since Cancun, India appears to have swung back again but without defaulting back to the very initial position. She has corralled the BASIC bloc more tightly, actively promoting exploration of new concepts of equity and fairness, such as 'Equitable Access to Sustainable Development'. What exactly such a paradigm might mean, or what it could offer, remains unclear. Whether such a paradigm could balance the country's development needs and its global aspirations is uncertain.

India's changing global aspirations, particularly the willingness to be more assertive internationally, may be nothing more than calculated self-interest to secure access to resources and trade routes. That goal, perhaps, shouldn't be doubted. But it is also more than that. On some days India appears as a self-confident country wanting to play a dominant international role. On other days, she appears as an uncertain country still carrying the heavy burden of its poverty.

The variations in India's global projections of herself mirrors the divided discourse about India as a poor country, as a rich country, as a country of opportunities, as a country of missed opportunities, as a country of destinies redeemed, as country of destinies waiting to be redeemed—all at the same time.

Acquiring the really cool faded Levi jeans ripped through in several places may not have been enough. India has a lot of work ahead. We all have a lot of work ahead of us. More needs to be done. '*There is no resting for any one of us till we redeem our pledge in full*,' Nehru had said.

Having one destiny would have made it a lot easier.

The Seven-Sister's Plight

—Ratnadip Choudhury

On the isolation of India's north-east, its dialectic relations with the national mainstream in past and the current status…

Thousands of kilometers of jungles, valleys, springs, rivers that run into the eastern Himalayas and the Arakans and the huge Indian Ocean makes India's most enchanting yet treacherous periphery. In this periphery live 39 million people, hailing from hundreds of varied tribes, speaking uncountable number of languages and dialects and occupying a land mass of nearly 2.62 lakh sq-km, which accounts for only 7.9 per cent of this vast nation. This periphery is called India's Northeast—a common identity for seven different states—Assam, Mizoram, Manipur, Nagaland, Meghalaya, Arunachal Pradesh and the tiny one Tripura. These days, peoples from these regions are being referred as 'Northeasterners' with their 'marginal stake' in the population (only 3.8 per cent of India's human count) however beyond the numbers, consideration of looking on the citizens in a democracy like India should be different and rational.

This periphery is bounded by five eastern neighbours—Nepal, Bhutan, Bangladesh, Myanmar and the dragon of the east—China. These porous and volatile borders make northeast 'strategically' very important in India's nation building framework. During the British Raj, colonialist expanded their reigns to Northeast, explored and exploited its human and natural resources—may it be its oil, coal or tea and set up its regional administrative headquarters in the hilly plateau of Shillong, a cool hill station that bears the insignia of colonial era in its lifestyle.

The British developed the area by bringing in road, rail and medium of communications like post, etc. The educated started getting jobs in the British administration and the tea gardens of Assam. Those days, Assam was by size double of what it is now. Meghalaya, Mizoram and Arunachal Pradesh (at that time it was known as Northeast Frontier Agency—NEFA) were part of it; Manipur and Tripura were princely states, British enjoyed only taking royalties from them. While the British did try to bring a lot of areas under its administration, largely into Assam, it kept a lot of tribal areas untouched, to be mastered by the village head or the clan chief. So the idea of allowing a sense of 'autonomy' in the tribal areas of Northeast was there from colonial times. Barring Manipur and Tripura—these two were princely states before their merger with India—the British had adopted the similar tactic throughout. Also with the Brits came the Christian missionaries and their free but questionable education.

Thus the Britishers gave northeast not only a consolidating term 'Northeast Frontier Region' but a lot more and before they left, they gave India, the Radcliffe Line. Radcliffe stretched northeast faraway from its mainland only to be connected by the 'Chicken Neck' corridor—a strip of land in North Bengal near the Siliguri town which is about 21 to 40 km in width, with the countries of Nepal, Bhutan and Bangladesh lying on either side of the corridor. This corridor now defines the main access gateway by rail and road to the Northeast—it defines the rest of land mass as India's Mainland and Northeast as its periphery, a rather troubled periphery. India continues its hangover of colonial rule even after its independence. Post Partition, New Delhi's policy towards Northeast had unfortunately remained the same as it was under the British colonial rule. Northeast was forced to be stereotyped as a far flung area full of hills, jungles and nomadic tribals, where the people of the valley areas always had the upper hand over the people of the hills. Thus the discourse on Northeast was jolly well started by the British Raj; New Delhi continued with the same irrational discourse post-Independence, even the semantics remained the same for a very long time. So the longstanding predicament of a sustained alienation that Northeast suffers perhaps started with the Partition when it all of a sudden lost its ancient trade routes, particularly in the Ganga-Brahmaputra basin where waterways were used at random, tea from Upper Assam sailed on vessels through the Brahmaputra into the waters of what is today Bangladesh for the final destination in Kolkata. Even before the British came up with the world famous Stillwell Road to join Assam with Myanmar and China during the Second World War, the indigenous people of Northeast had ancient links through the chain of mountain ranges. So unlike the hype, nothing was noble with Stillwell Road. Waterways were earlier too used to transport goods to Mandalay and Rangoon in Myanmar through the Chindwin and Irrawaddy river systems.

Among the tribals from Northeast, the Nagas, tucked on hills between Assam and Myanmar are the people who had to be the first to fight for their independence and self determination based on community ethics. Being a fighting race, they have been carrying an unusual legacy of head hunting, a practice of beheading and preserving a person's head, the Nagas of both Nagaland and Myanmar kept practising it for long. The practice has thinned away with the changing times and outside influence. The Nagas participated in the Second World War; they learned the modern warfare and carried those skills for waging civil war inside India for nearly six decades on the question of maintaining their 'unique identity'. Nothing substantial has been achieved so far and chances are blurred for India's soft stand on Naga's non-approachable demands, set by its opportunist leaders based in the comfort of western nations.

Although Christianity tried to bring the Nagas under one umbrella, the discord between different Naga tribes like the Mao, Sema, Angami, etc, ruled the scenes in the history of Naga rebellion. The twenty odd tribes who are commonly known as Nagas have contributed to this history of guns and blood but on ethnic lines, they remain under their rigid and isolationist community rules. Before embracing Christianity, the Nagas believed in animistic forms of worship, they used to live in villages, glued to their clan and family and fight for their village, retaining their culture and tradition. Christianity brought about social changes through modern education, health care; these drove Nagas closer to modern ways of life but in place of the 'unique cultural tradition' that the Nagas swear by in a rather 'confused state', to say the least. This sense of confusion has been one of the contributing factors for the long sustained insurgency in Nagaland.

The roots of unrest in Nagaland dated back to 1929 when the 'Naga Club' made a submission to the Simon Commission not to include Naga areas under the British administration reforms that were supposed to happen at that time. The demand got more voices. It was Naga National Council (NNC) that unilaterally declared Independent Naga Hills on August 14, 1947.

Angami Zapu Phizo led NNC in this tirade. In 1960 Nagaland was accorded a full state, but rebellion and call for secession continued. In 1975, the historic Shillong Accord was signed between the Naga rebels and New Delhi where the Naga rebels accepted to embrace Indian Constitution and a section surrendered but another section went on to form the National Socialist Council of Nagaland (NSCN).

NSCN also suffered a split. While one faction, the Issac-Muivah group, Isak Chisi Swu and Thuingaleng Muivah, decided to start negotiating with New Delhi, the other leader S.S. Khaplang, a Burmese Naga, opposed the idea and broke away. NSCN (IM) is involved in a peace parley for fifteen years; its core demand of creation of a Greater Nagaland by bringing all Nagas in habituated areas of Northeast together has been overruled. Khaplang's own faction has seen a vertical split with its top rank leader led by Zimomi Kitovi forming another faction. All these years what Nagaland has seen led to frequent fratricidal killings and astronomical cases of extortion.

The rest of the country started feeling that Nagaland is a place where every house has an insurgent. So a scope to promote Nagaland as a global tourism hot spot was outrightly dampened. With total organic farming, as part of its tradition, Nagaland could have been a delight for agricultural scientists across the world, but even today hardly one dares to set foot there.

The Naga's weaving art, range of weapons, lifestyle, traditional games and uniquely uninterrupted culture have been charming to many, even in their own way, and Nagas claimed themselves hospitable. A big chunk of the new generation is devoid of old superstitious or condemnable practices. Change is making a front there as modern Nagas now want to end the fratricidal killings, they want extortion to be stopped. But sadly in the disguise of insurgency, corruption is growing cancerous in Nagaland to say the least. Fifteen years' peace parley does not excite an average Naga as the call for greater Nagaland, also identical temptation could be noted in the Thankul areas and among the Nagas who stay in the hills of Manipur.

Manipur is called a 'failed state' these days. Whether it has failed or not, only its people will decide, but the state has an uncanny fortune or rather misfortune of normal conditions turning abnormal to the extent that Manipur is branded in media as something 'very chaotic'. Manipur was a princely state during the British Raj. After the exit of the Britishers, Manipur merged with the Indian Union on 15 October 1949, many in Manipur still believe that it was a 'forced merger'. They feel that the Manipuri royals were 'compelled' to sign the merger agreement. This feeling of 'forced' to be part of India is also among the age-old contributing factors to the decades of unrest in the land of jewels.

Manipur is conveniently divided into two regions, the valley and the hills. The traditionally Hindu tribal, the Meities live in the valley, the Christian Nagas and the Kukis live in the hills. Over the years, the divide between the hill areas and the valley is glaring. Traditionally, the governance in Manipur had remained more inclined towards the people from the valley, particularly for the Meities—for that, the hill peoples have cried foul and got alienated. Thus, while Manipur was in a phase of getting accustomed with the Indian federal structure, the call for sovereign Manipur was growing louder in the valleys. The groups like Peoples' Liberation Army (PLA), the armed wing of Revolutionary Peoples Front (RPF) and the United National Liberation Front (UNLF) led the armed fight for an independent Manipur. UNLF supremo Rajkumar Meghen who is now in Guwahati Central Jail hails from Manipur's royal family.

Under such a backdrop, the number of armed groups in valleys of Manipur went on increasing. In the hills, the two ethnic groups—the Nagas and the Kukis have a lot of distrust among themselves; there have been fierce ethnic clashes between the two tribal communities, so the Naga nationalism and the idea of greater Nagaland has takers in the hill areas in the Thankul Naga dominated districts of Senapati and Ukhrul. The General Secretary of the National Socialist Council of Nagaland (NSCN–IM) Th. Muivah who leads the outfit in the fifteen years long peace parley with New Delhi also hails from the hills of Manipur. This just goes to show why the Naga nationalism is so deep rooted among the Nagas of Manipur. As the Kukis were fighting with the Nagas for space in the Manipur hills, the Kukis also took up arms, demand of a separate Kuki homeland set in, Kuki nationalism was bound to come in.

So a multi-dimensional ethnic aspiration leading to bloodshed and unrest in the form of insurgency made way for huge deployment of security forces in Manipur like Kashmir. Armed with a draconian law called Armed Forces Special Powers Act 1954 (AFSPA), the security personnel performed the task ruthlessly and without any ethical check, which the basic democracy normally instructs to be followed in disturbed zones too. Innocent peoples are getting killed at will, girls are being raped, and violence and protest going hand in hand without any foreseeable clue for 'normalcy'. After a Manipuri lady Th. Manorama Devi was allegedly raped and murdered by the security personnel, Manipur protested like never before. The Manipuri mothers shouted 'Indian Army rape us' with their bare body in front of the historic Kangla Fort, shocking the world, defining the doldrums now called Manipur.

A lady, a poet, Irom Sharmila Chanu has been fasting for over a decade, asking for the repeal of AFSPA, Manipur is rallying behind her but hopes are only grounded in transition. Insurgency has turned into a cottage industry in the state marred by large scale administrative failures and almost no development at work. Rural minors were dropping out to take up arms and become child soldiers for the rebel outfits; Manipur is losing its plot. The hope thus remains only on its younger generation who have drifted away from violent endgame and are now seeking normalcy in life. They are excelling in sports, cinema, music and studies—today, more and more youngsters in Manipur are aspiring to become entrepreneurs, but even that makes it too early to say that the winds of change have come though a road ahead can be seen. This is not an ordinary feat, where despair is the norm to be followed through the obstinate stands maintained by a violent state and an ignorant bulk of its population.

Assam is breathing a spell of peace. Insurgency is on weaker legs unlike the last three decades, when Assam remained the hotbed of insurgency. For decades in Assam, insurgency was synonymous with the United Liberation Front of Assam or the ULFA. The banned outfit was founded on 7 April 1979, but it came to prominence only in 1983 with the new wave of participation based on the central argument shaped up through the feelings like 'son of soil'. The Assam Accord that was supposed to get Assam rid of New Delhi's neglect had been lately seen as an underachiever. While ULFA grew in prominence, the tribal communities in Assam were also feeling neglected of their rights. The Bodos were the first among them to call for separation from Assam; the All Bodo Students Union (ABSU) led by Upendranath Brahma started a mass movement that became violent demanding separate Bodoland. The Bodo nationalism gave rise to Bodo extremism. Rebel outfits like Bodo Liberation Tigers (BLT) and later National Liberation Front of Bodoland (NDFB) came into being. The BLT surrendered en-masse through the Bodoland accord, the ABSU decided to withdraw its demand for a separate Bodoland to allow the autonomous structure—the Bodoland Territorial Council to function. NDFB continued with its armed movement, in the name of a sovereign Bodo nation. The outfit suffered a split, the progressive group declared ceasefire and came under the ambit of peace talks. They clamped down their demand from sovereignty to a separate Bodo state.

Like the Bodos, other tribal groups of Assam like the Karbis, the Dimasas, have picked up arms in the past, fought the Indian state in a bid to achieve their rights of self determination. But the movements were not sustained long, some are now in peace parley with the Assam Government, some have settled for packages of autonomy though with many restrictions.

Even the Adivasis, the tribals from tea garden areas of Assam, people from Jharkhand who were brought to work as labourers in Assam for tea plantations by the Britishers, have constituted for long as easily secured vote bank for Congress that enabled and are still helping it to form the government in the state. But these marginalised labourers wanted the Scheduled Tribe status that has been eluding them for decades, thus the Adivasis also moved to join insurgency. At a high point of time, not less than seven Adivasi outfits were operating in the region; all of them have now declared ceasefire.

But it has been ULFA all the way that has impacted the fate of Assam for the last three decades. The outfit once has faced one of the most ruthless military operations done by India against its own people. First ULFA lost its main bases in Assam, the camps at Saraipung and Lakhipathar. It waved an olive branch in 1992 but that did not work out because ULFA chief Paresh Barua was more interested in regrouping the alienated cadres, which he eventually did in the hills of Bhutan. The Bodo rebels also went up to the hills in Bhutan to set up their own separate base. But Bhutan naturally turned hostile as being confident of India, so ULFA and other Northeast rebel groups had to move to Bangladesh. In the 1990s, India had a mixed sort of overtures with Bangladesh, therefore ULFA got time and space to perform at its will. Things turned hostile once the present government of Sheikh Hasina finally showed her loyalty to India by cracking down on ULFA's top wing. While sheltered in Bangladesh, the character of many of the outfits has changed. In 2009, Bangladesh started its operation against these outfits on India's insistence; they banned top insurgents and handed them over to India. ULFA had been badly hit this time. Now the outfit is split in two parts, the larger one is the pro-talk faction led by Chairman Arabinda Rajkhowa who is already talking to India by dropping the core demands of sovereign Assam; the other faction is led by the underground Commander-in-Chief Paresh Barua, who is still waging the war against India by shifting his base to Myanmar.

But amidst all these, Assam has not been able to solve its nightmare—like the growing number of illegal migrants from Bangladesh. Congress in Assam is accused by the Asom Gana Parishad of sheltering the illegal migrants, but AGP's own political relevance has come into question with its incessant reckless ploys. This is not less ironic that 'pro-migrant' All India United Democratic Front (AIUDF) of perfume baron Maulana Badruddin Ajmal emerging as a political power centre. By the real dirt around in politics, even today Assam has no answer to the growing number of migrants.

Meghalaya's capital Shillong, had seen history, it has seen Northeast emerge out of several political and ethnic crisis. The hills where the Jaintia, Khasi and Garo tribes once resided were part of Assam, but soon the demand of their own right set in. In 1972, Meghalaya was carved out of Assam. In last three decades, Meghalaya has also seen ethnic insurgency and distrust between tribals and non-tribals of the state. Within the tribal communities, there is discontent over land, forest rights, coal and mines. These days, the Garo Hills of Meghalaya are witnessing escalation of violence by the Garo National Liberation Army (GNLA), so the land known for its hide and seek of cloud and sunshine is having its own troubles, majorly because the state has seen political instability since its foundation.

The tiny Northeastern state of Tripura was a princely state before it merged with the Indian Union. Tripura's tribal majority demography underwent huge changes as a result of unhindered migration from the former East Bengal and subsequently Bangladesh. Thus the tribals turned minority to the non-tribals in their own state giving rise to a sense of distress and alienation. Insurgency started as a protest movement against this phenomenon.

Insurgency shaped and grew when Bijoy Kumar Hrangkhawal founded the Tripura National Volunteers (TNV). Next, came into existence the All Tripura Tribal Force (ATTF), which changed its nomenclature as, All Tripura Tiger Force (ATTF) in the course of time. Later came into action, the deadliest of all—the National Liberation Front of Tripura (NLFT). All the outfits set up their bases in Bangladesh, since Tripura is surrounded by Bangladesh on all three sides. By such a scenario, between 1992 and 2010, at least 3,479 insurgency related fatalities were reported from Tripura. But Tripura now is one of the peaceful states in Northeast. The Left Front is in power for the last nineteen years and it has been able to curb down the insurgency by sustained counter insurgency.

Mizoram was one state where India used its Air Force against its own people. Mizoram has seen a bloody insurgency of MNF (Mizo National Front) led by Laldenga from the late 1960s till it ended with the signing of the Mizo Peace Accord in 1986. Former insurgent leaders were absorbed into the political stream in the State, and following that, the State has remained, more or less, peaceful, except for the peripheral conflicts. Though the Christian domination has been ridden with the frequent ethnic strife, a fierce ethnic conflict between the Mizos and the Brus left almost 50,000 Brus homeless in 1997. They remained sheltered in refugee camps in Northern parts of Tripura till 2010, when finally New Delhi got into the act to repatriate the Brus to Mizoram; the process is still stuck in limbo.

After the ethnic clashes, the Brus retaliated by forming rebel groups like the Bru National Liberation Front (BNLF) and subsequently, Bru Liberation Front of Mizoram (BLFM) emerged out of the camps and indulged in intermittent violence inside Mizoram and also in the border areas in Assam. None of these groups exist now—last few years have witnessed the sharp decline in factionalism. Other outfits like the Hmar People's Convention-Democracy (HPC-D), however, continues to carry out its activities beyond the borders of Mizoram, mostly inside Assam and Manipur. Mizoram has also emerged as the one state in India that is a transit point for small arms and narcotics. But credit to Mizoram to live up to the Mizo Peace Accord and that mainstream Mizo insurgency did never rise up again.

Arunachal and Sikkim are the two states that have their own pattern of development that makes them distinct from the rest of the five states of the region. These two states have never witnessed any ironical interceptions of insurgency or the state mismanaged security affairs in internal areas. So, at least Arunachal and Sikkim give hope to 'mainstream thinkers', while remaining five states of north east still carry some level of difficult socio-political equations.

Northeast has been suffering with all these plights for the last six and a half decades and still chances are remote that the apathy of centre and the misconducts of insurgents and local leaders will allow it to be genuinely normal on a developmental path.

Chess 3.0 in the Jungle: Mapping India's Engagement With the World in the 21st Century

—*Mayuri Mukherjee*

There is no good and evil. There is only power and those too weak to seek it.

Lord Voldemort, Harry Potter and the Philosopher's Stone.

On the face of it there may be many multilateral institutions, international norms and bilateral treaties that govern the behaviour of nation states in the global arena. But in effect it is the law of the jungle that holds supreme here. Now, this may make you uncomfortable but the fact is that unlike their citizens, nation states do not function under the overarching authority of a government-like structure. Sure, there are some rules and guidelines but countries across the world have often chosen not to follow them. Yet, if there is a sense of order and discipline that seems to prevail, it is because of the all-encompassing power equation that is constantly at play here just like it is in the jungle.

The game of international politics is really quite simple. There is only one aim and that is the accumulation of power—more power. Of course, no diplomat or government official in their right mind will ever publicly acknowledge this in any discussion on foreign policy, since doing so would cause irreparable damage to their country's prospects of winning the game. Instead, in situations such as these, the government's strategy on the global platform is carefully wrapped within feel-good narratives. So, when it comes to describing the aims of our foreign policy, we are told, for instance, that it is either furthering our national interests or promoting the country's defining principles such as democracy and pluralism.

That's balderdash

This essay does away with that smokescreen of a narrative and builds upon the premise that, just like it is the case with every other nation state, the foreign policy of this country in the twenty-first century too should have only one key aim: To ensure that the global 'balance of power' equation is, at all times, in India's favour.

Towards that end, the single most important principle that New Delhi must follow in the years ahead is the maintenance of strategic autonomy that will allow it to place the country's national interests ahead of all other considerations. Consequently, even as India engages with a world that is increasingly inter-connected on multiple levels, it must not only refrain from aligning itself Cold War-style, with any one country or bloc of countries, but also prevent fuzzy ideologies and fancy '-isms' from defining its foreign policy prerogatives. These can become limiting factors in the long run, particularly when placed within the paradigms of a fluid, dynamic, if not sometimes unstable, world order.

Adding to the complexity of this situation is the fact that the unipolar world order of the post-Cold War era is now giving way to one that will be decisively multi-polar in nature. Of course, traditional Great Powers like America and Britain will continue to wield enormous power as well as strongly influence international processes; but, emerging powers like India and Brazil too will have the opportunity to assert themselves. Consequently, instead of just having one or two power centres in the world, this century will eventually produce an international system pinned to several smaller regional power hubs.

In other words, in the years ahead, India's relationship with the world will become increasingly multi-dimensional—a complex mesh of sorts. There will be few, if any at all, black-and-white situations with clear cut choices. Instead, time and again New Delhi will have to produce a multi-layered response that will have to evolve with changing times and demands. In such a situation, single-point narratives produced by either ideological compulsions or power bloc loyalties should not be allowed to overshadow policy-making. There will be no one-size-fits-all solution; each response will have to be tailor-made to fit the situation at hand.

India's relations with the United States and Iran provides for an interesting study of this kind of diplomacy. After a lukewarm start in the late 1990s, ties between New Delhi and Washington have strengthened in this past decade. Today, they play out in multiple diplomatic theatres across the world from Beijing to Tehran and Riyadh and finally of course in Islamabad and Rawalpindi. The Bush administration freely courted New Delhi—their alliance culminating in the ground-breaking India-US civil nuclear energy agreement—throughout the mid-2000s but by the time the Obama administration came to power in 2009, the honeymoon was decidedly over. Washington's continued pandering to Islamabad, for one, was beginning to take a toll on its relations with New Delhi.

But things have now changed again with the US making it clear that it wishes for India to take on a greater role as a strategic partner. In fact, the US Secretary of Defence Leon Panetta during his visit to India in June 2012, described India as the 'linchpin' of the US's new military strategy envisioning a 'pivot to Asia'. Introduced in early 2012, the strategy is essentially America's response to China's alarming growth as an economic and military powerhouse that has come at a time when the US's own influence is waning. Today, as Washington attempts to re-calibrate its relations with Beijing, it has decided to hedge its bet with New Delhi.

Or has it? Do not forget that during his first Asia trip in November 2009, US President Barack Obama had called upon the leadership in Beijing to "work together to promote peace, stability and development" in South—not just South East—Asia. Four years later that sentiment seemed to have sharpened itself after outgoing US Assistant Secretary of State for East Asian Affairs Kurt Campbell observed at the Aspen Institute in January 2013: "China is predominant in every aspect of political, financial, economic and security relations in Asia. India is still a nascent player in Asia."

The point here is that the US will design its relations with both India and China keeping in mind its own strategic interests, and that's exactly how it should be. As for New Delhi, the ball is now in its court. How exactly it will respond remains a definite foreign policy challenge. Some believe that after decades of remaining 'non-aligned', India has now come to a crossroads where it will have to be 'aligned' and choose its friends and foes—a view that expectedly has many others up in arms.

From a realist's perspective, however, there is nothing wrong with India building closer ties with the US as long as New Delhi lays down certain ground rules.

For instance, India must make clear that under no circumstances will it proxy fight the US's war with China. To be sure, the crux of Washington's 'linchpin' narrative is that in case of a US-China standoff, New Delhi will stand by America's side. But India has its own issues with China. The twenty-first century has the two Asian giants competing against each other on multiple levels, while also coming closer than they have ever been in the recent past. That apart, India and China already have long-festering border disputes that do not look like they will be resolved any time soon. Tibetan dissent is also gaining ground and becoming increasingly aggressive—think of the spate of self-immolation cases by Buddhist monks.

And that's not all—the Chinese have also been pushing their luck with unnecessary belligerence in the South China Sea. Up until now, India has exercised a cautious restraint in its opposition to China's aggressive expansionist behaviour. But this approach only has limited viability especially if India is serious about strengthening its ties with the ASEAN countries, almost all of whom now have territorial disputes with China. To successfully secure its own interests in the South China Sea, New Delhi must establish closer naval ties with key littoral states such as Vietnam, Indonesia, Australia and particularly Japan where Shinzo Abe, one of India's strongest supporters, has returned as Prime Minister.

However, New Delhi must also take care not to unnecessarily ring alarm bells in Beijing which is already on edge. After all, while India must do all that it takes to protect its rights and interests; it will have to do so with tact so as to maintain a crucial balance between competition and cooperation, especially with China. The two countries share very close economic ties. Indeed, China is currently India's largest trading partner, bigger than the US even. Simply put, New Delhi cannot afford to have a confrontational relationship with Beijing. Here, pragmatism is the keyword and all players must be keenly aware of that.

Indeed, such an assertion of pragmatic policy-making is perhaps most evident in India's own relations with Iran. The two nations have historically shared strong ties but in today's globalised world, their relation must be understood alongside India's relations with the US, Israel and the Saudi Arabia led-Gulf Cooperation Council. All four are valuable allies to India.

But the problem here is that the US, Israel and Saudi Arabia are all openly antagonistic towards Iran primarily due to the latter's controversial nuclear programme and also due to other geo-political considerations. Since the Iranian Revolution of 1979, Washington has had no diplomatic ties with Tehran while Israel's once robust ties with Iran have now been replaced with hostility and bitter acrimony. Saudi Arabia, on its part, remains locked with Iran in a perennial battle for regional supremacy accentuated by sectarian tensions.

Understandably, India is often caught in the crossfire between its strategic allies. To complicate matters further, India also needs cheap Iranian oil to fuel its national growth machine. As a consequence, we have India's chequered relationship with Iran. Thrice, between 2005 and 2009, India voted against Iran at the International Atomic Energy Agency but also gladly hosted President Mahmoud Ahmadinejad in New Delhi in April 2008 much to the chagrin of Washington. In March 2012, India even sent a high-level trade delegation to Tehran hoping to double bilateral trade by 2015. Interestingly, the trip to Tehran came only weeks after an Israeli Embassy vehicle came under attack in New Delhi. Investigations into the attack revealed an 'Iranian hand' while Israeli authorities said that the incident was part of a coordinated attack on Israeli targets in Georgia, India and Thailand.

But trade and terrorism apart, it is oil and the nuclear bomb that remain the key areas of contention between India and its Western allies when it comes to Iran. The US wants India to cut down on its oil imports from Iran so as to squeeze Tehran into giving up its nuclear programme. It had even threatened to impose sanctions if New Delhi did not 'significantly' reduce the import. Such diplomatic bullying of course did not go down well with India which neither wants to be seen as kowtowing to American demands nor can afford to wholly give up on Iranian oil.

Hence, in typical Indian fashion, a middle ground has been found. Without engaging in the West's high-pitched criticism of the

Iranian nuclear programme, and without publicly censuring Tehran as Washington would have perhaps liked, New Delhi slowly and quietly reduced its import of Iranian crude. From 21.81 million metric tonnes of crude import in 2008-2009, the number was down to 14.78 million metric tonnes for the period between April 2011 and January 2012. In April 2012, India imported only 279,000 barrels per day from Iran as compared to 410,000 barrels per day in March and 450,000 barrels per day in April 2011.

It is in return for this concession, it is believed, that the US assisted India in tracking down and arresting Zabiuddin Ansari alias Abu Jundal, the man who allegedly directed the terrorists from a control room in Karachi as they wreaked havoc on Mumbai on 26 November, 2008. Ansari's arrest has not only been a huge boost for Indian intelligence agencies but is perhaps the biggest step that has been taken towards putting those responsible for the Mumbai attacks behind bars.

However, it is also worth mentioning that one of the main reasons behind India's decision to cut down Iranian oil imports even though it increased the union government's subsidy bill considerably, as the then Union Minister for Finance Pranab Mukherjee pointed out to the US during his meetings at the International Monetary Fund and the World Bank, is seemingly a belief in the effectiveness of the multilateral sanctions. The US likes to believe that the only reason that Iran has now returned to the negotiating table is because the sanctions are really hurting. This is despite Tehran's past record that shows its enormous tenacity to withstand such pressure.

Nonetheless, India's decision to reduce its oil dependence on Iran and multi-source its energy requirements (from thirty other countries), coupled with New Delhi's 'pragmatic balance' approach is a step in the right direction. At least in the immediate future, this kind of a middle-ground approach will allow the country to best secure its national interests, be it in terms of energy security or defence enhancements, and maximise its potential. The question that remains though is how long India will be able to hold on to that middle-ground especially as tensions between the West and Iran continue to rise.

To borrow the analogy presented by another: The manner in which India engages with the world should not resemble a boxing match, where victory and defeat can be easily judged, but it should be like a game of chess where every move must be made keeping in mind the strategic placement of the other players and the moves that they may or may not make.

Now, allow me to take this analogy a few steps further and first, convert the single layered chessboard into one that has three layers, as envisioned by the legendary American political scientist Joseph Samuel Nye, Junior. In this modified game of chess, the top board represents military power, the middle board represents economic power and the bottom board represents, for want of a better term, power from 'everything else' that is largely outside government purview such as the media, arts and culture and other socio-political processes. Not only do different countries have varying degrees of advantage on different boards; the power equation on each level is different as well. Hence, the Military Board 1 is largely unipolar with the US at its helm. The Economic Board 2, however, is more multi-polar with emerging economies playing a dominant role as well. The Everything Else Board 3 has but no defined structure at all since power is dispersed throughout the board and across non-state actors.

To win this game of chess, both players have to be mindful of what is going on at each level or else they will lose the plot. That is Step 1. For Step 2, let us take the game out of our civilised society living rooms and into the jungle where, unlike on the game board, there are no rules except for one: Survival of the fittest. And this—a three-layered game of chess played in the lawless jungle—is what best describes India's complex foreign policy situation in its immediate neighbourhood.

Living in a neighbourhood that is as "resentful and dangerous" as South Asia, as the former Canadian Ambassador to India David Malone describes the region, is not an easy task. Of the eight countries with whom India shares land or maritime borders—Bangladesh, Bhutan, China, the Maldives, Myanmar, Nepal, Pakistan and Sri Lanka—most have experienced long periods of political instability. And among the countries that have been relatively peaceful such as Bhutan, Myanmar and the Maldives, the domestic situation has not been comforting everywhere. While Myanmar is only now emerging from years of military rule that isolated it for decades from the rest of the world, in Maldives, the first democratically elected President of the archipelago was toppled in what is widely accepted as a military coup in February 2012.

And then of course there is the war ravaged, Taliban-infested Afghanistan with whom India does not share an international border per se but that country is still considered to be an integral part of the greater Indian sub-continent. When viewed together, there is no denying that India's neighbours surely present themselves as a policy challenge to New Delhi. Unfortunately, the slipshod manner in which New Delhi has managed its foreign policy in the neighbourhood has resulted in India's failure to rise to the occasion and take up its place as a rightful regional leader despite its big size and huge population, higher economic growth, large military and the extensive reach of its 'soft power'.

India's relationship with Pakistan, especially as it evolved under the Congress-led United Progressive Alliance government, is a telling example of how a poorly thought out foreign policy may not only hurt the country's geo-political position in the neighbourhood but more importantly, significantly compromise on the country's national security concerns. For example, for some incomprehensible reason, India has refused to recognise the fact that for all practical purposes Pakistan today is a failed state. And, while there is little that New Delhi can do to change the situation on the other side of the border, it must nevertheless take every possible measure to ensure that the mess from Pakistan does not spill into India.

Unfortunately, this has not been the case in the recent past with India expressing a bizarre desperation to 'normalise' ties with Pakistan. Bilateral talks with that country had been suspended after the 26/11 attacks and their renewal was contingent upon Pakistan's cooperation in bringing the perpetrators to book. Yet, even though Pakistan had done little apart from stonewall the investigation into the attacks, Prime Minister Manmohan Singh nevertheless let Islamabad off the hook when he delinked the issue of terrorism from the composite dialogue process during his disastrous 2009 Sharm el Sheikh meeting with the then Pakistani Prime Minister Yousuf Raza Gilani.

This of course was only the first of a series of concessions–such as resuming cricketing ties with Pakistan in 2012—that India would make over the next few years, driven by little else apart from an inexplicable desire to look good before Pakistan The fact that these concessions come at a time when Pakistan has become increasingly isolated from the rest of the world, including its longstanding ally the US, makes the entire situation even more absurd.

Meanwhile, the mastermind of the Mumbai carnage Jammat-ud-Dawa'ah chief Hafiz Saeed not just walks freely around Pakistan but also holds million strong rallies where he continues to spew his patented anti-India venom. Islamabad remains wilfully blind to all of this including the volumes of evidence that India has presented pointing to the involvement of state actors in the Mumbai attacks. Worse still, it has now come to expect the same behaviour from New Delhi which it views as home to a gullible bunch of aman-wallahs preoccupied with lighting candles of peace at the border.

Indeed, so desperate New Delhi has been to have somehow established a semblance of peace between India and Pakistan that it no longer even cares to take Islamabad to task for the humanitarian crisis that is brewing in the Gilgit-Baltistan region of Pakistan-occupied Kashmir. In the absence of any effective government, the mullahs have been the de facto rulers in that region and for the past six decades they have openly flamed a sectarian conflict between the Shia majority and Sunni minority that has now engulfed one and all in a fatal embrace.

Such capitulation by New Delhi over a period of time has naturally dented India's claims to be a regional leader. Moreover, New Delhi's mistakes with Islamabad find reflection in its relations with Colombo, Dhaka and Kathmandu. Take for instance, India's decision to vote for the US/EU-sponsored resolution against Sri Lanka at the United Nations Human Rights Council in March 2012 in a supposed bid to push Colombo to 'promote accountability and reconciliation' in the island nation following the military defeat of the Tamil terrorist group LTTE. It was perhaps the biggest foreign policy blunder committed by New Delhi in recent times.

India should have strongly resisted the West's efforts to humiliate Sri Lanka especially at a time when the war-ravaged country was just about beginning to rebuild itself. Equally importantly, it should have called for a global acknowledgement of the fact that Sri Lanka is the only country in the world to have successfully defeated a terrorist organisation—a stellar achievement conspicuously ignored by the West that has been more keen to highlight the alleged war crimes committed by President Mahinda Rajapaksa's men during the final phase of the war.

The decision to publicly censure Sri Lanka was a direct result of the Manmohan Singh government giving in to the tantrums of a powerful regional ally, the Tamil Nadu-based Dravida Munnetra Kazhagam party. Worse still, this was not the first time that the union government had capitulated in such a manner that would eventually hurt national interest. In September 2011, New Delhi caved before Kolkata as a result of which the Teesta water sharing agreement–supposed to be signed during Prime Minister Singh's historic trip to Dhaka–fell through. This not only embarrassed the Prime Minister but also upset his counterpart in Dhaka, Sheikh Hasina.

The Bangladeshi premier had already done more than her fair share to help the Indian government when she handed over to New Delhi militants who had taken refuge in her country. But in turn, she received next to nothing even though she is facing a stiff re-election challenge and could well use the Teesta treaty to consolidate her position. Moreover, it is in India's interest to support Prime Minister Hasina's secular, democratic and strongly pro-India government (as opposed to one that could potentially be led by her rival Khaleda Zia who partners with Islamists and is not really a friend of New Delhi's.)

Unfortunately, India's foreign policy in the sub-continent has consistently suffered from an unacceptable degree of shortsightedness. In fact, even though India's ties with almost all its neighbours go back several hundred years, New Delhi has exhibited a rare ignorance of its immediate surroundings, resulting in a sclerotic foreign policy in the region.

However, this is not to say that all is lost. If on the one hand India is struggling to get a grip on the great game that is being played on the world stage, it has on the other hand done spectacularly well in the arena of soft power. Today, India's credentials as a peaceful, secular democracy allow it tremendous leverage while Indian music, art, culture, food and of course movies ensure that this country has already captured the global imagination.

Indeed, as India continues to script its growth story, it will have several opportunities to incorporate its neighbours into its own narrative. Importantly, it will also have newer tools of diplomacy at its disposal and these too can be effectively used to further the country's interests. Many have rightly observed that the union government's recent decision to set up an external aid agency marks India's coming of age on the international forum. Called the Indian Agency for Partnership in Development, it is to be modelled on the lines of its American predecessor USAID and is expected to handle aid worth Rs 50,000 crore or US$11.3 billion over the next five to seven years. The agency comes at a time when India has been giving out increasingly large amounts in aid money—It is one of the biggest donors in Afghanistan and Nepal; in January 2010, it also extended a US$1billion line of credit to Bangladesh as a reward for its co-operation in counter-terrorism and insurgency operations; it currently has 121 operational lines of credits to 54 countries worth US$6.43 billion as of June 2012; and is expected to give African countries a US$5 billion dollar credit over the next three years. One can only hope that the aid money will be used effectively to further Indian interests and fetch the country more goodwill.

Love, Loss and Longing: A Capital Affair

—Alokita Datta

A place does not merely exist, (that) it has to be invented in one's imagination...

Amitav Ghosh, *The Shadow Lines*

Although Delhi is the only city I can call home, it is usually with a fair amount of incredulous curiosity that fellow inhabitants colloquially enquire: *Kya aap Delhi se hi belong karti hain?* (Do you belong to Delhi?) While I instinctively respond in the affirmative, and emphatically so, their question is not unfounded. Not just because I am a Bengali but since 'everyone came (here) from someplace else', something that has been said of New York, albeit in a different context. Also, few people can (or would) claim Delhi as their 'own'; yet it feels like my own. Even as a melting pot of diverse cultures and (regional) ethnicities, the city bears witness to a distinct and conspicuous socio-cultural non synthesis, non integration. The coming together of different groups of people and divergent linguistic systems has rendered an urban agglomeration teeming with 1.7 crore people, today, who have established niche (mutually exclusive) ecosystems. This is a land where individuality is asserted by establishing a differential relationship with the rest of the city populace, a pronounced non affiliation; how we are unlike others—the subtext reads superior—and proudly so. But one overarching homogenising factor is the city's legacy of power, their relationship with it and its many connotations. As Ranjana Sengupta tacitly points out in her book, *Delhi Metropolitan: the Making of an Unlikely City*, 'The one persistent identity Delhi has always had is that of power'. From the Mughals to the British and today's bureaucratic *babus*, the city has wielded might, authority and political prowess. It is as much a part of the historical inheritance—a 'walled' city with imposing architecture, from the red sandstone legacies of Muslim dynasties to the imperial edifices that commemorate the days of the Raj—as it is ingrained in the psyche of the 'Dilliwala'; the manifestations of which range from real will (to bring about change), political clout, inflated personas, megalomania to the kind of characteristic aggression that helps identify a Delhiite from a random crowd of people. It is often with a cool sense of deliberate detachment that people appraise you once you step into the world outside the Capital's sceptred sway.

'But in this segregated city, everyone comes together on the roads,' says Rana Dasgupta in his seminal essay *Capital Gains* (written for the *Granta*) and true enough, the roads become an inevitable social leveller (for lack of choice) but witness a unique power dynamic between an Alto and an Audi (and what they represent in Delhi's social lexicon) and lessons in the importance of size, as DTC buses swagger about menacingly, belittling small cars and pedestrians across the city. That is a different ball game altogether, the semiotics of which is very telling indeed. The beauty of Delhi's roads lies not just in the impressive width of its highways or the swirling, swift freeway-like flyovers that have become the city's lifeline, but the fact that most roads chart their way into various tales and anecdotes, which take precedence over the haste to reach a certain destination—for me, anyway. In Lutyens' (central) Delhi, roads emerge radially and follow circuitous routes, held together by the magnetism of India Gate, and gravitate southwards. It isn't everywhere that Copernicus runs parallel to (Bal Gangadhar) Tilak, Shahjahan gives way to Aurangzeb, Max Muller and Lodhi (Lodi) intersect and Simon Bolivar and Sardar Patel meet at crossroads. They commemorate artists, (Amrita Shergill), writers (Leo Tolstoy), revolutionaries (Mustafa Kemal Ataturk, Ho Chi Minh, Benito Juarez, Nelson Mandela) and luminaries of the Revolt of 1857 (Rao Tula Ram) among numerous politicians and national leaders effected when a road renaming project was undertaken, presumably to shirk off colonial vestiges reflected in names such as Curzon Road. The streets are reverberating with history, if one chooses to engage. This is overtly romantic rhetoric on an urban transport system, of course, but Delhi allows you the space, opportunity and ambience to be romantic. There are monuments, memorials, mosques in plush, sprawling greenery even in the unlikeliest of places all over the city.

In championing their recommendation UNESCO states that: It is Delhi's surviving historic urbanscape comprising four precincts of Mehrauli, Nizamuddin, Shahjahanabad and New Delhi that still have an outstanding universal significance, that are being proposed for nomination as a World Heritage City. It goes on to delineate how, over several centuries, the city has defined its uniqueness in its ever evolving morphological and architectural styles as a result of its continuous amalgamation of ideas and ideologies. Such exigencies and syncretism have left a distinct mark on its tangible footprint with the development of new vocabulary of architecture where form, function and symbolism played an important role.

Yes, Delhi continues to charm architects, captivate archaeologists and the aesthetically inclined in general. We are mesmerised by the city's old world charm. Yet this admiration is heavily steeped in nostalgia; the pleasure of genealogy, sharing a vast, rich, multicultural heritage, which remains suffused in the air, the landscape, but is it really absorbed? But it exists, persists and even permeates. Delhi in its current situation is in a state of flux and may be known by many a sobriquet—heritage city may be the least popular—depending on who you are talking to. Therein resides the charm. It is a place where cigar bars and *chholle kulche* kiosks run parallel successfully, where Dunkin' Donuts and *dhabas* in Mehrauli would attract the same crowd and comments on social media (in numbers and composition), ostentation is the key, brand consciousness qualifies as a Jungian archetype, black money flows like rainwater on the slope of a hill, capitalism is cannibalistic, communists are confined in their state of sublimated idealism, intellectual discourses spill outside the walls of the academies as well and the arts are patronised. For every mall hopper splurging on Jimmy Choo, Fendi, Bvlgari and Zara's catacombs, there is a serial Mandi House thespian (even if it is just to update her Facebook check-in). With all its glaring contrasts and complexities, Delhi allows you to choose your circle, and remain ensconced there. It is feudal, aristocratic but the difference is that social mobility can be bought out with cash; the same can't be said for respect. We revel in our little sub cultures and often revile those who don't belong to ours. Delhi has been a planned city, meticulously developed and conscious of maintaining a high image quotient, politically and otherwise, and each stage has observed enrichment in the conglomeration that defines Delhi today. Is a reconciliation between the current histories of erstwhile Shahjahanabad (Old Delhi) and Shahpur Jat possible; but more importantly, is it really necessary?

Edwin Lutyens and Herbert Baker's New Delhi may have been inaugurated in 1931, but the grand narrative of a 'new' Delhi was written with the influx of over 500,000 refugees who migrated from West Punjab situated in the newly created Pakistan in 1947. Before that Delhi comprised about 300,000 people. The Independence Day rally at Princess Park, now known as India Gate, was followed by mass scale riots and the subsequent mushrooming of refugee camps and resettlement colonies, transformations that people such as S.S. Chibber, a retired professor of the University of Delhi, have observed and analysed having shared a long, tumultuous association with the city. 'Along the roadside, particularly in places like Gurudwara Road, refugees earmarked a plot of land, built a wooden structure where they would live and started their business,' he recollects. As migrants began to acclimatise themselves with Delhi, a wave of commercialisation engulfed the city. Ajmal Khan Road (within Karol Bagh) used to be an entirely residential colony; today it is abuzz with a conundrum like ghetto of shops selling items from dry fruits to brand knock-offs to hardware, and the roots of these business can be traced back to the Punjabi migrants who established themselves and the city thereby post Partition. Chibber muses how the culture of eating out emerged as numerous *dhabas* (modest, road-side eating places) spawned all over. In fact, Pandara Road, a tangential offshoot of India Gate, became a designated area for all the *dhabas* that had haphazardly cropped around the monument and its imposing force field. It was around this time that the man from Peshawar decided to acquaint Delhi with tandoori chicken, as he strolled into Darya Ganj, nestled in the Walled City. Kundan Lal Gujral would be better known by the chain of highly successful Moti Mahal restaurants (which now has around ninety franchises across the county) he started. There was no stopping him or the poultry bird that took flight across the world and perched itself prettily within the British culinary scene, in particular.

'The only change is that while Jawahar Lal Nehru would visit Moti Mahal, in a red beacon free white ambassador, today, Moti Mahal would have to be brought to Manmohan Singh,' Chibber remarks with a distinct sense of ironic detachment. The average Dilliwala's Saturday night, 'family dinner' is incomplete without butter chicken and when it comes to food in general, affluence doesn't overtake authenticity, as it were: the Honda Cities and Skoda Rapids outside Kake-da-Dhaba bear testimony to the fact that the pub wanderer would scrimmage through by-lanes and bottlenecks, when it comes to the pursuit of the palate.

In 1911, when the capital of India was shifted from Calcutta to Delhi, a large number of Bengalis came to the city and were soon employed in government services. With that came the quintessentially Bengali need to engender an environment conducive for the education and intellectual stimulation of Delhi's new guests from the east. The Raisina Bengali School (1925) is one such example. In the late 1940s and early 1950s however, people from southern India, Keralites, Tamil Brahmins, began to replace the Bengalis as clerks and secretaries in government offices when C. Rajagopalachari and later V.P. Menon held central office. Thus an era of multiculturalism began palpably. The Bengalis continued to reside here and they largely comprise the population that predates the creation of Chittaranjan Park. It is with a great sense of pride and an oblique amount of amusement that my (Bengali) friend talks about how she often passes by the hospital where her grandmother was born, in north Delhi. The tangible cord of lineage makes the bond with her grandmother and the city significantly special. Delhi has always benefited from invasions (however tyrannical or tragic) with the intermingling of new and residual cultures. Anthropologically, societies that have undergone disparate influences are said to develop faster. One of the first harbingers of change was the amalgamation of Punjabi in Hindi and the formation of new linguistic patterns. However, the gradual demise and imminent obliteration of Urdu was a denigrating occurrence. Khushwant Singh upholds that the Muslim exodus that was necessitated by the creation of Pakistan saw the drain of courtesy and refinement as well. Urdu today is survived in a diluted and sporadic manner for the mainstream population through the lyrics of Hindi film songs. Mirza Ghalib's decrepit haveli in Ballimaran (Chandni Chowk) is a coveted tourist destination but his *shayari* has sparse patrons. Yet Delhi, even today, is one of the few places where Urdu is studied, serenaded and celebrated with formidable gusto; even if couplets resonate within closed perimeters.

The other vital aspect of societal development—one that is consciously manmade—is urban planning. With Lutyens' Delhi as the nucleus, the city was cradled between Raigarh Pura (Karol Bagh) and Kashmere Gate in the north till 1947. The only Central government officers and staff colony to exist pre-Independence was Lodi Colony and was designed by William Henry Medd. The early 1950s initiated the Central Public Works Department's (CPWD) project that led to the creation of the Diplomatic Enclave of Chanakyapuri—the bureaucratic ethos which is demarcated for embassies, chanceries, high commissions and the residences of ambassadors, around the expansive central vista of Shanti Path. The magnanimous new bungalows soon ushered in a reinvention of decadence among the Delhi nobility. Sadia Dehlvi (her surname literally means 'from Delhi'), in an essay called *Dilli ka Dastarkhwan*, reminisces how 'Shama Kothi', their house in Diplomatic Enclave, became the venue for hosting '*mushairas*, *qawwalis*, dance and music *mehfils*' in the true spirit of *mahmannawasi*. The idea of enclaves fascinates Delhi, evidently since the city abounds in them—Safdarjung Enclave, Hauz Khas Enclave, Sadhna Enclave, Qutab Enclave, among a few others. Conceptually, enclaves suggest the dualities of embeddedness and isolation; places that are surmounted yet inwardly self indulgent as pockets that are (socio-culturally) divorced from the area that encompasses them. Hauz Khas (translates as the Royal Tank, which dates back to the Khilji dynasty) a posh, botanically blessed, upscale commercial and residential complex interspersed with 13th century tombs, and mosques from the Sultanate period, along the lake that defines it, which attracts nature lovers, the archeologically intrigued and art aficionados, was developed. The enclave was built by Delhi Land and Finance (DLF) in the 1960s, a private colony that exists in solitude. Safdarjung Enclave also came into existence around this time when DLF acquired farm lands from the Humayunpur Village. The second phase of extension in New Delhi, started in the late 1950s by acquiring land from Munirka farmers, developed by CPWD. Its development continued till the 1970s, when R. K. Puram, one of the largest residential colonies of the time was established. Farm land acquisition has been instrumental in Delhi's real estate politics and has inculcated the land owner mindset among its people that ranges from the self conferred sophistication of Chhattarpur farmhouse owners to the deliberately uncouth anarchism of the rich Jats who live across the Yamuna, the eastern part of the city (in and around Shahdara), and rule over small time malls and periodically encroach areas in Ghazipur village, for instance. It is modern, neo-feudalism flanked by the aplomb of rank consciousness. The creation of the Delhi Development Authority (DDA) in 1957, pushed real estate back in the hands of the state and private players, DLF primarily, embarked on a farmland purchasing mission in Haryana from thereon.

In 1956, Delhi was recognised as a Union Territory and the 1950s and 60s were a time of resettlement in Delhi. The city was accommodating, realigning itself with the immigrant population. To begin with, refugee camps were set up in Purana Qila (Old Fort). People were eventually allotted plots in areas such as Lajpat Nagar, Patel Nagar, and Rajendra Nagar. The plots were of 15x60 feet constructed like army barracks. The houses were all single storey, with asbestos roofs, but now most of the houses are multi-storeyed, stately and have skyrocketed several manifold in commercial value and social worth. Lajpat Nagar is probably one of the few refugee colonies where the camp like civic infrastructure is physically discernible even now. It was developed in the 1950s in four parts and was then known as Cheap Colony or Cheap Cantonment. Malviya Nagar was another colony which saw the influx of refugees and consists of a significant proportion of Punjabi, Sindhi, Haryanvi and even Rajasthani people. Jangpura (originally Youngpura, named after a Colonel Young) added an 'Extension' which has since then been the habitat of Jangpura Extension's Sikh population who hail largely from the villages of Rawalpindi; so is Tilak Nagar, where the population comprises Sikhs from Peshawar, besides Rawalpindi. Originally named East Pakistan Displaced Persons Colony, and established in the 1960s, Chittaranjan Park (thus named in the 1980s) has been a flourishing Bengali colony, a metonymic representation of Kolkata in most ways. Incidentally, it was Lajpat Nagar that housed a refugee camp for Bengali widows called Kasturba Ashram earlier. The ironic contrasts between life in Lajpat Nagar and C.R. Park, less than five kilometres away from each other, is demonstrative of how geographical proximity doesn't necessarily allow for cultural integration; a fact rather effortlessly delineated in the recent film *Vicky Donor*. Alongside these immigrant colonies, as it were, there was the concomitant rise of urban residential colonies, under DLF, such as South Extension, Greater Kailash. The latter came to be occupied by a large number of Indian Oil Corporation officers, during the 1970s. Interestingly, even after the sun had set on the British Empire, we continued to live in colonies. Perhaps the same way we live and travel in and around myriad '*sarais*' even if they remain a crumbling edifice of their former selves, after the Mughals have long gone. Perhaps not because colonies are as much a mental construct as they are physical entities and the former is invariably stronger.

My father first came to Delhi in the early 1970s, the reason was purely academic and one that continues to lure students from various parts of the country, especially the East—the plethora of options for post graduate education that exist in the capital. He, among many others from the North East, after completing his graduation from Cotton College, Guwahati, made a beeline for the city, ardently took to the University of Delhi, the coffee house culture and the enamour of dilapidated and relatively downplayed Khyber Pass and the world that thrives between Darya Ganj and Chandni Chowk. Through his fleeting associations with the city over the years, he marvels at the fact that he could always relate and return to the image of the city that remains consecrated in his mind. He's never alienated. Delhi doesn't self efface the past and is therefore characterised by a cultural sedimentation which doesn't quite sever the unique relationship you may have held with it, at any given point in time. The externalities may have changed but essence, I am given to understand, pervades all experiences entwined in memory. That is not to say in any way that Delhi's cultural milieu hasn't changed; there is always a dominant and residual culture and that is chronologically interchanged. In this respect, my father mourns the gradual relinquishment of what he calls the *tehzeeb* culture, which had an intangible but real presence in the city, behind the cloud of garishness that seems to have enveloped it. But there would still be some recesses in the city where one might discover what was once thought to have ceased in existence. Some phenomena in the city are impervious to change and exist in a timeless realm—the Sufis of Nizamuddin and their Thursday night qawwali, Amir Khusrau and the dargah, and the captivating and exasperating labyrinth that is Chandni Chowk; from Fatehpuri to Turkman Gate. From the point of view of city governance, this area poses a challenge and therefore due to the twin justifications of charm and congestion, *Purani Dilli* has remained in a scintillating time capsule amidst wholesale trade and grey market goods all along boasting of a kind of syncretism that captures the whims of many visitors. While the flood of 1978 wreaked unprecedented havoc it had transformed Ring Road into a cascading waterway as the rescue mission boats ferried people across the city. A passive recollection evokes the historical imagery of how the Yamuna would have flowed through the Red Fort when the latter was built by Shah Jahan.

With the establishment of Jawahar Lal Nehru University and the National School of Drama (under the Sangeet Natak Akademi and later autonomous in 1975) in 1959, Delhi began to cultivate its intellectual and artistic echelons. However, the architect of modernity, in more ways than one, who carved the hub for Delhi's intelligentsia in and around Lodi estate, is commemorated by the patrons of 'Steinabad'. Joseph Allen Stein came to Delhi in 1955 and over the next four decades designed some of the most stalwartly buildings that are conspicuous in their style of multi-dimensional space utilisation and stone lattices which were the hallmark of his architecture. One of the first ones was Triveni Kala Sangam (1957) followed by The India International Centre (IIC, inaugurated in 1962), the Ford Foundation, UNICEF building and the India Habitat Centre (IHC) in the 1980s. The IIC was instituted with the idea of 'quickening and deepening true and thoughtful understanding between peoples of nations'. Whether that has even begun to be achieved is a bigger question to answer, but what the Centre has in fact achieved in creating is a canopied enclosure, elite in an elegant, non exclusivist manner, which finds ambassadors, foreign diplomats, veteran journalists, aspiring and established writers diligently engaged in debates and discussions, rhetorical renditions, on grandiose subjects and pressing politics that spark interest, if not change. Yet it is one of the few genuinely stimulating forums where the cultural paparazzi haven't made its presence yet. Scholarly inclinations demarcate class boundaries here. On the other hand, the very ideas of mass ideological proliferation brought about the birth of Janam, Jana Natya Manch in 1973. It is estimated that between 1970-71 and 1990-91, industrial employment escalated by 300 per cent and the 1970s and 80s saw an unprecedented growth in population, vehicles and small scale industries—the handloom/handicrafts industries of Nand Nagri or the rubber factories in Seelampur and the development of the industrial units in Sahibabad (Ghaziabad, UP). People from Uttar Pradesh constituted the largest section of migrants coming to Delhi for work (49.61 per cent between 1981 and 1991, according to the Census). With their play *Machine* (1978) Janam unleashed a new narrative of street theatre that addressed the exploitation of the industrial class. Simultaneously, proscenium plays entered a definitive phase under Ebrahim Alkazi's dramatic oeuvre and set in motion the reparatory aspect of Delhi's theatrical legacy.

It was the 1980s that ushered in the era of township building; the sub city of Rohini was created by the DDA, as part of the urban extension programme and the aim to create residential localities that housed people from various income groups. The Dwarka project was also initiated around this time. It was a phase of white collar modernity, therefore, commercial complexes such as Nehru Place came into existence, as people moved from villas to apartments and multi-storied 'societies' threatened the equanimity of tree lined bungalows. The Asian Games (1982) metamorphosed the inheritance of the Khilji Dynasty with the incumbent need to create the Asiad Village in the Siri Fort Area which came to house ministry officials, PSU officers and public servants. The same year Pragati Maidan was founded with a (global) trade centric focus—thus divorced from the aesthetic revelry that dominated Delhi's fast springing art galleries—and remains Delhi's largest exhibition space.

One thing I have realised, having grown up and lived in Delhi, is that I (like many others from the city) tend to calibrate my views of the world in its likeness and dissimilarities with the city. It is a shared egocentricity, despite the obvious oxymoron inherent in that phrase. So, it doesn't disconcert us, for instance, that Delhi University admissions make national headlines—the fact that mainstream media is headquartered here (with the exception of the Times Group) isn't really a strong defence—it is the natural extension of our way of life. The rest of India is unlike us, and categorised by the degrees of incompatibility with the centre. Ironically, there has never really been an overarching sentiment of solidarity or the bond of nativity that unites the people of life in Delhi. The city is subject to a kind of 'block mentality' (pun intended)—most nagars, vihars, enclaves and colonies are divided into blocks, particularly under the master strokes of the DDA Master Plan (1962) which ensured the construction of local markets, shopping centres within each residential area; hence, the involution. Yet there is a somewhat united perception of the city that precedes an actual experience of life here—certain myths, in the sense that Levi Strauss promulgated the concept of mythology.

Towards the end of last year a certain blog-post by an irate *Madrasan* (as she is alluded to by our culturally insensitive city, we are told) wrote an 'open letter to a Delhi boy' which became quite a rage. It was sharp, succinct, and articulate and meanders along the lines of spite, vitriol, blatant and unabashed disrespect and genuine hilarity. But her impassioned harangue reinforced some of the most commonly held opinions about the city: boorish, chauvinistic cash flaunting men, luxury craving bimbos of South Delhi, the illusionary sense of independence women live with as well as the linguistic insufficiencies that dominate modern day vernacular. It was a hurtful post to which most Delhites responded by exploiting some of the stereotypes associated with Bangalore and Chennai—match point? Yet it was difficult to refute the generalisations because they are rooted well within the reality of Delhi in 2012. The gnawing question is that when and why did *they* come to represent the face of Delhi? The etymology of this cultural phenomenon could be traced back to Khushwant Singh's theory on the evolution of flashy flamboyance in the city. Having seen the city transform, enrich and deplete from almost the turn of the 20th century, Singh's narratives, much like his abode in stately Sujan Singh Park, delineate the city with authority. He believes that post Partition the new entrants from West Punjab were zealous about showing off how well they had done for themselves; making a fast buck in a new city and hence the practice of flaunting wealth became a norm. As a cultural meme it has probably been successively inherited by each generation of the Delhi's Punjabis, one could argue. But it was post liberalisation (1991 and thereon) that Delhi adorned its incandescent demeanour and saw the progression of the super rich. However, the middlemen—agents, brokers, mediators—they go by many names started to flourish around this time. Forming the much important nexus between ministers and business, the public and the private, wooing foreign entrants into the newly created market catapulted them to profitability. In an interview with *The Caravan*, Mahmood Farooqui recalls how in the mid 1990s, the amount of money being made from government connections were mainly through contracts leased out to private players; this ushered in an era of numerous scams and black money scandals. Mumbai has always been Delhi's arch nemesis and even if it is the financial capital of the country, Delhi is more money-minded. The difference probably is that while people in Mumbai strive to make money, the Dilliwala's prerogative is wealth acquisition and all the aristocratic privileges that come with it. Land as a tool of wealth generation has been utilised in this city more than anywhere else.

In Delhi you are judged by how you 'keep up appearances' and that applies unilaterally. A shopkeeper would find it extremely prudent to appraise you once and remark that the clothes he is selling is beyond your budget. Thus your apparel needs to be congruent with your bank balance. In the broader context it is a city that has always regaled in inequality—the symbols of superciliousness could be a Delhi School of Economics education or a Ducati depending on the context. The unequal balance of power needs to remain undisturbed at any cost. Maybe, this explains the recent infiltration of noveau riche progenies in 'cultural' events such as classical music recitals and literary festivals who make no qualms about leveraging brand equity. It of course gives them an edge over their other Punjabi Bagh club peers who were unfortunately engaged in collecting money for their next kitty party, and thus their socialisation takes on a new rank. It irks Kamani Auditorium and Sri Ram Centre devotees the most who see this as a debilitating depletion of our rich, cultural heritage. Paradoxically, inclusion in this case is a form of dilution but does this render Delhi a sham of its former self, where the burden of pretension weighs heavy in trying to uphold a facade that has hollowed? That is an elitist notion, though not necessarily untrue. Even if the people are buying Satish Gujral's contemporary art only to decorate their office and impress clients, for example, it cannot diminish the art critic's admiration for it. But harmonisation was never really a sought after virtue here. Rank consciousness goes well beyond the bureaucracy. The interesting aspect of Delhi's political make-up is that state level politics gets co-opted with central administration. There is no sense of peripheral entities that holds a dialogue with the centre. Student union politics is engineered by ruling or opposition party agendas. Progress has been the by-product of individual or nationalistic ambition because for the ministers Delhi would be the report card on which their next semester's performance depends. Corruption here however, is most decentralised and exists in the most insidious permutations.

My real bond with Delhi started to develop in 1996 when I returned after spending four glorious years in Mumbai. At the age of ten, I had other priorities in life and understanding the city was the least of them but the stark differences between my two favourite cities were apparent nonetheless. Delhi doesn't overwhelm you the way Mumbai sweeps you in its ambit before you have even realised it. Delhi remained cool and distant but if you don't resist, it will make place for you. But there is never really a feeling of warmth that emanates from the city; it is the waft of imbibed familiarly that pulls you towards it. It is often difficult to explain to people why and what you like about Delhi; it is usually the successive layers of history and their physical manifestations that form my typical answer. Of course the sprawling physical infrastructure and lush greenery, more importantly how they co-exist without compromising one another has its own charm. All these things go into the creation of my version of Delhi that is ever so dynamic as it is constant and is coloured in my experiences marked by alienation and acceptance. Driving past India Gate at night I often wonder why I love Delhi as much as I do; it doesn't love me back but I can live with that.

Hunger on Celluloid: Through Satyajit Ray's Ashani Sanket and Beyond!

—Santanu Banerjee, Subhadeep Ray

Indian Cinema completes its 100 years in 2013, considering *Raja Harishchandra*, by Dadasaheb Phalke, released on 3 May 1913, as the first full length *swadeshi* feature film. Historically the most recent to evolve, and aesthetically the most dynamic among the dramatic forms, with the potential to reach out to the different layers of human experience, film has undergone a very complicated course of development in this sub-continent. Although drawing its primary impetus from mythology and classical literature, the sense of any pan-Indian cinema has always been challenged by the demands to address what Satyajit Ray calls 'the broad cultural pattern that is India, a thousand disparities in behavior, habits, rituals, dress, topography, language and so on'[1], accounting for the various regional film industries. This also involves a continuous search for differing versions of cinematic language, which could employ the existing cultural codes in a particular province with significant effects on the growth of national cinema. Cinema, being one of the most popular art forms in the modern history, also invokes the contesting meanings of *popular* as both commercial and related to common life.

A 'new wave' in Indian film-making was thus generated from Bengal with the release of Satyajit Ray's *Pather Panchali* (*Song of The Road*) in 1955. Using Bibhutibhusan Banerjee's novel as a source text the film transcribes the poverty ridden life of a Bengali village into a commentary on universal humanism with the greatest artistic economy and subtlety. This was followed by a series of 'parallel cinema,' characterised by a strong social content and incorporation of the major experiments in Western realist film. The three Bengali film-makers who form diverging perspectives that define this movement are Ray, Mrinal Sen and Ritwik Ghatak.

The present essay would try to examine how post-Independence social crisis of starvation affects a central film of the above movement, Satyajit Ray's *Ashani Sanket* (*Distant Thunder*), 1973, as a case-study. The history of public hunger in Bengal had somehow overlapped the Independence, and preoccupied Bengali cinema at various levels: symbolically represented by Goopy and Bagha's feeding of Halla's hungry soldiers with the ghost-king's boon in Ray's *Goopy Gyne o Bagha Byne* (*The Adventures of Goopy and Bagha*), 1969. This trend continued till 1980, with Sen's *Akaler Shandhaney* (*In Search of Famine*). Therefore, a comprehensive reading of the main threads of cultural and political influences on Bengali cinema helps to understand the dynamics of flow and frame in a specific film producing a distinct kind of realism.

Realism in art attempts to depict life in an objective manner. As a term it is also applied to a movement in eighteenth and nineteenth century Western fiction by Defoe, Dickens, George Eliot, Tolstoy, Dostoevsky, Balzac, Flaubert and others; whose novel is distinctive in 'the amount of attention it habitually accords both to the individualisation of its characters and to the detailed presentations of their environment'[2]. Having originated through novelistic realism, the mainstream cinema attempts to present vivid characters in powerful dramatic situations. In early twentieth century D.W. Griffith in USA virtually perfected the language of motion-picture single-handedly; the crosscutting between the subplots in his *A Corner in Wheat*, 1909, imbibes Dickensian narrative technique. What follows Griffith is 'a phenomenal growth' in cinematic rhetoric, and the 'development of [filmic] language from [him] to Godard … is roughly equivalent to that from Chaucer to Joyce in English literature—a matter of 600 years as against 60 in the cinema'[3]. In film history, Sergei Eisenstein's works in Russia are the most significant achievements after Griffith. Eisenstein's *Strike*, 1924, and *The Battleship Potemkin*, 1925, move away from the practices of conventional cinema by dealing with historical situations that dramatise human oppression, using characters as representatives of different classes, turning masses into the protagonist, and technically juxtaposing apparently unrelated images and moments with rapid shifts in rhythm.

By cutting and editing, placing alternative movements side by side, and thereby reaching new synthesis, such films create 'dialectic montage'. After the October Revolution of 1917, under Lenin's leadership and pursuing Gorki's socialist realism, a new revolutionary use of camera for social analysis developed in Eisenstein, Pudovkin and Dovzhenko, whose works have taught later directors to catch 'the profound social and historical conditions and movements' enabling one to 'speak with some fullness of voice, of a human history'[4].

In a separate development French 'poetic realists' drifted from the traditional *film d'art*, and the impressionistic avant-garde of the 1920s and surreal school of Dali and Bunuel. Vigo's *L'Atalnte*, 1934, for example, elaborates the river-journey of two newly-weds, whose simple story of love, hate and maturity sets the tune of the masterpieces of Jean Renoir, portraying the lives of ordinary men and women in everyday setting. Renoir's study of contemporary cultural dynamics is evident in *Rules of the Game*, 1939—a film distinguished by robust humanism, and employment of deep-focus. Once the film was banned by French Right-wing state, Renoir immigrated to Hollywood. In 1950 when he came to India for shooting his colourful lyric, *The River*, Satyajit Ray accompanied him in journeying across Bengali countryside. The latter recalls, 'Renoir told me: "You don't have to have too many elements in a film, but whatever you do, must be the right elements, the expressive elements"'[5].

Luchino Visconti, Renoir's assistant in Paris, extended the scope of 'poetic realism' by focusing his camera on the rough visuals of villages and casting local residents. Visconti's disciple Cezare Zavattini, a professed Marxist, initiated 'neo-realism' in Italian cinema by scripting *Shoeshine*, 1946, *Bicycle Thieves*, 1948 and *Umberto D*, 1952, along with Vittorio De Sica, the director of these films. Rejecting the norms of commercial cinema, their works call for accurate and detailed representation of daily life of the mass, struggling under the Fascist rule. Playing the role of 'organic' intellectual Visconti engaged himself in the Left-wing political campaigns after World War II. With Italian 'neo-realistic cinema' film becomes a weapon of anti-imperialist struggle across national borders.

The state of Bengali cinema in the early twentieth century is portrayed by Satyajit Ray: 'the performers appeared plastered with makeup. Right from the start, speech was taken as the primary means of conveying information…Songs and melodrama…were direct imports from the stage'[6]. Bengalis' entry into realistic film was marked by Bimal Roy's *Udayer Pathe*, 1944. An actor in *Tathapi*, 1950, written by Roy, Ritwik Ghatak created *Nagarik* in 1953, but failed to release it due to legal complications. And, it was at this juncture *Pather Panchali* shook the world film-goers with a radically new kind of idiom. However, without an ideological involvement in the social turmoil of post-Partition Bengal, haunted by poverty and injustice, Satyajit could not identify his aesthetics with the living experiences of ordinary people in his debut film.

On several occasions Satyajit expressed his artistic indebtedness to Bibhutibhusan. Actually, while reappropriating Western traditions, the concerned directors found their national root in Bengali realist fiction. Unlike film-making, Bengal has cherished a long legacy of modern novel since Rabindranath. Thus, being mainly urban in their approach to life, Satyajit or Ritwik had to rely on the fictional portrayals of rural, marginalised people and their life-struggle. The social depth of their works owe much to the writings of the Banerjee trio—Bibhutibhusan, Tarashankar and Manik—along with Advaita Mallavarmana, Satinath Bhaduri and others. And when Mrinal Sen initiated another 'new-cinema' with *Bhuvan Some* in 1969, he drew upon one of the finest short-story writers of Bengal, Balai Chand Mukherjee. Involved entirely with the trivial and ordinary, yet having a sense of the immensity of time and space, these writers with a clear eye for minute details and utter humanism record the life of Bengali masses.

In an interview Satyajit states unambiguously that film making, and for that matter any creative work, cannot change a social order alone: 'It is very easy to attack certain targets like the establishment. You are attacking people who don't care. The establishment will remain totally untouched by what you're saying. So what is the point? Films cannot change society.' Referring to Eisenstein, Ray further says that 'In the midst of a revolution, a filmmaker has a positive role; he can do something for the revolution'[7]. Though pointing out that an Indian film-maker lacks the political setting congenial to work for social change, Satyajit's commitments to people's causes in his own films had remained unflinching since the making of

Pather Panchali. *Ashani Sanket* was originally planned to be produced in the mid-sixties—and had to be postponed for certain reasons—that is in the midst of the Food Movement. Ray's artistic self thus took part in this activism by reviewing 1943's man-made famine, where the film further decodes a set of signifiers for the social experiences in post-colonial Bengal. This is directly related to the complex relation between form and content of Satyajit's work.

That it had been a historical necessity to look back at the famine of the forties during the heady days of mid twentieth century was reflected in the address of the Communist leader, Jyoti Basu to a mass gathering revolting against state brutalities at Calcutta in 1959: 'In 1943 hearing of the devastating famine, Nehru had reported that so many people died without protesting, this time Jawaharlal cannot make this complaint. People of Bengal have wiped out that allegation, this time; they have fought till they are dead'[8]. With bitter irony, this speech explains that inspite of the establishment of Indian democracy supposed to ensure the entitlement of people to the rights of free citizenship, even the basic needs of life remained a distant dream for them, continuing the inheritance of suffering as the only option for poor: something poignantly caught by a title card in the opening montage of Mrinal Sen's *Kolkata 71*, 1972: 'History. History of poverty. History of deprivation. History of exploitation.'

Food-crisis and price-rise had begun to affect Bengalis since 1951, supported by the neo-colonial strategies adopted by the ruling class in the interest of the rich. This completely undermined the struggle of the victims of the forties' Famine, whom the last shot of *Ashani Sanket* show in silhouette as the camera is continuously drawn back to focus first on dozen and then on thousands of starving men and women. Passing through a phase of discrete protests, Food Movement took an organised shape around 1957-58 under the leadership of *Krishaksabha*. During this whole period the post-colonial rulers were found to be no less atrocious towards people than their imperial counterparts. The number of martyrs grew up continually in different districts of West Bengal.

The price of rice and other rations rose up to an alarming height in the late-fifties, symptoms of famine being shown everywhere, people were forced to decide, as declared then by the left organ *Swadhinata*, 'there is no other way, so struggle is inevitable'[9]. Replying to the state government's decision to deregulate the price of rice on 22 June 1959, peasant organisations took the path of civil disobedience[10]. Next came 31 August 1959: the Jallianwallabagh of independent India. After a huge mass demonstration, comprising peasant workers, women, industrial labourers and even professionals at Kolkata demanding the end of hunger and exploitation, a procession moved towards the Writers Building only to be suddenly lathi-charged by the police, as a result of which 80 people died, 100 went missing and 3000 were injured, a number of whom had ironically survived the Famine of forties[11]. Such a moment in political struggle obviously deserved the creative artist to reconsider 'the lives of the great majority of people,' which had been 'almost wholly disregarded by most arts,' and 'film could at once move beyond these limitations' by the simple virtue of camera that it 'could be taken and set up anywhere'[12]. Thus, when a second-wave of food-crisis and resultant revolts struck from 1964-65, Bengali film-makers started thinking on framing this total course of history in various ways.

In Congress's Patna session in 1962, 'Pandit Nehru was emphatic that socialism would ultimately come through, not only in India but the world over'[13]. Paradoxically, such belief in the redemptive power of socialism was uttered against the backdrop of extreme social discrimination, lack of primary amenities among common people partly due to the Indo-China war, and nationwide drive against socialists. In Bengal, food-crisis became acute again in 1965; with peasant organisations continuously demanding rice, kerosene and proper rationing service; the government turned coercive: at least 54 persons were killed in 1966[14]. People responded finally by voting Congress out and electing the first United-Front Government in 1967. However, the United-Front Government, too, mismanaged the food-problem and fell to upper-classes' traps, resulting again in social unrest. This led to another passage of history through Emergency, and a rediscovery of people's democracy.

Therefore, it was when the toiling mass of Bengal was fighting out its destiny, Satyajit returned to his favourite narrator in *Aṣhani Sanket*. It was his 'first substantive return to the Bengali village scene, burdened with the fearful problem of achieving the reality of *Pather Panchali* without the benefit of the primitive passion of the "first fine careless rapture"'[15]. But his own logic was strong behind such project: he could explore the hidden potentials of Bengali viewers' "love of narrative" according to contemporary situation; and, this satisfies the fact that "every film is *about* something—usually about people, who pass through various phases and events which give the film a shape'[16].

It is easy to follow in *Ashani Sanket* the peaceful life of Gangacharan, poor Brahmin priest, school-teacher cum doctor, with his beautiful wife Ananga, their subsequent hardships because of scarcity of food and extensive price-rise, and realisation of human helplessness against physical, social and psychological forces in a deterministic world order. But, this much from Bibhutibhusan's novel turned into film with necessary improvisations could not ascribe Satyajit's work with the kind of effect it produces. 'The Apu Trilogy' taught Ray to think of film-making as a matter of being both true to original and translating it into a new medium. In the case of *Ashani Sanket* he had to work harder in finding a suitable sub-text in the requirements of a modern film.

The film is located in a small, sort of prototype Bengali village. Such use of generalised setting interestingly differ *Ashani Sanket* from its contemporary films like Mrinal Sen's *Kolkata 71* and Ritwik Ghatak's *Titas Ekti Nadir Naam*, (*A River Called Titas*), 1973. Ritwik's film is situated at the bank of a river, and thus occupies a particular geographical territory where a fishing tribe lives, as clearly identified in Mallabarmana's novel. Ray's village and its men and women stand in an almost equal distance from Sen's identifiable streets and slums of Calcutta, crowded by people belonging to a distinct spatiotemporal frame, which in the film through a complex web of montage, are seen as a representative part of human history. On the other hand, Ray's Gangacharan, Ananga, Chutki, Moti all first appear as universal-characters, who seem to have been peacefully living in rural Bengal for a long span of time like the vibrating Nature surrounding them.

The representation of Nature in the most expressive of terms with the use of colour becomes a trope in Ray's film; and the complex relation between man and Nature provides clues to some of the work's deep import. Bibhutibhusan's plot is actually set against a disintegrating feudal society, with most of its social values remaining intact, and always interacting with the intervention of newly arising finance capital. Thus, the only Brahmin priest in the village is allowed to live on others until there is a meagre availability of food. The chief source of food, the paddy field, is shown throughout the film, although human condition changes from modest living to extreme misery. This should be noted that 'the sensuous world' of Nature is to be conceived 'as the total living sensuous *activity* of the individuals composing it'[17]. It is in this sense; human labour becomes a central concern in Ray's film. As Andrew Robinson opines, 'Hands are a motif of *Distant Thunder*', but the direct relation between hands and labour is hard to miss. However, the sense of time and space arrive with the lush paddy field which is a product of the villagers, being gradually taken away from them for some reasons they cannot perceive. The main use of colour in the film 'as to point up the contrast between Nature's throbbing vitality and lushness, and the gradual ebbing away of life from human beings'[18], thus raises 'the statement of ownership of food by persons' into which 'starvation statements translate'[19]. At this very point, by reaffirming their claim on food produced by their toil, the movements of fifties and sixties gave a fitting reply to the politics of famine.

Ray's village is placed on a road allowing people to come from other villages in search of food, or to pass through this village and from it to the city. Gangacharan himself uses the road at the time of prosperity for earning his livelihood, as well as at the time of suffering to collect food. But neither Ganga nor his wife thinks of leaving the village where they had come after some hurdle, until a final hit of hunger forces them to join the collective mass of beggars. Exploiting Bibhutibhusan's romanticism, based on old feudal dignity, Ray makes the film's central couple to emblem a stout optimism, which becomes both a point of reference and a point of departure of the human actions. The film then throws light on the passing of consciousness through actual life process.

Ashani Sanket is really not about famine, but about the pre-conditions of famine being growingly visible. This is also a film on the very moment when the perennial Bengali village life entered into the particular history of imperial exploitation. The title being a metaphorical one, the 'thunder' is seen at a distance. In these terms, the cinema brings out a contrast between what has been suggested above as a generalised vision of Bengali rural life and the stark reality of hunger. In *Bishoy Chalachchitra* Satyajit argues that colour can articulate reality convincingly, and even poverty has its own colour. This is perhaps best suggested by the different shades of colour in the film, Nature being both blushful and wild, and the frequent use of silhouettes, and at a certain point of action, with a Brechtian method of self-disruption, the film cuts the flow of colourful scenes in a montage of intervening black and white slides on facts and images of 'the great Bengal famine'. Action of the film, too, follows a rhythm of conflict, shaped within certain situations, of which a few could be examined. In each of these situations, shots are selected in leading the viewer's gaze to new levels of reality. For instance, the scenes of Chutki and Ananga husking rice, intermingles the rhythm of their bodies with that of the machine, creating a natural effect of the productive process. This is ideologically set against the destitution of women huskers during forties' famine, and also the peasant rebellion against Government's decision of closing small husking mills to serve the bigger ones and *majutdars* in nineteen sixties[20].

Chutki and Ananga, two central ladies of the film, are associated with blossoming Nature as well as its wilderness. In another moving scene, Ananga turns practical in deciding to accompany Chutki and another woman into the woods to collect wild potatoes, defying the social taboos for a Brahmin *badhu*. Mothers and sisters of Bengal were first to react to the compelling situation of steady scarcity of food during famine, and also to rise against the neo-colonial administrative policies, and sacrificed their lives. Lacking the efficiency of the other two Ananga cannot join them in extracting the potato; the film represents woman vitality in powerful labour through a close-up of their hands. While returning Ananga again lags behind, and a man attacks and molests her. The whole shot is taken from the back of the man, whose identity remains undisclosed. After a few seconds the voyeuristic gaze achieved by placing the female at her utter distress and helplessness under eyes of the male molester, who shares the view *with* the audience, is smashed in a change of shot and action. Chutki kills the man by boldly hitting his head with an iron rod. The colour of the nearby stream changes into red with his blood. Significantly Ananga never discusses this incident with her husband. Although sharing Ananga's repulsion against such sexual advances, Chutki later leaves the village with a physically distorted man who secretly stocks rice to possess her, and promises her a good life in the town. Andrew Robinson refers to Ray's comments on the colour of that man's blue shirt as indicative of his foreign origin, as against the colours of the women's saris, well blended with environment[21].

Much has been stated on the event of the death of Moti, an under-caste, and Gangacharan's reaction to it, including Satyajit's own readings on the rise of this formerly shrewd type Brahmin priest to a human being, touching the untouchable after her death and thinking of her cremation. What interests here is the realisation of death through the changes it causes in living relationships. Moti dies with the timeless dream of Bengalis for *bhat, macher jhol* and *chachchori*, which turns into a goal of revolt during the making of the film. The master film-maker said once, 'In life, there is so much death'[22], and it is this celebration of life that makes his films so appealing. *Ashani Sanket* thus ends with Ananga's announcement of the advent of her baby, may be belonging to the next generation social fighters.

May not be literally a political worker, Satyajit Ray, along with contemporary directors fought for social change by responsibly accomplishing what they thought to be their cultural tasks. Marxist thinker Hiren Mukherjee recognises Ray as a revolutionary in the 'grand-historical' sense of the term[23]. Bengali socially conscious cinemas not only remain crucial in our understanding of Bengal's cultural and political milieu and cinematic experiments, but their universality lies in still contributing to the on-going struggle against imperial cultural hegemony—here the paradigms could be seen in the broadness. Thus, their true legacy is to be realised in a never-ending fight for humanity, equality and self-determination.

Endnote

1. Ray, Satyajit. Deep Focus: *Refections on Cinema*. Ed. Sandip Ray. Foreword. Shyam Benegal. HarperCollins Pub. India with The India Today Group, 2011. Pg. 90.
2. Watt, Ian. *The Rise of the Novel: Studies in Defoe, Richardson and Fielding*. Pimlico, 2000. Pg.17-18.
3. Ray, Satyajit. *Our Films Their Films*. Orient Black Swan, 2009. Pg. 94.
4. Williams, Raymond. "Cinema and Socialism." *Politics of Modernism: Against the New Conformists*. Verso, 2007. Pg.116.
5. Ray, Satyajit. "My Life, My work." *Satyajit Ray: A Portrait in Black and White*. Photographs by Tarapada Banerjee. Foreword. Raghubir Sigh. Viking, 1993. Pg.22.
6. Ray, Satyajit. "My Life, My work." Satyajit Ray: *A Portrait in Black and White*. Photographs by Tarapada Banerjee. Foreword. Raghubir Sigh. Viking, 1993. Pg.21.
7. Ray, Satyajit. Interview to The Cineaste. Interviews: On the Art and Politics of the Cinema. Ed. Georgaks, Dan and Lenny Rubenstein. Chicago: Lake View Press, 1982. Web. 15.04.12. Microsoft ® Encarta ® 2007. Pg.04.
8. "Fact file about the Historical Food Movement (1959) and Witnesses account." N. Pag. Web. 18.04.12 http://westbengalnews.blogspot.in/2009/08/fact-file-historical-food.html.
9. "Fact file about the Historical Food Movement (1959) and Witnesses account." N. Pag. Web. 18.04.12 http://westbengalnews.blogspot.in/2009/08/fact-file-historical-food.html.
10. Bhattacharya, Jayanta. *Paschimbanger Krishak Andolaner Dhara*. National Book Agency, 1991. Pg.26.
11. "Fact file about the Historical Food Movement (1959) and Witnesses account." N. Pag. Web. 18.04.12 http://westbengalnews.blogspot.in/2009/08/fact-file-historical-food.html.
12. Williams, Raymond. "Cinema and Socialism." *Politics of Modernism: Against the New Conformists*. Verso, 2007. Pg.116, 114.
13. Editorials. "From 50 years ago The Economic Weekly: Congress and Jan Sangh." EPW: XLVII.2. January 14, 2012. Pg.09.
14. Bhattacharya, Jayanta. *Paschimbanger Krishak Andolaner Dhara*. National Book Agency, 1991. Pg.28-29.
15. Das Gupta, Chidananda. *The Cinema of Satyajit Ray*. National Book Trust, 2001. Pg.110.
16. Ray, Satyajit. *Our Films Their Films*. Orient Black Swan, 2009. Pg. 94-95.
17. Marx, Karl and Frederick Engels. *The German Ideology*. Moscow: Progress Publishers, 1976. Pg.47.
18. Robinson, Andrew. *Satyajit Ray: The Inner Eye: The Biography of a Master Film-Maker*. Oxford UP, 2004. Pg.225.
19. Sen, Amartya. *Poverty and Famines: An Essay on Entitlement and Deprivation*. Delhi: Oxford UP, 1982. Pg.01.
20. Bhattacharya, Jayanta. *Paschimbanger Krishak Andolaner Dhara*. National Book Agency, 1991. Pg.31-32.
21. Robinson, Andrew. *Satyajit Ray: The Inner Eye: The Biography of a Master Film-Maker*. Oxford UP, 2004. Pg.226.
22. Ray, Satyajit. Comments. *Satyajit Ray: A Portrait in Black and White*. Photographs by Tarapada Banerjee. Foreword. Raghubir Sigh. Viking, 1993. Pg.114.
23. Mukherjee, Hiren. "Shatam Jiba." *Satyajit Ray: Sottor Bachar Purti Upalakshe Shraddhanjali*. Nandan, 1992. Pg.04.

Immortal Picture Stories: Growing up with Indian Comics

—Aditya Mani Jha

Prologue

In the 2000 film *Unbreakable*, (written and directed by Manoj Night Shyamalan), Samuel L. Jackson's character Elijah is a comic book aficionado, and has a fittingly large, impeccably archived collection of comics down the years. In a crucial scene, he tries to make the case for comic books as an ongoing, uninterrupted historical account of the times we live in, from Egyptian hieroglyphics all the way down to Superman and others of his ilk. It is clear that Elijah has very strong views on the subject; and in his passionate, let-me-tell-you-a-secret dialogue delivery, we the audience share a bit of the skepticism which comes Elijah's way on most occasions like these.

While I did not set out to compile an unbroken account, (as Elijah did) I did figure out that one way to chronicle the evolution and the influence of comic books in modern India would be to look back at my own childhood (I'm twenty-three right now), and focus on the reading options which young people had back then, as compared to now. It would be superfluous to emphasise the subtlety and the elegance of telling a story using words and pictures here; instead, just remember (if you can) that happy summer where you started maintaining and updating a stash of shiny comic books.

Childhood (Uncle Pai and the village elders)

On 17 September, 2011, Google brought out a new doodle featured on its home page; honouring Anant Pai, (or Uncle Pai, as he was better known) the legendary Indian comics creator and founder of *Amar Chitra Katha*, one of the most popular and long-running series in Indian comics.

(Pai had passed away following a heart attack earlier in February). The doodle featured the prolific Pai at work in his office, with racks and racks of his creations peering back at him. It was a touching tribute, on the birthday of the man who did more for Indian comics than perhaps anybody else. When I looked at the doodle on that evening, the first thing which flashed in front of my eyes was a huge, bound volume, comprising of scores of old issues of *Tinkle* (the illustrated children's magazine started by Pai in 1980). My parents had them bound after I'd stubbornly refused to clear out the old ones from my room; pack rat that I was, unwilling to accept the idea that I might have grown too old for them.

I mention this because unfortunately, comic books have always been seen as something which one eventually outgrows; they are doomed to be forever associated with yellowed pages and dog ears. They will inevitably be found in bedrooms discarded by college-bound teenagers, in almirahs where the grandkids left them as they went home after the vacations. Much in the way certain comic book characters never seem to age, the comics themselves are thus frozen in time.

For people of my generation, kids growing up in the 1990s and the 2000s, *Amar Chitra Katha* (Wikipedia translates it, somewhat improbably, as *Immortal Picture Stories*) was a veritable treasure trove of stories; mythological and sometimes historical. Hundreds of comic books, lavishly illustrated, and on most of them you'd be sure to see a familiar name, credited as co-writer or editor—Anant Pai. Uncle Pai, whose role in our lives was fittingly avuncular; even his alter-ego in *Tinkle* was a bearded, bespectacled character called Uncle Anu, who would teach scientific principles to a gang of kids, taking pains to make sure the kids have fun in the process.

Okay, so the language seemed out of our preachy Moral Education textbooks at times. As I grew up, I found out other historical inconsistencies, like its portrayal of Muslims and women, one particular instance involving the *jauhar* (self-immolation) committed by Rani Padmini, to protect her honour from the invading Muslim monarch Alauddin Khilji. But despite these occasional blemishes, *Amar Chitra Katha* was a huge presence on our bookshelves.

Tinkle is Uncle Pai's other enduring masterpiece. Started in April 1980, it combined the mythological flair of a *Chandamama*, the goofy slapstick of a *Champak* and *Amar Chitra Katha's* own brand of 'educational storytelling' to create perhaps the most engaging children's magazine in India. (Pai credited the Marathi writer B.R. Bhagwat for the idea behind the name *Amar Chitra Katha*; Bhagwat's *Faster Fene* adventure stories would later appear in *Tinkle*, in comics form.) Most of the recurring characters in the *Tinkle* ensemble of the 1990s could be roughly divided into two categories: The first being the brain-above-brawn protagonists, who would prize wits and wisdom above all else; time and again they would rescue themselves and their friends by simply thinking on their feet. These included Kalia the Crow, the cat-and-dog detective duo Mopes and Purr; and memorably, Nasruddin Hodja. (Based on Nasreddin, a Sufi figure featured in numerous popular philosophical stories across Central Asia and the Middle East.)

The second would be the happy-go-lucky hero with little or no talent, but with a constant optimism about the world, and an endearing way of committing a *faux pas* at the worst possible moments. Leading the pack here was Suppandi the simpleton, (who is still going strong) along with Shikari Shambhu, an Inspector Clouseau-like fumbling hunter who has, till date, never actually killed an animal.

Both these stereotypes, utopian as they were, had strong resonances with the work of cartoonist Pran Kumar Sharma, better known as simply Pran, who'd started writing the *Chacha Chaudhary* stories as early as 1969, more than a decade before the first issue of *Tinkle* came out in 1980. Even today, Chacha Chaudhary remains the most identifiable character in all of Indian comics.

A thin, elderly, frail-looking man with an oversized red turban, and seemingly limitless intellectual acumen, Chacha Chaudhary (with a little help from Sabu, the giant from Jupiter) exuded a rustic, old-world defiance, a self-belief which verged on the vainglorious (the most famous line of the series runs: '*Chacha Chaudhary kaa dimaag computer se bhi tez chalta hai*' or 'Chacha Chaudhary's brain works faster than a computer). Thus with Pran and Uncle Pai, kids of my generation had their own village elders, raconteurs extraordinaire. Like Tolkien's wizard Gandalf the Grey, they were the wisest of the wise. They were, quite simply, a safe place to go to, whether you needed advice or mirth. That is, of course, until you decided to grow up.

Boyhood (The many hues of hero worship)

Violence as a rite of passage into adulthood is an old trope employed in various narratives across the world. Comic book fans will recall an oft-discussed scene in Frank Miller's *300*, where a Spartan soldier tells the tale of how their king Leonidas killed a huge, menacing wolf while still a boy, as part of a ritual where he was abandoned, naked and hungry in a forest from where he would '*return a Spartan, or not at all*'. While *300*, and indeed, most of Frank Miller's oeuvre features more machismo and stylised, slickly drawn violence than most comic books; it's hardly unusual to find echoes of this theme in superhero comics anywhere.

Growing up in Ranchi in the late 1990s (then part of an undivided Bihar), I soon realised that there lay a world beyond the genteel pages of *Tinkle* and *Chacha Chaudhary*. Cable TV, too, had begun to play its part by then, and it was getting increasingly tougher for parents to shield their children from violent imagery. When I first stumbled on to *Nagraj*, *Super Commando Dhruv*, *Doga* and other Indian superhero comics, I was immediately taken by how the makers were certainly not interested in pulling their punches. There was an endearing sincerity to their efforts, even when they descended to cliché. Many gory scenes, outrageous sound effects, lovingly drawn biceps and improbable plotlines later, I was hooked; devouring *Super Commando Dhruv* in particular, who's an urban vigilante *without* an alter-ego. (Eat your heart out, Bruce Wayne and Peter Parker!)

Raj Comics, which started both *Nagraj* and *Dhruv* in the late 1980s, (they currently have over twenty recurring titles) cashed in on an undeniable fact: Indian comics did not have even a halfway successful superhero. In fact, barring Aabid Surti's *Bahadur*, first published by Indrajal Comics in 1976, there were no Indian vigilantes anywhere at all. Indrajal Comics, owned by Bennett, Coleman & Co., (who also own *Times of India*) was started in 1964, not necessarily to come up with original comics, but with an eye towards acquiring the rights to reprint popular American titles like *Flash Gordon*, *The Phantom* and *Mandrake the Magician*. In *Chitrakatha*, an upcoming documentary by

Alok Sharma (Former illustrator for Gotham Comics, better known by his blogosphere alias Toonfactory), Uncle Pai himself reminisces, 'You'll be surprised...but Indrajal Comics was started just to keep the rotogravure machines at Times of India working...these machines used to print calendars at the end of the year.'

Pai, employed there as a junior executive at the time, was entrusted with selecting the most popular foreign titles, which would then be reprinted under the name Indrajal Comics. Indrajal, with *Bahadur*, couldn't quite succeed in launching its own brand of Indian superheroes/vigilantes; but it did inspire the Gupta brothers (Sanjay, Manoj and Manish) to start Raj Comics, with all-new range of Indian superheroes. Nagraj, an ageless, super-strong *ichchaa-dhaari naag* (shape-shifting snake) with microscopic snakes in his body for white blood cells, quickly became their best-selling character; followed closely by Super Commando Dhruv, an expert martial artist with no superhuman powers (except the ability to communicate with animals).

Nagraj/Dhruv formed a sort of Superman/Batman double team for Indian comics, often sharing the same adventures, or making guest appearances in each others' stories. At the height of their popularity (and, I suspect, sales figures), I distinctly remember seeing an animated TV ad featuring the two, albeit one with very primitive animation, even for those times (I was eleven then, circa 1999). But the fun was wearing thin; Nagraj and Dhruv began spouting lines which sounded like things Bollywood left on the editing table. Their adversaries began to be less and less memorable; either all bluster and no real menace, or thinly disguised rip-offs.

Regarding the latter, Raj Comics titles were pretty in-your-face: Any kid who had ever watched cartoons on television would have seen Teenage Mutant Ninja Turtles (TMNT) at least in passing, and so *Fighter Toads*, a bunch of four masked crime-fighting anthropomorphic toads left one far from impressed. With the advent of mainstream Marvel/DC characters as cartoons on TV; and as competitively priced reprints, transgressions such as these were bound to be pointed out more and more often. To point but a small example: Super Commando Dhruv's dead parents were circus performers; and years later, in his vigilante avatar, Dhruv takes a vow to never use firearms—thus completing a weird composite tribute to (or rip-off from, depending upon where you stand) Batman and Robin.

In 2008, Raj Comics released *Nagayana*, a version of the Hindu epic Ramayana set in the future, with versions of Nagraj and Dhruv playing the parts of Ram and Laxman, respectively. Not long ago, in 2006, Liquid Comics, (then called Virgin Comics, the brainchild of renowned director Shekhar Kapur, author Deepak Chopra and entrepreneur Richard Branson, among other people) had launched, amidst much fanfare, a new title named *Ramayana 3392 A.D.* It's a very entertaining science fiction cover version of Ramayana, complete with post-apocalyptic shenanigans, cannibalistic mutant bad guys and gun-toting, *bidi*-smoking killer apes.

Nagraj, during a special 'World Terrorism Series' of titles, (Nagraj was initially conceived in the late eighties as an enemy of terrorism, following the events leading up to Prime Minister Indira Gandhi's assassination and the Delhi riots) has adventures like *Omerta-The code of silence*, *Ronin* and even *Kame Kazi*. I know correlation does not imply causation, but for the conscientious reader, constant allusion is a vexing thing indeed.

I rather enjoyed reading *The Ecstasy of Influence*, a long essay by American author Jonathan Lethem. It is a passionate, articulate defence of plagiarism in art. Moreover, as adolescents (the age at which Nagraj and Dhruv mattered to us); a lot of what we passed off as our own authentic selves was a collage of our accumulated plagiarisms, the yearbook of our influences, really. Looking back, though, I think it wasn't a coincidence that my brief divorce from the world of comics (I'd return to it in college, through a friend who's a comics nerd) coincided with what was creatively a dark phase for the Indian superhero. I guess hero worship did extract a price, after all.

Youth (Of Barn Owls, Graphic Novels and the Thought Crimes of the future)

When I came across the work of Sarnath Banerjee for the first time, a few years ago in college, I was enjoying an extended period of reading some brilliant comics. A good friend of mine; an artist himself, had introduced me to Frank Miller, and soon enough I read copious amounts of comics on my computer, magisterial works by writers such as Alan Moore, Neil Gaiman, Art Spiegelman, Will Eisner and others, not to mention artists like Dave McKean, Jill Thompson, Eddie Campbell and Glenn Fabry. Banerjee's debut book *Corridor*, published by Penguin in 2004, featured the words '*a graphic novel*' on the cover, something which you couldn't miss. The publishers had also marketed it as '*India's first graphic novel.*' (This is simply not true, as has been noted elsewhere—That honour belongs to *River of Stories*, Orijit Sen's 1994 novel inspired by the much-disputed Narmada river valley projects, and funded by Kalpavriksha, a non-profit organisation dedicated to environmental conservation.)

Comics legend Will Eisner (whose *A Contract with God* (1978) was one of the first books to call itself a graphic novel) had gently made fun of the new nomenclature in a speech. Alan Moore, writer of classics like *Watchmen* and *V for Vendetta*, was deeply skeptical of the phrase as well, and called the whole thing a marketing gimmick. While starting *Corridor*, I admit I was a little wary of these unholy connotations from this world of PR, blurbs and book launches, fearing an overhyped story which would be too clever for its own good.

I couldn't have been further from the truth, for I've read *Corridor* several times since that first hasty read while waiting between lectures. Inventive, wickedly funny and thoroughly postmodern, Banerjee's debut book ripped into the hypocrisies and the fragmented realities of urban India with panache. Combining a caricaturist's witty, unerring eye with an eclectic range of cultural allusions and stereotypes, (From Keats, Barthes, Bob Marley and Baudrillard to Hitchcock, Woody Guthrie, Bruce Lee, *Mother India*, Jyoti Basu and Mao Zedong) *Corridor* signalled the arrival of a major new talent. The slices of life presented here (through the eyes of Jehangir Rangoonwalla, Old Delhi bookseller) are as original and the irony as fine-tuned as anything else I've read in contemporary Indian literature. And yes, that includes books without pictures. To me, *Corridor* captures the angst beneath the urban youth's slick irreverence like few books have in recent times.

Banerjee's subsequent books, *The Barn Owl's Wondrous Capers* (2007) and *The Harappa Files* (2011) have confirmed his status as a major talent, with Banerjee's artwork, in particular, getting better and better. To many, they also signal a new direction for Indian comics; as books which take their status as works of art very seriously indeed. In an interview published in *The Hindu*, Banerjee described how the dynamic interplay between words and images in comics made for a different, more complex reading experience. He said, 'Reading comics is a complex process. Therefore, it is mostly consumed by a sophisticated reader. Art Spiegelman, the creator of the Pulitzer-winning, Auschwitz-based "Maus", has a word for them—the post-literate. From where I stand, adult comics are probably never going to be for the masses. At best, they could be at the mainstream end of the alternate.'

Following *Corridor*, there have been quite a few Indian graphic novels which deserve a far wider readership than they currently enjoy. Amruta Patil's *Kari* (2008) tells the story of the eponymous protagonist, a young woman working as a small-time copywriter in Mumbai, (memorably referred to as '*Smog City*' at one point in the book) who cannot come to terms with being separated from her sweetheart Ruth. Not only does *Kari* handle female homosexuality (among other things) in an unflinching, sensitive manner; it also weaves together some stirring visual sequences.

Two pages from the book are seared into my mind forever. The very first page of the novel, a tribute to legendary artist Frida Kahlo's painting *The Two Fridas*, depicts Kari and Ruth sitting, hands clasped, with their hearts exposed to the elements, joined by a lone artery. The accompanying words at the bottom of the page: '*There are two of us, not one. Despite a slipshod surgical procedure, we are joined still.*' I distinctly remember getting goose bumps when I saw this page for the first time. In another panel, equally memorable, depicting how Kari and Ruth met for the first time; there's a poster of Shah Rukh Khan's 1995 blockbuster *Dilwale Dulhaniya Le Jayenge* in the background. The lesbian lovers and the epitome of utterly kosher, heterosexual upper middle-class daydreaming; the irony couldn't have been any sweeter.

There have been other bright spots as well; Parismita Singh's *The Hotel at the End of the World*, Vishwajyoti Ghosh's *Delhi Calm*, Naseer Ahmed and Saurabh Singh's *Kashmir Pending*, and more recently, *Bhimayana: Experiences of Untouchability* (Yes, as far as India's concerned, *Ramayana* will take some beating in the allusions counter), a collection of illustrated vignettes from the life of Bhimrao Ambedkar. Drawn by Gond artists (the Gonds are a tribe indigenous to Central India) Durgabai and Subhash Vyam, *Bhimayana,* which was published last year, has rightly drawn rich praise for its dazzling, unconventional artwork.

Prateek Thomas and Rajiv Eipe's 32-page graphic story *Hush*, published by Manta Ray in 2010, is a novella with an immediately noticeable oddity—it features no words at all, relying on the artwork alone to guide the reader through the circumstances behind what appears to be another arbitrary high school shooting. Although at that time I'd never read something like this; I've since then read Peter Kuper's *Sticks and Stones* (2004) and *The Arrival* (2007) by Shaun Tan—both silent graphic novels. It is safe to say that sustaining an entire graphic narrative minus words is no laughing matter at all, and requires considerable technique and skill.

To be sure, Indian comics have come a long way since I first counted up to a hundred issues of *Tinkle* in my bedroom stash; all little boys are magpies to an extent. At the second annual Comic Con India held in Delhi recently, Robert Crumb, the renowned comics creator and father of the underground comix (deliberately spelt with an 'x' to distinguish them from mainstream comics) movement of the late 60s and 70s; was present as the guest of honour. He appeared to be pleasantly surprised at the growing number of comics readers in this part of the world. He would've been positively touched by the ever-increasing readership of webcomics—Manta Ray (the creators of *Hush*) is also behind a weekly strip called *The Small Picture* for *Mint Lounge*, mostly based on current affairs.

Given the number of technocrats India produces every year, the popularity of webcomics like *XKCD*, *Saturday Morning Breakfast Cereal* and *PHD (Piled Higher and Deeper) Comics* is hardly surprising—webcomics are geek gold, as far as modern-day pop culture's concerned. If comics were to be taken as mainstream, (which they aren't in India yet—by a long way) then webcomics are fast becoming the alternate end of the mainstream, (to subvert Sarnath Banerjee's phrase) thanks to the Internet. Last year, I was surprised to discover the cult following (mostly through Facebook) of a webcomic which a friend's brother published online. Named *The Thought Crime*, after a typically Orwellian phrase which appears in the novel *1984*, its last update (in May 2011), *Osamageddon* had over 2,700 'likes' on Facebook. Interestingly, it had a gag featuring bin Laden plotting to kill Steve Jobs—months before Jobs passed away in October.

There's a palpable sense of excitement in the Indian comics industry today, but it isn't because sales have suddenly skyrocketed—they haven't; nor is it because a bunch of publishers decided that '*graphic novel*' sounded more grown-up than '*comic book*'. It is because of that elusive, indescribably happy feeling you get when you see people appreciating art on its merits alone, without preconceptions. Anant Pai knew this, as does Pran, as do other, less fancied creators across India, looking to commit the next great thought crime of the twenty-first century.

And that's why I would imagine this to be a very, very interesting time to be growing up with Indian comics.

Connecting India

—Mahima Kaul

The seventh largest country in the world and the second most populated, India has always been a bit of an enigma to the rest of the world—and to itself! There are sixteen official languages and a number of religious communities, not to mention the average age of the Indian is twenty-six years, of whom only thirty per cent live in urban areas. Imagine these numbers stretching right from the southern coasts through the rolling planes of the Ganges, alongside deserts in the West, the valleys in the East and the Himalayas in the North, and it makes for a complicated picture. As a functioning democracy, reaching each citizen and counting their vote has been an exhaustive exercise enough, but ensuring that the state can stay in continued contact with them has been fraught with challenges. Governance has especially failed rural India, with much of the country still mired in poverty and the lack of opportunity. But a new hope is being pinned on technology that fosters connectivity, governance and dialogue. And that new hope—which seems almost old now—is the Internet!

Many of the changes India has experienced since the 1990s—when the government liberalised numerous sectors of the economy to usher in more competition—have changed the face of the country as we know it today. The same can be said of telecom, which is steadily gaining more and more customers with fast changing technologies. However, in the forty years that preceded this revolution, the Indian public listened, watched and talked in a very limited capacity. The All India Radio was the mainstay of India, a way to get the news of the day. Most people who owned televisions were limited to public service broadcasting—Doordarshan—and a lucky few had landlines that were run by the government. The social significance of what was lost in the 1940s years of limited telecom has to do with limited connectivity, time delays and isolation. Even a simple long distance phone call needed to be booked in advance, without a guarantee of its quality. Families could not keep in touch unless it was through the post, and large areas of the country remained disconnected with their urban counterparts, unaware of the changes being experienced in cities. Immediate and urgent messages, both business and personal, were sent through telegram. The Internet did not exist in those days.

Things began to change in the 1980s. During Prime Minister Rajiv Gandhi's tenure, public sector organisations like the VSNL and MTNL were set up under the Department of Telecommunications (DoT). However, foreign players were not yet allowed into India's telecom landscape. By 1994, under Prime Minister Narasimha Rao, the growing demand for telephones had led to a National Telecommunications Policy that brought changes in the areas of ownership, service and regulation of the telecommunications infrastructure. Foreign players were now allowed up to 49 per cent of stake in telecom companies. Over time, with more liberalisation, private companies entered the long distance carrier business and mobile phones were introduced in a limited fashion. The Telecom Regulatory Authority of India (TRAI) was set up in 1995, much to DoT's opposition, to decide policy and tariffs. By 1999, the government had changed and the NDA, under Prime Minister Atal Bihari Vajpayee, came into power; liberalisation carried on, including splitting DoT into two separate entities. While foreign stake in companies was increased to 74 per cent in 2000, the idea was proposed back in 1995 when it was defeated by opposition parties. All this churning meant that costs kept coming lower, as the number of subscribers kept increasing. Today, the numbers speak for themselves. With mobile subscriptions reaching 951 million in March 2012, there is no doubt that a telecom revolution has taken place in the country! Most households, even in the villages, have one family member with a mobile phone as Indians have understood the personal and business value of being connected.

Similarly, television has seen many changes since 1947. While the public service broadcaster, Doordarshan, was the main channel available to Indians for a long time, it was only in 1992, under Prime Minister Narasimha Rao, that liberalisation led to opening up the country to cable television. Both international and private TV channels have blossomed, and technology has improved as well. Many households have shifted from old school cable to satellite, foregoing cable lines for set-top-boxes. What this has meant is that Indian viewers have a wide range of programming to choose from. And that they are exercising this choice is clear by the numbers: it is estimated that 148 million homes have televisions, while 94 million have basic cable, 41 million have 'Direct to Home', 88 million have analog while the rest have digital connections. The genius of television, being a mass medium, is that it has been used as an agent of education and change through intelligent programming. This is not to say shows with pure entertainment and no academic value do not exist, but that many shows shine a light on cultural problems faced by Indians and try and teach them to make better decisions. It is a tool for connecting with citizens, while remaining a commercial venture.

The latest technological innovation to take India by storm, in terms of connecting citizens and the potential for good it has—is the Internet—now fifteen years old in India. Its potential as a tool for information gathering, connecting and improving governance cannot be questioned, but these changes will only happen if it is encouraged, developed and regulated in a positive manner. In its initial years, it seemed every household would access the Internet via computers but now it seems most people will access the Internet on-the-go, via mobile phones and smaller tablets. All these changes come with challenges as well as opportunities.

In 1995, the government announced that the Internet was available to users through VSNL's dial up service in six cities. The next year, the first dot com was registered from India—Rediff.com. In 1998, private Internet service providers were allowed, and Sify rose to become India's first private ISP. Over time, many public call operator shops morphed into Internet cafes, and the wait for a connection became shorter. In the next few years, private businesses started launching websites, and India centric websites like www.samachar.com popped up online. By 2001, the Indian government had put railway ticketing online, a service wildly popular with the Indians.

But behind the scenes, monumental efforts were required to go from the days of only a government Internet service provider to the choices and tariffs we have today. In 1992, when the government allowed Value Added Services to be offered via license, there was no real policy framework to guide this. As recounted by Amitabh Singhal, at the time, email license holders had to pay INR 5 million for the first year and INR 2 million for subsequent years. The licenses were valid for five years. Adding to their woes were additional costs such as port charges, and upto a nine month wait to get a 64 kbps line. Private companies then gathered together to form India's Email and Internet Service Providers Association (EISPA) in 1994-95 to influence policy, and go from email service providers to Internet service providers. However, in 1995, government owned VSNL became the sole Internet service provider in the country. In 1997 when TRAI was established as an independent telecom regulator, DoT's monopoly came to an end. After many meetings between DoT, TRAI and EISPAI (which then became ISPAI), finally, decisions were taken which allowed a 'bandwidth hungry country' to become one with private telecom giants like Tata, Reliance, Bharti, etc. Over the next few years, pricing, tariffs and quality of service was examined and worked upon.

The next few years saw other forms of progress. In 2002, TRAI began to focus on setting up Internet exchanges to develop infrastructural capacity and improving Internet access in India. The National Internet Exchange of India, headed by a government official, was set up for the purpose. This body also started registering websites under the domain .IN in 2005.

However, while policy made strides in the first decade of the Internet in India, the result has also been that a handful of Internet Service Providers have captured largely urban settings, and this leaves the question of providing universal access to all citizens of India, through the idea of last mile connectivity.

At this juncture, the application of ICTs information and communication technologies in India should be examined. Since 1947, there has been a gradual decline in the agricultural and manufacturing sectors of India, and a steep hike in the service sector industry. In particular, the BPO industry has grown rapidly, offering white-collar jobs in satellite towns and huge opportunities to young Indians. These jobs would never have been possible without the telecommunications revolution. Even the very nature of government is slowly beginning to change, with websites, online transactions and information available at a click. It has allowed the information pyramid to become, at least slightly, a little more squarish in nature.

The two sides to ICTs in development (often called ICTD) are access and appropriate content application. Having an Internet or mobile connection just isn't enough; it's learning what to do with it. Looking at the challenges of access first, if you look at the government's telecom policies over the years, it is quite obvious that it has missed its targets time and time again. For example, targets set in 1994 under the telecom policy—all villages should have telephone lines, and also that telephones should be available on demand was not met by 1999. Further, targets in 1999, providing Internet to administrative headquarters in all districts as well as providing high speed data to all towns with a population over 200,000, were not met by 2011. But what did happen was that the teledensity rose from a targeted 4 per cent in 2010 to an astounding 26.5 per cent by the end of 2011. Unfortunately, the data also revealed that the teledensity was rising in the urban centres, like cities and towns, and villages were by and large still disconnected.

The government has come up with ways to fix this problem, but not with a great deal of success. In 2002, the Department of Telecom set up the Universal Service Obligation Fund, which was meant to get private telecom players to enter rural markets. In 2004, two years later, it amended the rules to enable disbursal from the USO Fund to reimburse telecom operators for rural telephony. In 2006, another amendment supported mobile services and broadband in rural and remote parts of the country. Despite the incentives given to corporates to provide rural connections, the scheme did not work. It seems the reasons these operators later tried to escape the license conditions, some of whom bid aggressively to be part of USOF, was because the projects were commercially unviable. Some of the towns had very small populations, or were too far tough to reach, and it was easier to pay the penalty imposed by the government for abandoning the project.

Now, the government has decided to lay out fiber optic cables across the length and breadth of the country to ensure last mile connectivity.

There have been problems with application of ICTs as well. The government has implemented other schemes to promote ICTs, such as using Public Private Partnership models, where village entrepreneurs and software companies join hands to start Internet kiosks. These kiosks, under the 'Common Service Centre' scheme also serve as front end delivery points for various government services such as payment of utility bills (water, electricity, telephone), certificates (birth, death, income) and other services like train tickets, mobile phone top ups and so on. Through the CSCs the government was going to take the Internet to every village in India. However, right off the bat, a few practical problems slowed down the project. One such problem was the irregular supply of electricity. The other was the project design. The village level entrepreneur cannot make a profit by simply offering government services as they are accessed only on a monthly (and sometimes even more infrequent) basis. Instead, they had to find new ways of monetising the Internet (for example, offering browsing) in small towns and villages where people had not yet any real use for the Internet. Unfortunately, the CSC scheme has slowed down because it has been noted that there is lack of interest by the private partners and slow implementation by state governments. This is in part fuelled by the fact that private partners do not profit from only offering government services, but need to offer enough private services that can help them earn a profit. In fact, a 2009 World Bank report has calculated that a 10 per cent increase in broadband penetration leads to a 1.38 per cent increase in GDP in developing countries. However, on-the-ground experience has demonstrated that merely furnishing broadband connections does not automatically lead to productivity.

This project falls under the National e-governance Plan (NeGP). Other schemes include digitising other aspects of ministries to make them more efficient, such as, land records or subsidy disbursal. In fact, e-governance, as a concept, has caught on very well in India with many different schemes being implemented by state governments for the delivery of citizen services. On paper, India has made many strides towards providing better governance (mainly by improving efficiency and cutting corruption by the use of ICTs) but the success rate varies from project to project.

What has been very encouraging, however, is the manner in which civil society and the corporate world has embraced ICTs to design projects which help the Indian population connect to not just the world outside their communities, but to also connect in deeper and more meaningful ways within their communities. For example, a simple community SMS newsletter called SMS One, sends texts to members of geographical communities about special offers from stores, requests for blood donations, news about job opportunities and so on. Mouthshut, a web based consumer platform, enables people to write and read product reviews so that they can be informed customers. E-commerce websites like Flipkart have allowed customers to order a number of products online, with the option of paying in cash on delivery. This model is popular in India because people are still uncomfortable with feeding their bank details online for fear of fraud. Community media projects, such as Video Volunteer's India Unheard, make it possible for anyone with an Internet connection to view stories produced by community members from all corners of India. These, and countless other small projects, are the real success of ICTs because they help empower people in ways that benefit their lives directly.

There is also the power of social media, which has been documented in great detail in the press. Allowing people to virtually connect in real time to discuss issues of common concern has enabled concerned citizens to not just gather knowledge, but often, to organise themselves in real life to communicate with their governments. India is not an exception to the global trend, where all sort of issues are being proliferated and discussed over the vast network of social media that is leaving a huge impact in shaping public opinion. The slow proliferation of regional language content (starting with keypads) is also helping the cause of digital inclusion.

However, there is a danger in extolling the virtues of 'inevitable' democracy, communication and profit through ICTs. One should pause and examine many of the problems that plague it. The Congress government under Manmohan Singh might be pushing the NeGP, but it is the same government that has seen massive scams in the spectrum allocation of 2G spectrum leading to cancellation of licenses. These delays due to government corruption are inexcusable given that the government itself has made connectivity a priority. Another concern is the increasing censorship coming from the government. Ostensibly to protect the feelings of religious communities and stop child pornography, it has been discovered that most of the requests by the government to big Internet giants like Google, Facebook and Yahoo have been to remove criticism of the government itself. For the world's largest democracy, this is a very unwelcome trend and needs to be carefully watched.

Another very important facet, which has been touched upon earlier, is that ICTs are a potential tool to bring out the kind of development most developing countries have been unsuccessfully trying to bring to all their corners. As the Internet/mobile landscape of India develops, we must ensure that it does not take on a shape that benefits those in power and leaves the poor masses of the country, yet again, at the mercy of the rich. For example, it is better for the government to encourage an Internet based distance education scheme rather than a scheme that simply encourages crass consumerism. I'm sure both can co-exist, but with the weight of many corporates behind schemes like the latter, it is essential that human development is the core focus of governments and NGOs. After all, the entire point of glorifying ICTs is about digital inclusion, not exclusion.

India's Tryst with Destiny in Sports

—Subhadeep Paul

The other day while travelling in the Metro, I happened to overhear a seemingly college-going boy chatting with a friend on his cell phone. Thin and shabby, apparently from the suburbs, donning worn out track boots, this guy was understandably a football enthusiast. However, I might have turned my attention away if I could have afforded not to be a party to the conversation he was having with his confidant in Bangla, my mother tongue. He grudged: 'This *football-tootball byapar shapar* was okay but it is getting increasingly difficult for me to stay over at the city in my PG with the food, boarding, college, tuition and the various other miscellaneous adjacent costs that accrue to my daily subsistence. I need a job as soon as possible. But then how can an ordinary guy like me, barely with his intermediate level over, aspire to the same?!' This was a question to which perhaps no one had an answer. I went down memory lane to recollect how my real education in life began after I had stepped out of the precincts of my university life and was faced with the compulsion to fend for my family. I realised that if things were so hard for me, a postgraduate, then, how hard things must have been going for him, having to face a predicament which even made him contemplate abandoning his soccer dreams forever!

Statistics wise, perhaps there is much to show about India's achievements in sports since Independence. The 1951 Asian Games, 1982 Asian Games, the 1987 Cricket World Cup and 1996 Cricket World Cup, the 2003 Afro-Asian Games, the 2010 Hockey World Cup, the 2010 Commonwealth Games, and the 2011 Cricket World Cup. The Chennai Open, Mumbai Marathon, Delhi Half Marathon, and the Indian Masters would count as major international sporting events that have taken place in the heart of the subcontinent. Though India has never been a notable sporting power, India has some noteworthy achievements in the realm of sports: eight Olympic gold medals in hockey, India has been a major stakeholder in the game of cricket and has won both one day and T-20 World Cup victories in cricket, several Grand Slam titles attained by Leander Paes and Mahesh Bhupathi in Tennis along with several other brilliant, though sporadic performances by Indian athletes such as Milkha Singh, P.T. Usha and Anju Bobby George. Vishwanathan Anand has been the World Chess Champion and India has maintained its impressive position in billiards and snooker too.

Special mention should also be made about some famous firsts, viz. 'The Flying Sikh' Milkha Singh who was the first Indian athlete to reach the Olympic finals (1960, Rome). Singh finished fourth in the finals of the 400 m and clocked a timing of 45.6 seconds, missing the bronze medal by just a difference of 0.1 second! However, subsequently he set new milestones with 200 and 400 meters record in the National Games at Cuttack and in the same year, in the Asian Games at Tokyo, in the same category. He also won the gold medal in the 1958 Commonwealth Games at Cardiff. Anju Bobby George is the first Indian athlete to win a medal in World Athletics Championship, who entered the record books when she won the bronze medal in Long Jump at the 2003 World Championships in Athletics in Paris, with a jump of 6.70 m in the penultimate round. From Heptathlon, she moved over to Long Jump and Triple Jump. Anju broke her own record in Long Jump with an effort of 6.74 m in the National Circuit Meet at Thiruvananthapuram, won the bronze medal at the 2002 Commonwealth Games at Manchester, gold medal at the Asian Games in Busan and finished sixth at the 2004 Athens Olympics but achieved a personal best of 6.83 m. Prakash Padukone was the first Indian to win the All England Badminton Championship. He won the coveted All England Open title in 1980 with a victory over Liem Swie King of Indonesia. He won the National Junior Title and Senior Title in the year 1972 and thereafter he won the National Title consecutively for the next seven years, until 1979. Padukone won his first major international title in 1979 at the Commonwealth games and the London Masters' Open, the Danish Open and the Swedish Open. It should be brought to the fore that the backing he received from his father Ramesh Padukone, the Secretary of the Mysore Badminton Association, did give him a distinct edge over other badminton aspirants. Similarly Leander Paes, the first Indian to Win Junior US Open Title, was highly benefited in his early years because of support from his father Vece Paes, a midfielder in the bronze medal-winning Indian field hockey team at the 1972 Munich Olympics and his mother, who captained the Indian basketball team in the 1980 Asian basketball championship. Family encouragement aside, his exposure to tennis since the age of eight at the Calcutta (Kolkata) South Club courts under Anwar Ali, brother of former Davis Cupper and national coach Akhtar Ali, played a decisive role. The company of Akhtar, Jaidip Mukherjee, Akhtar's son Zeeshan and a few seniors to him who later went to play the Davis Cup, cast a positive influence on Paes. For lack of a proper coaching system in Kolkata, Paes (lovingly called Lee) enrolled with the Britannia Amritraj Tennis Academy in Chennai in 1985 and was coached by Dave O'Meara. Paes won the US Open championship in 1991 by defeating Karim Alami of Morocco 6-4, 6-4. He is also credited with other major victories like the 1990 Wimbledon Junior title, the Davis Cup, a bronze medal for India at the 1996 Atlanta Olympics and multiple Grand Slams doubles titles with Mahesh Bhupati and mixed doubles with Sania Mirza.

The legendary Ramanathan Krishnan is the first Indian (and Asian too) to win Wimbledon Junior Singles title in 1954 by beating Ashley Cooper in the finals. Krishnan won the national senior title for eight consecutive years, was rated among the top ten in the world on five different occasions, was seeded 4 in the Wimbledon of 1962 and was also a member of the Indian team which reached the final of the Davis Cup in the year 1966. In 1960, Krishnan reached the semifinals of the Wimbledon but lost to the eventual champion Fraser and in the following year too he could make it to the semifinals, only to be beaten by Rod Laver. With Krishnan too, the tutelage of his father T.K. Ramanathan, made a lot of difference.

The 'Payyoli Express' P.T. Usha, who made her debut in the 1980 Moscow Olympics, won silver medals in 100 m and 200 m in the 1982 Delhi Asian Games. At the Asian Track and Field Championship at Kuwait in 1983, she took gold in the 400 m and set a new Asian record. In 1986 Seoul Asian Games, P.T. Usha won four golds and one silver medal in the track and field events and created new Asian Games records in all the events she participated. Usha was lucky to have O.M. Nambiar as her coach.

None can forget India's first Olympic Gold Medal in 1928 Olympics in hockey. India defeated the host country Holland 3-0 and the legendary Dhyan Chand scored two goals in the final. Indian goalkeeper Richard Allen had the unique distinction of not conceding a single goal throughout the tournament. The gold medal won by the Indian hockey team in 1928 was the first Olympic gold medal won by Asia in the modern Olympics. India has won a total of eight gold medals in hockey at Olympics. From 1928 Amsterdam Olympics to 1956 Melbourne Olympics India won six consecutive gold medals at hockey. The two other gold medals for India came in the 1964 Tokyo Olympics and the 1980 Moscow Olympics.

Viswanathan Anand, India's first grandmaster claimed that feat at the age of eighteen. He had already won the National Sub-Junior Chess Championship with a score of 9/9 in 1983 at the age of fourteen, won the National Championship at the age of sixteen and in 1984 became the youngest Indian to win the International Master Title at the age of fifteen. In 1987, Anand became the first Indian to win the World Junior Chess Championship. Anand won the FIDE World Chess Championship in 2000 after defeating Alexei Shirov 3.5 - 0.5 in the finals at Teheran, and became the first Indian to do so. He is one of only four players in the history of chess to break the 2800 mark on the FIDE rating list. Parimarjan Negi is the youngest Grandmaster (GM) in India and the world's youngest International Master (IM).

Indians of a cross-cultural heritage have also distinguished themselves at many levels. Norman G Pritchard, an Anglo-Indian athlete from Calcutta, was the first Indian to take part in Olympic Games. He was not the official representative of India. He was holidaying in Paris and participated on his own at the 1900 Paris Olympic Games and competed in four events—100m, 200m, 110m hurdles and 200m hurdles. He bagged two silver medals, one each in 200m and 200m hurdles. He won his first medal on 16 July, 1900 when he finished second only to the American athlete Alvin Kraenzlein in 200m hurdles. Hennery Rebello qualified for the final of the Triple Jump in 1948 London Olympics. Sprinter Lavy Pinto reached the semi finals of 100 m and 200 m events at Helsinki in 1952.

Down the line and over the years, there have been many additions to the illustrated afore-mentioned name chart. The champions have been distinguished with several awards—the Arjuna Award, the Rajiv Gandhi Khel Ratna Award, the Padma Shri, the Padma Bhushan, et al. Yet, every success story that makes it to the headlines is not even the tip of the iceberg, since there are thousands of others whose dreams are nipped in the bud. Sports are not just about the victors who proverbially don the laurel-crown as was the literal practice in the earliest Olympics. It is also about those who, to quote, follow the dictum as enshrined in the Pink Floyd song *Hey You—Don't give in without a fight*. Of course, for sportspersons, the '*jo jita wahi sikander*' ideal holds good. But since, no one is born a champ but has to make oneself so, it is obligatory that the nation, the corporate world, the local community and every enlightened person of the civilised society should come forward towards helping those who make the nation proud. The trend of conferring an award upon someone, only after he or she has made a mark in sports, is not a healthy one. In many a case, the burning need of the hour for the aspirant is to receive the cherished sponsorships during that phase of their career when they are at their struggling worst. Unfortunately, we in India still idealise (and idolise!) someone only when the concerned person has made a mark (preferably in the international circuit) but seldom when he is an unrecognised nobody. This is true and applicable to every field but as far as sports is concerned, it becomes all the more a lamentable syndrome, given the fact that sports is a field where motivation and inspiration can literally make a heaven of hell. The pessimistic but brutally honest one liner in Peter Gabriel and Kate Bush's highly influential song *Don't Give Up*—'*But no one wants you when you lose*', can be completely overhauled when some agency stands beside the struggler and says—'Don't give up/You're not beaten yet/Don't give up/ I know you can make it good.'

Corporate India too has been slow in promoting a truly international level sports culture in India, which unfortunately, is still lacking. It is only of late that certain promotionals are noticeable, but even then, their numbers are paltry. For instance, the recent Airtel Rising Stars' talent hunt, which is India's largest under-16 soccer talent hunt, has promised to give twelve promising youngsters the chance-of-a-lifetime to train with Manchester United Soccer School and kick-off a career in professional football. From mid-July 2012, this three-month long training involved participation from over 10,000 young soccer players across sixteen cities in India and hand-picked the best performers in skill tests, real time match simulations, coaching clinics with Manchester United Soccer School coaches, etc. But with changing times perhaps, the equation between sports and brand sponsorships is being better understood. One need not be a top-level marketing or ad-honcho to guess that brands steal the spotlight when the sport that benefits from the money, also comes into the limelight. In the second largest multicultural nation of the world where the art of branding is an activity that is growing leaps and bounds every day, it should not be impossible to raise the status quo of any given sport if its worth, nature and niche participants/audience be decisively targeted.

India's erstwhile real life pride in hockey now finds a diminutive position in a reel life cutpiece in the movie *Chak De India*. The 2010 CWG (Commonwealth Games) debacle has earned the shame of political cartoons and graffiti caricatures. There is no dearth of newspaper coverage every now and then, showing a governmental agency or a politician scurrying forth to prize an '*arabpati*' M.S. Dhoni or a Sachin Tendulkar with a Hayabusa bike, a gold memento or a cash reward running into lakhs. But when Indian hockey players go on strike for nonpayment of their arrears that often run into lakhs of rupees, they are strangely booked as unpatriotic and even ordered or cautioned to leave the conditioning camp within 48 hours, if the 'modest' twenty-five thousand offered in lieu of their arrears were not claimed by them. The unity and support of the juniors for the seniors grabbed public and media attention and hence the rotting IOA (Indian Olympic Association) and the equally horrendous Hockey India, began acting right. Perhaps this is how it happens in India. Honour and pride find no place in a nation where the victors of the Asia Cup (2007), Azlan Shah Cup (2009) and the bronze medal bagger at the 2009 Champions Challenge, have to squabble for their rights and dues from the corrupt fiefdoms of politicians for whom vote based hoopla and media moulding carry greater weight than talent and/or performance.

What is most lamentable is the fact that even the dignity of established sportsmen do not escape the caprices of governmental sports associations. The name of Abhinav Bindra is a pointer of how in India, vanity sponsorship is the chief recourse to many a sporting pursuit. Son of an affluent Sikh Punjabi family, Bindra could afford to get an indoor shooting range installed at their home in Patiala! After winning the gold in the 10 m Air Rifle event at the 2008 Beijing Olympic Games, he became the first Indian to win an individual gold medal at the Olympic Games. It was also India's first gold medal since 1980, when the Men's Field Hockey Team won the gold. Yet the National Rifle Association of India (NRAI) behaved badly with him and even debarred him from participating in a Commonwealth Shooting Championship, on grounds of discipline. The IOA, then chaired by Suresh Kalmadi, intervened and when the 2010 Commonwealth Games were held in New-Delhi, Bindra got the honour of being the Indian contingent's flag-bearer at the opening ceremony and taking the athletes' oath on behalf of the 6,700 participants from 71 countries and territories on that occasion. Strange indeed are the ways of the government and administration of this country!

Ahead, Bindra received cash prizes from the Mittal Champions Trust, the Central Government, the BCCI, the Steel Ministry of India, Golds Gym, the Railway Ministry of India, the Pune Municipal Corporation and the State governments of Haryana, Bihar, Karnataka, Madhya Pradesh, Maharashtra, Odisha, Tamil Nadu and Kerala. Even the Patna Indoor Stadium was renamed after him! Yet nothing could perhaps take away from him, the bitter hurt of his early years, when there was no one other than his parents to back him up. In an interview with *The Telegraph* in August, 2008 ('Abhi-nerve cures a nation's yellow fever'), the 'Shooting Star' hoped that his countrymen and their government would now show "a little more belief in athletes, a little more patience when they were down, instead of an eagerness to hustle them into oblivion." We hope that the Abhinav Bindra Foundation would do more in the recent future what the government failed to do in all these years.

Boxer Vijender Singh defeated Carlos Góngora of Ecuador 9-4 in the quarterfinals which guaranteed him a bronze medal—the first ever Olympic medal for an Indian boxer. Other accolades also preceded and succeeded this historic win but he was not so much into news for his commendable hooks and uppercut that is comparable with the style of actor Sylvester Stallone as the character Rocky Balboa in the *Rocky* film series. Rather, as the latest pin up boy, a parallel modelling and film career, game and dance reality shows et al, he became quite a household name. However, the boxer has taken the brouhaha in good spirit and a public platform for the promotion of boxing as a sport and in a media interview has openly lambasted the lopsided favouritism for cricket in this country, where sports academies for specialised sports are severely in dearth. When Vijender pointed out the name of Saina Nehwal as a contemporary badminton genius who deserved greater support, the media also started focusing upon her. This is a very commendable example of how one sportsperson can promote another sportsperson (not necessarily in the same field), in a milieu where the general tendency is towards backstabbing and slander-mongering.

Vijender's censure of the unwarranted cricket mania in the sub-continent definitely deserves a critical introspection. If we consider cricket's present and its well-nigh possible future, a lot has to be said, given the fact of its sub-continental popularity. The lineage of the game can be traced from the days of the British Raj, accompanied by the sense of elitism that went with it. The evolution of the game till the present day, as its long history suggests, is exciting but it is questionable whether it is utopian. The trajectory of development from Test cricket to ODI's to the Twenty20 competition format has brought in mixed blessings. The 1983 Prudential World Cup and the 2011 Cricket World Cup were the zenith, till gritty sports bowed down to gimmicky entertainment and money spinning machines. Indian Premier League or Indian Paisa League—the IPL has perhaps emerged more of a bane than a boon. It is a veritable symbol of the grotesque edifice of Indian capitalism tethering upon its own weight. The controversies associated with it cannot be overlooked so easily and they have much more to do than simply the habitual match-fixing revelations, the SRK-MCA brawl and the most recent Delhi hotel incident.

Domestic competitions like the Ranji Trophy, the Duleep Trophy, the Deodhar Trophy, the Irani Trophy and even the Challenger Series have now been relegated to the background as events that might get covered by a languishing Doordarshan, to be watched by the superannuated and the hopeless alike. The illogical distribution of franchises and financial discrepancies in their allotment is definitely a very serious topic of discussion. The scheduling and length of the whole tournament is also an issue, as mostly it takes a toll on the fitness of main players. There is also a crying need for a total revamp in the model how BCCI functions as the sole controller of cricket in India. The Gentleman's Game is losing its gentlemanly nature and bowing down before the logic of late capitalism (to borrow Frederic Jameson's idea). This is not surprising, given the high mercenary nature of our present day milieu. What passes off in the name of an innovation of format is actually a crazy zest for the unlimited that reads like a bastardised version of the great American Dream. It is not without reason that one of the most noted historians and cricket writers of this country—Ramachandra Guha, had abhorred from writing on cricket, given the clear fact that the mantra of 'earn while you can' and 'perform or perish' had most adversely affected the players themselves.

The ultimate achievement of any team in any form of the game is to win as many numbers of games as possible. But if we go by statistics, we will find that after winning the first T20 World Cup in 2007 followed by the inaugural edition of the IPL, India has always performed dismally to say the least in each and every T20 World Cup that has followed, as well as other T20 internationals. Of course the entertainment factor cannot (and perhaps should not) be completely criticised. People can cheer, shout, rant and dance for any number of reasons (viz. my hometown's victory when KKR wins!). But an entertainment that comes at the risk of a star player's very fitness becomes severely questionable. Moreover, an out-and-out cricket competition is always miles above a tailor-made entertainment ritual. Against the vivid collective memory of the miraculous innings of V.V.S Laxman, along with the daring resistance of Rahul Dravid against Australia in Eden Garden (2001), hardly anyone will be likely to remember the struggling Laxman or vulnerable Dravid of 20/20 Cricket! If cricket becomes solely like a Bollywood masala

Blockbuster, governed by a carpe diem mindset and having the shelf-life of a B-grade cine flick, the legacy of injured performers and fatigued heroes will be all that will be left for us. Guha's satirical renaming of the IPL as 'Smash-And-Grab Crony League' exposes how the replacement of 'creative capitalism' by 'crony capitalism', spells disaster, not just for Indian cricket but for a whole host of other vital areas and avenues of Indian life and living. Phony and boorish movie and corporate celebs should not be the role models of the youth brigade but rather those very sportspersons who believe in being champions first and stars afterwards. When the closet secrets come tumbling out, the stylised euphoria of such designer cricket matches do not seem that worthwhile after all!

Cronyism is there in almost every sector in India and sports would naturally be no exception to the norm. Still, I am proud of the sporting legends of my land; proud of the fact that despite all the poverty, neglect and squalor, there is no dearth of private enterprise. After all, Australia with a population of two crore plus can win multiple golds as much as China, with the world's largest population, wins hundreds of gold. We have the population and the money alike but not the right attitude towards sports—something this long trajectory since 1947 has not been perhaps yet able to claim zealously. As participant, spectator or volunteer, we must recognise that 'sport' has the ability to transcend across nations, cultures, socio-economic and political boundaries and can be invoked with success in virtually every global community. The malaise of the neglect of sports in India has to be recognised and its citizens should become more demanding in these matters. Like those mentioned above, there are many other games that wait being delivered out of the closets of local *mohalla*s. Some are dying even there, viz., hopscotch, *chouka/attha chouk*, *lattu/bagari*, *lagori*, *kancha/goti/goli*, *gilli danda*, *akhada*, *pehlwani* and even *kabaddi*. Else, we will constantly have to hear, see and lament about budding sportspersons, like the one I saw in the metro, completely clueless about how a sporting dream can actually turn into a reality someday!

About the Contributors

Aditya Mani Jha is New Delhi based journalist, presently working with *The Sunday Guardian.*

Alokita Datta is a New Delhi based journalist. Her account of Delhi is first hand and comes through her avid interest in its landmarks and people.

Anupam Mishra is the President of Gandhi Peace Foundation, New Delhi and is a well-known environmentalist.

Atul Kumar Thakur is a New Delhi based journalist. He is the editor of this volume, his first book.

B.G. Verghese is a columnist and author and was earlier editor of the *Hindustan Times* and, subsequently, of *The Indian Express*.

Banibrata Mahanta is the author of a book *Joseph Conrad: The Gothic Imagination*. He has published widely in national and international journals. He teaches English Literature at Benaras Hindu University, Varanasi.

Benoy K. Behl is a leading art critic and author based in Delhi.

Bibek Debroy is a Professor of Economics at Centre for Policy Research, New Delhi and Consulting Editor, *The Economic Times.*

Bimal Jalan is an economist, former Governor of the Reserve Bank of India and a distinguished policy maker.

Bishal Thapa is an international business consultant. He previously served as the India Head of ICF International.

Jagmohan is a former Governor of Jammu and Kashmir, a former Union Cabinet Minister of India and has also held the position of Lt. Governor of Delhi.

Jean Drèze is Visiting Professor, Department of Economics, Allahabad University. Nobel laureate **Amartya Sen** is Lamont University professor and Professor of Economics and Philosophy at Harvard University.

Kunwar Natwar Singh is the former foreign minister of India; he is one of the most authentic voices on India's Foreign Policy.

Mahima Kaul is a New Delhi based journalist, she has been working on the digital inclusion.

Mayuri Mukherjee is a New Delhi based journalist and an IR enthusiast. She works as Senior Assistant Editor at *The Pioneer*.

Ninad D. Sheth is a strategic expert, senior journalist and visiting Fellow, Institute of Chinese Studies, New Delhi.

Pran Nevile is a career diplomat and a renowned scholar on cultural matters; he has authored many books and papers.

Prem Shankar Jha is a veteran journalist, columnist and a writer of more than a dozen books. In his career spanning five decades, he has worked with the United Nations, and later with *The Economic Times, The Hindustan Times* and *The Financial Express* as editor.

Rafia Zakaria is columnist with *The Dawn*, Pakistan.

Rakhshanda Jalil is a New Delhi based writer, literary critic and translator; she writes the columns in the leading publications of South Asia on culture, cinema, literature and related topics.

Ramchandra Guha is a leading social historian and public intellectual; he is the author of *India after Gandhi*.

Ratnadip Choudhury is a Guwahati based journalist. He is the Principal Correspondent with *Tehelka* and has covered the north eastern states very remarkably.

Santanu Banerjee and **Subhadeep Roy** teach English at the University of Burdwan, West Bengal, and are the editors of a National level refereed journal on language and literature studies, *Impressions of Eternity*.

Saugata Ghosh is a writer and translator. His recent translation works include *BT Road and The Hollow-Two Novellas* by Samaresh Basu.

Shashi Tharoor is a minister with the central government, a former Under Secretary General of the United Nations and an acclaimed writer.

Subhadeep Paul is a literary critic and sports enthusiast based in Kolkata.

Sumana Roy lives in Siliguri, the Chicken's Neck region, India. Her poems, fiction and essays have appeared in *Guernica, Asian Cha, Caravan, Pratilipi, Seminar, Open, Biblio and Himal Southasian,* among others.

Sunita Narain is a leading environmentalist. She is the Director General of Centre for Science and Environment and Editor of *Down to Earth.*

Udaya Narayana Singh is a distinguished linguist and litterateur, a former Director of Central Institute of Indian Languages, Mysore, and now a Professor, Rabindra Bhavana, Visva-Bharati, Santiniketan.

Yamini Mishra and Navanita Sinha are with UN Women South Asia Sub Regional Office.

Acknowledgements

Being a non-fiction aficionado, a book on modern India was on my mind for years. But it was during the winter of early 2012 that I changed my plans and decided to come up first with an anthology, written with broad overviews on the diversified themes that indeed matter to India and its people. An anthology possesses a different kind of character than the usual solo book; here greater cohesion is required from all the related components.

I can easily admit that this book rises from the collaborative inputs of all writers, who have contributed to this anthology. I am immensely thankful to each one of them. Moreover, my literary consultant and friend, Kanishka Gupta and Editors at Niyogi Books (Gita Rajan, Jyoti Kumari and others) deserve all praise for working so hard along with me for making this book truly remarkable. It was great to work with a professional publisher like Niyogi Books at the beginning of my writing career.

For the valuable feedback given in the initial stages of the compilation, I am very thankful to Ramchandra Guha, Jean Drèze, Prem Shankar Jha, B.G. Verghese, K Natwar Singh, Jagmohan, Bimal Jalan, Shashi Tharoor, Sunita Narain, Rakhshanda Jalil, Mahasweta Devi, Nandini Sundar, Ram Kirti Shukla, Pankaj Mishra, Amit Chaudhuri, Rajkamal Jha, Tabish Khair, Siddhartha Varadrajan, Venkitesh Ramakrishnan, Rasheed Kidwai, Trithesh Nandan, Ashish Mehta, B.V. Rao, Ajai Singh, Rajesh Singh, Rajen Kumar, Siddhartha Gigoo, Raza Rumi, Rajiv Jayaram, Omair Ahmed, T.K. Arun, Rajeev Bhattacharjee, Prasenjit Bose, Taj Hasan, Amitabh Thakur, Nipun Vinayak, Ramesh Chandra Deka, Ajoy Ashirwad Mahaprastha, Sopan Joshi, Hemender

Sharma, Sushil Srivastava, Rajiv Jha, Rakesh Singh (Harmony Book Shop, Banaras), Vijay Bahadur Singh-Amitabh Singh (Universal Book Shop, Banaras), Mahesh Acharya, Rupesh Acharya.

Since this is my first book, so simply recalling my immediate and extended family's support in my voyage will not be enough to appreciate what they have done for me but I am trying. I especially appreciate the valuable enthusiasm for my writing from my parents (Dhrub Narayan Thakur and Baby Thakur), Prabhat Mishra, Manoj Jha, Ashutosh Thakur, Manglesh Thakur, Dipesh Thakur, Rina Thakur, Archana Jha, Pooja Thakur, Prashant Mishra, Bhavesh Nandan Jha, Rinky, Anu, Abhishek Jha, Ravindra Jha, Ravi Ranjan Thakur, Prabhat Ranjan Thakur, Alka Jha, Ayush Jha and Avanish Mishra. I would also like to acknowledge the interest in this book shown by Urmimala Bhattacharjee, Ghazala, Saira, Malabika Biswas, Supriya Dhaliwal, Shariq and Abhinav Thakur. I am also thankful to many others who are waiting to read this book and have faith in my intellectual pursuits.

I am missing my grandfather and grandmother (Late Upendra Thakur and Gita Thakur), who are not alive anymore to see my first book. But I am glad my maternal grandparents (Bimlendra Mishra and Vinita Mishra) are looking forward to read *India since1947*.

The news vendors and street booksellers of Madhubani, Patna, Banaras, Kolkata and Delhi have been thoroughly supportive in keeping my unrelenting reading habit intact—I have gratitude for them, and also for the staff of various libraries. Last but not least, my three excellent years in Banaras Hindu University and subsequent time in Delhi, which I spent honestly like a knowledge seeker, inside the library or beyond.